Becoming American, Remaining Jewish

Cultural Studies of Delaware and the Eastern Shore

1973
Carol Hoffecker, ed., *Readings in Delaware History*

1977
Harold Hancock, *The Loyalties of Revolutionary Delaware*

1983
C. A. Weslager, *The Nanticoke Indians—Past and Present*

1984
John A. Munroe, *History of Delaware* (2nd edition)

1984
Jay F. Custer, *Delaware Prehistoric Archaeology: An Ecological Approach*

1986
Claudia L. Bushman, Harold B. Hancock and Elizabeth Moyne Homsey, eds., *Proceedings of the Assembly of the Lower Counties on Delaware 1770–1776, of the Constitutional Convention of 1776, and of the House of Assembly of the Delaware State 1776–1781.*
Jay F. Custer, ed., *Late Woodland Cultures of the Middle Atlantic Region*

1988
Claudia L. Bushman, Harold B. Hancock and Elizabeth Moyne Homsey, eds., *Minutes of the House of Assembly of the Delaware State, 1781–1792*

1989
Jay F. Custer, *Prehistoric Cultures of the Delmarva Peninsula: An Archaeological Study*
John A. Sweeney, *Grandeur on the Appoquinimink: The House of William Corbit at Odessa, Delaware*

1993
John A. Munroe, *History of Delaware* (third edition)

1995
Carol E. Hoffecker, Richard Waldron, Lorraine E. Williams, and Barbara E. Benson, eds., *New Sweden in America*

1999
Toni Young, *Becoming American, Remaining Jewish: The Story of Wilmington, Delaware's First Jewish Community, 1879–1924*

2000
Jane Harrington Scott, *A Gentleman as Well as a Whig*
Carol E. Hoffecker, *Honest John Williams: US Senator from Delaware*

Becoming American, Remaining Jewish

The Story of Wilmington, Delaware's First Jewish Community, 1879–1924

Toni Young

DELAWARE

Newark: University of Delaware Press
London: Associated University Presses

Associated University Presses
440 Forsgate Drive
Cranbury, NJ 08512

Associated University Presses
16 Barter Street
London WC1A 2AH, England

Associated University Presses
P.O. Box 338, Port Credit
Mississauga, Ontario
Canada L5G 4L8

The paper used in this publication meets the requirements of the American National Standard for Permanence of Paper for Printed Library Materials Z39.48–1984.

Library of Congress Cataloging-in-Publication Data

Young, Toni.
    Becoming American, remaining Jewish : the story of Wilmington, Delaware's first Jewish community, 1879–1924 / Toni Young.
        p.   cm. — (Cultural studies of Delaware and the Eastern Shore)
    Includes bibliographical references and index.
    ISBN 0-87413-694-6 (alk. paper)
    1. Jews—Delaware—Wilmington—History.   2. Wilmington (Del.)—Ethnic relations.   I. Title.   II. Series.
F174.W79J59   1999
975.1'2—dc21   99-26914
                                                                       CIP

To Mom and Dad, Nana and Papa,
Who Taught Me to Love My Roots

Contents

Preface

DESPITE THEIR DISTINCTIVE PROBLEMS, ALL IMMIGRANTS TO THE United States face the same basic challenge: how to preserve their heritage and, at the same time, become American. Is one a better American by becoming more similar to everyone else or by maintaining a unique identity? The specifics and intensity of the dilemma change for the descendants of immigrants, but the essential issue remains the same.

At the end of the twentieth century, the question of identity has heightened importance to the Jews of America because we find ourselves at a difficult juncture. More than 90 percent of American Jews are born in the United States. Many feel more American than Jewish, which is not surprising because studies show that the longer a family resides in America, the more remote its later generations become from Judaism. Today, more than 50 percent of American Jews marry non-Jews. Will assimilation become so prevalent that Jews no longer maintain their identity as a separate group in America?

Many people suggest that we should no longer speak about one American Jewish community but instead should speak about American Jewish communities. Some people define the Jewish community as a religious community, some as a political one, while others emphasize the ethnic grouping. Within each of these Jewish communities, opinions range so widely that it has become increasingly difficult to find points of agreement. Does the tension between Jewish groups mean that the amorphous entity known as the American Jewish community is moving towards its demise?

One way to clarify the position of American Jews and the American Jewish community is to examine the past. In *Becoming American: Remaining Jewish* we will study the first permanent Jewish community in Wilmington, Delaware, which began as a collection of one hundred Jews in 1879, and grew to a community of over four thousand by the early 1920s, when the immigration laws changed and the growth slowed down.[1] My purpose is to trace the development of Wilmington's Jewish community in order to understand what the Jews created and why, what values were reflected in the institutions they established and the causes they advocated, and what changed over the years. In order to examine fully the purposes of institutions, it is necessary to understand the personal background and needs of the founders; therefore, significant time is devoted to information about individual Jews. By understanding the values that inspired immigrant Jews to build a community, we can better define the essence of a Jewish community. Perhaps recognizing the early immigrants' values will assist us in defining our identities and community today.

To the outside world, the early Wilmington Jews were one group, yet the diversity among them in country of origin, language, religious rituals, and economic and educational backgrounds was tremendous. Because the outside world saw them as one minority, they were labeled the Jewish community. Were they really one group in the sense that they shared a body of values or was this concept imposed from the outside? How does their situation compare to ours today, when we live in a more open society and are no longer newcomers in a foreign land?

This volume will not examine the early Wilmington Jewish community as a vibrant center of Jewish learning that made major contributions to Jewish life in the United States. Two neighboring cities, Philadelphia and Baltimore, have distinguished themselves in that light. Rather, we will study the first Jewish community of Wilmington as a model of how Jews in America successfully balanced the demands of adapting to the American culture and preserving their heritage. Through compromise, the early Jewish immigrants both lost and gained, while creating a new entity: the Delaware Jew, an individual different than the European counterpart, but still clearly recognizable as a Jew.

In my opinion, the challenge facing American Jews today, balancing the demands of being American and Jewish, is the same one that faced our ancestors. Whether we will be as successful as they were in defining ourselves and our role in the United States remains to be seen.

Clearly, I could not have written this book without the archives of the Jewish Historical Society of Delaware; therefore, I thank Rabbi David Geffen, the late Bill Frank, and the late Harry Bluestone for their foresight in organizing the archives in the 1970s and for their generosity in sharing their knowledge of Delaware Jewish history with me. A special thank you to those who have sustained the JHSD, particularly Marvin Balick, president, Helen Goldberg, past president, Mutzie Bellak and Ralph Tomases, active board members with a wealth of information on the early Jewish community; and Julian Preisler, our energetic archivist. The Emile Topkis Collection of the JHSD has been invaluable. During the 1950s, Topkis worked on a history of the early Jewish community. His copious notes, lists of nineteenth-century Jews, and interviews with children of the founders became vital primary sources. Interviews with descendants of the founders became an important source of information, and I am grateful to the people listed in the bibliography for their time and insights.

I am deeply indebted to three people who have offered continual encouragement and advice. Rabbi David Geffen kindled my interest in Delaware Jewish history nearly twenty-five years ago. Since then he has served as teacher, mentor, and critic. At an early stage, Dr. Carol Hoffecker offered valuable suggestions on what to include in the manuscript and how to write history for the general public. She generously answered all my questions concerning Delaware history. Dr. Barbara Benson demonstrated confidence in my ability to write this book. When details threatened to consume me, she wisely advised me to begin writing so that ideas would not be lost. Each of them read the manuscript and offered excellent suggestions. Dr. Sara R. Horowitz also read the manuscript and offered valuable ideas.

At Delaware's research libraries I have been welcomed and assisted by kind, patient people. In particular, I would like to thank Ellen Rendle and Constance J. Cooper at the Historical Society of Delaware; Jo Ann Mattern, Doris Carignan, and Bruce Haafe at the Delaware Public Archives; Jean Kaufman, Ben Prestianni, and Thomas Morabito at the Wilmington Institute Public Library; Marge McNinch at Eleutherian Mills Hagley Foundation; Jane Goldberg at the New Castle County Recorder of Deeds, and Alan Schoenberg. I would also like to thank Kevin Profitt at the American Jewish Archives and the librarians at the Balch Institute for Ethnic Studies, the American Jewish Historical Society, the Jewish Theological Seminary, and the Chicago Institute.

I would like to thank the Historical Society of Delaware and the Jewish Historical Society of Delaware for permission to use their photographs. The kindness and expertise of everyone at Associated University Presses has made the process of publishing this book most enjoyable.

Finally, a special thank you to Stuart, Mitchell, and Ann for their patience and for understanding why the people from a century ago often took me away from them. And an extra note of gratitude to Ann for her meticulous work in reviewing names in the manuscript and on the lists.

Author's Note to the Reader

Historic events don't simply happen. People make them happen. Without the dreams and motivations of individuals, the world would not progress. Furthermore, historic events don't occur in a vacuum but rather reflect the conditions of a given moment as well as all that has come before.

In order to emphasize these two basic but essential facts, I have written this book in a nontraditional manner. Instead of dividing the work into thematic units with a separate section of biographies, I have integrated background information about individuals into the story of what they created so the reader can understand the connection between the individual's motivating factors and the institution that was created.

I have also developed the stories of various synagogues and institutions simultaneously so that the primary interests of the community become clear, and each person and institution is seen as part of the whole. The existence of each institution affected the development of the others; therefore, the most effective way to understand the identity of the community is to examine the developments chronologically.

If you, my reader, are interested in a specific individual, institution, or subject, the contents and index will help you locate all the relevant sections. However, I suggest that you concentrate on the story of the community and the relationships between different events and people. While the multitude of details may be overwhelming at moments, if you focus on the sense of community, you will complete the story with a vivid picture of Wilmington's first Jewish community and an understanding of the way various components of a community combine to form something larger than any one part.

A major technical difficulty in a study of this sort, involving hundreds of long-deceased individuals, is ascertaining who is Jewish. The lists of Jews who arrived in Wilmington each decade and the statistics about Wilmington's Jewish population include only those people whose Judaism can be substantiated through definite

13

sources. Birth, death, marriage, and cemetery records, obituaries, early synagogue records, interviews done by Emile Topkis during the 1950s, and interviews with Delawareans today are my sources for establishing Jewish identity. Even the census was most helpful because Wilmington census-takers often wrote "Yiddish" in the language column on the 1910 census. Undoubtedly, the lists do not include all Jews, and the estimates are probably low because numerous individuals, whose names sound Jewish and whose countries of origin suggest a Jewish background, have not been included for lack of definite proof. If I have omitted some people who should have been included, I apologize, but omission seemed a lesser error than inclusion of someone who was not Jewish.

Becoming American,
Remaining Jewish

1

By Way of Background

WHY BEGIN IN 1879?

ALTHOUGH JEWS LIVED IN THE TERRITORY THAT BECAME DELAWARE as early as 1671, Judaism did not flourish in the area during the next two centuries, and Delaware became the last of the original colonies to have an organized Jewish community and worship services in the state for the high holidays.[1] In 1671, Jacob Fiana bought 188 acres of land near the Appoquinimink Creek. The following year he sold his property, legalizing the sale by marking the document with a Star of David.[2] During the next two hundred years, only a small number of Jewish immigrants moved to the area, and they appear to have converted, allowed their Judaism to lapse, or moved out of Delaware within a few years.[3] There is no evidence that any of these early Jews attempted to form Jewish organizations, or that there were enough Jews at any one time to establish a Jewish community.

Among the Jews who lived in Delaware between 1671 and 1850 was Daniel Nunez, Jr., who lived in Lewes in the mid-eighteenth century, married into a well-known non-Jewish family, and was baptized. A surveyor's report of 1750 referred to him as "Nunes the Jew."[4] The merchant Abraham Judah lived in Wilmington for ten years in the mid-eighteenth century and then moved to Philadelphia. Jacob and Daniel Solis ran a dry goods store in Wilmington in 1815, but both brothers had left Wilmington by 1821. Captain Henry B. Nones, offspring of a prominent Philadelphia Jewish family, lived in Wilmington from 1843 until his death in 1868. While Nones did not convert, he married a non-Jew, did not participate in Jewish activities, and was buried in unconsecrated ground at the Brandywine and Wilmington cemetery. Several immigrants with Jewish-sounding names resided briefly in Delaware, but none lived in the state long enough to leave any proof of Jewish background.[5]

During the 1850s and 1860s, approximately twenty Jewish merchants from neighboring Baltimore and Philadelphia opened small businesses on lower Market Street in Wilmington. Some stayed only a few years; others remained and provided the nucleus for a community. In 1879, these merchants organized the Moses Montefiore Society, thereby beginning the first formal Jewish community, the foundation of today's Jewish community. By the time Wilmington's Jewish community was organized, there were nearly one thousand points of significant Jewish settlement in at least thirty-two of the thirty-eight states, four territories, and Washington, D.C.[6]

WILMINGTON IN THE LAST THIRD OF THE NINETEENTH CENTURY

Wilmington, the largest city in the state of Delaware, was founded by Quakers in the 1730s and remained a small milling and shipping village through the early years of the nineteenth century.[7] Between 1840 and the Civil War, the city grew rapidly into an industrial center with railroad car manufacturing, iron casting, carriage making, leather tanning, and coopering as its largest industries.[8] By the 1880s, Wilmington's major industries were heavy metal fabrication, ship and railroad car construction, and tanning.[9] Given Wilmington's industrial nature, it's not surprising that the city hadn't attracted a lot of Jews. An industrial environment, which required skilled workers, was not the ideal setting for the Jewish immigrant, who in the mid-nineteenth century generally engaged in two major petty trades, peddling and tailoring. Jews in America had fewer people working in factories and workshops than other immigrant groups during the mid-nineteenth century.[10]

Because of the industrialization of Wilmington, between 1840 and 1870 the population of the city increased dramatically by more than 350 percent, from 8,452 in 1840 to 30,841 in 1870. Continued prosperity and expansion caused the population of the city to increase 40 to 50 percent every decade from 1860 to 1900.[11] However, the foreign-born percentage of the population did not increase; in fact, it decreased. The foreign-born population of Wilmington accounted for 18.9 percent of the city's population in 1860, but for only 13 percent by 1880 and 1900.[12]

Wilmington had a much smaller foreign-born population than many other cities on the eastern seacoast. In 1860, Wilmington ranked fourth lowest in percentage of foreign-born among twenty-seven cities with populations between 20,000 and 50,000.[13] In 1880, Philadelphia's foreign-born population was 24 percent of the

Wilmington, Market and Second Streets, c. 1867. (Historical Society of Delaware).

total population, New York's was 40 percent, and Baltimore had 17 percent foreign-born population.[14] Philadelphia and Baltimore had more diversified economies and offered greater employment to immigrant families.[15] Camden and Trenton, two medium-sized industrial cities in the Delaware River Valley, also had larger foreign-born populations than Wilmington in 1880.[16]

One factor that may have accounted for Wilmington's lower immigrant population was the presence of a statistically significant black community, which could provide a pool of unskilled laborers.[17] During the second half of the nineteenth century, blacks averaged about 10 percent of Wilmington's population, making them the largest single minority in the city.[18] The presence of a large black population may have restricted the growth of an immigrant population because blacks and immigrants competed for the same unskilled laboring jobs.[19]

The immigrants who did settle in Wilmington in large numbers prior to 1880 came from groups that had few assimilation problems. The Irish, many of whom came to Delaware to work in the Dupont Company's powder mills and other Brandywine River industries, were the largest immigrant group.[20] The British and the Germans, many of whom were skilled workers, were the next-largest immigrant groups. Few German immigrants of the eighteenth century reached Wilmington; in 1810, there were only some 250 Germans in Wilmington. However, during the second half of the nineteenth century, when artisans, tradesman, and political refugees began to emigrate from Germany, many such individuals came to Wilmington, and the German population of Wilmington grew significantly, from 343 in 1850 to 1263 in 1860.[21] Wilmington's German immigrants arrived at roughly the same time as the German Jewish immigrants, a fact that made it easier for those who wanted to lose their Jewish identity to do so.

Not only was Wilmington an industrial city, but it was a city where ancestry mattered, a place that could support its own endeavors because of the prosperity of old families. In 1870 a local magazine commented that "in almost all industries of the city, you are struck by the ancestral aspect of trades, the continuance of a business from father to son or the gradual change of firms by the absorption of partners."[22]

Although the foreign-born population of Wilmington was low in comparison to neighboring cities, by Delaware standards, Wilmington had a diverse ethnic and religious mix.[23] In 1880, 94 percent of Delawareans were native-born, and only 6 percent were foreign-born.[24] In contrast, Wilmington's foreign-born population was 13 percent. The vast majority of native-born Americans in Wilmington and throughout the state had been born in Delaware.[25]

Religious factors also made Wilmington undesirable for Jewish immigrants, who were continually warned against settling in small towns where there were no established Jewish congregations. Inter-marriage and conversion were widespread in such locations, and Jews were lost to the faith within a few years.[26] Therefore, although the majority of Americans lived in rural areas in the nineteenth cen-tury, Jews chose to be city-dwellers. As early as 1840, one-quarter of Jews in the United States lived in New York, Philadelphia, and Baltimore.[27] By 1880, 83 percent of American Jews lived in urban centers with populations of five thousand or more, though such cen-ters were home to only 25 percent of Americans.[28] Jews in New York, Chicago, Philadelphia, Boston, and Baltimore were in "large enough concentration to shape public institutions and make a full-scale Jewish culture possible."[29] In those cities, Jews could be Jew-ish without much concern about what the Americans would say.

In the mid-nineteenth century, Wilmington had no Jewish organi-zations and no organized Jewish community. In contrast, Philadel-phia, a mere twenty-seven miles north of Wilmington, had a thriving Jewish community. By 1860, approximately 8,000 Jews, out of a total United States Jewish population of 150,000 Jews, lived in Philadelphia.[30] There were eleven synagogues in Philadel-phia in 1875. The earliest one, Mikveh Israel, had been established formally in 1782 from a loose association of observant Jews who held religious services as early as 1740.[31] Rodeph Shalom, the first American synagogue to use the German or Askenazic rite, was es-tablished in Philadelphia in 1795.[32] Numerous charitable and educa-tional institutions including Rebecca Gratz' Sunday School Class, the first Jewish Publication Society, the Hebrew Education Society, the Hebrew Relief Society, and the Jewish Foster Home and Orphan Asylum were active in the city. Influential rabbis like Isaac Leeser, Sabato Morais, and Marcus Jastrow as well as creative lay leaders like Rebecca Gratz, Abraham Hart, Moses Aaron, and Mayer Sulz-berger lived and worked in Philadelphia, making it a vital center of Jewish life. During the last decades of the nineteenth century, an enviable community of cultured Jewish laymen and rabbis, known as the Philadelphia Group, played a key role in shaping America's emerging Jewish cultural institutions.[33] Working in Philadelphia or neighboring cities, they created the basic institutions, characteris-tics, and standards of twentieth century American Jewish culture that reached almost to contemporary times.[34] "From 1829 when Rabbi Isaac Leeser took the pulpit of Mikveh Israel until 1906 when the American Jewish Committee was formed in New York, the Philadelphia Jewish community was innovating, pioneering, and in many ways the most influential Jewry in the United States."[35]

Baltimore's Jewish population grew rapidly to over eight thousand by 1860.[36] The city, seventy miles south of Wilmington, became a center of religious debate because several influential rabbis representing conflicting ideologies held leadership positions in the city. In 1840, the Orthodox Baltimore Hebrew Congregation, the city's first synagogue, hired Rabbi Abraham Rice, who became the first ordained rabbi to live in the United States.[37] In 1842, several members of Baltimore Hebrew Congregation resigned in protest over Rice's strict orthodoxy and formed the Har Zion Congregation, which became the first lasting Reform congregation in the United States. At first Har Zion remained somewhat traditional; men and women sat separately, and Hebrew was the predominant language of worship. However, in 1855, David Einhorn, who had been trained at an Orthodox European yeshiva became rabbi of Har Zion. A radical reformer, Einhorn made Baltimore a center of Reform thinking.[38] In 1859, Rabbi Benjamin Szold became rabbi of Oheb Shalom and he served for the next forty-three years.[39] A great scholar, Szold believed in an approach midway between Orthodox and ultra-Reform that later became known as Conservative. The replacement of traditional prayer books from the Old World with new ones published in America was one of the important changes in Judaism in America.[40] Two of the earliest American prayer books were published by Baltimore rabbis. In 1856 Rabbi Einhorn published *Olat Talmud,* (Perpetual offering), and in 1864, Rabbi Benjamin Szold published *Abodath Israel,* (Service of Israel).[41] Baltimore also had numerous Jewish charities, including the Hebrew Benevolent Society (established in 1856 from smaller assistance organizations), several private Jewish schools and synagogue schools, a Society to educate poor and orphan children, and the first YMHA in the country (established in 1854).[42] Baltimore Jews began collecting money for Jews in Palestine as early as 1840, and the city became an important center of Zionist activity.[43] Even nearby Trenton, which had attracted German settlers in the 1840s, established a synagogue, the Har Sinai Hebrew Congregation in 1858.[44]

Given all this Jewish activity in the surrounding cities, a religiously observant Jew who wanted to live in the Mid-Atlantic area among Jewish people, would most likely have chosen Philadelphia or Baltimore over Wilmington. Clearly, given the nature of the dominant economy, the large native-born population, and the lack of a Jewish presence, Wilmington was not the ideal place for the new Jewish immigrant. Those Jews who arrived in Wilmington between the 1850s and 1860s for business reasons had made a deliberate choice to accept life in a city without Jewish amenities. Several retailers who had worked in Baltimore or Philadelphia before coming to Wilmington returned to those cities for their religious needs.[45]

AMERICAN JEWRY IN THE LAST THIRD OF THE NINETEENTH CENTURY

Religious Life

By the 1870s, when Wilmington's Jews began to organize, Judaism in America had become something very different from traditional European Judaism, which was based on a "highly structured community empowered to enforce the proper behavior" and religious piety on individuals.[46] In America, the state was indifferent to religious behavior, and "even the most hierarchical religious groups saw lay members challenge established authority, question beliefs and demand changes in ritual."[47] American Jews were part of the general trend. Hoping "to harmonize Judaism and modern American life," they made changes in the practice of Judaism that would help Jews blend in with American norms and appear less foreign.[48]

Formal interest in reforming Judaism existed in America as early as 1824, when forty-seven members of South Carolina's Congregation Beth Elohim petitioned for several reforms in order to bring back those fellow Jews who "are now wandering gradually from the true God and daily losing strong ties to the faith."[49] The petitioners requested the translation of some prayers into English so they could be understood, a shortened service, and a weekly English "discourse" expounding the basic texts and principles of Judaism. Denied their requests in 1825, the discontented members formed the Reformed Society of Israelites, which instituted many reforms including the use of a choir, instrumental music, the practice of men praying without head coverings, a prayer book with the first radical changes in liturgy, and extensive use of English.[50] The Society of Israelites ceased formal existence by the 1830s, but the impulse for reform grew stronger as the century progressed.

By 1855, Charleston, Baltimore, New York, Albany, and Cincinnati had congregations with some reformed rituals.[51] Since the goals of American Jewish laymen were respectability and Americanization, they modified the strict rituals of traditional European and earlier American synagogues to reflect the tastes of a respectable, acculturated constituency.[52] Reformers advocated the use of English, stricter decorum at services, the abandonment of hats, mixed seating of men and women, and the elimination of the second day of holidays.[53] By 1877 there were some 277 synagogues in the United States, and most had introduced some reforms.[54] It was apparent that "with greater or lesser rapidity nearly all of American Jewry was moving toward a moderate Reform."[55] Although there were some enclaves of Orthodoxy in the East, the general feeling was that they would not resist for long.

The American interest in reform was also influenced by the Reform movement in Germany.[56] Beginning in the early nineteenth century, each state within Germany emancipated its Jews.[57] By 1871 the last of the civil and political laws restricting where Jews could live, who they could marry, and what occupations they could pursue, had been removed and Jews could become equal citizens in German society.[58] As a result, more Jews lived near non-Jewish neighbors, integrated into the larger culture, and felt pressure to become more like other German citizens. In other words, Jews in Germany experienced the confrontation of Jewish culture and secular culture just like the Jews in America. One of the most sweeping German reforms had been to force all rabbis to receive a university education.[59] Once the university-trained rabbis became aware of the conflict of traditional Judaism and the secular world, they began to reform Judaism in order to preserve Judaism, by giving people a choice other than moving to Christianity.

After midcentury, German-trained rabbis like Isaac Mayer Wise, David Einhorn, Max Lilienthal, Samuel Adler, and Kaufmann Kohler emigrated to America, bringing the theoretical framework developed by the German Reform movement with them and spurring the interest in reform.[60] More German Jews were emancipated as the century progressed; therefore, most of the German immigrants who arrived in America after 1850 carried German cultural experiences with them.[61] German Jews proudly accepted the identity of Germans and took pride in the culture of the fatherland.[62]

The Reform movement in America was divided on how much emphasis to give to German culture and language. Rabbi Isaac Wise, who did not actively identify himself as a German Jew, emphasized the Jewish acculturation to America. He believed the United States was the center of modernization.[63] In 1857, in an attempt to create unity among all American synagogues, Isaac Mayer

Wise published a prayer book, *Minhag America*, which was quickly adopted by many synagogues.[64] Rabbi David Einhorn, the great "Germanizer," believed that Americans should follow Germany, the center of reform. In 1869, a meeting in neighboring Philadelphia of eleven reform rabbis clearly established American Reform thinking as something different than German Reform. One significant area of disagreement between the two groups concerned the position of women and the wedding vow. The Germans maintained that although a wife might be equal to her husband, she occupied a different position in society, and the man was the master of the house; therefore only the man should say the vow, and the woman should passively whisper "yes."[65] The Philadelphia conference voted that as a symbol of the equality of husband and wife, the bride would be allowed to respond to the wedding vow by repeating the same words as the groom, with a change in gender.

During the early part of the nineteenth century, American intellectuals and Jews had tremendous respect for German culture. Jews from Germany were considered more influential than both American-born Jews and the Sephardic Jews, who had arrived earlier. However, by the late 1870s, vicious outbreaks of anti-Semitism had erupted in Germany.[66] In spite of the centuries-old, underlying German belief that Jews were alien bodies, many liberal Germans had supported the concept of Jewish emancipation with hopes that once free, the Jews would renounce their Jewishness and become more like their fellow Germans. By the last third of the nineteenth century, it had become apparent that this strategy had not worked, and the entire German society became more anti-Semitic.[67] American Jews found it increasingly difficult to speak favorably of Germany when it had failed to control its vicious anti-Semitism. During the 1870s and 1880s, as the new American Judaism grew stronger, the German influence that had been predominant in both religious and cultural matters for nearly a century began to wane.[68] By the 1880s, German Jews in America felt that "the lessons to be learned from the Jews of Germany were mostly negative."[69] Ironically, while the German Jewish influence in America was in decline, Wilmington's German Jewish population was responsible for organizing the first synagogue and aid society. During the late nineteenth and early twentieth centuries, the general Wilmington community still looked with favor on the German population.

Organizational Life

As the largest and most active group of Jews in America, by the 1880s Jews of German descent had built a network of viable institutions and organizations across the continent, had established a multilingual press, and had attracted a body of able-bodied, European-ordained rabbis.

In the Old World, the synagogue had been the center of Jewish society, but in America, which did not have rabbis to serve as ecclesiastic heads of the community in the early days, the synagogue ceased to be comprehensive and many functions fell to secular institutions.[70] Generally, organizations dealt with three basic areas of concern: dying, disaster work and support of families, and association with friends.[71] In forming these organizations, the Jews followed other immigrant groups, who found that forming associations of others like themselves lessened their sense of loneliness and helplessness.[72]

In New York in 1822, a group called the Hebrew Benevolent Society was formed to serve and aid the growing number of destitute newcomers who were not affiliated with a synagogue.[73] By creating an organization without a synagogue connection, Jewish leaders established the concept of communal organizations assisting needy Jews, regardless of their religious affiliation. They recognized a standard for humanity, not just religion. Whether these organizations were based on the Talmudic teaching of responsibility for one's fellow man or on the practical desire to keep the Jewish poor from becoming a burden in the United States, thereby giving Jews a bad name, is debatable. The fact is that Jews developed a strong tradition of communal organizations, without synagogue ties, to assist needy Jews. B'nai B'rith was founded in New York in 1843. Modeled upon Freemasonry, B'nai B'rith was a fraternal organization which provided philanthropy for Jews in need.[74] Its fraternal nature seemed to some rabbis "an indication of American Jews' drift away from normative Judaism to the bland and pleasant atmosphere of a club room."[75] Isaac Lesser's original Jewish Publication Society, which existed from 1840–1851, was another example of a voluntary organization working outside the synagogue.

The concept of community is basic to the Jewish religion. Individuals normally do not pray alone. Traditionally, in order to hold a religious service, a *minyan* of at least ten men has to be present.[76] Given the primacy of community in Judaism, the development of community organizations to assist members of the group was a logical step.

American Jews established themselves as part of an international group that would speak up publicly when Jews anywhere in the world were threatened.[77] In the infamous Damascus Affair of 1840, Syrian Jews were accused of killing a priest and his Muslim servant in order to use their blood in making matzah. Sir Moses Montefiore, the revered English Jew, who was knighted for his service to humanitarian causes, led a successful effort to have the Jews released. In New York, Mordecai Manual Noah, a well-respected Sephardic leader, addressed a large gathering at the Askenazic synagogue and announced "we are one people bound by the same religious ties. . . . The cause of one is the cause of all."[78]

Throughout the nineteenth century, American Jews more than other immigrant groups shied away from injecting ethnic interests into the political arena.[79] The generally accepted guideline was that it was wrong for Jews to ban together in political clubs, that rabbis and Jewish agencies had no right to advise people how to vote, and that Jews should not support candidates just because they were Jewish. During the Civil War, American Jews were divided on the question of slavery; Jews lined up according to the section of the country they lived in. Despite the sectional loyalties of the Jews, neither side really accepted them.[80]

During the war, many merchants tried to make their fortunes by speculating in cotton. They bought cotton in the South, which needed money, and sold it in the North, which needed cotton.[81] According to official documents, civilian and military personnel in many areas were involved in cotton speculation. President Abraham Lincoln and the national government were strongly against cotton speculation because it diverted attention from the war effort. In December 1862, General Ulysses S. Grant singled the Jews out as scapegoats. He issued Grant's Military Order No. 11, which expelled all Jews from the military immediately. The order stated: "The Jews, as a class violating every regulation of trade established by the Treasury Department and also department orders, are hereby expelled from the military department within twenty four hours from the receipt of this order."[82] At the request of the Jewish community, President Lincoln interceded for the Jews and instructed Grant to revoke the order because it proscribed an entire class, some of whom were loyal fighters. Following the President's request, Grant did rescind the order, but he never actually apologized. In fact, a Jewish delegation that visited President Lincoln to thank him reportedly was shown a letter in which Grant's anti-Semitism was clear: "Mr. President, as you have directed me, I will rescind the order, but I wish you to understand that these people are the descendants of those who crucified the Savior and from the specimens I have here, the race has not improved."[83]

When Grant ran for president in 1868, the whole issue came to the forefront again. The idea of a Jewish vote and the question of a candidate's anti-Semitism became a central political issue. Should the Jews declare that their religion and Americanism were separate and vote on party lines and political beliefs, or should they vote as Jews? The ideal of political neutrality prevailed, and Jews appeared in support and in opposition to Grant.[84]

By the time Wilmington's Jewish community began to organize, patterns of charitable organizations and political behavior had been established throughout the country. Wilmington's Jews, who had lived in other places in America, used their knowledge of Jewish life elsewhere as a model for building the Jewish community in Wilmington.

Religion or Race

Throughout the nineteenth century, most American Jews thought of themselves first and foremost as a religious group.[85] Such a definition allowed them to maintain their Judaism and to adapt to a country that respected religious diversity.[86] Rabbi Isaac Mayer Wise expressed their sentiment well when he announced, "We are Jews in the synagogue and Americans everywhere."[87] However, by the last decades of the nineteenth century, when racial categories were in wide use in America and the Jews faced unprecedented opportunities for social integration, many Jews feared that assimilation would destroy their group integrity. In order to express their desire to maintain a distinct identity without unwanted political connections, they embraced a racial definition, which distinguished Jews from others by cultural differences as well as biology, shared ancestry, and blood.[88] In the last decades of the nineteenth century, when Wilmington's Jewish community began, American Jews differed on whether to define themselves as a race or a religion.[89]

Ironically, the use of race became a factor in the restrictionist movement that led to the end of immigration. The welcoming attitude of the United States towards immigrants, which had dominated the nineteenth century, was based on the assumption that the quality of men was determined not by birth but by environment.[90] All immigrants would come with minds and spirits fresh for new impressions and being in America would make Americans of them. However, at the end of the nineteenth century, racist ideas about the division of people into biologically distinct groups had seeped deep into the thinking of many Americans.[91] Restrictionists used the "realities of race" to bolster their arguments against the admission of new immigrants.

WILMINGTON'S JEWS IN THE MID-NINETEENTH CENTURY

In the 1850s, Jewish merchants from the neighboring cities of Baltimore and later Philadelphia began to open stores in Wilmington.[92] Often the stores were branches of businesses that other family members continued to operate in the original cities.

Joseph Row, a native of Bavaria who had emigrated to Baltimore, arrived in Wilmington in 1853 to open a clothing store with his nephew Sol Brenner. Row, a master mason, also remained in business in Baltimore, where he was a member of the Baltimore Hebrew Synagogue. Other relatives—including his brother Bernard Row and brothers-in-law Moritz Landower, Louis Richenberger, and Emanuel Richenberger—came to Wilmington in the late 1850s and early 1860s. They engaged in the clothing business in Wilmington together or separately for more than twenty years. During much of the period, Joseph Row, Landower, and the Richenbergers retained residencies in Baltimore and most likely returned home for religious observances.

Another Jewish clothing firm, Bacharach, Goldstein and Company, opened on Market Street during the late 1850s. The partners in this firm also retained their out-of-state residencies: Solomon Bacharach and Herman Goldstein lived in New York, while Julius Lowenstein lived in Havre de Grace, Maryland.

During the 1860s, at least seventeen Jewish merchants from Philadelphia tried their luck at business in Wilmington. Most opened their shops for some brief time and were gone again by 1870. Many of them maintained their residences in Philadelphia. However, a few—Nathan Lieberman, Jacob DeWolf, Kaufman Sondheimer, and Henry Buxbaum—established successful clothing businesses and remained in Wilmington. Most likely during the early years of their Delaware life, these families returned to Philadelphia to worship, but as business became profitable and they decided to remain in Wilmington, these men helped organize Jewish life here.

In 1872, about twenty Jews who lived or worked in Wilmington attempted to form a synagogue. Jacob DeWolf was elected president, Nathan Lieberman vice-president, and Joseph Row corresponding secretary. Although Row was not a permanent resident, he had been in business longer than any other Jew in Wilmington and had family here. Nathan Lieberman, Henry Buxbaum, and a newcomer from Philadelphia, Frederick L. Frank, sold subscriptions to the proposed synagogue at their clothing stores. The reaction from the general community was favorable: "Nearly every faith has here its house of worship, and it is quite time that the most

Nathan Lieberman. (Jewish Historical Society of Delaware.)

ancient of them all had its tabernacle."[93] One of the major needs of the Jews was a burial ground. Jewish customs forbid burying the dead in a Christian cemetery, so when an observant Jew died in Wilmington his remains were always taken to Philadelphia for internment.[94]

Unfortunately, subscriptions did not sell well, and the synagogue was not formed.[95] However, services for the High Holidays were held in different stores for several years. The failure of the synagogue might have caused some Jews to leave Wilmington. Within a few years of the synagogue's failure, Joseph Row and Landower returned to Baltimore and Frederick L. Frank returned to Philadelphia.

The Row-Landower-Richenberger family seems to have split after Joseph's return to Baltimore. In earlier days, family members had traveled back and forth between the two cities. However, Joseph's daughter Carrie, born in 1869, only remembered her father in Baltimore. She did not remember her uncle Bernard or any Wilmington cousins.[96]

After Joseph Row returned to Baltimore, he remained a strong Jew. His daughter Carrie recalled large Sabbath dinners with at least twelve people at the table. Row knew many ship captains because his tailoring shop was down by the wharf, and on Friday night, there was always at least one ship captain at the Shabbat dinner table. At the same time, Joseph became chaplain of his Masonic lodge. Brother Bernard, who remained in Wilmington, never formally renounced his Judaism; however, Bernard was not an active member of the Jewish community. Bernard's son Isaac married a non-Jewish woman. Another son renounced his Judaism in order to become chaplain of one of the Masonic orders, requiring allegiance to Jesus Christ. Bernard, his wife Sophie, and their children Isaac, Clara, Joseph, and Harry were all buried in an unmarked plot in Riverview Cemetery. Brother-in-law Manual Richenberger also married a non-Jew.

The branch of the family that remained in Wilmington lost its Jewish identity. The branch that returned to Baltimore remained Jewish. Perhaps Joseph had such a premonition when he left Wilmington. Clearly, it was dangerous business to live in a community without any other Jews. This thought must have been primary in the minds of the Jews who chose to begin the Moses Montefiore Society in 1879. Living in a community with no formal Jewish presence was not the way to balance the demands of becoming American and remaining Jewish.

2

In the Beginning

On the evening preceding Yom Kippur, the day of atonement, 1879, about thirty Jews, "including four or five women and a dozen children," attended Kol Nidre services conducted by Rabbi Julius Weil of Philadelphia in the Morrow Building.[1]

In September 1879, the Jews of Wilmington numbered roughly ninety-four people, including sixteen married couples, two men married to non-Jewish women, ten single men over the age of twenty, and some fifty children.[2] To most Jews, Yom Kippur is the most sacred day of the year. Observant Jews refrain from all work, maintain a fast, and attend synagogue from sundown one evening, Kol Nidre, until sundown the following evening. The fact that only thirty Jews out of a citywide Jewish population of some ninety-four people attended Kol Nidre services indicates that some Wilmington Jews were not particularly observant, or that many Jews still observed the major holidays with their relatives in neighboring cities.

Although only thirty people in a city with a population of some 42,500 attended the service, the holy day was described in great detail by an article on the front page of the *Every Evening* newspaper. Clearly, the Jews had made their presence felt or at least had aroused some curiosity. Expressions of admiration about the way Jews kept their archaic faith alive were prevalent throughout America even in areas that did not have Jewish populations.[3]

None of the Jewish rituals were familiar to the reporter, who admitted that the "exercises appeared very strange to a reporter visiting a Jewish synagogue for the first time." The rabbi's talit was unfamiliar to the reporter, who explained "Reverend Julius Weil . . . had a shawl like garment apparently made of white silk bordered with dark blue stripes thrown over his shoulders."[4] Two or three of the congregation wore similar shawls. All the men kept on their hats, most of them wearing neatly brushed, glossy head coverings of the stovepipe variety.

In describing the traveling ark and Torah, the reporter wrote:

Leaning against the front wall of the room was a box containing the Hebrew Pentateuch written on some material, most probably parchment and arranged to roll up as large maps generally do. This roll was covered with yellow cloth, and a scarlet curtain inscribed with Hebraic characters was drawn across the front of the box.[5]

The service began with a prayer in German and continued with scriptural selections and chants, all in Hebrew. Some prayers were spoken in a very low, almost inaudible voice while others were recited in loud voice and still others were sung in unmelodious measures.

After describing the service, the reporter explained that the Jews were attempting to induce Rabbi Weil to locate in Wilmington and to start a school for their children. There was also a "movement afoot" to form a beneficial organization that would "aid indigent and unfortunate brethren."[6]

Indeed, there was more than a movement afoot; a movement was about to burst forth. On Sunday evening, the day after Yom Kippur, several Hebrew citizens met at the home of Nathan Lieberman, 503 Shipley Street, for the purpose of organizing a benevolent society that would serve religious, educational, and charitable functions. Eighteen men formed the Moses Montefiore Society, which pledged to aid all needy Jews and Gentiles who applied to them for assistance and, in the course of time, to erect a synagogue.[7] The new organization also intended to "accumulate funds for the payment of sick benefits to members and funeral benefits to his family."[8]

In selecting the name Moses Montefiore Society, Wilmington Jews paid tribute to the man who was seen by American Jews as the ideal model of a modern, emancipated, yet traditional Jew.[9] Throughout the United States in the nineteenth century, so many organizations were named after Sir Moses Montefiore that they probably equal all of those named for other Jews of historic importance added together.[10]

George A. Jacobs was elected president, Julius Fisher secretary, and Kaufman Sondheimer treasurer. Messrs. Kahn, Fellheimer, and DeWolf were appointed to the by laws and constitution committee. Thanks were given to Messrs. Lieberman, Meyers, and Rosenblatt for their efforts in bringing the organization into existence.[11] The identity of the other nine founders has been lost in time. In all likelihood, they were all men because the nine members mentioned by name were men, all articles about the Moses Montefiore Society in the following years mentioned men, and throughout America at this time, men were dominant in Jewish organizations.

THE FOUNDERS

Nathan Lieberman, who hosted the meeting of the Moses Montefiore Society, was the most prominent Jew in Wilmington in 1879. He had been in the country for more than two decades, had fought in the Civil War, had been in Wilmington since the mid-1860s, and had been a United States citizen since 1872.[12] At forty-three years of age, he was one of the oldest Wilmington Jews.

Born in Bavaria in 1836, Lieberman lived in Saginaw, Michigan, and Philadelphia before he arrived in Wilmington and opened the clothing store, Goodman & Lieberman, with his uncle Daniel Goodman, who also ran a store in Philadelphia. By 1868, Lieberman ran N. Lieberman and Company at 426 Market, and both Goodman and Isaac Richman, another early partner, had disappeared from the Wilmington scene. Nathan Lieberman married Rosa Arnold, a native of Württemberg, Germany in 1866. Abe, the first of their eight children, was born in Wilmington in 1868.

N. Lieberman and Company was a very successful store with the "largest stock of clothing in the city and a selection as fine as that of any pretentious establishment of Philadelphia at lower prices."[13] Barkers outside the store tried to prevent a pedestrian from passing the door without coming in. Once a customer entered, Lieberman's policy was never to let a shopper go away empty-handed. Bargaining became an art.

It was sort of understood that when a man entered the store, he was a buyer and every effort was made possible by a wide range of prices for

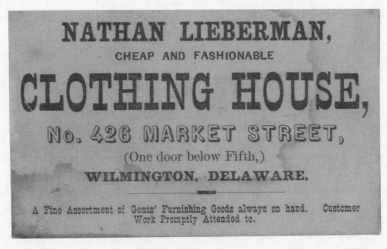

Business card of Nathan Lieberman, 1870s. (Jewish Historical Society of Delaware.)

The Prices we Have Inaugurated

Have caused a revolution in the trade, and Clothing Dealers are at their wits end to account for the way we do it. Our patrons are both surprised and delighted, and are loud in their praises of the

BEAUTY AND NOVELY OF OUR STYLES

and the unprecedently low prices at which they are offered at

Lieberman's Store at 5th and Market Streets. (Jewish Historical Society of Delaware.)

which clothing could be bought. Bickering often took an hour or more. Part of the policy of merchants was to sell goods at any figure above their cost if it were necessary to make sales.[14]

Since the store specialized in an exclusive line of men's clothing and haberdashery, it was the place that many duPont children were outfitted in the 1860s. Lieberman's was so successful that it was not unusual for $4,000 to be taken in on a Saturday. Mrs. Lieberman came down on Saturday after supper and took charge of the cash, which piled up high in her apron.[15] The fact that Mrs. Lieberman came down after supper suggests that the Liebermans had worked out a compromise about the Sabbath: the store was open but they refrained from work themselves until sundown.

Lieberman had been one of the forces behind the attempted synagogue in 1872. Although the synagogue had not been established, the need for worship services in Delaware had been proven, and Nathan Lieberman provided space on the second floor of his store for the "divine services" during the High Holidays of 1873. By the time of the High Holidays in 1875, Lieberman's business had increased beyond expectations, and the second floor of his building had been incorporated into the store as a sales room for children's clothing, so services for the holidays were held in the Morrow Building at 211 Market Street. In the 1870s the Knights of Pythias had a hall on the third floor of the Morrow Building at 211 Market Street. As treasurer of one chapter of the Knights of Pythias, Lieberman probably made the arrangements for services to be held in their quarters in the Morrow Building.

In April 1878, Nathan Lieberman was given the contract to furnish the local police with new uniforms, which he would provide at $3 per suit less than any house in Philadelphia could supply them.[16] By 1880 Lieberman was known as the "principal dealer of clothing on Market Street, with superior abilities for transactions of this special business."[17] The reference to superior talents might have been intended as a compliment, but like so many statements of admiration, it conveyed the idea that Jews were somehow different than everyone else.[18]

Lieberman was also active in the broader community. Within a few years of his arrival in Wilmington, he became an active member of a local chapter of the Knights of Pythias, a benevolent society that aimed to alleviate the suffering of a brother, to succor the unfortunate, and to watch at the bedside of the sick. The Knights of Pythias was open to all men who believed in a Supreme Being. Lieberman served as treasurer of the Castle Lodge of Knights of Pythias from the time of its inception, before 1870, until his death in 1906.

Jacob De Wolf, who had been elected president of the attempted 1872 synagogue, attended the meeting and became a member of the bylaws committee. DeWolf, a native of England, had come to Wilmington from Philadelphia in the 1860s in order to open a clothing store.[19] His store at 308 Market Street, one block away

Jacob DeWolf. (Jewish Historical Society of Delaware.)

from Lieberman's store, had ready-made and custom-made clothing. DeWolf's boasted one of the finest cutters in the country. Just
a few years after DeWolf opened his store, an article on "Where to
Get the Best Clothes at the Lowest Prices in Wilmington" recommended DeWolf: "DeWolf competes with everyone in selling
cheap and can suit any gentleman as to quality. Economize by buying at DeWolf's."[20]

Jacob DeWolf and his wife Fanny Isaacs DeWolf, also a native of
England, were among the few Wilmington Jews who could trace
their roots to Sephardic Jewry. Jacob's parents were born in Holland; they had married when his mother was fifteen, and emigrated
to England. Fannie's mother's family had left Spain for England at
the time of the Inquisition. The family of Fannie's father, Isaac
Isaacs, had emigrated from Australia to England. Jacob had come
to the United States when he was six, and Fannie arrived when she
was ten.[21] Isaac Isaacs lived with the DeWolf family, and at sev-
enty-six years of age was the oldest Jew in Wilmington. His grand-
daughter remembered him as a "lovely Jewish man with a white
beard and white hair, who looked like the old Bible."[22]

Fannie and Jacob DeWolf were married in 1865, by the renowned
Sabato Morais, who at the time was the *chazan* (cantor) of Mikveh
Israel, Philadelphia's Sephardic synagogue. The two older DeWolf
sons, William and Isaac, were born in Pennsylvania, and the next
three children were born in Delaware. DeWolf returned to Philadelphia just before the Centennial in an attempt to make money during
the celebration. Most likely, part of the reason DeWolf left Wilmington was the failed synagogue of 1872. Two children were born
in Philadelphia before Jacob DeWolf returned to Wilmington,
where the family grew to include fifteen children.

Calling the Dewolfs "a mother and father to be proud of," Estella
Hoffman described her mother as a "beautiful lady who looked like
the Spanish type" and was very self-sacrificing. Her father was "a
Bible and Hebrew student, self-taught, and a man you could ask
any questions, very well read." Jacob DeWolf was religious in a
free way. He prayed with his talit on his shoulders, but never laid
tefellim.[23] Estella had been told that while her father was in Wilmington, he and his friends "organized a place of worship and a
Sunday school for children."[24] DeWolf was also accepted in the
larger community. He was initiated as a Master Mason into the
Grand Lodge of Delaware in 1872.

Like Lieberman and DeWolf, Kaufman Sondheimer ran a clothing store on Market Street and had been in Wilmington for more
than a decade.[25] In the 1850s Sondheimer, a native of Bavaria, ran

a clothing store in Freehold, New Jersey and bought merchandise for his store from another Bavarian, Morris Stern of Philadelphia. He met Morris's sister Barbara and married her in Philadelphia in 1861. Rabbi David Einhorn, recognized as one of the leaders of reform Judaism in America, performed the ceremony. Kaufman and Barbara's first child Ben was born in New Jersey. In 1866 Kaufman and his wife Barbara moved to Wilmington to be near Barbara's sister Mrs. Hirnheimer, who lived in Smyrna, a city about forty miles south of Wilmington. After they moved to Wilmington, five other children were born to the Sondheimers. Monroe Sondheimer, the youngest of the children, described his father as a man of about 5'7", with a beard and a heavy German accent. Both his parents were Reform Jews. At the meeting, Kaufman Sondheimer was elected treasurer of the Moses Montefiore Society. He was the only officer who had been in Wilmington for more than a decade.

Another Market Street clothier, Meyer Meyers, was thanked along with Nathan Lieberman and Barney Rosenblatt for bringing the organization into existence. Born in Bavaria in 1848, Meyers had been in the United States since the early 1860s.[26] His wife Selena was born in Switzerland. Meyers had opened a one-price clothing store on Market Street in the mid-1860s, but because he ran several other stores in neighboring states, he did not actually live in Wilmington until the late 1870s. The Meyers lived in New Jersey, where four of their children were born between 1873 and 1878. The fact that Meyers finally decided to settle in Wilmington at the same time the Montefiore Society was formed suggests that there was a connection between Meyers' decision to live here and the fact that there would be some formal Jewish communal life.

Since Meyers supplied his stores with clothing manufactured at a factory in which he had an interest, the store prices were low. *Delaware Industries* claimed there was "not a better or more favorably known house than that of Meyer Meyers."[27]

An innovative merchant, Meyers was one of the first ten merchants in Wilmington to install electric lights in his store. In 1883, the *Sunday Star* newspaper reported "Goods can now be seen at night as well as in the daytime. Goods are still cheaper than cheap."[28]

Meyers' technique was to advertise clearing-out sales. For instance, in 1885 he advertised 120 men's suits at $3.75 each because he was forced to make changes in his business. In 1888, Meyers sent up a balloon with his letterhead and said whoever found it and brought it to his store would get a present.

Barney Rosenblatt, who presided over the September 28 organi-

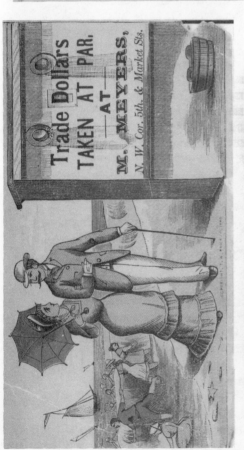

Business cards and advertisements of Meyer Meyers, 1880s. (Jewish Historical Society of Delaware.)

zational meeting, was not a clothier but a hairdresser.[29] Arriving in Wilmington in 1879, shortly before the Moses Montefiore Society was formed, Rosenblatt immediately became a catalyst for the formation of the new organization.

Born in Poland in 1844, Rosenblatt had arrived in the United States in time to fight in the Civil War. During the 1870s, he and his wife Rachel, a native of Bavaria, lived in California, where their children Benjamin and Rebecca were born. However, Rosenblatt did not like the Chinese, and he left California in order to get away from them. Because of the California Gold Rush, large numbers of Chinese laborers had immigrated to California. Between 1860 and 1880, the population of California was some 9 percent Chinese.[30] In 1869, when the Union Pacific Railroad was completed, jobs began to decline and a strong anti-Chinese movement developed. In 1879 Rosenblatt told the *Every Evening* newspaper "the Chinese must go. I left California to get away from them and don't want to find them here."[31] Perhaps as a veteran of the Civil War, Rosenblatt felt totally integrated into American society. Perhaps he thought he would strength his position by belittling someone else. Clearly, Rosenblatt did not recognize that discrimination against one ethnic group would eventually lead to discrimination against other minorities.

Rosenblatt was an outspoken character and attracted much attention during 1879–1880. Once he wrote a resolution to City Council requesting a new lamppost outside his barbershop. Another time he was named as a possible candidate of the Dooly Warden Party for City Council. In March 1880, a few months after Rosenblatt presided at the founding meeting of the Moses Montefiore Society, he held a meeting at his home to organize a Veterans Corps for Civil War soldiers. The *Every Evening* suggested that Rosenblatt deserved the title "the great organizer."[32]

In 1880, Rosenblatt began building a two-story brick building adjoining his barbershop at East 7th Street. He said the upper story would be used as a Russian bath house.[33] Apparently, he was more of a dreamer than a pragmatist because by 1881, Rosenblatt had left Wilmington, and in 1883, he was in distress in Baltimore. His wife was hospitalized, two of his children were sick, and his right hand was disabled.[34]

George A. Jacobs, who was elected president of the Moses Montefiore Society, remains more mysterious. Along with his wife Amelia, who was English, and their son Ezekiel, born in Pennsylvania in 1875, he moved to Wilmington before daughter Sarah was born in 1878.[35] Several months after the census was taken in 1880, the Jacobs' second son Jacob was born and circumcised. The census of 1880 says Jacobs was also born in England, but his death certificate says he was born in Delaware. Jacobs died in Laurel, Delaware in 1888, and the funeral service was held in Philadelphia.[36] Jacobs was such an honored member of the Montefiore Society that the entire membership of the society attended his funeral. He was then buried in Sussex County, a fact that suggests family connections in Sussex County.[37] While there were several Jacobs families in southern Delaware, none were still Jewish in the 1870s and 1880s. However, there would have been no reason for a burial in Sussex County unless family members had been buried there in the past.

Julius Fisher, who was elected Secretary of the Moses Montefiore Society, never became a permanent part of the Wilmington community. In 1878, when he married Sarah Nogler, the daughter of Wilmington clothing manufacturer Sam Nogler, Fisher was in business with his father-in-law but lived in New Jersey.[38] There is no record of the Fishers living in Wilmington, but their wedding on March 5, 1878 at Saenger Hall was called "the first public Jewish wedding in the city."[39] Both Julius Fisher and Sam Nogler left Wilmington before the Moses Montefiore Society's incorporation in 1883.

Mayer and/or Gerson Kahn attended the meeting at Lieberman's home, and one of them joined the bylaws and constitution committee. The Kahn brothers arrived in Wilmington from Baltimore in 1879 to open a clothing store at 218 Market Street.[40] Gershon boarded at the U.S. Hotel and Mayer boarded at the Clayton House. Mayer was born in Maryland; Gershon had lived in Maryland at least since 1853. Both Mayer and Gershon left Wilmington before 1882.

Both Marx and Louis Fellheimer were most likely among the eighteen men who joined the Moses Montefiore Society that first night, but whether the Fellheimer on the bylaws committee was Marx or his eldest son Louis, who was twenty-two years old at the time, is not known. In 1879, Marx was fifty-five, older than all other Jews in Wilmington except Isaac Isaacs and Bernard Row, who was not a practicing Jew. Instead of taking an active role in the new organization, he might have suggested his son Louis for the bylaws committee. Louis, who had been born in Pennsylvania, worked in his father's clothing store but lived independently.[41]

Marx Fellheimer was born in Württemberg, Germany in a small town called Jebenkausen, or possibly as his daughter remembered a town called Fellheim, and came to America as a child. His family first settled in Chambersburg, Pennsylvania but was burned out by rebels during the Battle of Gettysburg. After living in Philadelphia

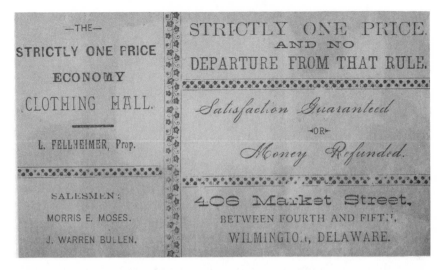

—THE—

STRICTLY ONE PRICE

ECONOMY

CLOTHING HALL.

L. FELLHEIMER, Prop.

SALESMEN:

MORRIS E. MOSES.

J. WARREN BULLEN.

STRICTLY ONE PRICE,

AND NO

DEPARTURE FROM THAT RULE,

Satisfaction Guaranteed

—OR—

Money Refunded.

406 Market Street,

BETWEEN FOURTH AND FIFTH,

WILMINGTON, DELAWARE.

Business cards of Louis Fellheimer, early 1880s. (Jewish Historical Society of Delaware.)

for some years, Marx, his wife Ellen Yeisenberg Fellheimer, and seven of their children moved to Wilmington around 1871. Marx opened a clothing store at 310 Market Street. Bertie Fellheimer, the tenth of Marx and Ellen Fellheimer's eleven children, said that her father was "not a religious man but he did assist with services on the high holidays." Their combination store and home had a retail portion facing Market Street, a dining room and parlor in the rear, and bedrooms upstairs. It was "a rendezvous for traveling Jewish men." Marx Fellheimer was a jovial man who sat on the curb and sang.[42]

Like Lieberman and DeWolf, Marx Fellheimer was an accepted part of the larger community. He was a member of the Knights of Pythias organization. Like Lieberman and DeWolf, he had many children who needed a Jewish education.

The remaining men who joined the organization were not mentioned by name. Any of the Jewish men in Wilmington in September 1879 could have been founders, but five seem to be leading possibilities because they were part of the committees for the first Montefiore ball a few months later. Charles Italie, who was married to Dora Nogler, was a brother-in-law of secretary Julius Fisher and son-in-law of Sam Nogler.[43] An optician from the Netherlands, Italie worked in Wilmington by 1878. In his office at 218 Market, he examined people who had problems with sight, particularly those who had problems because of inferior glasses. His office was opened on Wednesday and Saturday and every evening. Although Italie's business was in Wilmington, he may not have lived there at this time, since the son born in early 1880 was born in Pennsylvania.

Another optician, Ferdinand Bishof, his wife Harriet, and their three children arrived in Wilmington by 1878. Ferdinand, a native of Prussia, and his wife, a native of France, had both arrived in the United States before 1864. The children had been born in New York; a fourth child, Eva, was born in Delaware in 1879.[44] Bishof's store was at 714 Market Street.

Samuel Levi of Germany participated in the grand march at the first Montefiore Ball. In 1880, he lived with Louis Fellheimer and and was a clerk, most likely in Fellheimer's store.

Bernard Wolfson, the only East European Jew besides Rosenblatt, was a native of Russia, and had arrived in the United States in the 1860s.[45] His wife Mina was from Germany. The Wolfsons' older children, Simon and Abraham, were born in Massachusetts, but by 1874 Bernard opened a clothing store at 14 East Front Street in Wilmington. The next three Wolfson children were born in Delaware. Wolfson was elected messenger of the Moses Montefiore Society in September 1880 and signed the Moses Montefiore Society's papers of incorporation in 1883. Although he believed in a more Orthodox interpretation of Judaism than the others, he most likely was one of the eighteen men who joined that first night in 1879.

Manual Richenberger, originally from Bavaria, arrived in Wilmington from Baltimore in 1865 to join family members. Richenberger's sister Sarah was married to Joseph Row and his sister Sophia was married to Bernard Row.[46] In the 1870s he left the clothing business, becoming first a furrier and then the manager of Sharpe's Hotel. Although Manual married a non-Jewish woman, Margaret, he was one of the charter members of the Moses Montefiore Society when it was incorporated in 1883, and he might very well have attended the 1879 meeting.

Manual was remembered by Wilmingtonians as a "handsome, dapper dresser, never without a diamond pin in his shirt."[47] He was a sportsman who managed an amateur baseball club and ran hunts from his hotel. When he was in court once, Richenberger insisted on swearing on the five books of Moses. Richenberger supposedly told Sondheimer that he had made one serious mistake in his life: he had married out of his religion.

Other possible original members were Adolph Arnold, Mrs. Nathan Lieberman's brother, who managed Nathan Lieberman's store in the late 1870s; Isaac Isaacs, the father of Fannie DeWolf; Samuel Cohen, who opened a clothing store at 211 Market Street in 1877; Samuel Hocheimer, who had a dry goods store on First (Front) Street; and Aaron Cohen of Prussia, who moved to Wilmington from Pennsylvania with his wife in 1879 or 1880. Cohen was a merchant tailor with a store at 200 Market Street. In September 1880, Cohen was elected one of the trustees of the "Hebrew church and school."[48] Wilmington's first resident rabbi, Rabbi Simon Rosenberg, lived with the Cohens in 1880.

The First Community

A spectator watching the group congregate at Lieberman's home might have assumed they were forming some type of business union. Sixteen of the likely attendees were in the clothing business on lower Market Street. They were joined by others who were in business on or near lower Market Street. At the time, there were two opticians, one tailor, one cigar maker, one carriage maker, one hairdresser, and one dry goods retailer.

It's not surprising that clothiers dominated the meeting because of the twenty-eight Jewish men in Wilmington, twenty were employed in the clothing business. In 1880 Wilmington had seventeen clothing stores and nine were run by Jews.[49] Therefore, though Jews accounted for less than a fraction of 1 percent of Wilmington's population, they owned half of the clothing stores in Wilmington. Throughout America in the post–Civil War days, Jews dominated clothing manufacturing and distribution. In the years before the Civil War, the garment industry was small, but whatever industry existed was in Jewish hands.[50] The Civil War demonstrated the importance of ready-made clothing, and when the industry grew after the war, Jews were positioned to manufacture and distribute clothing by family networks. In New York City, which took the lead as a garment center, men's clothing had a product value of $34 million by 1870.[51] A good part of the clothing industry was owned by German Jews who had arrived in midcentury. In an 1863 edition of the *New York Herald*, Jewish names appeared in twenty-three out of twenty-five ads for firms handling ready-made and secondhand clothing.[52] The Wilmington Jews' businesses were successful because the larger community patronized their stores. In Wilmington, Jews did not live in an isolated ghetto, like Jews often did in larger cities like New York, but rather were interspersed among other ethnic groups.

All of the twenty-eight Jewish men in Wilmington in 1879 were gainfully employed, except Isaac Isaacs, who was elderly and retired. Therefore, no one saw them as a burden on the population, which could have increased negative feelings against them. Not only were the Jews employed, but they were very comfortable. Eight of the eighteen married families had a servant.[53]

The community could almost be described as a collection of families. Close to half of the population, forty-six individuals, belonged to just six families. In 1879, the DeWolfs and Fellheimers each had seven children, the Liebermans and Sondheimers each had six children, and the Meyers and Wolfsons each had four children. All of the adults in these families except Bernard Wolfson were born in the United States or Central or Western Europe. All of the largest families were in the clothing business within a few blocks of each other on Market Street. Four of the largest families—Lieberman, Sondheimer, Meyer, and DeWolf—had been in business here since the 1860s, giving them not only the largest numbers but also seniority.

The Jews of Wilmington were an acculturated group. Approximately 20 percent of the adults, five men and five women, were Americans by birth. Of those born in Europe, all the women and all but two of the men were born in Western or Central Europe. The largest number of immigrants were from parts of what had become Germany, previously known as Bavaria, Prussia, or Württemberg. In Western and Central Europe, they had witnessed the dramatic changes of the Enlightenment and the French Revolution, which encouraged societies to become more secular and open; but as Jews they had been denied freedom to participate.[54] After they arrived in America, they used their freedom to break with the past, to become part of the American society, and "to realize their political, economic and social aspirations."[55] The children were all native-born Americans.

The community was youthful. Children accounted for slightly more than half the population. Even the adult portion of the population was young. Of the twenty-six men about whom information is available, only three individuals were older than fifty, six were in their forties, seven were in their thirties, and eight were in their twenties.[56] Of the fifteen Jewish married women about whom information is available, only two were in their forties, six were in their thirties, five were in their twenties, and one was nineteen.

The immigrants were experienced with life in the United States because they had been in this country either since a young age or for at least a decade. At least 80 percent of those who were immigrants had lived in other states, including Pennsylvania, Maryland, New York, New Jersey, California, Massachusetts, and Michigan, before settling in Wilmington.[57] The largest number had lived in Pennsylvania. By living in other states, they had become comfortable with American ways; they had seen how Jews could organize to help themselves, and they had learned to speak English. They did not arrive in Wilmington as penniless peddlers but rather had capital and could enter business directly.

Each of these immigrants shared another vital characteristic: a commitment to Judaism. They had made successful transitions to life in America; they earned good livings, and they were accepted by the secular community. Nevertheless, they believed in the religious and social teachings of Judaism enough to preserve them even though they recognized that the easier path, which many Jews took, was to abandon their religion and become part of mainstream America.

Given the familiarity of the community, the founders knew that Manual Richenberger had married a non-Jewish woman and that Bernard Row, a Master Mason who bought five shares of stock in the corporation that built the Masonic Temple and Grand Opera House in 1871, did not participate in Jewish organizations.[58] They also knew Samuel Kerns, the manager of the novelty Carriage House, which had a full and varied stock of buggies, phaetons, and carriages and occupied five floors at 217 East Front Street.[59] Kerns' first wife had been Jewish, and his daughters married Jewish men. Kerns' second wife was not Jewish, and Kerns never aligned himself with the Jewish people. However, on his deathbed he called for Rabbi Rezits.[60]

In addition to Row, Kerns, and Richenberger, the Wilmington Jews must have been aware of many Jews who chose to lose their identity when they moved to Wilmington. In Germany, the Jews had been persecuted and denied certain rights because of their religion. When they moved to a new country, one that respected German culture, it was attractive to emphasize their German side and ignore their Jewish roots. Many German Jews clung to German culture, wanted German schools for their children and participated in German clubs and associations.[61] The largest German immigration to Wilmington came in the 1850s and 1860s.[62] Since the Jews were beginning to arrive at the same time, the process of losing Jewish identity was even easier. Several immigrants whose names, parents' names, countries of origin, and occupations suggest they were Jewish never joined any Jewish activities or were married in churches.

During the 1860s and 1870s, several of the leading Jewish merchants had employed young Jewish clerks, who had stayed in Wilmington for a few years and then returned to Philadelphia. Some merchants had opened stores for a few years and then left Wilmington. Frederick L. Frank and Joseph Row, who had worked to establish Jewish organizations in earlier years, had returned to cities with larger Jewish populations. Jews who had been in Wilmington for a decade or more had seen that many Jews would not establish permanent residence in a city with no Jewish institutions. The founding members of the Moses Montefiore Society, who wanted to retain their heritage, recognized the importance of beginning a Jewish community in order to stem the tide of assimilation, to maintain the influx of younger Jewish families who had moved to Wilmington in the late 1870s, and to educate their own children.

DEFINITION AND COMPROMISE

During the first year of the Moses Montefiore Society's existence, the founders established a Hebrew school and a synagogue in addition to providing aid. While defining themselves as something different, they made compromises which showed their desire to adjust to life in America.

Unlike many immigrants who immediately established their churches in America as a way of holding on to an aspect of old-world life, the founders of the Moses Montefiore Society had lived in Wilmington without organized religion for some time.[63] Undoubtedly, one of the major reasons they decided to establish the Montefiore Society was to educate their children. On February 8, 1880, the Montefiore Society opened a Hebrew Sunday School that met at 3 P.M. The following evening, the society opened a Hebrew night school, to teach children Hebrew and German.[64] Some fifteen to twenty students attended the school.[65] In 1879, six of the Montefiore's founding families—DeWolf, Sondheimer, Lieberman, Meyers, Wolfson, and Fellheimer—had twenty-five children under the age of thirteen. There was a critical mass of children who needed to learn about Judaism. Traveling to neighboring cities a few times a year for High Holidays might have satisfied the adults, but clearly it was not possible to educate youth or to observe the Sabbath as a family without a synagogue and school in Wilmington. By establishing a school to educate their children, the founders believed they would preserve the children's Jewishness.

In deciding to educate their children about Judaism at night or on Sunday and to use the public schools, the founding Jews accepted a compromise made by most American Jews at the time.[66] They embraced the public school as an indispensable training ground for American citizenship.[67] Earlier in the nineteenth century, when few public schools existed and those that did were more overtly evangelical, Jewish children often attended Jewish day schools. However, as public schools advanced, more Jews attended public school. Throughout America, in their Jewish Sunday and evening schools, the Jews also adopted American models of education, which recognized that children were not adults and needed special educational materials.[68] In Europe, children had begun their studies in the original sources and were given Torah, Talmud, and Hebrew commentary at a very young age. Although no information on the teaching methods of the Montefiore Society's schools is extant, the founders' decision to teach German in their school shows that they still considered German the language of refinement and cultural sophistication. Until the late 1870s, when the first American-trained rabbis were ordained by Hebrew Union College, all rabbis were imported from Europe and by and large spoke German.[69]

In February 1880, the *Every Evening* announced that the new rabbi, Simon Rosenberg, had also become the *shochet*, the butcher and ritual slaughterer.[70] Rabbi Rosenberg killed animals according to a special procedure, using only the forequarters of the animal and carefully inspecting all the meat. He sold his kosher meat through David Megill's stall in the market on Second Street. However, after a few days, Megill announced that the Jews were not purchasing the meat and he would retire from the trade.[71] As a group, the Jews in Wilmington were not religious enough to keep kosher; however, a month later during Passover, they ate unleavened bread.[72] Like other American Jews at this time, Wilmington's Jews selected the practices they wanted to follow.

Rabbi Rosenberg, a native of Prussia, had lived in Philadelphia, but he was not a leader of any of the major synagogues there. At fifty-three years of age, Rosenberg was one of the oldest Jews in Wilmington. Rosenberg's tenure was brief; by the fall of 1881, he had been replaced by Rabbi Morris Faber. Rabbi Rosenberg might have returned briefly to Wilmington because in 1888, after Rabbi Faber left the community, the High Holiday services were conducted by a Rabbi Rosenberg.

The Moses Montefiore Society held its first annual Purim ball on February 26, 1880, in order to raise funds for the erection of a synagogue, the employment of a Hebrew teacher, and to promote the interests of the race.[73] The concept of a charity ball was an innovation. In Europe, each Jewish community was governed by a *kahal*, which taxed individuals in order to maintain services to the needy. The system was based on *tzedakah*, the concept of giving as an obligation based on justice. Here in America, Jews quickly adapted the American custom of a charity ball, and the "tzedakah concept gave way to the charity concept."[74] Purim was an ideal time for a ball, as the Jews in New York and other cities had seen.[75]

The social status of the Wilmington Jews is evident in the description of the ball, which was held at the Grand Opera House, in the rooms of Webster's Dancing Academy, a very prominent place to hold a dance. Among the numerous organizations who used the space were the Washington Assembly for an annual ball in honor of President George Washington, the Knights of Pythias, and Webster himself for fancy dress carnivals.[76] Ritchie's seven-piece orchestra, which performed at many society balls, provided the dance music. Festivities began at 9:30 P.M. with a grand march of some fifty couples. The *Every Evening* newspaper said: "the scene was such as is witnessed only among these people or Germans, that of gray-headed men and little children mingling and joining with the reveling and merry throng."[77] Guests included people from Philadelphia, Chester, Dover, and West Chester and many people from outside the Jewish race. Nathan Lieberman, Jacob De Wolf, F. K. Fisher, M. Fellheimer, K. Sondheimer, and G. L. Kahn were on the committee of arrangements. Samuel Levy, Reuben Wolters, F. Bishof, and Charles Italie were assistants.[78]

The ball was financially successful and the synagogue, which was located on the third floor of Nathan Lieberman's clothing store at Fifth and Market Streets, was redecorated. On March 19, 1880, the Ohabe Shalom synagogue was dedicated. Rabbi Simon Rosenberg and Mr. Isaac Isaacs, "the oldest Wilmington Israelite," wore talit and long white vestments.[79] Mr. Isaacs carried the Torah. The men walked around the altar with the Torah several times while a chant filled the air. When the chant was finished, the Torah was deposited in the ark. During the service, the rabbi was presented with a *yad*, a pointer used in reading the Torah. Rabbi Rosenberg addressed the group in German, but he gave his blessing in English. The congregants were observant enough that no one would turn out the lights so "an uncircumcised newspaperman turned off the gas jets and the congregation dispersed." Sabbath services for the next day began at 7 A.M.

Attempts to determine the religious practices at Ohabe Shalom are hindered by the fact that there are no extant records. We do know that by 1885, Ohabe Shalom was not traditional enough for the new Russian immigrants. Furthermore, when Rabbi Morris

Faber, rabbi of Ohabe Shalom from 1880–1887, left Wilmington in 1887, he became rabbi of a Reform synagogue in Titusville, Pennsylvania and advised at least one congregant to "abandon kosher meat."[80] The fact that Ohabe Shalom was established by Americans and acculturated European Jews at a time when most American synagogues had introduced some reforms suggests that Ohabe Shalom was not strictly traditional but was more typical of the changing American synagogue. Given the fact that most of the founders of the Ohabe Shalom were German, the synagogue undoubtedly followed the Askenazic ritual.

The meaning of the labels Reform, Conservative, and Orthodox has shifted considerably with time. In the 1950s Emile Topkis interviewed several descendants of the founders of Ohabe Shalom. Monroe Sondheimer, son of Kaufman Sondheimer, labeled the synagogue Orthodox but described his parents as Reform Jews who had been married by Rabbi David Einhorn of Philadelphia's Reform synagogue, Knesseth Israel. Sondheimer's description clearly demonstrates the problem of labeling these early synagogues. Ohabe Shalom's ritual might have been progressive or too nontraditional for the new East European immigrants in 1880, but by 1950 it was so much stricter than what had evolved in many United States synagogues that Monroe Sondheimer remembered it as Orthodox.

Marx Fellheimer, who assisted in the services at Ohabe Shalom, was described half a century later by his daughter Bertie as "not religious." Jacob De Wolf, another early member of the synagogue, was described by his grandson as "not overly religious but able to speak Hebrew and Yiddish and eager to preserve his Jewish heritage."[81]

Another indication that the Jews of Wilmington were Reform-minded was given by an *Every Evening* reporter in August 1880. When a converted rabbi, Professor Reider, gave a lecture in August 1880, he wore an ancient rabbinical costume that the orthodox still wore, but the reporter had learned that "none of the Jews of Wilmington are so orthodox as to wear it, being more what are called reform Jews."[82]

The Thanksgiving service held in November 1880, was another adaptation to the American way. Obviously, such a service had not been part of the European Jewish tradition, but in America most religious denominations held services on Thanksgiving so Wilmington's Jews incorporated it in order to be like their neighbors. The service, which was held at three o'clock in the afternoon, attracted nearly all the Jewish people of the city."[83] Rabbi Faber, who had replaced Rabbi Rosenberg, spoke about the prosperity of the country during the past year, and offered a prayer for the president and vice-president and the people.

Within a year of the formation of the Moses Montefiore Society, the Jews of Wilmington had a synagogue, a Hebrew school, a rabbi, and an organization ready to help those in need. They had formulated the rudiments of a community just in time for the new immigration, which would bring tremendous change to the community.

3

With Increased Diversity—The 1880s

DURING THE 1880S, THE JEWISH POPULATION OF WILMINGTON expanded quickly to some five hundred people. In the first years of the decade, the new Jewish arrivals continued to be immigrants from Central and Western Europe, individuals born in America, and people who had lived in other states before coming to Delaware. They came to Wilmington for business reasons or to join family. However, by the middle of the decade, the majority of the new arrivals were natives of Eastern Europe. The newcomers immediately established a more traditional synagogue, Adas Kodesch.

As the number of immigrants to the United States continued to increase, concern about their effect on the country led to the first restrictions against immigration. Clearly, new immigrants would have to prove they would not become burdens on the society if they wanted to be accepted in America.

The East European Jews arrived in Wilmington in such large numbers that by 1890, only approximately 32 percent of the adult Jewish population was German, Western European, or American while some 68 percent was Russian and East European. Despite the fact that the East European Jews were more numerous, the German, Western European, and American Jews continued to be influential beyond their numbers because they had more experience, money, and better connections in the community.

Although the new immigrants from Eastern Europe were very different than the Jews who had arrived earlier, the general community saw them as one group. Recognizing their interdependence, the more established Jews helped the newcomers find homes and jobs.

GROWTH THROUGH BUSINESS AND FAMILY CONNECTIONS

During the early 1880s, the Moses Montefiore Society and its synagogue Ohabe Shalom continued to be the only Jewish institutions in Wilmington. The founders of the Moses Montefiore Society successfully maintained a synagogue with Morris Faber as rabbi, purchased a burial ground, and raised funds for the indigent. Through all of these actions they affirmed their desire to remain Jewish.

The annual ball continued to be a highlight of the Jewish social season. In January 1883, the ball was an enjoyable affair attended by a large crowd. Thirty-seven couples participated in the grand march led by Master of Ceremonies Louis Fellheimer and Miss Henrietta Fellheimer. If the weather had been fair, the reception would have been better attended, but in spite of the weather, the ball raised $350, which was used to purchase a Jewish burial ground.[1] Until this time, Jews either had to be buried in Philadelphia or in unconsecrated ground, which was an unacceptable solution. Taking the deceased to a Jewish cemetery in Philadelphia was costly and was an additional hardship on mourners.[2] Therefore, providing a Jewish burial ground in Wilmington was one of the basic needs of the fledgling community. Among all immigrant groups, the first concern of mutual aid societies was death.[3]

On February 13, 1883, the Moses Montefiore Society purchased a small parcel of land on the south side of Fifth Street, between Rodney and Hawley Streets, from William and Sarah Brightman for $250. The plot was judged large enough for a single house or one hundred graves, packed in. Years later, Joe Martin of the *Sunday Star* described the cemetery as "the most dismal place imaginable; the entire area was fenced in with a board fence at least six feet in height, painted black."[4] The Moses Montefiore Society had been formally incorporated for the purpose of "procuring suitable land for the establishment of a cemetery and to provide for the mutual benefit of members in cases of financial aid on February 2."[5] Eleven men signed the incorporation papers. Nine of them, Jacob DeWolf, Marx and Louis Fellheimer, Charles Italie, George Jacobs, Meyer Meyers, Manual Richenberger, Kaufman Sondheimer, and Bernard Wolfson, had lived in Wilmington in 1879.[6] Barney Rosenblatt, the Kahn brothers, Julius Fisher, Ferdinand Bishof, and Sam Nogler no longer lived in Wilmington. Nathan Lieberman did not sign, most likely because of a personal tragedy, the death of the Liebermans' three-year-old son Adolph on February 3, 1883.[7] Two newcomers, Max Ephraim and Julius Cabe, also signed as incorporators.

Max Ephraim came to Wilmington as part of the Wolters family group. A native of New York, Max had lived with the Wolters family for several years when he was a child, before going to a foster home.[8] He arrived in Wilmington in 1880 to manage a new clothing store, Wolters & Company, which the cousins Reuben and Abe Wolters had opened at 114 Market Street, a site formerly occupied by the store of Julius Fisher and Sam Nogler. Ephraim immediately became active in the Moses Montefiore Society and at the second ball in 1881, he led the grand march. The Wolters cousins and Ephraim were most likely aided and advised by Reuben's father, Wolf Wolters, who ran a successful clothing store in Philadelphia.

By 1882, Reuben Wolters ran a clothing store at 408 Market Street, formerly the store of Leon Saphir, and Reuben's father Wolf Wolters worked with Abe Wolters and Max Ephraim at 114 Market Street. Wolf Wolters, a native of Holland, and his wife, a native of Germany, had actually helped raise Abe after Abe's parents died of cholera when Abe was just three years old.[9] By 1884, Harry Pizor, who had married Wolf's daughter Mary Wolters, ran the store at 114 Market Street, and Otto Wolters ran a clothing store at 123–125 Market Street. The following year, Otto was no longer in Wilmington, and Reuben had taken over 123–125 Market while Wolf Wolters ran the original store at 114 Market Street. However, Wolf Wolters did not remain in Wilmington at this time. He returned to his own clothing store in Philadelphia and only moved back to Wilmington upon his retirement and the death of his wife just after the turn of the century. Harry Pizor remained in Wilmington and later ran a store at 116 Market Street with his brother Charles. Abraham Wolters returned to Philadelphia in 1886 and eventually became a very successful manufacturer. By 1886, Max Ephraim worked for Harry Hart clothing. The Ephraim-Wolters-Pizor clan, which came to Wilmington for business reasons, expanded in a pattern typical throughout immigrant America.

Julius Cabe came to Wilmington in the early 1880s to run a clothing store at 118 Market Street.[10] At the time of the second Montefiore ball, February 16, 1881, Cabe was on the ball committee. A native of Germany, Julius was naturalized in 1882. By the time of the 1883 ball, Julius was married and he and his wife were listed as one of the couples in the grand promenade. The following year, Cabe was the master of ceremonies of the ball. By 1885, Julius Cabe had left Wilmington. Like so many transients, although he only lived in Wilmington briefly, Cabe made a contribution to Wilmington's Jewish community.

Aaron Harris, a Russian Jew, who had been in business in New York since the 1860s, arrived in Wilmington by 1882.[11] Harris came by horse and buggy from New York looking for a place to land. His first wife had died, but he arrived with his second wife and three

children, Louis, Samuel, and Fannie. Harris opened a clothing store
at 218 Market Street, where the Kahn brothers had formerly been
in business. In 1884 he bought the building for $11,000. Harris
quickly became a leader among merchants and a major influence in
matters of religion. In the early days, when someone died, a *minyan*
was often held at Harris' home. Harris' arrival proved fortuitous because as a Russian Jew with a good understanding of the United
States, he was ready to assume a position of leadership when the
newer Russians arrived.

Samuel Mann opened a clothing store at 1 East Fourth Street in
1883 and boarded at the Clayton House. The following year, Solomon Mann worked at the store as a salesman and boarded with
Samuel at the Clayton House. In 1885, the shop at 315 Market
Street was known as I. Mann & Brothers. Israel Mann, the named
partner, maintained his residence in Philadelphia. By 1886, the
store had been sold to Henry Hart, and the Manns had "gone
West."[12]

Rabbi Morris Faber most likely came to Delaware directly from
Europe in 1880. Certainly he hadn't been in the United States long
because he was only twenty-six, and he had graduated from a Hungarian Talmudic college and received a rabbinical diploma from
Rabbi Wolf Tannebaum in Hungary.[13] In 1880 Rabbi Faber, his
wife Regina, and their child were the only known Hungarian Jews
in Wilmington. The Fabers' second child, Fanny, was born in 1882,
and a son, Harry, was born in 1883.[14] Rabbi Morris Faber continued
to lead the Ohabe Shalom synagogue from the fall of 1880 until
1887, with a brief hiatus in 1885 after his wife Regina died at the
age of twenty-nine.

In order to earn enough money to support his growing family,
Rabbi Faber always had an additional occupation, and like many
immigrants, he changed this occupation often. In 1881 Faber was a
teacher and his wife Regina ran a trimming store. In 1882, Faber
ran a variety store at 416 ½ Market. In 1883–84, the rabbi and his
nephew ran a furnishing store on King Street, but by the next year
the store had failed and Morris Faber was listed as a peddler. In
1885, he was a teacher of languages. The following year, the rabbi
was a clerk for a musical instrument store, a branch of a Philadelphia store whose owner, William Blasium, lived in Philadelphia. In
1887, his final year in Wilmington, Rabbi Faber was an agent for a
sewing machine company.

As soon as the Fabers were established, relatives began to join
them in Wilmington. By 1883, Rabbi Faber's cousins or nephews,
Jacob and Simon Faber, were in Wilmington.[15] Simon was in busi-

ness with the rabbi at M. & S. Faber furnishings. Seventeen-year-old Jacob, who had come to Wilmington directly from Temisvar, Hungary, lived with his brother Simon and ran a dry goods store.

David and Johanna Abramson, Benjamin and Anna Fischer, and Samuel and Lena Slessinger all arrived in Wilmington from Hungary by 1883.[16] Another Hungarian, Ignatz Roth and his wife Rosie, arrived in Wilmington shortly afterwards. Rosie Roth was Benjamin Fischer's sister. These Hungarian Jews came to Wilmington without money to begin a business. Abramson, Roth, and Fischer all began as peddlars. Since peddling could be done in numerous locations, not necessarily Delaware, there might have been another reason, like kinship or friendship with Faber, that brought the men here. David Abramson helped Rabbi Faber with High Holiday services in 1884 shortly after his arrival in Wilmington. Within a year of their arrival, Abramson and Slessinger ran an installment house together. They separated by 1886; Abramson was a tailor and Slessinger ran the installment house. David Abramson's brother Michael, who became known as Max, joined his brother as a tailor in Wilmington a few years later.

All the new Hungarians were young. In 1884, Slessinger was the oldest at thirty-four, David Abramson the youngest at twenty-eight. The Abramsons, Fischers, and Slessingers all had a child born in Delaware in 1884. In fact, Gidor Abramson and Jacob Fisher were both born in June 1884. In 1879, there were no known Hungarian Jews in Wilmington, but by 1884 there were at least sixteen.

INFLUX OF EASTERN EUROPEAN JEWS

The movement of Jews to Wilmington for business and family reasons probably would have continued as a tiny trickle were it not for the mass immigration of Jews from Eastern Europe that began in 1881. The erosion of the peasant-based economies of Eastern Europe in the late nineteenth century, and the subsequent anti-Semitism focusing on the Jews as scapegoats for the instability made life increasingly difficult for the nearly six million Jews who lived in Eastern Europe.[17] After Czar Alexander II of Russia was assassinated in March 1881, government-inspired pogroms against Jews erupted throughout Russia, and Jewish immigrants began to arrive in America in large numbers several months later.[18] By early 1882, many Russian Jews had arrived in Philadelphia. At the end of February 1882, subscriptions for the benefit of Russian Jews in Philadelphia were up to $14,480 and a large number of people had visited the refugees.[19] Days later, employment had been found for seventy-five more of the Jewish refugees and contributions were up to $16,236.[20]

Most of the Jewish refugees who recently arrived in Philadelphia had never seen a black man until they arrived in this country.[21] When two of the "dusky gentlemen" walked into Penn Station, they created considerable excitement. One of the refugees reportedly asked, "What's the matter with those men?"[22] Most of the refugees shrunk away, and the children ran in terror. The young blacks enjoyed the sport and tried to talk gibberish to the exiles.

In July 1882, the first Russian Jews, nineteen refugees who had come to Philadelphia from Odessa, arrived in Wilmington.[23] The eight men, five with wives, and some children were placed in the care of Nathan Lieberman by a Mr. Levy of the Philadelphia committee. Lieberman found employment for three of the refugees at the Bower & Duer Company, a car-building company. T. W. Bowers and Henry F. Duer lived on the 900 block of West Street, one block from Lieberman. The other refugees found work unloading ice for the Kennebec Ice Company, the largest establishment of its kind in the state with between one hundred and two hundred employees, depending on the season.[24] All the refugees were well-educated and could speak German and Russian fluently. All were excellent artisans; one was a fresco painter. The refugees were living at a house on Claymont Street over the Third Street bridge. They were ill-clothed and needed donations of apparel.

Nathan Lieberman, the central Jewish presence in Wilmington, was the ideal person to assist the new immigrants. He was a wealthy man with business connections that could help him find employment for the newcomers. He also owned real estate, which could help provide housing. In 1882, the Liebermans moved into a beautiful three-story home at 814 West Street. The house had two bathrooms, complete with copper tubs, which was unusual in those times.[25] There was a large stable in the rear of the house and a number of chestnut trees in the yard.

In 1883, after running a successful clothing store for nearly twenty years, Nathan Lieberman sold his clothing store to two of his clerks, Thomas Pennock and Thomas Foreman, and entered the real estate business.[26] Actually, Lieberman had been successfully dealing in real estate for many years. In 1868, he purchased his first property, on Market Street between Fourth and Fifth Streets, most likely his store at 426 Market, from William H. Tatnall, a real estate agent. From that time until 1897, Nathan Lieberman was involved in more than seventy real estate transactions.[27]

At first his properties were in the main business district on Market, Shipley, and Madison streets. In early 1870 he purchased the lot at Fifth and Market streets, which later became his store. In 1872, he paid $5,000 for 503 Shipley Street, which was his home until he moved to 814 West. In the late 1870s and 1880s, Lieberman began to buy properties in two more industrial areas: in the northeast near the Brandywine River from Seventh to Thirteenth between Walnut Street and Railroad Avenue, and in a more southern area between Front and Third Streets in the area of Franklin, Conrad and Van Buren Streets. The Pullman Palace Car Company and the Bowers and Duer car-building company were in the first area. Several small morocco plants were in the second area. In 1883 alone, Lieberman bought five properties between Thirteenth and Fifteenth around Poplar, Lombard, Pine, and Claymont. By 1888, Lieberman's real estate holdings in the city of Wilmington were valued at more than $65,000.[28] Lieberman appears to have paid for his properties outright with no need for mortgages. He bought several of the properties with partners Patrick Neary and John Dickey, a former clerk in his clothing store. In addition to his real estate in downtown Wilmington, Lieberman owned two farms, one in New Castle, Delaware and one in Kennett Square, Pennsylvania. Lieberman used to drive around in his horse and buggy to collect rents.[29]

The number of lots with homes owned by Lieberman and his known interest in the general welfare of the Jewish immigrants suggest that he may have owned many of the houses later occupied by indigent immigrants. In 1883, just after the first Russian immigrants arrived, Lieberman bought a property at Thirteenth and Claymont Streets, and in June he built a row of eight houses on the property.[30] Although the newspaper said the immigrants were on Claymont Street over the Third Street bridge, it may have been the bridge at Thirteenth Street. In 1883, Joseph Levy, one of the early immigrants, lived at Eleventh and Claymont.[31]

Unfortunately, the names of the first nineteen Jewish refugees have been lost. None of them are listed in the city directories of 1883 or 1884, which is not unusual: when new immigrants came to an area, it often took several years for them to establish themselves in a business and to list themselves in a directory. One new Russian couple, Bertha Bernisky Levy and Joseph Levy, is known through the birth record of their son. The Levys expressed their joy in arriving in the United States by naming their first child, a son born on February 22, 1883, George Washington Levy.

Nathan Barsky, a Russian who listed himself as a peddler, lived with Joseph Levy in 1885.[32] Barsky, who later became a stalwart of the Wilmington Jewish community, arrived in the U.S. in 1882, on the same boat as Rosa Topkis, and might very well have been one of the original nineteen refugees.

Rosa and Jacob Topkis were not part of the group that reached Wilmington in July 1882 because Jacob was sent initially to Chester, Pennsylvania to work in the ironworks. The men in the mills didn't like working with Jacob Topkis because they couldn't understand him.[33] By 1884, when son Harry was born, Jacob, Rosa, and their children David, Louis, William, Sallie, and Charles lived in Wilmington.[34] Jacob became a peddler and he was "charitable to a fault."[35] As Sallie Topkis Ginns recalled: "One day when I was about eight, he walked into the kitchen and informed my mother, 'We must look to God for our supper. I have given away my last $2. That family needed it more than I did.' "[36]

Often, after a full day of peddling, Jacob Topkis would return with empty baskets but very little money. He trusted everyone. Before the end of the decade Rosa, Jacob, and the younger children left for New Castle, where they lived until about 1894.[37] Older brothers David and Louis Topkis remained in Wilmington.

Other Russian Jews who had arrived in Wilmington by 1887 and might have been part of the first group sent to Nathan Lieberman were Wolf L. Friedman, Louis Brofsky, Philip Cohen, Isaac Goldstein, Samuel Levy, Abraham Adelman, Benjamin Rosenblatt, and Marcus Nonky.

At least one Russian family—Baer Hindin, age forty-six, his wife Sarah, age forty, Chana Hindin, age twenty-seven, and two young children, Abraham, age seven and Sarah, age six—were sent to Wilmington by the Philadelphia Association for the protection of Jewish Immigrations, a forerunner of HIAS, the Hebrew Immigrant Aid Society in 1887.[38]

The Eastern European Jews who arrived in Wilmington in the mid-1880s found employment in very different areas than the Jews who were already here. Three were peddlers, one was a laborer. Those who tried retail businesses sold tinware and picture frames. One who began selling clothing became a peddler; one who was a watchmaker left within the year. Wolf Friedman was a rabbi who officiated at the marriage of his daughter Ellen to Marcus Taenenbaum in December 1885.[39]

On February 5, 1885 the Moses Montefiore Society held its annual ball, which was called "one of the most brilliant affairs of the season. Nearly all the guests were in full evening dress and the costumes of the ladies were especially rich and elegant. Silks, satins, velvets, and diamonds were seen on every hand."[40] Among the

guests were eighteen couples from Chester, five couples from Philadelphia, and three couples from New York. By 1885, there were two
vastly different groups of Jewish immigrants in Wilmington, those
who danced in satin at fancy balls, and those who struggled to make
a living in a new land. In taking responsibility for their brethren,
Lieberman and the members of the Moses Montefiore Society accepted a basic tenet of Judaism, and reaffirmed their desire to remain Jewish.

Religious Rivalry: A New Alternative

Most of the immigrants who arrived from Eastern Europe in the
1880s had lived in traditional Jewish communities, which were
governed by Jewish law and were untouched by modernity.[41] In
1885, there were at least twenty Jewish families in Wilmington who
wanted a more Orthodox synagogue. The Eastern Europeans did
not feel that Ohabe Shalom was traditional enough to meet their
religious needs.

> The massacre of Russian Jews brought refugees to Delaware to pursue
> an honest living and to serve God according to their conscience. The
> somewhat reform tendencies of the Moses Montefiore Synagogue did
> not correspond with the Orthodox feelings for which adherence to the
> new ones had almost given up their lives. They wanted to serve God
> according to the old teachings and succeeded through the untiring ef-
> forts of Bernard Wolfson. . . .[42]

Bernard Wolfson, who had been outnumbered by the large German population in the 1870s, became president of the new synagogue. Wolfson had been an incorporator of the Moses Montefiore
Society and had assisted Rabbi Faber at the services for the High
Holidays in 1884, but as more Eastern European Jews arrived, he
was ready to lead them in a different direction.

Aaron Harris, who arrived in Wilmington by horse and buggy
from New York, became vice-president of the new synagogue and
donated the ark. The other named officers were newly arrived: Benjamin Fischer, Ignatz Roth, Simon Cohen, and Morris Levy.[43]
Brothers-in-law, Fischer and Roth had both come from Hungary. In
1885, Fischer was a junk dealer and Roth was a peddler. Simon
Cohen, a twenty-six-year-old Russian, had just arrived in Wilmington and opened a tinware and furnishing store. Morris Levy was a
peddler.

The new synagogue, Adas Kodesch, was dedicated at 308 West Front Street on August 16, 1885.[44] Sabato Morais, *chazan* of Philadelphia's Mikveh Israel from 1851–1897, conducted the dedicatory service. In his early days, Morais was well known for being a traditionalist who wanted to maintain Orthodoxy in Judaism. In 1869, when a constituency of Mikveh Israel was urging the synagogue to change rapidly and adapt American ways in order to bring in more worshipers, Morais gave an eloquent address explaining why he was against changes that would "Christianize Judaism" and be "at the cost of the ancestral faith."[45] While many advocated the use of organ music, Morais claimed "the pealing of the organ in a synagogue is the death knell of Jewish rites and tenets." Morais was also against the practice of hiring mercenary chorists. Both of these practices were introduced at Philadelphia's Rodeph Shalom in the late 1860s. However, by the time he dedicated Adas Kodesch, Morais was integrally involved in the formation of the Jewish Theological Seminary, a school to train rabbis in a new type of Judaism, known as Historical or Conservative Judaism, which believed in tradition and the primacy of texts but also wanted to respond to modernity and rationalism, particularly to the changing conditions in America.[46] Taking elements from the orthodox and reform, historical Judaism accepted the importance of Jewish law from the orthodox and of moral purpose from the reform.[47] It believed that growth and change were necessary, but that change had to be evolutionary, not radical. In other words, Jewish texts had to be explored before innovations were made so that changes would not violate the basic spirit of Jewish legal principles. Followers of the historical school believed in the unity of all Jews and hoped to attract moderate reform and liberal orthodox to their movement.[48] They sought to compromise between the ghetto-oriented Orthodox branch and the assimilationist Reform movement.[49] Five months after he dedicated Adas Kodesch, Sabato Morais was part of a small group that formed the Jewish Theological Seminary Association. The school opened officially in January 1887.[50]

At the dedication of Adas Kodesch, Morais addressed an important issue for the congregants, many of whom were brand-new to the United States, the question of how a Jew could be a patriot but also believe in the Holy Land. Defending the ability of the Jew to be both a good citizen and a lover of Zion, Morais claimed:

> There is ever longing among Jews for Zion, but I rebut the attack of those who claim that a Jew by reason of this cannot be a patriot. A Jew

wherever he resides is a true man and law abiding citizen except when persecution attempts to make him odious.[51]

In Morais's opinion, a Jew could be a good citizen, but he could never accept the radical idea that the United States was the Holy Land, an idea that gained many adherents in the less traditional forms of Judaism, or that George Washington was the Messiah.[52]

The subject of Morais's address, and his selection as speaker when he was a leader of Conservative Judaism, suggest that although the Russians in Wilmington wanted a synagogue that was more traditional than Ohabe Shalom, they were not rigidly Orthodox and were willing to accept change in their new synagogue. The community was tiny, and its leaders hoped they could maintain unity. Undoubtedly they recognized that if Adas Kodesch adopted the historical approach, the possibility of all Jews remaining in one synagogue was stronger. In order to engage as many Jews as possible, Reverend Avigdor Caro of Philadelphia's House of Israel Congregation was asked to lead the regular afternoon service. House of Israel had been established in 1840 by people of German persuasion in accordance with the "old German and Polish customs" and conducted on the principle of the Great Synagogue in London. In other words, it was founded on principles that many German Jews found more acceptable. During Caro's tenure at House of Israel, several innovations of the "reform" school were made.[53] Caro, a contemporary of Faber from Hungary, spoke in German.

There were fundamental differences between the Eastern European Jews and the earlier German Jews. A leader of the movement was quoted as saying, "There is just as much difference between the old congregation and the new as there is between Catholic and Protestant."[54] Many of these differences had to do with ritual and observance. The more reform-minded accepted mixed seating, a weekly sermon in English, and congregational participation. Despite their differences, the newcomers were similar to the earlier immigrants in one important aspect. They remained committed to Judaism. The new Russian immigrants had been persecuted and forced to flee their homeland. Instead of ridding themselves of their religion, the cause of their suffering, in the new land, they reconfirmed their belief in their religion and duplicated their former rituals as precisely as possible. In maintaining their faith, they followed their German predecessors who had come to a strange city with no organized Jewish rituals and had chosen to remain Jewish.

Unfortunately, the religious differences between the two groups could not be resolved. A month after Adas Kodesch's dedication, services for the Jewish High Holidays were held at two synagogues, the reform Ohabe Shalom synagogue in the Morrow building and the new Adas Kodesch. There were differences in degree of observance, but all Jews of the city closed their stores on September 10th to observe the New Year.[55]

The newer immigrants, who were more traditional, wanted kosher meat. Although David Megill's attempt to sell kosher meat in 1880 had not met with success, by 1885 Gould's Slaughter House had kosher meat that was killed by Reverend Lasar Heilperin of Philadelphia.[56]

Within a year of its formation, Adas Kodesch ran into problems. In May 1886, Aaron Harris, treasurer of the synagogue, was involved in a lawsuit against the synagogue. Harris claimed the surety of $200 could only be used for the scrolls, but some members wanted it to be used for rent. According to the newspaper, the suit was decided in favor of the synagogue, but Harris was going to appeal.[57] The matter, which had caused great interest among the Jews of the city, was not publicly resolved. In 1886, the more liberal Hebrews rented German Hall where they observed one day of Rosh Hashanah while the Orthodox observed two days at Adas Kodesch.[58]

In late 1886 or early 1887, Adas Kodesch hired Herman Rezits, a twenty-two-year-old cantor and rabbi, to lead the congregation. Rezits had recently graduated from a Russian seminary, had received a rabbinical diploma from Rabbi Isaac Elchanan of Kovno, and had been a student of Cantor Rachovsky.[59] Rabbi and his wife Lena had just recently arrived in America. All of their children were subsequently born in Delaware. Rezits served as cantor, *shochet*, and ritual leader of Adas Kodesch until his death in 1930, becoming an integral part of the Jewish community. "[H]e was part of the blood and sinew of every Jewish home for nigh onto 45 years. Every Jewish family was his family. He had been moel at the circumcision of nearly every Jewish son, been at Bar Mitzvahs and weddings."[60]

The dispute between Aaron Harris and Adas Kodesch was not over. By 1888, Harris had organized a second Orthodox synagogue, Ahavath Achim, described as an offshoot of Adas Kodesch, which had split with Adas Kodesch because of financial transactions. Aaron Harris was so unhappy with Adas Kodesch that though he was a very religious man who actually kept the Torah at his home at one time, when his daughter Fannie married Barnet Gluckman in December 1887, the ceremony was conducted by Mayor C. B. Rhoades rather than by Rabbi Rezits.[61] In explaining the existence of the second Orthodox synagogue years later, Barnet Gluckman,

RABBI HYMAN REZITS,
Who has been Cantor and Reader of this Synagogue since 1887.

Rabbi Rezits of Adas Kodesch. (Jewish Historical Society of Delaware.)

wrote, "the disease of division among mankind is so prevalent that it pervaded even among denominations."[62]

On Rosh Hashanah 1888, there were three congregations of Hebrews, two Orthodox and one Reform, embracing about four hundred persons.[63] The second orthodox congregation, which met in the Crosby & Hill Building, a dry goods store on Market Street, observed the same services as the Adas Kodesch, which met at the third floor of the Morrow Building.

On the first day of Rosh Hashanah 1888, the scene at the Orthodox congregation was very foreign.[64] The room was full of Jews, very few looking as if they had been in the United States long. The group was comprised exclusively of Russian, Polish, and Hungarian natives, very few of whom could speak English. There were no women in the group, the men were on their knees in front of high stands, the room was filled with loud incantations, and the observers' faces were filled with mental agony. The observers had not eaten before the services, which began at 4 A.M., nor would they eat again until they left. The congregants would worship from 6 A.M. to noon on the second day of Rosh Hashanah as well. They would attend services every morning at 6 A.M. until Yom Kippur, when services would be held from 6 A.M. to 6 P.M.

In the *Evening Journal*'s opinion, there was a vast division between the Reform and Orthodox groups, and it did not attempt to hide its opinion.

> The Reformed Hebrews in this city comprise in the main the best elements of the race, and they are almost all of them German. (They believe in) the abolition of most of the forms and customs of years ago and in further reforming their religious customs.[65]

In the fall of 1889, the Adas Kodesch congregation was incorporated in order to maintain an Orthodox house of religion. Since Delaware law at that time did not provide for the incorporation of a Jewish house of worship, the synagogue was incorporated as a church. Bernard Wolfson, Abraham Smith, Solomon Friedman, Morris Miller, and Solomon Grossman signed the papers of incorporation.[66] The fact that Aaron Harris did not sign indicates that the rift had not been healed. Harris's synagogue, Ahavath Achim, was in half-existence in 1889, but the union of the two synagogues was inevitable because one could not financially exist without the other.[67]

Bernard Wolfson, the driving force behind Adas Kodesch, was elected to a three-year term. Another trustee, Solomon Grossman,

Incorporation paper of Adas Kodesch. (Jewish Historical Society of Delaware.)

had emigrated to the United States from Russia in 1880 and was a shoemaker in Wilmington by 1885. Grossman became a grocer in 1890 and by the turn of the century he was a salesman of dry goods. Solomon Friedman had arrived in Wilmington around 1887 and seems to have left again by 1890. Morris Miller, a Russian, married Betta Friedman here in 1888 and was gone by 1890. Abraham Smith, born in England, arrived in Wilmington as a tailor in 1887 and appears to have left soon after. Not only had four of the incorporators arrived recently, three did not stay long. The Jewish community was so new that transients had an immediate impact.

ATTITUDES TOWARD IMMIGRANTS

As more Eastern Europeans poured into America, the attitude towards immigrants began to change. During the first century of its existence, the United States had welcomed immigrants of all nations.[68] The country, immensely rich in natural resources, was underpopulated and needed people. Furthermore, the United States had been founded on the principle that the country was a land of opportunity for all, and the restriction of immigration would have proven that freedom for all was an unattainable goal. The receptive attitude was also based on the belief that since "the quality of men" was determined by environment, not birth, immigrants "would come to America with minds and spirits for new impressions and being in America would make Americans of them."[69] As late as the 1870s the attitude to immigration was open, except in California where a large number of unemployed Chinese, who had immigrated to the state to work on the railroad, became the victims of attack. By the early 1880s, philanthropic leaders of several Eastern seaboard states, concerned about the growing burden of maintaining immigrants, began urging the federal government to establish controls over immigration.[70] The nativism that developed during the 1880s took the "hordes of new immigrants" as its target.[71]

In 1882 an act "suspending" immigration from China for ten years was passed. The same year, the federal government also passed a law that gave the secretary of the treasury executive authority over immigration, but left state agencies in charge of actual inspections.[72] Convicts, lunatics, idiots, and persons likely to become a public charge were denied admission. The new law also required fifty cents from each immigrant to begin an immigrant welfare fund. The 1882 law was the first decisive step away from laissez-faire.

Unaffected by growing nativism, Delaware welcomed immigrants. On April 10, 1883, the Delaware General Assembly passed a law establishing a three-person Board of Immigration in order to "induce immigration into the state." The preamble to the law cited the importance of agricultural interests to the state and the need for more people to cultivate the lands. The farm lands of Delaware were "sparsely-populated" and would benefit from increased people.[73] The law clearly stated that the board should prevent improper persons from immigration. "The board shall at all times exercise due care to prevent the bringing into the state of any person or persons who might endanger the public morals, health or peace or good order of its citizens."[74]

Although the official law of the state encouraged immigration, the clear message was that immigrants were needed to farm the land, and they were welcome to the degree that they conformed to the larger group and could do farm work. An underlying assumption of Americans at this time was that as immigrants worked in America, they would fuse with the larger society; in other words, assimilate.[75] In an article describing the need for immigrants, a *Sunday Star* reporter announced that those immigrants who assimilate most quickly and easily are Germans and Irish. He never even mentioned the Eastern Europeans or Russians, and he made unflattering comments about other groups.[76]

In the United States, where any religion was good if it inculcated good morals, the Jew was on equal footing with other citizens.[77] Unlike the Jews of Europe, who had suffered anti-Semitism for centuries, the Jews in America lived in an atmosphere of acceptance, in a country that protected their constitutional right to live as Jews and to enjoy the same privileges as other citizens. Nothing made this point more clearly than the actions of President Grover Cleveland and his secretary of state, Thomas Bayard, during the hearings concerning the appointment of Anthony M. Keiley to the Court of Austria-Hungary in 1885.[78] The story, which attracted national attention, was followed closely in Delaware partly because Thomas F. Bayard, Delaware's popular former senator, played a key role. Bayard was so well respected that he was seriously considered as the Democrat candidate for President in 1876,1880, and 1884. In fact, Bayard accepted the position as Cleveland's secretary of state largely to add much-needed prestige to President Cleveland's cabinet.[79] As Cleveland's secretary of state, Bayard prepared the statements about Keiley and worked closely with the president.

In the spring of 1885, shortly after he became president, Cleveland named Anthony M. Keiley, a former mayor of Richmond, to the position of minister to Italy. In April, the Italian government declined to receive Keiley because of statements he had made in a speech in 1871, denouncing the cruel and causeless invasion of the Papal States by King Victor Emmanuel.[80] According to the Italian government, Keiley's speech had been an unforgettable insult to the king. A week after the Italian government rejected him, Keiley withdrew his name. An editorial in the *New York Evening Post* said that Keiley should stay in Richmond because he was not fit to be a foreign minister. However, a few days later, President Cleveland appointed Keiley ambassador to Austria-Hungary. The court of Austria-Hungary refused to accept his appointment because Keiley's wife was Jewish. As Baron Schaeffer of the Austro-Hungarian Empire explained, "a foreign envoy wedded to a Jewess by civil marriage would be untenable and even impossible in Vienna."[81] President Cleveland was incensed by the refusal based on religion, and in a statement prepared by Bayard, he emphatically denied the relevance of the question of religious faith or sect: "The Supreme law of our land is that no religious test shall ever be required as a qualifier to any office or public trust in the United States."[82] Emphasizing the Constitutional legality of the fact that the United States had no religious test for holding public office, the statement continued, "To suffer an infraction of this essential principle would lead to disenfranchisement of our citizens because of their religious beliefs and would thus impair or destroy the most important end which our Constitution was intended to secure."[83]

The position did not surprise those who knew Bayard. During his years in the Senate, he was well known as a supporter and defender of the Constitution against its domestic enemies.[84]

When the Austrian government realized its religious explanation was not favorably accepted, it tried a different explanation: given the friendship between Austria-Hungary and Italy, the Austrians could not accept someone whom their friends the Italians found unacceptable.

The high moral ground of the President's position was lost because so many people were against naming a man like Keiley a second time. The reaction from Republican and Independent newspapers was unfavorable. "Keiley should be not be appointed anywhere but to oblivion," said one. The *New York Evening Post* rationalized by saying Austria was the next best thing to Richmond because no serious business was likely to occur in Vienna.[85] The *Wilmington Morning News* criticized the State Department as absurd for insisting on Keiley's appointment, but pragmatically stated that the Austrians wouldn't change: "Keiley would never be acceptable in Vienna because he was married to a Jew. Neither Jew nor Jewess had ever been received at the Austrian Court."[86] Some people may have felt that Keiley would be acceptable because his wife converted, but the insightful *Morning News* editorial continued: "the old social disabilities of the Jews, of which this court at Vienna is a relic, ran against the race more than the religion. Once a Jew always a Jew was the familiar formula."[87]

After several months, Keiley withdrew his name in order to end the controversy. President Cleveland was so angry about the Austrian court's attitude that he left the position of ambassador open for nearly two years before he appointed Alexander R. Lawton in April 1887.[88] In 1886, Keiley was made a judge on the international court of First Instance at Cairo, Egypt. He was successful and was promoted in 1894 to the Court of Appeals in Alexandria.[89]

The Keiley story, which attracted national attention, undoubtedly reflected well on Delaware. Bayard, a favorite political son, had shown himself to be a strong proponent of the freedom of religion and was willing to extend the American viewpoint to the United States' dealings with foreign nations.

Although the Jews in America were far better off than they had been in Europe, as the Protestant revival gained ground, the Sunday laws became a problem. During colonial times, laws had been enacted to require the observance of Sunday as the day of rest. Although such blue laws had remained on the books in some states, by the eighteenth century they were not enforced and had become largely anachronistic.[90] However, in the mid-nineteenth century, the revival of religious zeal and the upsurge in American Protestantism as a reaction to the perceived lack of morality in America revived interest in enforcing the Sunday laws.[91]

In October 1889, Samuel Gluck, a Hungarian Jewish immigrant who had recently arrived in Wilmington from New York with his wife Rosa (Rebecca) and three children, was taken to court and accused by Emerson Noble, a baker in the downtown area, of selling bread on the Lord's Day.[92] Another neighborhood baker, William Kersler, brought a loaf of unleavened bread to court and "shook it in the Israelite's trembling face."

Gluck admitted that it was his bread and that he had sold it on Sunday. He explained that Saturday was the Jewish Sabbath, which he duly observed, but that he he was obligated to do business on the Christian Sabbath to accommodate those of his faith. The judge declared, "There is only one Sunday in Delaware," and fined Gluck $4 plus court costs.[93]

The law in Delaware at the time said "If any person shall perform any worldly employment, labor, or business on the Sabbath day, works of necessity and charity excepted, he shall be fined $4."[94] So Gluck defended himself using the words of the law, and referring to the Sabbath. But the words meant something different than what they said. According to the judge's interpretation the words Sabbath and Sunday were synonymous. Even the newspaper confused the two words, resulting in the humorous claim that Gluck had said "Saturday is the Jewish Sunday." Perhaps that's why the newspaper also referred to the incident as an amusing trial. While it might have been funny to some, the trial demonstrated to the Jews that they had a long way to go before they achieved equality or true freedom of religion in Wilmington.

During the nineteenth century, many such cases were brought to courts. Like Gluck, Jews generally defended themselves by trying to exempt themselves from the regulations rather than to appeal for the repeal of a discriminatory law.[95] Gluck's argument, that he would be deprived of two days' income if he observed the Christian Sabbath, was the usual defense in such cases.

As more foreigners flocked to America, some citizens worried more about the burden of maintaining immigrants. The anti-immigrant feelings weren't directed against Jews as a religious group, but against all foreigners who kept American citizens from getting jobs. In September 1889 there was a race riot in Dobbinsville, a small village about one-half a mile below the heart of New Castle. The town, which was composed of four long rows of two-story brick houses, had been built by Richard J. Dobbins of Philadelphia for employees of the Delaware Iron Company, also known as Tasker Works.[96] The middle row of the town was inhabited almost entirely by Poles and Hungarians, whose ranks had grown rapidly during the last two years. The American laborers accepted the Poles, but they couldn't stand the Hungarians, who they accused of being dirty, unkempt, and of living like pigs. The foreigners were paid about the same as the Americans, $6.50 to $7.50 a week, or as high as $14 for those who could speak English. According to the more established citizens, the American laborers' resentment was based on the belief that the foreigners were interlopers who reduced the number of Americans who would be hired.

One Saturday night in September 1889, after both groups were out drinking at Wilmington bars, the rough American group decided to clean out the Hungarian quarter. They used heavy axes to knock down doors and attacked people in their homes with bricks and stones. One young Pole, Frank Jankovsky, was shot at short range. Jankovsky was not Jewish; his funeral was at St. Peter's

Roman Catholic Church. There is no evidence that any of the foreigners were Jewish; however, the death of an innocent immigrant and the prejudicial attitude shown towards newcomers was certainly of concern to all immigrants. When the case came to court, the man representing the interest of the foreigners was William Seitterbaum, a Polish Jewish attorney from Philadelphia. Jacob and Rosa Topkis, who at the time lived in New Castle, had opened a small, second store in Dobbinsville in order to capture the trade of all the workers who were brought from Eastern Europe to work in the mills.[97] Their presence suggests that some of the workers might have been Jewish.

The respectable citizens of New Castle, who were annoyed by the unpleasant notoriety of their usually quiet city, blamed both the Hungarians and the natives. In their opinions, most at fault was the policy that brought the scum of Europe to work in the great manufacturing cities of this country in competition with native working men, thereby cutting wages and bringing other workmen to their level. However, all agreed that while the Poles and Hungarians were here, they were entitled to protection afforded by laws.[98]

Another example of increased problems for the new immigrants occurred a few months later at the Jackson and Sharpe Company. David Mex, a cabinetmaker, was struck unconscious by a fellow worker one Friday in February 1890. Mex, a Russian Hebrew immigrant who spoke broken English, was in Wilmington trying to earn enough money to bring his wife and six children from Russia to this country. He earned $11 a week and sent $7 a week to his wife in Russia.[99]

Mex claimed that young apprentices at the company were constantly annoying Germans and Hebrews. On the day of the accident, one of the employees began calling Mex "sheeny" and other names. Then he picked up a heavy plane and struck Mex over the head. Mex, who was alone in his room with no heat, was reported to be near death.

When Job H. Jackson, owner of the shipbuilding company, heard about the incident, he instructed the superintendent to immediately discharge anyone who intimidated or annoyed foreigners in his employ. However, when the case came to court a week later, a witness for the defense said Mex had started the trouble by cursing the other employee and threatening to strike him. Judge Ball concluded that Mex was the aggressor. He discharged the employee and told Jackson and Sharpe to take care of its own disturbances.[100]

Tensions between some Americans and the new immigrants were high. The immigrant was not a sympathetic figure to those struggling to make a living. Constitutional rights were protected, and the Jews were better off than anywhere else, but public opinion could not be ignored. Successful immigrants would have to prove to those who had been here longer that they were assets, not burdens. They would have to become contributing members of American society.

THE JEWISH COMMUNITY IN 1890

By 1890 approximately five hundred Jews lived in Wilmington.[101] Since some 61,400 people lived in Wilmington in 1890, the Jews were a tiny minority, not even 1 percent of the population.[102] In fact, the Jews only accounted for some 5 percent of the foreign-born population, which was dominated by Irish, German, Italian, and Polish immigrants.[103]

Nearly two-thirds of the Jewish adults living in Wilmington in 1890, 66 percent of the men and 60 percent of the women, were from Eastern Europe.[104] The dramatic shift had occurred because the majority of Jewish arrivals in the 1880s were from Russia, Poland, Lithuania, and Hungary, and only about 30 percent of the Jews who settled in Wilmington in the 1880s were from Germany, Western Europe, or the United States. Furthermore, many of the founders of the community had died or left Wilmington. Marx Fellheimer, Leon Saphir, and George Jacobs had died during the 1880s.[105] Jacob De Wolf returned to Philadelphia. Not only did the adults themselves leave Wilmington, but their children, who had grown up in Wilmington in the 1870s, left the city as well.

The strong German domination of the Jewish community was gone by the end of the 1880s. The only German leaders of the original community who were still active in Wilmington Jewish causes in 1890 were Nathan Lieberman, Kaufman Sondheimer, Meyer Meyers, and Samuel Hocheimer.[106] Manual Richenberger, Samuel Kerns, Bernard Row, and Isaac Row had drifted farther from Judaism. Unlike many neighboring East Coast cities whose Jewish populations were founded and led by Germans for most of the nineteenth century, Wilmington's German population dominated for less than a decade. The German Jews established the Moses Montefiore Society and the first synagogue, but they did not remain dominant long enough to establish the numerous service organizations later founded by a largely East European community. By 1890, the German Jewish influence throughout America had lessened. Although the German Jews were still influential, they did not dominate the American Jewish scene as they had throughout much of the century.[107]

While the adult Jewish population had become more foreign, the children of the new immigrants as well as the children of the earlier immigrants' families were born in the United States so the division between a foreign adult population and a native-born young generation was even more pronounced than it had been in 1879.

Only ten observant Jewish people—Mr. and Mrs. Nathan Lieberman, Mr. and Mrs. Meyer Meyers, Mr. and Mrs. Kaufman Sondheimer, Mr. and Mrs. Bernard Wolfson, and Mr. and Mrs. Samuel Hocheimer—had lived in Wilmington for more than ten years. More than 70 percent of the Jews had arrived within the last five years, with the majority arriving in the last two years.[108] The fact that the Jewish community was so new meant that there were no strong traditions. Newcomers participated immediately in the development of the community. Furthermore, at least 25 percent of the Jews who had passed through Wilmington in the 1880s had not remained here, so there was a sense of transience. Those immigrants who moved through Wilmington brought information about how Jewish life was organized in other places to the Wilmington Jews.

Within a few years of their arrivals in Wilmington, about thirty-five of the new immigrants began the process of becoming American citizens. In 1890, to qualify for naturalization the immigrant to Delaware had to have lived in the United States for upwards of five years and in Delaware for at least one year immediately preceding the final petition. Previous to filing a petition for naturalization, the immigrant had to have filed a declaration of intention in which he renounced loyalty to the ruler of his former country. Once a husband became a citizen, his wife and children received derivatory citizenship. By 1890, about seven of the newer arrivals, including Sam Slessinger, Jacob Faber, and Nathan Barsky, were American citizens. Others had completed the first step of declaring their intention.[109]

The adult community was youthful. Less than 20 percent of the men were older than forty, and some 80 percent were in their teens, twenties, or thirties. Women were slightly younger than the men.[110] The oldest Jews—Lieberman, Sondheimer, Hocheimer, Wolfson, and Aaron Harris—were in their fifties.[111] There were a large number of single men in Wilmington; however, there were no known unmarried women. The Jews from Eastern Europe tended to be younger than those from Germany and Western Europe and those born in America. Sixty-five percent of the Russians who came to

Wilmington in the 1880s were in their teens and twenties. Of the fourteen men forty or older, only four were from Russia and Hungary. All the Germans here were thirty-five or older. Many of the young people had come to the United States without their parents and elders. The people who took them in as boarders or sales help were the older, Western European and German Jews, who in a very real sense helped the newer Eastern Europeans learn the ropes of American life.

The founders had been in retail businesses, primarily the clothing business. In 1890 Jews continued to operate clothing shops; in fact twelve of the nineteen clothiers listed in the 1890 Wilmington City Directory were Jewish.[112] More than half of the clothiers were those who had been in Wilmington for a while: Kaufman Sondheimer, Meyer Meyers, Bernard Row, Reuben Wolters, Max Ephraim, Aaron and Louis Harris. The four new clothing stores, run by Russian immigrants (Sarah Cohen, Jacob Dolphman, Herman Goldstein, and S. Levy) were smaller enterprises on Front Street. Some Eastern European immigrants began as clerks or salesmen in clothing stores. Three became tailors. More than half of the new Eastern European immigrants earned their livelihoods in the clothing industry. Like their compatriots who immigrated to New York City, the Jews were experienced with the clothing trades, which had been one of the few industries open to Jews in Europe and had provided a livelihood for one of every three arriving Jewish workers.[113] Jewish workers also chose the clothing industry because Jewish employers allowed them to refrain from work on Saturdays, and tailoring and weaving were named as desirable occupations in the Talmud. In New York City, the newer immigrants edged the older German ones out of the garment industry.[114] However, in Wilmington, because so many German clothiers and their children left the city, the clothing trades were wide open for the newer immigrants from Eastern Europe.

While the clothing trades continued to be the most common occupation for Jews, employing more than thirty people, the newer immigrants branched out to other areas. They became shoemakers, tailors, laborers, carpenters, cabinetmakers, upholsterers, pocketbook makers, and peddlers.[115] Those who tried retail stores opened different types of stores: bakeries, groceries, dry goods, and millinery shops. In the 1870s, the first wave of Jewish businesses had opened on lower Market Street; in 1890, many of the newer immigrants clustered together on Front Street. The clothier Sarah Cohen was at 7 East Front, D. M. Lurge, a watchmaker, was at 9 East Front, Herman Goldstein, a clothier, worked at 15 East Front, and lived on the next block of Front Street, where Philip Sklut, a shoe-maker, was at 103–105 East Front, Nathan Hurshman, a shoemaker, was at 109 East Front, and Jacob Faber, a barber, was at 117 East Front.

Peddling became an almost universal male Jewish experience in nineteenth-century America. It was a bridge occupation for new im-migrants who knew its values and approach from Europe.[116] For im-migrants from Russia, who came to the United States with considerable entrepreneurial experience but little ready cash, ped-dling was a logical choice.[117] During the 1880s at least fifteen new-comers made their livings as peddlers, which made peddling second only to the clothing industry. Most likely many more Jews worked as peddlers but did not list themselves in the Wilmington City Di-rectory; some peddlers were probably in the city so briefly that there is no record of them.

Changes in Delaware law reflect the increase in peddlers. The re-vised 1887 law began with a clear definition of a peddler: "any per-son who shall drive a carriage, wagon, cart or other vehicle from which personal property is retailed or shall carry a pack from which personal property is retailed shall be considered a peddlar."[118]

An earlier law had been unfavorable to noncitizens. Not only did the noncitizen have to pay $50 for a foot peddler's license, for which a bona fide citizen paid $8, but also the noncitizen had to pay $100 extra for each and every county in which he want to peddle. In keeping with the spirit of encouraging immigration, the 1887 law removed the distinction between citizen and noncitizen, but all the fees were much higher: $50 for a foot peddler or peddler with one horse, $75 for traveling with two horses, each additional horse $25. In addition, the peddler had to enter into a bond with the State for $500.

The revised 1887 law required the peddler to "display his license in a prominent and conspicuous place" and to allow authorities to search his pack or vehicle.[119] The peddler was not permitted to lend or borrow a license. This strict new addition most likely was added to the law because many individuals tried to peddle without pur-chasing licenses. In keeping with the spirit of promoting agriculture in Delaware, the law exempted all who peddled anything manufac-tured or grown by an individual in the state.

In the mid-nineteenth century, when many new immigrants began peddling, they traveled throughout the countryside bringing goods to rural areas. However, in the 1880s several of Wilming-ton's peddlers chose not to travel great distances with their goods, but to stand in one place on Market Street in the heart of the business district. Wilmington's businessmen did not look favorably on these peddlers who sold goods similar to their own without paying rent. In 1888, some sixty merchants signed a petition asking the government to enforce the law against selling on the streets.[120] Calling themselves taxpayers and legitimate tradesmen, the merchants claimed that by not enforcing the law, government officials favored the few, and the few had given confidence to hundreds of others to sell in a like manner. Despite the fact that most of the Jewish merchants had stores in this section of town, none of the signers was a known Jew. At least one store owner, Reuben Wolters, took care of the peddlers, giving them credit and helping them in any way he could.[121] Wolters permitted many Jews of that time, including Baer, Faber, Barsky, and David Topkis, who had arrived from Europe with practically no capital, to buy from him on credit.[122] All the peddlers loved him.

Government officials did begin to get stricter about peddlers having licenses. In June 1889, Morris Cohen was arrested for peddling without a license and was given bail of $200. The bail was raised to $500 two days later. In July, after he had been to Philadelphia, Mr. Cohen produced a license and was discharged.[123]

Later that month Ed Livingstone, a sixteen-year-old who had left Russia two years before, Aaron Rosenbloom, Bernard Bulwick, Hyman Greenstein, and Joseph Sollad were arrested for peddling matches and writing paper in King Street. They were discharged with a warning to stop this illegal activity.[124]

Livingstone was arrested peddling matches again without a license in October 1889. He produced a license but complained about buying it because he needed his one dollar to get into the synagogue for Yom Kippur. "No one gets in unless he pays the dollar," Livingstone explained to the authorities.[125]

In February 1890, Joseph Moskovitch was arrested for peddling toys he had manufactured. Since Moskovitch had just arrived the day before from New York, he was set free with the promise that he would leave the city.[126]

At the same time some Jewish immigrants faced such difficulties, the more acculturated Jews enjoyed the life of the well-to-do. Nathan Lieberman's daughter Carrie was married to Harry Lipper in October 1889. Among the three hundred guests at the elaborate supper at Philadelphia's Mercantile Hall were the former governor of Pennsylvania, Robert E. Pattison, and the mayor of Wilmington, Austin Harrington. Rabbi Joseph Krauskopf, a leader of the Reform movement in Philadelphia, performed the ceremony.[127]

By 1890, Wilmington's Jews included peddlers and real estate entrepreneurs, greenhorns who spoke no English and American-born or naturalized citizens, Orthodox and Reform-leaning Jews, illiterate peasants and well-educated scholars. Not all the nationals of one country had the same characteristics, but the differences in economic class, cultural background, language, and religious orientation often were related to country of origin, with the more acculturated Jews coming from Germany and Western Europe.

Despite their pronounced differences, the outside world saw the Jews as one group. When David Topkis and Hannah Ray Tiger were married in December 1888, the *Morning News* reported that the wedding was "attended by nearly all the Jews of the city and was to them a social event of importance."[128] Many Germans were invited so "there was also a large supply of wines and liquors including the German's favorite beverage, lager beer." The distinction between the Jews and the readers of the newspaper was clearly drawn. "The men sat at table with their hats on, *a custom peculiar to the Jews.*" The article also referred to "the wedding feast, always an important part of social events *among these people.*"[129]

In many American Jewish communities, there was friction between the German and Eastern European Jews. The tension between the two groups went back to Europe, where "German Jews habitually viewed Eastern Jews as unenlightened medievals and Eastern Jews in turn viewed them as assimilated and godless."[130] In the 1880s many German Jews saw the new Eastern European immigrants as social inferiors and feared that their mass immigration would provoke anti-Semitism.[131]

While Wilmington's Jews were acutely aware of their differences and disagreed on religious observance, they recognized their mutual dependence. The founders, knowing they lived in a tiny community with a dwindling German Jewish population, needed the influx of their co-religionists to develop a community. Their sense of obligation to help their brethren succeed as Jews and as Americans was reinforced by growing sentiment against immigration and by their own increasing recognition of the persecution of Jews in Eastern Europe. The more observant Eastern Europeans met a new type of Jew, one who lived comfortably as an accepted part of the wider community and freely practiced Judaism. They saw a model worthy of imitation. From the beginning the Jews of Wilmington recognized that what they had in common overrode their differences, and they worked together.

4

Taking Care of Their Own—
The 1890s

DURING THE 1890S, TWO-THIRDS OF THE NEW JEWISH ARRIVALS TO Wilmington continued to be Eastern Europeans; few Jewish immigrants from Germany and England arrived in Wilmington, and members of the founding families left the city. By the turn of the century, the adult Wilmington Jewish population was largely Eastern European. Many of the new immigrants found employment in the thriving industries of Wilmington; however, each struggled to make a living. Their lifestyles were very different than those of the successful merchants.

By the middle of the 1890s, disagreements about religious observance led to independent efforts by the Orthodox and the Reform to build synagogues. To the surprise of many, the Orthodox were successful, while the Reform were not. Although the Orthodox had little money, they had more people, absolute determination, as well as the assistance of the wealthier Reform Jews.

In spite of significant cultural, economic, and religious differences, the more established Jews and the newcomers worked side by side in the important task of assisting those in need. They created the Hebrew Library Association, a local chapter of B'nai B'rith, the Hebrew Charity Association, and the earliest version of the Ladies Bichor Cholem Society. Several Jews became active in the Zionist movement.

As more immigrants flocked to the United States, the mood of the country began to change, and the anti-immigration movement gained momentum. The United States Congress debated the possibility of a literacy requirement for entrance to the country at the same time Delaware's constitutional convention made literacy a requirement to vote. Immigrants to Delaware recognized that in order to be accepted as Americans, they would have to learn English and lose some of their foreign ways.

NEW OCCUPATIONS IN A CITY OF OPPORTUNITY

On New Year's Day 1890, the *Every Evening* newspaper described the encouraging advancement of the city in the last decade and its bright hopes for the future.[1] Wilmington's population had grown from some 42,000 in 1880 to more than 60,000 in 1890. The city's industrial development had been rapid. New ventures included the Pullman works and at least a half-dozen new morocco manufacturers. Telephone, telegraph, and electric light, which had been comparatively unknown in 1880, were in wide use. The number of churches, public schools, places of entertainment, and railroad stations had grown tremendously.

In addition to material progress, Wilmington enjoyed a sense of community and the recognition by one social class of its responsibilities to the other, as indicated by the record number of local associations for prison reform, free kindergartens, and care for the poor and distressed.[2] The arts and letters flourished with many literary, dramatic, and musical organizations. Wilmington had excellent street architecture, well-paved streets, efficient electric passenger service, telephones, and electric lights. In other words, Wilmington was a city of opportunity for the Jews and all other newcomers.

Eager for employment of any type, many new Jewish immigrants found jobs in the flourishing industries of the city. Morocco production, the tanning of choice kidskins, had grown into a major Wilmington industry after the first leather factory, Pusey and Scott, was founded in 1845. By the 1890s, there were some seventeen morocco plants in Wilmington employing "thousands of hands" and producing 520,000 dozens of skins annually.[3] Wilmington was second only to Philadelphia in the morocco industry.[4] In 1893, F. Blumenthal and Company hired Richard Patzowsky, the Jewish owner of Patzowsky and Company in New York, as its superintendent.[5]

Patzowsky was born near Prague, Bohemia around 1857 and emigrated to the United States at age eighteen.[6] He went to Chicago, became a foreman in a tannery, and within two years was promoted to superintendent. Patzowsky then went to New York City and founded Patzowsky and Company. No reports about the new management mentioned Patzowsky's Jewishness. His name does not appear in the official records of Jewish synagogues and organizations; however, Dr. Ostro, who arrived in Wilmington at about the same time as Patzowsky, reported, "Patzowsky was definitely Jewish, absolutely."[7] Patzowsky was seen at Adas Kodesch many times, and his children married Jews. Ostro recalled a meeting of the building committee of the Temple of Truth after the turn of the century that consisted of himself, D. L. Levy, another morocco worker, and Patzowsky. In his will, Patzowsky contributed to the Hebrew Charity Association, the Delaware Anti-Tuberculosis Society, and the Associated Charities of Wilmington. Although Patzowsky's second wife was not Jewish, she employed Jewish help at home because she liked them; she patronized Jewish stores, and gave to needy Jews.

Richard Patzowsky was already financially successful when he arrived in Wilmington. His home at 819 West was right near Nathan Lieberman's home. When he gave a party for his daughters Antoinette and Louisa in 1894, the only Jewish guest among the seventeen young people was Joe Lieberman, son of Nathan and Rose.[8] The following month, Patzowsky introduced a tradition of giving a ball for all employees of Blumenthal's, in order to bring labor and management together. At the ball held on February 5, 1897, more than one hundred couples participated in the grand march.[9]

Patzowsky brought eleven foremen and approximately 450 of his old employees to Wilmington with him, though most of the old hands in the factory were retained. Extensive alterations costing between $25,000 and $35,000 took place at the plant, located at Front and Monroe Streets, in the following weeks. Thirteen carloads of heavy machinery, capable of turning out more work, were shipped from New York. Later in the spring, many of the buildings were enlarged. The expansion of Blumenthal's came at an opportune time because a business depression the following winter caused many factories, like the Woolen Mills of New Castle and the Delaware Iron Works, to close, and many workers were unemployed.[10]

Most likely, some of the 450 employees who came with Patzowsky from New York were Jewish. Sam Hendler, whose daughter Rosa was born in Wilmington in 1893, is the only one who was definitely in Wilmington in 1893.[11] However, in 1894 and 1895 at least ten men (including Benjamin Fischer, Morris Friedman, Isaac Greenberg, Thomas Handleman, Louis Horowitz, Julius Kramer, Jacob Lipkin, Morris Muscovitch, Abraham Rosenthal, and Morris Silberger) also worked at Blumenthal's.[12] Of the eleven men in the initial group, only Sam Hendler, Morris Silberger, and Benjamin Fischer appear to have remained in Wilmington more than a few years. In 1900, only Morris Silberger still listed his occupation as morocco worker at Blumenthal's. Hendler was listed as a grocer and Benjamin Fischer as an agent.[13]

In the seven and a half years Patzowsky served as superintendent of Blumenthal's, at least forty Jewish morocco workers, a significant number, came to Wilmington. At least twenty-two worked at

Blumenthal's for some period of time; others worked for American Leather. David Levy, who became president of Liberty Leather in 1921, began his Wilmington career at Blumenthal's in 1898.[14] Abraham Hirshout was sent to Wilmington from Austria for a job at Blumenthal's because a friend of his brother was head of the company.[15] Only about ten of the morocco workers who arrived in the 1890s were still in Wilmington in 1910. In addition to Patzowsky and Levy, only Meyer Briefman still listed his occupation as morocco worker. The others may still have worked in the factories but they also had retail shops in order to increase their incomes. Jacob Millman, Abraham Hirshout, Michael Hendler, and Morris Ezrailson were grocers; Thomas Handleman owned the Colonial Quick Lunch; Charles Jellinek became a salesman.[16] Many laborers considered morocco work unpleasant because of the poor wages, terrible color stain on the hands, and the bad smell.[17] They were eager to move out of the leather business into retail businesses as soon as possible.

In August 1900, after making F. Blumenthal and Company the largest morocco factory in Wilmington, Richard Patzowsky resigned as manager.[18] The factory, which was as fine as any in the country, had grown from several hundred to 2500 workers.[19] After resting for a few months, Patzowsky formed his own morocco company, the New Castle Leather Company.

The early morocco workers often were boarders. In 1895, Morris Muscovitch lived at 824 Read Street in the home of Jacob Wineberger; Julius Kramer lived at 404 Front Street in the home of George Johnson, who ran a liquor store; Louis Horowitz lived at 7 Justison Street in the home of Nathan Reiner, who sold baskets; and Morris Silberger lived at 10 East Front Street with Peter and Anna Tucker.[20]

The Pullman Palace Car Company, which was based in Illinois, opened a large plant with five buildings in Wilmington in 1886–87.[21] The company employed about eight hundred workers from every class of skilled labor, from blacksmith to seamstress, and Jews who were skilled laborers found employment there. Gidel Podolsky, a Russian Jewish immigrant first listed as Zidel Podolski, arrived in the United States in 1886 with his wife, Minnie, and three Russian-born children, Charles, Sarah, and Isaac.[22] Daughters Maggie, Jessie, and Bessie were born in Delaware between 1888 and 1893. Podolsky's first job was as a laborer for the Pullman Palace Car Company. A year later he worked for the company as a cabinetmaker. For several years in the 1890s Podolsky was in the clothing business at 416 West Front Street, but at the end of the decade he again worked for Pullman Palace Car Company.

Gidel Podolsky became an important member of the Jewish community, offering a first home to many new immigrants By 1890, a few years after Gidel's arrival, his brother Max, a peddler, boarded at Gidel's home at 318 East Second Street.[23] Within a couple of years, Max had established himself in the hat business, and in 1895 he bought his own three-story brick house on South Second Street between Market and King. In 1892, Gidel lived at 416 Front Street. The following year he purchased a parcel of land on Front Street between West and Washington for $2,000.[24] By 1895 three Jewish men, Joseph Raisman, Benjamin Fisher, and Lazarus Price, and their families lived at 416 Front, and Podolsky himself lived at 424 Front Street, suggesting that he used the property at 416 to provide housing to new immigrants.

David Finkelstein's family lived with the Podolskys when they first arrived from Philadelphia.[25] Finkelstein had begun his life in the United States as a tailor in New York City; however, when the union went on strike, he moved to Philadelphia to avoid being a strike breaker. After several years in Philadelphia the unions took over, and again there was a strike. Finkelstein did not want to be a strike breaker so he answered an ad in the Wilmington paper about an opening for a tailor at Mullin's, a large clothing store. "Finkelstein went to see Carol Mullin and somehow or other they fell in love, and the family moved to Wilmington." I. B. Finkelstein, who was about nine years old when his family moved to Wilmington, remembered that "a great many Jewish people when they came to Wilmington, came to Podolsky on West Front Street. That was the usual thing, the gathering place."[26] Three Friedman families, all involved in morocco, also lived with Podolsky.

After a short time, the Finkelstein family of five people moved nearby to 113½ Justison Street with the Friedman family, which included Jacob, a morocco worker, his wife Sarah, and their three children. Morris Friedman and wife, Katie, lived at the same address by 1894 when their daughter was born, but by then the others had moved. HIAS sent Fusel Kramer, a twenty-year-old female, to the Podolsky home in 1892.[27]

Samuel A. Berger, Max Gold, Morris Gross, Barney Goldstein, Joseph Rosenblatt, Jacob Singer, and Louis Wolfman also arrived in Wilmington in the late 1890s and all worked at the Pullman Car Company.[28] Sam Berger, born in Russia around 1877, lived in Philadelphia before coming to Wilmington as an upholsterer for Pullman.[29] While he worked for the railroad, Berger always had a

1893- Esther Finkelstein Keffie, Rae, Isaac and Lena

Esther Finkelstein with Keffie, Rae, Isaac, and Lena, ca. 1893. (Jewish Historical Society of Delaware.)

grocery store or used furniture store on the side.[30] Elizabeth Berger, who had "tremendous common sense and business acumen did much of the work in the stores."[31] Elizabeth and Sam also raised thirteen children and their family was reputed to be the largest Jewish family in the state. Jacob Singer and his wife Rosa came to the United States by 1888, when their son Sam was born in New Jersey.[32] Jacob, who was a car builder and a cabinetmaker, worked at Pullman at least until 1900. Max Gold was a carpenter at Pullman by 1898.[33] He still lived in Wilmington in 1910. Morris Gross and his wife Sarah were in Wilmington by the mid-1890s, when their fifth child, Joseph, was born. By 1898, Morris worked at the Pullman Company, and by 1900 he called himself a cabinetmaker. Barney Goldstein was a laborer in 1895, but by the end of the decade he was a cabinetmaker for Pullman.[34] Louis Wolfman was a cabinetmaker for Pullman, and later became a grocer.[35] Several newly arrived immigrants listed themselves as laborers at first, but later became morocco workers or Pullman employees.

David Finkelstein was one of about nineteen Jewish immigrants who came to Wilmington in the 1890s and earned a livelihood through tailoring. At least half of the new tailors were from Eastern Europe.[36] An equal number began as shoemakers. Like their brethren in New York City, the Russian Jews followed the path of the German Jews and gravitated to skilled labor, shopkeeping, and peddling.[37] Although 56 percent of the Jews in New York City in 1880 did manual labor, less than 1 percent of them were unskilled and only 5 percent were semiskilled. The skilled laborers were glaziers, jewelers, shoemakers, carpenters, and most often tailors.[38] In contrast, the Italian and Irish immigrants to New York City found employment in domestic service and common labor.[39]

Many new Jewish immigrants chose peddling because they were experienced in commerce but had no cash.[40] Some became peddlers until they could find other jobs or for short periods of time when they were between jobs. In February 1891, R. R. Morris of Sussex County submitted a petition to have the peddling license law that was enacted at the last session repealed.[41] Morris and his co-signers felt the cost of the peddler's license was too high. They argued that storekeepers in different towns competed with peddlers by going around the countryside securing orders that they later filled with delivery wagons. The revised code of 1893 did not change the basic cost of a peddler's license except for peddlers of fruit, vegetables, and produce, whose costs were reduced in order to encourage agricultural interests.[42]

Tension between peddlers and merchants was high. In March

1895, three peddlers, identified as Hebrews, were brought to municipal court for selling mops on Second Street without a license.[43] Both Harry Davidson and Ignatz Roth admitted that they had purchased mops from the peddlers. The defendants, who were morocco shavers by trade and were out of work for the first time, claimed they weren't aware that they needed licenses. The city solicitor recommended they be dismissed with the understanding they they would be punished if it happened again. Judge Ball emphasized that it was unfair for peddlers to sell wares without a license when reputable merchants were compelled to pay for a license and taxes to maintain the government. The merchants were entitled to protection.

Simon Cohen became the first Jew to join the Wilmington police force in June 1891. He was described as a "well built Hebrew" who along with the new Italian policeman was a "good man."[44] By 1894, Cohen had left the police force and run into problems. When a Jewish clothier arrested on charges of receiving stolen goods jumped bail, Cohen revealed the fugitive's whereabouts for a fee of $25. After admitting what he had done, Cohen left town presumably to escape the anger of his fellow countrymen.[45] When his son William was born in May 1895, Cohen was a salesman.

At the same time increased numbers of Jewish laborers and peddlers came to Wilmington, the first three Jewish doctors arrived. Michael Ostrowsky came to Wilmington in 1891–92 as a graduate of the School of Pharmacy at the University of Kiev. After passing the Delaware State Pharmacy Exam in 1892, he worked for Bennett Downes, a physician and druggist at Eighth and Poplar Streets.[46] A few years later he went to medical school at Baltimore University School of Medicine, later known as Johns Hopkins, but he continued to be listed in the Wilmington City Directories.[47] After passing the Delaware State Medical Board exam in 1899, Dr. Ostro took a special course in obstetrics in New York and then resumed practice in Wilmington.[48] Beginning in 1900, Dr. Michael Ostro (as he became known) was a physician and druggist at 6th and Pine.[49]

Sigmund Werner graduated from Jefferson Medical College in 1897 and established a practice in Wilmington in 1898.[50] Dr. Albert Robin holds the distinction of being the first, and perhaps the only, Jew invited to come to the state of Delaware. Avraim Rabinovitch was born in Uman, a small town in the Ukraine, on April 12, 1874.[51] After he completed public school, he was not permitted to attend high school because he was Jewish. Relatives in Pittsburgh, learning of Avraim's great ability, urged him to migrate to America to avoid conscription in the Russian army. After arriving in Pittsburgh and working briefly in his uncle's pharmacy, Rabinovitch enrolled in Western Pennsylvania Medical School under the name Abraham Robin. After graduating from the Medical School in 1897 and practicing medicine briefly, Robin decided to take a special course in pathology and bacteriology with Professor MacFarlane at the Polyclinic Medical School in Philadelphia.

In 1899, the President of the Delaware Board of Health wrote to Professor MacFarlane "asking him to recommend a young doctor to head the laboratory which they were about to establish in connection with the University at Newark, for the purpose of helping the general practitioners make more accurate diagnoses."[52] MacFarlane heartily recommended Albert Robin (as he became known). So Dr. Robin and his new bride Eva came to Delaware for the "stupendous salary of one thousand dollars a year."[53]

RETAIL SUCCESS IN A CITY OF OPPORTUNITY

Wilmington offered excellent opportunities to those in retail business. "A noticeable and praiseworthy awakening of retail business in Wilmington" had occurred between the 1870s and the early 1890s.[54] Wilmington's retailers had increased trade with the surrounding country and peninsula, and now it was an everyday occurrence for people to come from all parts of the peninsula, Pennsylvania, and New Jersey to shop in Wilmington stores. Market Street, which was the hub of retail businesses, had changed dramatically, with buildings of several stories replacing the ugly barracks formerly lining the street.[55] However, proximity to Philadelphia still hampered the city's trade.

The largest number of Jewish immigrants, including nearly all of those who had arrived before 1890, continued to work in retail businesses or petty trades on lower Market and Front Streets. Unlike the vast majority of immigrants to America, who had worked the land in the Old World, Jewish immigrants had been prohibited from owning land and had therefore been involved in petty trade. They found themselves better prepared for life in the towns and cities of America.[56]

Some new Jewish immigrants tried different types of retailing. Barnet Gluckman entered the cigar business soon after he arrived in Wilmington. Born in Popelany Schawl, Lithuania in 1867, Gluckman first appeared in Wilmington in 1887 when he married Fannie Harris, Aaron's daughter.[57] Gluckman had studied for the rabbinate before emigrating to the United States, so he was well-versed in Hebrew and the Talmud. He was also a master of English, Polish, Russian, Yiddish, and German. On his journey from Lithuania to the United States, Gluckman had learned two trades, telegraphy and cigar making.[58] By 1889 Barnet was in the cigar business. His store at 913 Market Street, which featured Cuban handmade cigars and a full line of tobacco and smokers' articles, employed four skilled workmen and produced 18,000 cigars monthly. The store was singled out for praise: "Few establishments have acquired the popularity that Mr. Gluckman has so quickly. Mr Gluckman is a German by birth, but he has been a prominent and well known resident of this section for some time."[59]

The description is rather curious because Gluckman was neither German nor a long-term resident, but it demonstrates the fact that the word "German" was considered a compliment and was meant to convey length of time, educational level, and prosperity. "German" was misused just as "Sunday" had been confused with "Sabbath" earlier.

Despite the glowing description of the store, Gluckman had trouble earning a living and decided to try his luck in New York. However, by 1895, Fannie, Barnet, and their two New York-born children had returned to Wilmington, where Fannie ran a clothing store.

Simon Gordon opened a restaurant at 116 Market Street. Considered one of the best restaurants in the city, with nearly perfect cuisine, the restaurant was spacious, with seating for about fifty people. He also offered rooms for rent. Gordon, who had run a similar business in Philadelphia, left Wilmington by the end of the decade.[60] Although Gordon was not in Wilmington for a long time, he contributed liberally to the *mikveh*, the ritual bath, when it was built. He also contributed the first books owned by Adas Kodesch.[61]

Moses Weil, usually referred to as Professor Weil, was a scientific optician at 305 Market Street.[62] Educated at the most renowned schools in Germany and France, Weil had proven himself to be a most skillful optician. In February 1892, Weil reported that in the previous month, he had relieved 250 cases of defective vision, including farsightedness, nearsightedness, and astigmatism with his celebrated Scotch pebbler glasses. Weil made the O.E.P. lens, the hardest, clearest, whitest lens invented. Weil, who had agents throughout the country, was respected by prominent people throughout the United States. He was a veteran of the Civil War and an active member of the Grand Army of the Republic. Weil had lived in Cincinnati and New York before settling in Wilmington around 1888. His store was one of the five "Jewish" stores men-

tioned in the 1891 book *Delaware Industries*. In 1892, when Grant
Post No. 13 of the Grand Army (named after Ulysses S. Grant) was
formed, Weil was elected commander. He was the only Jewish officer.[63]

Most Jewish retailers continued to operate clothing stores. Meyer
Meyers, who had been in the clothing business in Wilmington since
the 1860s, ran a clothing store at 406 Market Street. In his large,
two-floor store, Meyers had a full line of men's and boy's ready-
made clothing and furnishing goods as well as a large custom department. Meyers was identified with the A.O.U.W., Ancient Order
of United Workmen, Knights of Gold Eagle, and Masonic fraternities. He was a member of various German societies as well.[64] In
1890, when the German societies met to celebrate the two hundredth anniversary of the arrival of Germans in America, Meyers
represented the Liberty Lodge.[65]

Aaron Harris and his son Samuel continued to work long hours
at the clothing and pawnbroker business they had opened upon their
arrival from New York. In August 1892, the Harrises received a
hateful letter, which the *Sunday Star* printed in its entirety.

Dear Father and Son,
If you don't close up at 6 o'clock, we will taar and feather yo and white
wash yo and your son. If you will, it will save us the trouble. The cisen
of this City is made up their mind to do this.

Your res
White Caps No. 49[66]

Mr. Harris claimed that the threatening letter was the outcome of
a proposition made to him by certain clothiers of Wilmington to
close down at six. Harris insisted that he and his son owned the
property at 218 Market Street and would manage it their own way.
After the senior Harris's death, Samuel Harris continued operating
the clothing store until after the turn of the century.[67] Aaron Harris's older son, Louis Harris, had opened his own clothing store at
114 Market Street.[68] By 1900, the store was called Minnie Harris
Pawnbroker, and both Louis and his son Henry were employed
there.[69]

Kaufman Sondheimer operated his clothing store at 230 Market
Street until after the turn of the century, but in 1895 the family
moved back to Philadelphia.[70]

Max Ephraim, who had begun as a salesman in Wolters Clothing
Store, ran his own successful clothing store at 316 Market Street.

In the Columbus Day parade of 1892, he had a float that reflected credit on his taste and enterprise.[71] By 1900 Max Ephraim was at 504 Market Street in a business known as the New York Clothing House.

I. Hamburger and Sons, which advertised itself as the largest clothing store and factory in Baltimore, opened a branch store in Wilmington in 1888.[72] Henry Hamburger, who ran the store, first boarded at the Clayton House, suggesting that he was testing business here before becoming a permanent resident. By 1890 the Hamburger firm sold clothing at 220 Market Street and shoes at 209 Market Street. In 1895, the store was at 220 and 222 Market. From its beginning, the store ranked among Wilmington's foremost business houses. However, in 1898, the firm announced that it was selling its entire stock and returning to Baltimore. The firm had concluded that there was "more money in Baltimore business."

In 1890, Sam Mitchell and his brother-in-law William Bash ran a millinery store at 219 Market Street.[73] Sam Mitchell, who had recently married William's sister Freda, still lived in Philadelphia. In 1892 the Mitchells and Bash lived at 207 West. William Bash came with his sister and her husband so they would all have family nearby. "Having close kin nearby was very important then, when Jews in small communities were very few." By 1894, Mitchell and Bash had introduced a novel way of holding sales. Each day of the week, a different assortment of goods was on sale. Apparently the technique was successful because it was "interesting for the ladies" and kept them busy in January.[74]

Only a few of the very largest stores in the country produced such elaborate decorative displays as Mitchell and Bash.[75] At each successive opening—referring to the seasonal openings that were traditional at the time—the displays were distinctive and wonderful. For the October 1896 opening, the store was decorated with Japanese lanterns, curtains, and screens. Banks of plumes in the center made it a veritable flower garden. Large crowds attended the opening and some two thousand souvenirs were carried away by purchasers. By 1897, Mitchell and Bash also ran a store in Chester, Pennsylvania.[76] Like many new immigrants who became involved in the community, Sam Mitchell was active in the Moses Montefiore Society, though the Mitchells had only lived in Wilmington for five or six years. After the Mitchells and Bash left Wilmington, they went into business in Baltimore, where they were successful in a business specializing in fur coats and capes.[77]

Sam Slessinger, who had arrived in Wilmington from Hungary in 1884 and opened an installment house with David Abramson, expanded his business continually and became enormously successful. By 1894, Slessinger advertised his installment house at 706 French Street, as an old established firm well-known for an easy payment system.[78] Not hurt by the poor business times, Slessinger said "the shortage of cash this year makes it desirable for many to avail themselves of the credit house." Four years later, Slessinger advertised two locations, 706 French Street and 506 Market, as "Greater Wilmington's Biggest Department Store."[79] He sold ready-made and made-to-order clothing for men, women, and children as well as dry goods, carpet, and furniture. In 1899, Slessinger expanded to a third location, 209 Market Street, where he ran a wholesale clothing store. The new business spread quickly through Delaware, Maryland, Virginia, and part of Pennsylvania with the aid of three traveling salesmen.[80]

After Jacob and Rosa Topkis and their younger children moved to New Castle in the late 1880s, they ran a store in the old Delaware House, a former hotel. The store was in one parlor, another parlor was rented to the Republican committee, and the third floor was rented to the Young Republicans for fifty cents a week. Jacob Topkis, who had studied studied math, Latin, French, Russian, and grammatical Hebrew at a school in Odessa until he was twelve, also opened a general merchandising store in Dobbinsville to serve the mill workers of the River Road Mill, many of whom were from Eastern Europe.[81] With his keen mind, he soon spoke the languages of his customers and acquired fame as an interpreter in Mayor Herbert's court.[82] He could converse well in seven different languages, "an accomplishment few men in the state could boast of."[83]

Louis and William Topkis opened a dry goods wholesale and retail store at 417 King Street in March 1894. A year later, Louis sold his share to his mother Rosa, and the whole family moved back to Wilmington. By 1897, Jacob, Sallie, and William all worked at Rosa Topkis Dry Goods, and Louis was manager of Samuel Slessinger's Delaware Wholesale Notion shop.

Throughout the United States, many Jewish immigrants carried a variety of clothing, dry goods, shoes, and notions in their stores. The concept of multipurpose stores developed logically from the fact that many retailers had begun as foot peddlers carrying a wide range of goods.[84] The largest of these multipurpose stores became known as department stores. Straus, Rich, Bonwit, Gimbel, Saks, and Filene were among the Jews who established well-known American department stores. The large, all-purpose stores that originated in Wilmington never reached the level of such national department stores, but one store, Snellenburg's, a branch of the

Philadelphia firm of N. Snellenburg and Company, achieved new heights. N. Snellenburg and Company, founded in 1869, employed over three thousand people and was the largest maker of clothing in the world. Since the firm made its own clothing in Philadelphia and sold directly from workroom to wearer, the clothing was sold for less.[85] By the 1890s, the Snellenburgs were leaders in Philadelphia's Jewish community.

In 1895, the partnership led by S. Snellenburg, F. F. Snellenburg, and S. L. Black, decided to open a Wilmington branch and purchased a lot and building for the new store at Seventh and Market Streets for $25,950.[86] At the end of the year the company purchased another nearby lot for $22,000. The firm sent the young German-born David Snellenburg, who had worked in the Philadelphia store since his arrival in the U.S. in 1890, to Wilmington to manage the new store.[87]

Snellenburg and Company's opening days were Friday, September 20, and Saturday, September 21, 1895.[88] On Friday, the store was full all day. The large windows were full of flowers and displays that attracted great interest. Electric light was used Friday evening. Apparently the store was crowded on Saturday as well. Perhaps Friday was an important retail day and therefore a good day to open a new store; however, it was an odd day to open a Jewish store. Not only was Friday evening the beginning of the weekly Sabbath, but Friday, September 20 was the second day of Rosh Hashanah, the Jewish New Year. Nothing demonstrates more clearly the vast gap between the reform Jews and the newly arrived Orthodox ones. Reform Jews did not celebrate two days of the New Year and did not observe the Sabbath by closing their stores.

Snellenburg and Company was noted for innovation throughout the next decades. In March 1898, Snellenburg's offered to give a free magazine, *Home Talk*, to all who sent their name to the store.[89] The concept attracted much favorable comment and many names were submitted. From the beginning, David Snellenburg tied the store's success to Wilmington's growth. An 1899 ad proclaimed "We Believe in Wilmington." Stating that Wilmington had an irresistible destiny to become a great and powerful industrial center, Snellenburg offered $1000 toward a fund to induce capital investment to the city.[90]

There was a big difference between the Jewish immigrants who laborered for meager wages and those who were self-employed and financially successful. Despite their differences, to the broader community they were all one Jewish community.

Snellenburg's c. 1905 (Collection of the author.)

RELIGIOUS RIVALRY: DUCATS VERSUS NUMBERS

The 1890s began with unity among the Orthodox factions. A new cemetery was needed because the Moses Montefiore Society's plot at Fifth and Rodman was too small. On August 8, 1890, a joint committee of Adas Kodesch and Ahavath Achim purchased a lot in Lombardy Cemetery for $457.20.[91] The purchase of the cemetery lot brought the union of the two Orthodox synagogues into one synagogue, Adas Kodesch K'nesseth Israel, with sixty members.

Orthodox services for Rosh Hashanah 1890 were conducted at 211 Market Street and lead by Rabbi Israel Goldstein.[92] The second floor was filled by males and females, the latter occupying a railed-off division at the lower part of the room. Everyone present, including the Gentiles, wore hats. The congregants sang rapidly; even little children read from the prayer book in Hebrew. Married men wore long white garments striped with black. The rabbi and the elders had their heads and bodies completely enveloped in these garments.[93]

At the same time, the Reform Jews of the Moses Montefiore synagogue worshipped at 406 Market Street, on the second floor of Meyer Meyers' clothing store. Rabbi Pizer, who had emigrated from Poland to England and then to the United States, conducted the services. He was not a rabbi but a learned Jew who was regarded by the community as a holy man.[94] The integrated Jews felt the need for worship accompanied by a greater degree of decorum than prevailed at the Orthodox synagogue.[95]

During the early 1890s, the Reform and Orthodox synagogues held services at different stores on lower Market and Front Streets. For a few years, Adas Kodesch leased space at Third and Shipley Streets. The parlor was a place of worship and the back part was a ritual bath. Jacob Topkis, a coppersmith by training, contributed the copper lining and actually did the work.[96] The need for a large, permanent space was evident every Rosh Hashanah. However, most of the population had to "eke out a livelihood, and there were not many dollars for a large synagogue."[97]

No information about the fate of the Moses Montefiore Society's school of 1880 is extant. However, in 1893, the Adas Kodesch synagogue began a traditional Hebrew School with the aim of giving children more education in the language and religion of their fathers than could be given in limited home instruction.[98] Only Hebrew was taught. Following the traditional belief in the separation of men and women at religious services, there was one teacher for girls and another for boys. The school was free to all Hebrew children, but all Hebrews were asked to pledge monthly gifts to the school. The Board of Education was also asked for assistance.

Isaac Goldstein, a Russian by birth, was elected president of the new Hebrew school. Goldstein may very well have been the "rabbi" who led services in 1890. He had arrived in the United States in 1883 at the age of twenty-one, and was in Wilmington by 1886, when he married Rachel Leshem.[99] In 1893, Goldstein was a merchant. He and his wife had three children. Samuel Gluck of Hungary, the baker who defended his Sabbath in court, was elected secretary. Rosa and Sam Gluck had five children by 1893.[100] Solomon Grossman, a trustee of Adas Kodesch when it was incorporated in 1889, was elected treasurer. Solomon and Mary Grossman had six children by 1893. The three families all remained in Wilmington for some time, and their families kept expanding. Eventually, the Goldsteins had five children, the Glucks had nine children, and the Grossmans had seven. Like the founders of the Ohabe Shalom Hebrew School in 1880, their interest in starting a Hebrew school was personal as well as communal. Ensuring the preservation of Judaism in their families and in Wilmington was important to them.

Apparently, J. Harry Gordon began a Sunday School at about the same time. Gordon was "the only one who established and superin-

tended a Sunday School from 1892 until 1907 when the old building was razed."[101] Evidently, the school struggled to survive; in
1898 Gordon expressed hope that the congregation would decide
that a Sunday and religious school should be suitably maintained.[102]
Gordon spoke about the importance of the Sunday school in shaping a child's future and referred to many children who are not receiving any religious instruction whatsoever. In 1899, Adas
Kodesch hired Reverend Silverman to be the cantor of Adas Kodesch and to teach in the Hebrew Sunday School.[103]

Establishing a Hebrew school was very important because children had to be taught about their heritage. As more youngsters entered the public schools, they were exposed to a broader world,
which many thought of as superior.[104] The public school became a
rival source of authority that separated the child from his or her elders and heritage.[105] After observing Yom Kippur with his family,
young Isaac B. Finkelstein was shocked to return to his public
school and discover that nothing had happened to the children who
attended school on Yom Kippur.[106] "It threw some doubt into my
mind," he explained years later. "How could anyone go to school
on Yom Kippur and live?"[107]

Throughout the early 1890s, Jewish leaders hoped the Reform
and Orthodox factions could be brought together in order to build
one handsome temple, which might cost as much as ten thousand
dollars.[108] However, by March 1895 the hopes of building one synagogue were doomed because of the differences between "the reformed and orthodox Jews of the city relative to the management
of the new synagogue."[109] The groups disagreed on several items
that were "seemingly trifling but of vital importance to the sons of
Abraham."

[The Reform Jews] believe in being comfortable when they worship. In
place of shutting off women and children in a latticed balcony, they
want them in their pews. In place of keeping on their hats in church,
they see no problem in removing them. In place of a male choir and no
instrumental accompaniment, they think an organ and a good mixed
choir would add to the services. Then they want hymns or sermons in
English . . . the orthodox which has numbers but not so many ducats,
adheres to wearing hats, the isolation of women and children, the use of
Hebrew in services, and the banishment of music.[110]

The Reform Jews were usually the wealthier Jews. "While they
were inferior in numbers, they had the best in the money line."[111]
Both groups held meetings to discuss new synagogues on March

3, 1895. The Reform Jews met in the Smith Building, formed a congregation with about forty-five members, and raised considerable money.[112] The new synagogue was named Ohabe Shalom. The fact that the six trustees of the Ohabe Shalom synagogue met "for the purpose of forming a religious society" suggests that the original Ohabe Shalom had ceased to function, but it could also mean that the new temple was a reorganization of the former one. In May, the *American Israelite* predicted "there is no doubt that within a few months, almost every Israelite in the city will be a member of the Ohabe Shalom synagogue."[113] The *Jewish Messenger* reported that the Reform faction of the Hebrews was building its own synagogue because it had failed to agree with Conservative brethren on the question of whether the services should be said in English or chanted in Hebrew.[114] In all accounts of the split, reporters suggested that the Reform group would be successful because it had more money.

Reports on who was elected to lead the congregation differ, but all those mentioned—David Abramson, Solomon Baeringer, Nathan Barsky, Max Ephraim, Abraham Greenbaum, Samuel Harris, Morris Levy, Nathan Levy, Joseph Lictenbaum, Nathan Lieberman, Jacob Schless, Sam Slessinger, and Moses Weil—were in retail businesses, earned good livings, and were presumed to have the resources to establish a synagogue.[115] With such men in leadership positions, the general public was confident that Ohabe Shalom was destined for success.

Furthermore, many of the leaders of the Reform synagogue had been in Wilmington for a relatively long time; therefore, they were more familiar to the rest of Wilmington, which felt more comfortable with them. Nathan Lieberman, the patriarch of Wilmington Jewry, had been in Wilmington for some thirty years. Abramson, Barsky, Ephraim, Harris, and Slessinger had been in Wilmington for more than a decade. Moses Weil had been here six or seven years, but had been in the United States since before the Civil War. Nathan Levy and his wife Ettie had only arrived in Wilmington in 1893, but he too had fought in the Civil War.[116] Nathan and Ettie Levy and their nine children arrived in Wilmington after living in Grand Rapids, Michigan, and Auburn, New York. When he first arrived, Levy ran Turk's Clothing Company, but by 1895 he and his wife had established a pawnbroker business.

Two other men, while new to Wilmington, had connections to the early families. Solomon Baeringer had married Julia Wolters, sister of Reuben Wolters, and ran a ladies' furnishing store at 231 Market Street.[117] Morris Levy, who had lived in New York since he was a young child in 1870, married Leah Stern, sister of Reuben Wolters' wife Rebecca.[118] After he married Leah Stern, Levy moved to Wilmington and sold feather dusters, but he soon bought the shoe store of Martin Schlager and renamed the store Morris Levy Shoe Company.

In addition to the well-known merchants, Jacob Schless was in the jewelry business at 319 Market with his family. Abraham Greenbaum ran a dry goods store at 209 Market. Joseph Lictenbaum ran an installment house at 315 Tatnall. Samuel Harris, who was in business with his father, became an active member of the Reform group even though his father, Aaron, was elected president of the Orthodox group. Harris's action was typical of what happened throughout America as the younger generation matured.

The names of Ohabe Shalom's specific officers are less important than the fact that men of differing backgrounds, with substantial experience in America, came together to form the new synagogue. Abramson and Slessinger were from Hungary; Barsky, Lictenbaum, Morris Levy, and Samuel Harris were born in Russia, but Morris Levy and Samuel Harris had come to New York as young children. Nathan Levy, Nathan Lieberman, and Moses Weil were from Germany and had been in the United States for more than thirty years. Ephraim and Baeringer were born in New York. All had been in the United States long enough to have become somewhat Americanized. Jews from different countries and traditions came together to form new patterns in America. Although the Wilmington newspapers tended incorrectly to use the words "German" and "Reform" almost synonymously, the implication that all Reform Jews were German was not correct. It might have been more accurate to correlate length of time in the United States and degree of religious observance. Not all the nationals of one country could be characterized as similar in their religious beliefs, but many of those who had been in the country longer tended toward reform.

The predictions that Ohabe Shalom would be successful were also based on the fact that during the last decades of the nineteenth century, the emphasis in many religious movements was on adjustment to conditions in the United States, which involved a sacrifice of some traditional rituals, conformity to some of the modes of the Protestant sects, and an extreme view of religion as primarily a system of ethical precepts.[119] The Jews of the United States followed the pattern of the Catholics, Lutherans, and other religious groups and moved towards reform. However, in Wilmington, which had a diminishing Western European population and a tremendous influx of Eastern European Jews, the predictions of success for the Reform synagogue proved mistaken.

When the Orthodox Jews met on March 3, 1895, they named ten people to a constitution committee and raised $100, bringing their total financial resources to $700.[120] Aaron Harris was named president, his son-in-law Barnet Gluckman was named secretary, and Philip Sklut was named treasurer. All three were established in business: Harris at his clothing store, Barnet Gluckman at his cigar store, and Philip Sklut as a butcher, after selling both shoes and clothing. The three men were from Russia, but Harris and Gluckman had been here for many years. Aaron Harris's election as president suggests that the tension of the 1880s had been left behind.[121] Unfortunately, one month after his election, Aaron Harris died suddenly of paralysis of the heart.

Continuing its preference for the Reform movement, the Wilmington newspapers paid more attention to their activities than those of the Orthodox. In April and May 1895, Dr. Jacob Korn, Ohabe Shalom's new rabbi, delivered public lectures on Sunday afternoons, conducted services, and organized a Jewish Women's Aid Society. Many of Wilmington's most prominent Jewish women— including the wives of Nathan Lieberman, Nathan Levy, Samuel Harris, Max Ephraim, Jacob Schless, Sam Slessinger, and Abraham Greenbaum—joined the new Aid Society.

Reform services for the Jewish New Year in 1895 were well attended and were concluded at the end of one day.[122] A special novelty of the holiday were New Year's cards bearing the motto Happy New Year in English and Hebrew.[123]

The Jews observed Yom Kippur strictly: "Every Hebrew, except invalids and those under thirteen, was expected to abstain from food and drink from sunset yesterday until tonight and business was generally suspended."[124] Many Jews made a practice of visiting various synagogues to inquire of friends how they were fasting. The musical program at the "progressive" synagogues was long and impressive, with selections by recent composers as well as Psalm tunes and hymns from antiquity. In the strict Orthodox temples, the traditional melodies made up the entire program and were sung by choirs of men and boys, without organ accompaniment.[125]

Rabbi Korn also began a Sunday School, which continued at least through 1896.[126] However, Rabbi Korn left Wilmington at the end of 1896, and public discussion of building a new Reform synagogue ceased.

Services for Rosh Hashanah and Yom Kippur 1897 were held at both the Orthodox and Reform synagogues. Rabbis L. Pizer and

A. B. Cohen were engaged to officiate at the Reform services held at Eighth and Orange Streets.[127] There was a cheerful aspect to the observance; many social features were similar to those that distinguish the first day of January."[128] Most Jews lived together in a small area at lower Market, Front, and Second Streets so that section of the city had a distinctive holiday appearance on the Jewish New Year. Many of the businesses were closed and bore the legend "Closed on account of holiday." The city was thronged with men and women in festive attire and throughout the afternoon, there were many visits and a number of receptions of the social kind.[129] While the evening papers compared Rosh Hashanah to the New Year, the *Sunday Star* believed that "socially, the method of celebration is much the same as that of Christmas."[130] By comparing the Jewish holidays to holidays well-known to all Americans, the newspapers suggested that the Jews were not really so foreign, but rather had holidays similar to those of the general public.

Shortly after the High Holidays of 1897, Gidel Podolsky, the president of Adas Kodesch, was elected chairman of a building committee that included Louis Brown, Albert Dannenberg, Albert Greenstein, Morris Gross, Solomon Grossman, Benjamin Handleman, Adlai Shapiro, Israel Wainer, and Rabbi Rezits.[131] In stark contrast to the Ohabe Shalom group, the members of the Adas Kodesch building committee were all from Russia. With the exception of Solomon Grossman, who had been in Wilmington for a decade, the others had been here six years or less. Grossman was an agent and Benjamin Handleman sold picture frames. The others were laborers, tailors, and shoemakers.

A few months later, the committee reported that the Zion Lutheran church at Sixth and French Streets was available for the sum of $5,625.[132] The task of raising that much money in 1897 was extremely difficult, "not only because many of the Jews had only been in this country for four or five years and did not have much money but also because there had been a general business panic for several years, and the Jews were not in a position to contribute." Israel Wainer, Albert Greenstein, and Solomon Grossman led the effort to raise funds, which included a ball held in January 1898. Although Morris Levy favored a Reform synagogue, he and his wife led the grand march.

On July 8, 1898, Adas Kodesch bought the Zion Lutheran Church.[133] One month later, on August 4, 1898, the new synagogue was dedicated.[134] About one hundred persons assembled at the synagogue's temporary quarters at 418 Shipley Street and marched to the new one, accompanied by a band and an American flag.[135] During the dedication, Rabbi Rezits offered a prayer for President Mc-Kinley and for the success of the American armies in the Spanish-American War. During the 1890s, as nationalism became stronger, Jews found it necessary to "prove their patriotism" at all times and to emphasize their loyalty to America.[136] Rabbi Rezits officiated at the dedication, and the cantor Hyman Cohen conducted the services in Hebrew. Between 80 and 120 children as well as members of the general community attended the dedication. At the time of the dedication, the name of the synagogue was changed from Adas Kodesch K'nesseth Israel to Adas Kodesch Baron de Hirsch in honor of the great philanthropist who enabled so many of his suffering co-religionists to leave Russia.[137]

Adas Kodesch had about one hundred members, men over the age of twenty, and many of them paid for participation in the dedication exercises. Sam Gluck paid $10 for the honor of carrying the flag in the procession. Jacob Knopf paid $25 for the honor of opening the door to the synagogue. Mr. Adolph Frank paid the same amount for the privilege of drawing the curtain of the ark. Mr. and Mrs. Daniel Leshem donated the covers for the Torahs, and various members paid for the privilege of placing the covers on the scrolls.[138] At least one new scroll had been donated to the synagogue by the Moses Montefiore Society. About $200 were raised through contributions for participation in the dedication.

Although the more established Jews wanted to build a Reform synagogue, they believed the continuation of Judaism in any form was so important that they supported the new Adas Kodesch. Perhaps their participation also reflected the realization that the Reform element was becoming less numerous. Nathan Lieberman, Nathan Levy, Morris Levy, and Joseph Lictenbaum, moving forces behind the Reform synagogue, all paid to enter the procession around the new Orthodox synagogue. In fact, the committee in charge of the building and reception included Nathan Barsky, Morris Levy, and Nathan Lieberman. When Nathan Barsky proposed raising funds for the synagogue by selling windows, Nathan Levy offered $50.

A few months after the dedication, in October 1898, Nathan Lieberman was a candidate for the presidency of Adas Kodesch. However, Adas Kodesch's president, Albert Greenstein, ruled that no one could be eligible for the presidency unless he had been a member for not less than six months. Since Lieberman had not been a member that long, Sam Gluck, the baker who defended his Sabbath in court, became president.[139] The Orthodox Jews' decision to deny Nathan Lieberman, a highly respected and wealthy long-term resident, the presidency of Adas Kodesch shows the independence of the new immigrants, who insisted on being in charge of their own synagogue.

For several years after Adas Kodesch was dedicated, newspaper articles written by A. B. Cohen, the rabbi who had come to Ohabe Shalom after Rabbi Korn, were the only public Reform presence in Wilmington. Early in the twentieth century, Cohen was in Wilmington and involved in Zionist issues, but there is no mention of Reform worship services. His articles refer to two synagogues: which must have been Adas Kodesch and Chesed Shel Emeth. Although the Reform Jews had more financial resources, they were not successful in starting a Reform synagogue until 1906.

The 1895 predictions of success for the Reform movement were incorrect because they did not take into account the changing Jewish population of Wilmington. During the 1890s some 280 Jewish men and 217 Jewish women arrived in Wilmington.[140] About 70 percent of those whose nationalities are known were from Russia, Hungary, Poland, and Romania.[141] In contrast, only about 12 percent of the men and women were from Germany, and only about 6 percent were born in America. The success of the Orthodox synagogue reflected the background of the vast majority of Wilmington's Jewish immigrants, who wanted a more traditional approach to religion. The intensity of their effort and their large numbers proved more important than their lack of financial resources.

ASSISTING NEW IMMIGRANTS

At the same time employment opportunities expanded in Wilmington, anti-Semitism and violence against the Jews in Russia and Eastern Europe increased, which caused large numbers of Jews to seek better lives in the United States. By 1891, Jews were expelled from several Russian cities, and the press continued a campaign of unbridled anti-Semitic propaganda.[142] Some eight hundred Jewish families were ordered to get out of Odessa in the early months of 1891.[143] Baron de Hirsch donated $15,000 to begin an effort to transfer Jews from Poland and southeast Europe to Brazil and Australia. Later that year, the London correspondent of the *New York Times* reported that Russia was a bankrupt empire, and within a month there would be commercial panic.[144] Dr. Walter Kempster, British immigration commissioner, returned to London from Russia with startling tales of Russian barbarism. Kempster, who had the highest opinion of the Jewish population, particularly of their farming colonies, was boiling with indignation and horror at the treatment the Jews were receiving from the Russians.

In February 1892, Delaware's governor, Robert J. Reynolds, issued a proclamation urging the citizens of Delaware to assist the Russian Family Relief Committee of the United States, which was raising funds to assist sufferers. He requested all citizens, societies, committees, and agencies who could offer assistance to put themselves in communication with the committee, which was working with the American National Red Cross.[145]

Many Jews assisted new immigrants by welcoming members of their extended families into their homes. Nathan Barsky married Rosa Ostrosky in 1890. Two years later, Michael and Lizzie Ostrosky were living with the Barskys. By 1900 Jacob Ostrosky was also there.[146] Philip Sklut was the first of the large Sklut family to settle in Wilmington.[147] After working briefly in the shoe business and the clothing business, he became a butcher. When his brother Abe Sklut came to Wilmington, Philip taught him the butchering business. However, Abe didn't like life in Wilmington so he went back to Russia, got married, and had children. Later he returned to Wilmington to avoid service in the Russian army.[148] Philip married Fanny (Frances) Frumen in 1892, and shortly afterwards, Fannie's young sister Bessie came to Wilmington to live with the Skluts.[149]

Reuben Lepidos, who came from Radishkavich, the same Russian town as the Skluts, came to Wilmington after being sponsored by his brother-in-law Adlai Shapiro, a shoemaker.[150] Like many immigrants, when he arrived at Ellis Island, Lepidos received a new name.

> —The clerk asked his name, and he answered Lepidos.
> —Spell it.
> —I don't know how to spell it. I don't know English.
> —Your name is Levy. L-E-V-Y.[151]

After living in Wilmington for many years, Reuben earned enough money to bring over his wife Rifka and their children, Abe, Florence, Isadore, Israel, and Charles.[152]

Very often older brothers arrived in the United States and then paid for the younger siblings to emigrate. Abraham Fineman brought his fifteen-year-old brother Benjamin to the United States and Wilmington in 1888.[153] The boys' mother had died when the youngest son, Israel, was an infant. Their father had remarried a woman who already had a family and threw them out of the house. After studying at a yeshiva, each of the Fineman brothers fled to

America. Each arrived successively, the next brother being brought over by the one who came before. Benjamin described his trip from Philadelphia.

> In the early morning I paid fifty cents to be taken to the wharf of the Wilson Line on the Delaware River from which I traveled by excursion boat to Wilmington. In those days, the railroad tracks were on a level with the pavement at Church Street. The bed of the tracks covered all of Water Street. Down the middle of these tracks I walked with a flour bag containing all my belongings thrown over my shoulder. In my other hand a card which was printed, "Abe Fineman 624 W Front." I was dressed in the typical garb of the yeshiva Bocher, a loosely fitted mohair jacket that ran from skins. Lined with cotton wadding. The day was insufferably hot, on my head a broad rimmed black hat. The first persons I saw was your grandfather Topkis and your Uncle Louthen about 17. They recognized my garb and knew I need help. They read my card and took me to my brother's house. I was just given a decent meal and then sent down to Wolfson's to be fitted with American clothes from head to foot.[154]

Although Abraham stayed in Wilmington for the rest of his life, Benjamin did not like Wilmington and went to New York. From there he went to England, enlisted to fight in the Boer War, and was sent to Africa. Only after his marriage at the turn of the century did Benjamin return to Wilmington.[155]

The immigrants who had been here longer helped the newer arrivals find employment. When J. Harry Gordon arrived in Wilmington in the early 1890s, he worked for Moses Weil and lived in his house.[156] In later years, Reuben Wolters got Gordon a job at Bacharach Tailoring Company. Gordon also worked for Miller Brothers.[157] Jacob Faber, J. Harry Gordon, Harry Grossman, and Louis Topkis were among those who worked for Sam Slessinger during the 1890s. Many of the immigrants came without a trade and were taught by other Jews. For example, Julius Glantz taught Michael Sklut to be a tailor.[158] When a Jew was in need, other Jews offered help. David Abramson had been president of both the Moses Montefiore Society and the Montefiore Hebrew Cemetery from 1890 to 1894. During the depression of 1893–94, David Abramson's recently opened installment house failed, and Abramson was imprisoned for concealing property. Samuel Slessinger paid Abramson's bail. Abramson went to Philadelphia, where he became a successful manufacturer of shirts.[159] The concept of a close-knit community, modeled on the shtetl, where each is responsible for all and all are responsible for each, prevailed and brought obligations.[160] Jews hired Jews, gave charity to Jews, and as they moved into business, they pulled their co-religionists along into jobs.

Formal help came from organizations. When the Orthodox synagogues combined in 1890, the new Adas Kodesch K'nesseth Israel promised to give $5 a week to sick and needy families.[161] From its inception in 1879, the Moses Montefiore Society offered sick benefits to its members. The society held its eleventh annual reception on January 15, 1890, at Eden Hall, in Professor Webster's new dancing studio. About two hundred people attended the ball, which featured an orchestra, an elaborate supper, and dancing until the wee hours of the morning.[162] The men were in evening dress and the women's costumes were handsome. Unfortunately, the newspaper covered these balls as social events and did not report on specific uses of the contributed funds.

When the charity ball was given in 1896, it was called the Hebrew Charity Ball instead of the Montefiore Society Ball.[163] Most likely the name had been changed because the Montefiore Society was associated with the Reform synagogue, and for the purposes of charity the Jews wanted to reach out to everyone. The ball was held at Eden Hall with the usual format of an orchestra and a late dinner by Ainscow's. The word "charity" showed in electric lights over the door at one end of the hall. Most of the ball's organizers were the men who were working for the Reform synagogue. Mr. and Mrs. Nathan Lieberman led the grand march.

Reform leaders were so dominant in the Moses Montefiore Society that in January 1897, the *Sunday Star* and the *Every Evening* referred to the Charity Ball as the second annual Ohabe Shalom ball, which would raise funds for charitable purposes.[164] The *Morning News* explained that the ball was the equivalent of the charity ball in other cities and was always one of the events of the season. More than one hundred couples participated in the grand march, which was led by Sam Slessinger and Mrs. Samuel Harris. Many people from the general community attended. With the exception of David Topkis, the newer immigrants from Eastern Europe did not take leadership positions in the Moses Montefiore Society at this time.

In the shtetls of Eastern Europe, the concept of *tzedakah* (assistance based on justice and righteousness) prevailed, and Jews accepted the fact that they were interdependent and responsible for one another.[165] So upon arriving in America, even in communities that had large established German Jewish communities to assist them, the Eastern Europeans immediately "established a web of their own voluntary organizations and improvised a viable, decentralized pattern for their own collective existence."[166] In Wilmington, which did not have a large, established German Jewish community and continued to lose its founding families, the new Eastern European immigrants played a dominant role in building communal organizations.[167]

Because there were so few Jewish people in Wilmington, each person could have an impact immediately. In February 1892, three new Russian Jewish immigrants—Louis Finger, Albert Greenstein, and Nathan Shtofman—formed a Hebrew Library Association, the purpose of which was to improve the future of their countrymen by establishing a place "to educate members in and about the city and to afford a place of meeting for Hebrew citizens."[168] About thirty Jews joined the new organization.

Louis Finger was in Wilmington by March of 1888, when he married Esther Tartakovsky and was a puddler, a type of laborer.[169] By 1894, Finger was a letter carrier. The Fingers' first child, Matthew, was born in 1889; Aaron was born in 1890, Samuel in 1892, Freuda in 1894, and Reba in 1896. Albert Greenstein was a puddler in 1891 when he married Amelia Gilman.[170] In 1891, when daughter Jennie was born, the Greensteins lived at 9 East Front Street. Benjamin, Morris, Hillard, Joshua, Lewis, and David were born over the next sixteen years. Nathan Shtofman first appeared in Wilmington in 1891, living at 330 East Second; he was a tailor for Mullins.[171] Clara and Nathan's son Jacob was born in 1893, to be followed by Rebecca, Norman, and Samuel. The newspaper referred to the three men as leading Hebrews. Although earning a living was of paramount importance to these immigrant Jews, they took the long-term view and invested their energy in education as the way to help later generations.

In the 1890s many young Jewish women in Wilmington were recent immigrants living far from their families and friends. They were expected to bear many children. More than half of the women with children in 1900 had borne five or more.[172] At least half of those women also had experienced the death of at least one child.[173] Women who had fewer children had less chance of losing a child, but more than 35 percent of all mothers had lost a child. Since they were living near poverty, these young women had to assume full responsibility for the care of young children, feeding the family, and laundry. Furthermore, pregnant women usually remained in confinement for some time. Around 1897, Rosa Topkis and her friends and relatives felt the need to get together to do something for the poor Jewish women in Wilmington.[174] They began to go out in pairs to collect funds and groceries for women in confinement.

Rosa Topkis was born Rose Avrach in the village of Matsov in the Pindus Mountains in 1847. At times, the village was considered Greek, at other times Turkish.[175] Rosa was brought up by relatives after her mother died in childbirth and her father left Matsov for Odessa. Her grandfather was a *dyan*, a scholarly man who taught boys to become rabbis. Rosa was given the work and responsibility of an adult. From the beginning she knew the meaning of want and the importance of money. After a fire destroyed Matsov when she was seven, Rosa was sent to live with cousins who were in the fur business. They made her an accountant for the business, and she developed great business acumen. When she was twenty, which was very old for an unmarried woman, she married Yonker Hench Tubkin, Jacob Topkis, a coppersmith.

Rosa was described by Barnet Gluckman as a "woman frail of stature and body but with a greatness of mind, possessing a heart overflowing with sympathy and kindness."[176] According to her daughter Sallie, "carefree as was my father, so careworn was my mother. The financial responsibility of the family was hers."[177] As a mother of six children, Rose understood the difficulty of raising a family in a strange land under conditions of poverty.[178]

Rosa Topkis involved Nessie Tiger, mother of her daughter-in-law Hannah Ray Topkis, and Mrs. David (Esther) Finkelstein, in her efforts to help the new immigrants.[179] Nessie Tiger was born in Austria in 1844. She had come to the United States in 1885, just a few years after Rosa, and lived in Newark, New Jersey.[180] Nessie had borne eleven children, but only two, one of whom was Hannah Ray Topkis, were still living. Esther Baer Finkelstein had been born in Germany in 1856 and was married in 1882. She had borne six children, four of whom (Isaac B., Rachael, Lena, and Keffie) were living in 1900.[181] The women worked informally for some time, but just after the turn of the century more people needed assistance, and the women organized their assistance more formally in the Bichor Cholem Society.

At the time of the January 1898 ball to raise funds to build a new Adas Kodesch, which was supported by both the newer immigrants and the more established reform leaders, Jews in New York, Philadelphia, Baltimore, and other large cities helped new immigrants through an organization called B'nai B'rith, whose first local chapter had been organized in New York in the 1840s. Among its numerous activities, B'nai B'rith provided and maintained orphan asylums, manual training schools, and homes for the aged. Some major American Jewish leaders, including Mayer Sulzberger, Charles Adler, and Reverend Wise of Cincinnati, were guests at

Rosa Topkis. (Jewish Historical Society of Delaware.)

Adas Kodesch's ball.[182] They learned that Wilmington did not have a B'nai B'rith chapter and helped Wilmington's Jews form one.

Two months after the dance, in March 1898, Sulzberger was back in Wilmington along with B'nai B'rith Grand Master Charles Hoffman to aid in the formation of a Wilmington chapter of B'nai B'rith.[183] By March 21, thirty-two men had joined the new chapter called Wilmington Chapter International Order of B'nai B'rith #470. The majority of B'nai B'rith's new members were from Eastern Europe; twenty were from Russia and four were from Hungary, while three were born in the United States, two in Germany, and one each in Austria and Holland. In Wilmington, even an established organization like B'nai B'rith included Eastern Europeans. When the members met to select officers a month later, there were forty-five members.[184] Despite the fact that so many members were Russians, the only officer born in Russia was treasurer Morris Levy, who had lived most of his life in the United States. Moses Weil, from Germany, was installed as president; Sam Slessinger, from Hungary, was vice-president; J. Harry Gordon, born in the United States, was Secretary; and Dr. Sigmund Werner, from Austria, was recording secretary. Levy, Slessinger, and Weil had lived in Wilmington for a decade or more and were familiar to the general community as well as to the Jews. Slessinger was president of the William Penn Beneficial Association, which secured insurance and sick benefits to persons of modest means. Slessinger's name was synonymous with fairness, promptness, and honesty.[185] Dr. Werner had just arrived in Wilmington, but as one of the first Jewish doctors he brought tremendous prestige to the group. J. Harry Gordon, who was born in Georgia, arrived in Wilmington in the early 1890s. Among his earliest contributions was his work with the school at Adas Kodesch. Because Wilmington had such a small Jewish population, the more established Jews welcomed the participation of the Eastern Europeans, who in turn accepted the leadership abilities of the others.

At a December 1898 meeting of B'nai B'rith, A. B. Cohen, Abraham Tollin, Solomon Grossman, Israel Wainer and Dr. Sigmund Werner were appointed to a committee to formulate plans for a Hebrew Charity Association.[186] The community needed a new organization because differing interpretations of charity had begun to interfere with the operation of the Moses Montefiore Society.

Max Podolsky was sick and requested the $10 he was due from the Montefiore Society. Morris Levy, president of the Montefiore Society, visited Podolsky and found him sick, but the visiting committee failed to visit Podolsky the next week. At the society's meeting, when Levy recommended that Podolsky be paid his sick benefits, several members objected.[187] They alleged that Podolsky had violated the society's rules by washing the windows of his store while he was ill, and, therefore, did not deserve his $10.

Podolsky brought suit against the Moses Montefiore Benefit Society in Magistrate Daly's Court on January 8, 1899. Podolsky testified that he had been sick and was attended by four doctors. Professor Weil, a well-respected member of the community, testified that he did not know what sickness the man had, but he was sick. The court referees, "an Irishman, an American and a Hebrew," awarded Podolsky the $10.

Even before the case went to court, it had repercussions. On January 1, 1899, a group of thirty men, including Moses Montefiore's president Morris Levy, met to form a new charitable organization, the Hebrew Charity Association.[188] Levy was named temporary president and A. B. Cohen temporary secretary. The names of the original members of the Hebrew Charity Association are not extant; however, those mentioned in association with the first balls were often members of B'nai B'rith and were a mixture of Eastern Europeans and long-term residents.[189] The organization's purpose was to provide charity for needy people regardless of their religion, in accordance with the biblical precepts of "caring for thy brother, though he be a stranger, and opening thy hand unto thy brother, the poor and the needy in the land."[190] From the beginning, the Jews were anxious to be good American citizens and wanted to offer their help to all in need.

Within a month of the formation of the Hebrew Charity Association, its services were needed. In early February 1899, an unknown Hebrew man about twenty-one years of age was found frozen to death near the railroad, the victim of a snowstorm.[191] People thought that he had alighted from the train in Wilmington and attempted to walk to Philadelphia. The name Joseph was found on some papers in his pocket. One of Wilmington's Jewish clothiers, M. Stone, recalled that the young man had asked him for a job about three weeks before, but Stone had not needed assistance.

After several days, when no identification of the young man was forthcoming, the Hebrews of Wilmington paid to have him buried with all the ceremonies of the Hebrew church in the Hebrew cemetery on Lombardy. The Jewish societies in the city paid the expenses, about $50. The day after the burial, the young man's parents arrived from Philadelphia. The father identified his son, David Binder, through the clothes that had been saved. The older Mr. Binder, a tailor, had made the clothes himself.

Ironically, the Hebrew Charity Association's first ball was held on February 8, 1899, three days after David Binder was found. A crowd of some two hundred people, including many prominent Jews and non-Jews, attended the ball, which was opened by Bishop Coleman.[192] The unusual spectacle of a Gentile officiating at a Hebrew gathering attracted much attention. Bishop Coleman told the crowd that although he might differ with those present on some points, they agreed on charity:

> . . . "hardly anything gave me more enjoyment than this invitation," he explained, "because I knew by it that you trusted me. You knew when you invited me to come that nothing would fall from my lips to offend you. I learn that you give not only to members of your household but to those in need. In giving to charity you are not giving to the man or woman who solicits it but to mankind."[193]

The Hebrew Charity Association met quarterly at Eighth and Orange streets. A few months after its formation, President Morris Levy explained to the annual conference of Associated Charities at the New Century Club that the Hebrew Charity Association's work by force of circumstance was among "our own people." There was very little demand for assistance from the Jews in the Wilmington community, but the demand was primarily from people who wander here from other cities and are helped to secure situations or given transportation. Levy emphasized that the aim of the society was not to make mendicants of men but to make them self-supporting.[194] Based on Morris Levy's report, there were adequate employment opportunities in Wilmington, and people ready to work could find jobs.

A number of "Hebrew ladies" met in March 1899 to organize a benevolent association with the name Ladies' Montefiore Society, which all Jewish women in the city were invited to join. Mrs S. J. Baeringer was elected president, Mrs. Louis Harris vice-president, Miss M. C. Lurge secretary, and Miss J. Barsky treasurer. Twenty-five women joined the new organization.[195] Although named after Moses Montefiore, the new association probably had no connection to the Moses Montefiore Society because even Mrs. Max Podolsky, whose husband had just sued the Moses Montefiore Society, joined the new ladies' society.

The tradition of caring for those in need, which is a basic tenet of Judaism and was a strong part of life in Europe, flourished in Wilmington as soon as there were Jews who needed assistance. So many individuals offered help in a variety of areas that a network of community services developed quickly. As the anti-immigration movement in the United States gained strength, Jews intensified their work so that Jewish immigrants would not become a burden to the larger society.

LITERACY AS A REQUIREMENT

Before the 1890s, the restrictionist movement lacked strength because it was fragmented and its advocates couldn't agree on one plan.[196] However, during the 1890s the debate on immigration policy embarked on a course that eventually brought an end to immigration in the early 1920s.[197] In 1891 the Department of the Treasury passed an act that strengthened controls over immigration by creating a superintendent of immigration under federal control and gave the entire job of immigrant regulation and inspection to federal officials.[198] The act also banned the admission of all assisted immigrants, people who could not survive in the United States without help.[199] The fear that new immigrants would become public charges was one basis for numerous efforts to restrict immigration.[200] Simon Wolf, who represented the Board of Delegates of the Union of American Hebrew Congregations, was an outspoken advocate for open immigration. Along with Lewis Abrahams and representatives of several Jewish groups, Wolf prevailed upon Charles Forster, Secretary of the Treasury, to remove all aliens who were aided by private, charitable agencies from the category of assisted immigrants since they didn't use public welfare.[201] Thus began an intensified effort by Jewish philanthropic groups to take care of their own.

The Immigration Restriction League, organized in Boston in 1894, promoted the belief that hordes of inferior breeds were pouring into the country and would mix freely with the Anglo-Saxons, producing a deterioration of the species.[202] The league and its congressional advocate, Senator Henry Cabot Lodge, attempted to limit immigration by amending the immigration laws to include a literacy test for admission into the country.[203] During February 1897, Congress discussed a new immigration bill with a literacy provision requiring all persons over the age of sixteen to be able to read and write their own language, with the exception that admissible immigrants could bring with or send for illiterate wives, minor children, or parents and grandparents over fifty. While pretending to favor education, the bill, sponsored by the Immigration Restriction League, was actually discriminatory because it was designed to cut in half the number of immigrants from Southern and Eastern Europe without seriously interfering with the immigration from the parts of Europe where literacy was more widespread.[204] Congressional debates about the literacy requirement took place in February and early March 1897.

On February 9, 1897, the United States House of Representatives passed the immigration bill with a literacy requirement by a vote of 217 yeas, 36 nays, and 102 not voting. Congressman Jonathan Willis of Delaware did not vote.[205] The following day, the *Morning News* reported that the House had passed the immigration bill, 217 to 37, without mentioning the abstentions. "That makes the third proposition on that subject passed by the House," the article noted.[206]

On February 17, when members of the United States Senate were to vote on the immigration bill, the *Morning News* ran an extensive editorial on the importance of restricting immigration. The *Morning News* claimed

> there was widespread sentiment against the further admission of hordes of ignorant and therefore undesirable immigrants. . . . [T]he literacy test was simply a method of discouraging and restricting the shipment to the United States of armies of foreigners who can neither read nor write, who show no disposition to do either, who do not assimilate with the people already here, who have no interest in our institutions and who are a menace to society in every direction. . . . [I]lliteracy must be reduced as upon intelligence rests the future strength of our institutions.[207]

With all the prejudices inherent in restrictionists' lingo, the editorial equated foreigners who could neither read nor write with those who would not benefit the country. Opponents of the literacy requirement found such comparisons objectionable. They believed that a person's ability to read and write was no reflection on his character, his capacity to work, or his ability to be a good citizen.

The editorial did not convince Delaware's senators. Although the Senate passed the bill by a vote of thirty-four to thirty-one, Senator George Gray, a highly respected Delaware statesman who became a prominent judge, opposed the bill; Senator Richard Kinney did not vote.[208] Gray supposedly rejected the bill because it also prohibited the hiring of aliens who came to the United States for employment without declaring an intent to become citizens.[209]

On March 2, 1897, two days before he left office, President Cleveland vetoed the immigration bill claiming "violence and disorder do not originate with illiteracy."[210] Denying a connection between radical, unlawful behavior and illiteracy, Cleveland implied that supporters of the bill were using illiteracy as a pretext for other discrimination. An editorial in the *Morning News* noted that Cleveland was opposed to protection of any kind and suggested that "the next session of Congress ought to repass the bill, and President McKinley will not veto it."[211]

The following day the House overrode the President's veto. Again, Jonathan S. Willis of Delaware did not vote. The Senate did not override the veto, so the bill did not become law. In the following Congress, the 55th, the vetoed bill was again introduced and passed in the Senate, but the House refused to even consider it.[212] Immigrant groups themselves, led in part by the German-language press, helped defeat the literacy bill.[213] For twenty-five years while the immigration debate raged, American Jewish leaders were in the forefront of the effort to keep immigration open. In denying the importance of literacy for entrance into the country, the Jews advocated that new immigrants not be judged by their past but be given an opportunity to become part of American society.

Delaware held a constitutional convention between December 1896 and June 1897. One of the notable changes in the new constitution was the addition of a literacy requirement in order to vote.[214] Delaware's debate about the use of the literacy requirement for the franchise took place at precisely the same moment that the heated, national debate about a literacy requirement for new immigrants took place in Congress. The Delaware requirement—voters must be able to read the Constitution in English—was far stricter than the national one, which only required the ability to read or write in some language. Newspaper stories about Delaware's decision to make literacy a part of the franchise did not link Delaware's debate about literacy to the national debate.

In January 1897, at Delaware's constitutional convention, delegate James Gilchrist proposed an amendment with a literacy requirement as part of the basis for the franchise.

After January 1, 1900, no person shall have the right to vote or be eligible for office who shall not be able to read the Constitution in English and write his name, provided that no person be prevented by physical disability . . . nor does this apply to any person now with the vote.[215]

Representatives to Delaware's constitutional convention debated Gilchrist's amendment about a literacy requirement for the franchise on February 16, 1897. They were more interested in the tech-

nicalities of enforcing the new law, including how to determine if
the examiner had been fair, when to begin the new requirement, and
how to be certain it was applied to the correct person, than in the
actual meaning of the literacy requirement. All twenty-three of the
representatives who were present at the session voted in favor of
Gilchrist's amendment.[216]

Delaware's newspapers, which reported daily on the constitutional convention, did not focus on the literacy component of the
franchise before it was passed. Perhaps there was no discussion of
the literacy requirement because it was discussed at the same session as the issue of women's suffrage, a topic of more widespread
interest.[217] Perhaps the literacy requirement was not discussed because delegates to the convention thought it was an essential and
noncontroversial way to stop the rampant fraud that pervaded elec-
tions.[218]

Although the *Morning News* had written an editorial in favor of
using a literacy test to limit immigration, a few days after the literacy component was made part of the franchise requirement, the
Morning News expressed a more liberal view. It ran an editorial
entitled "Right of Suffrage" that claimed the constitutional convention should be very careful about the provision shutting out illiterates from the enjoyment of suffrage because such a provision would
raise a large element who would seek to overthrow it. The new constitution should have as little as possible in it that will cause public
objection from a large number of citizens, the editorial suggested.[219]

In June 1897, when Delaware's new constitution was passed with
the literacy requirement for the franchise, the new Jewish immigrants recognized that in order to be fully American, they would
have to learn English. In Delaware, Jews would not be treated as
second-class citizens as they had been in Europe; they would have
the same opportunities and privileges as other citizens, but they
would have to accept the institutions of the country and learn the
language of the country. Unlike the restrictionists, who believed
that those who came to the United States without knowing English
could never become good citizens, Delaware's leaders had confidence in the fact that illiterate immigrants wanted to become part
of a new country and were willing to learn the language.

ZIONISM

At the same time Wilmington's Jews provided assistance to immigrants in need, the question of how American Jews would relate

to Jews throughout the rest of the world assumed new importance. In 1896, Theodore Herzl published *Der Judenstaat (The Jewish State)* in which he persuasively argued for the restoration of a Jewish state. According to Herzl, the Jewish Question existed wherever Jews lived in perceptible numbers. This was the case in every country and would remain so until it was resolved on a political basis. Herzl urged that sovereignty be granted to the Jews over a portion of the globe large enough to satisfy the rightful requirements of a nation. Using Herzl's idea, the First Zionist Congress met in Basle, Switzerland in August 1897. The congress declared its aim to create for the Jewish people a home in Palestine, secured by public law.

Zionism was greeted by European Jews with great enthusiasm because it addressed itself to the problem of anti-Semitism, which had flourished in Europe for centuries and was seen as the cause of misery among Jews.[220] However, in America, there had been no long history of anti-Semitism. Jews were not singled out any more specifically than other dissident religious groups, such as Catholics or Quakers. Although some discrimination began in the latter part of the nineteenth century, it was by and large unrelated to religion. Rather it was part of the wider American problem dealing with large-scale immigration and economic maldistribution. The anti-Semitism of the nineteenth century bore little relation to the centuries old Jew-hatred of Europe; it grew out of distinctly American tensions and affected other immigrant and religious groups as well.[221] Furthermore, many immigrant Jews saw America as the new Zion. In 1885, the Reform leadership of America denounced any desire to return to the ancient homeland. The American Jewish Committee also opposed such an action. Advocates of both sides lived in Wilmington. Part of each person's reaction to Zionism was personal experience in the old world.

Louis Finger became an active part of the Jewish community shortly after his arrival in Wilmington. In 1899, the year the Moses Montefiore Society became overwhelmingly Russian, he was elected financial secretary of the society. In addition to his involvement in causes to improve Jewish life in America, Finger became an active Zionist.

In December 1898, Finger wrote to the Federation of American Zionists in New York to inform them that B'nai Zion of Wilmington was three weeks old and would like "to bring itself into alliance with the central organization."[222] On January 2, 1899, Finger wrote to Stephen S. Wise, secretary of the Federation of American Zionists, acknowledging receipt of his kind letter and circular. He requested that Wise send the shekel book.

Louis Finger. (Jewish Historical Society of Delaware.)

At a meeting of B'nai Zion on Sunday, January 29, Louis Finger read a paper entitled "The Aims of Zionism." Apparently the meeting was not a big success. The day after the meeting Finger wrote to Stephen Wise about the Wilmington Jews' lack of understanding of Zion.

> Unfortunately, I can't send more dollars. As hard as I have been working for Zion, I have not been able to increase the membership which numbers only ten though a hundred could easily be gotten, but we have not the mental talent that would bring the Jewish population of this city to their sense of duty towards Zionism.[223]

Despite the temporary setback, Finger explained that the members were resolved to hold a mass meeting on Sunday, February 12, and requested that either Stephen Wise or the Federation's president, Rabbi Richard Gottheil, attend the meeting.

For several months, Finger worked tirelessly to strengthen B'nai Zion. Finally, in May 1899, Finger wrote, "after a struggle of seven months, we at last succeeded in establishing a permanent organization with a roll of twenty full fledged members with bright prospects for an increase."[224]

One of the reasons establishing B'nai Zion was so difficult was that some prominent citizens were actively working against it. In one letter to Wise, Louis Finger advised him never to send any correspondence to 211 Orange Street because the person living there stood against the organization from the beginning, and only at the last meeting paid his per capita tax with hopes of hurting the organization by being a member and attending meetings.[225] Rabbi Wise's response to Louis Finger is apparent from Finger's next letter: "Thank you for your good advice to 'preserve peace.' I assure you that perfect harmony reigns in the work of our members."[226] The Federation of American Zionists and other groups were formed as a result of the Zionist Congress of 1897, but Zionism did not gain widespread, mainstream American Jewish support until World War I.[227]

THE COMMUNITY OF 1900

Perfect harmony did not reign among the Jews in Wilmington. Given the diversity of the population, that would not have been possible. But both Wise's admonition and Finger's response demonstrate the determination of all active members of the Jewish community to work together to help all Jews adjust to life in America.

Between 1890 and 1900, the Jewish population of Wilmington doubled, and by the turn of the century some 1200 Jews lived in Wilmington.[228] Therefore, though the Jews were still a small minority, they now accounted for about 1.4 percent of the population.[229] They had grown to account for 10 percent of the foreign-born population, which was dominated by Irish, German, and English immigrants.[230]

Two-thirds of the Jewish adults were Eastern European.[231] As the decade progressed, the new Eastern European families had become more influential and the German influence had declined. Among the long-term Germans, Nathan Lieberman and Manual Richenberger, who was not an observant Jew, were the only ones who still lived in Wilmington. Only about five Jewish men from Germany (Henry Kaufman, Harry Lang, Sam Mitchell, Andrew Schaller, and Moses Weil) had lived in Wilmington for more than ten years.

The community was still a young community. Nearly 70 percent of the adult men were in their late teens, twenties, or thirties. Of the 30 percent over forty years of age, only five men were older than sixty. Women were slightly younger.[232] By 1900 about 27 percent of the adults had become United States citizens.The youth were largely American-born. Many young immigrants married and began their families in the United States so their children were native-born. Other families arrived with young children born in the Old World and later had American-born children.

The community was more stable than it had been a decade earlier. In 1890 only six men had lived here for more than ten years. In 1900, some 25 percent of the adult Jewish men had been here for ten years or more.[233] Still, more than 55 percent had arrived within the last five years. Since 30 percent of those who had lived in Wilmington during the decade were no longer here by 1900, the community still had an air of transience.

In spite of the growing number of Jews who worked for the morocco factories, railroads, or as general laborers, the largest number of Jewish immigrants continued to earn their livings in retail business, with clothing and dry goods stores leading the way. In 1901, 70 percent of the clothing stores listed in the Wilmington City Directory were run by Jews.[234] Considering that not even 1.5 percent of the population was Jewish, Jewish clothiers far outnumbered their proportion of the population. The same pattern was true of dry goods stores; 70 percent of the dry goods stores in Wilmington were run by Jews. More than seventy Jews worked in the clothing and dry goods businesses, including all those who worked as clerks and salesman in the stores.

Many Jewish immigrants worked in the skilled trades. Eleven were shoemakers, accounting for 12 percent of all Wilmington shoemakers; twelve were tailors, accounting for 18 percent of all Wilmington tailors. There was a growth in the number of cigar makers and barbers. Jacob Faber, the nephew of Rabbi Morris Faber, had begun his life in Wilmington in the dry goods business, but by 1890 he was a barber.[235] The Leshem family—including father Daniel, sons Louis, Jacob, Charles, Joseph, and Philip, and cousins Robert and James J. Cohen—also became barbers. Abe Hinden, whose sister was married to Louis Leshem, and Max Friedman, who worked for Daniel, also became barbers.

At the turn of the century the Jews of Wilmington disagreed on religious observance and the role of religion, lived in different economic circumstances, spoke diverse languages, including English, German, Yiddish, and Russian, had dissimilar experiences with life in America, and were at different stages in their accommodation to life in America. Nevertheless, they united for the important work of taking care of their own. Some five hundred people, including nearly all the adult Jews in Wilmington, attended the annual Hebrew Charity Association ball held on January 18, 1900.[236]

In the eyes of the larger community, since all Jews followed the same religion and took care of their own needy, they were a separate people. The general public marveled at the way the Jews adhered to the religion of their fathers. In discussing their use of unleavened bread during Passover 1901, the *Sunday Star* noted, "There is no other example in history of a people, once a nation and subsequently scattered to every part of the earth, and yet maintaining their entity for many centuries."[237]

The article's note of tolerance and acceptance undoubtedly encouraged the Jewish community to establish a balance between Jewishness and Americanism. But at the same time, its clear statement that Jews were a separate entity implied that they were not fully American. The primary tension of immigrant life in America was between retention of the old ways and accommodation to life in America. Although there was tremendous difference in the rate at which Jews adjusted to life in America, at the turn of the century, the Jews who had lived in Wilmington longest and were most familiar to the general community had achieved a successful balance, and this reflected well on all the Jews.

5

Balancing Two Worlds—The 1900s

Dᴜʀɪɴɢ ᴛʜᴇ ꜰɪʀꜱᴛ ᴅᴇᴄᴀᴅᴇ ᴏꜰ ᴛʜᴇ ᴛᴡᴇɴᴛɪᴇᴛʜ ᴄᴇɴᴛᴜʀʏ, ꜱᴏᴍᴇ 650 adult Jewish immigrants arrived in Wilmington; approximately 75 percent of them were from Russia and Eastern Europe. The numbers of those from Central and Western Europe continued to decline. Increasingly, children of immigrants were born in Wilmington, so the young population became more American while the adult population became more foreign. Jewish immigrants earned their livings in a wider diversity of occupations. Some attained new heights as magistrates, while many newcomers began as laborers in the morocco factories.

Although the immigrants from Central and Western Europe remained active in Jewish organizations, the Eastern Europeans, many of whom were new to the community themselves, played a large role in caring for new immigrants and formed several new organizations, including the YMHA, Workmen's Circle, and Ahawas Israel, to meet additional needs. While the Jews worked together for charity, they had religious differences that led to the formation of two new synagogues, the Orthodox Chesed Shel Emeth and the Reform Temple of Truth.

As large numbers of immigrants from different parts of the world flooded into the United States, feelings against immigrants increased throughout the country. However, in Wilmington the Jews became a respected segment of the population. The Jewish community and the broader community worked together, in the finest American tradition, to protest the treatment of Jews in Russia and to assist sufferers from tuberculosis in the United States.

The new century began with optimism as economic prosperity returned to the country; however, the mood changed dramatically on September 6, 1901, when President William McKinley was shot. The president, who had been warned by Attorney General Griggs not to go out without a bodyguard, was shot at close range while greeting the public at the Temple of Music in Buffalo, New York.[1] The accused assassin, Leon F. Czolgosz, was of Polish Jewish descent. When interviewed, he claimed that he had been inspired to commit the crime by words he had heard from Emma Goldman, the well-known Jewish anarchist.[2] McKinley's assassination challenged the fragile balance the Jews had achieved.

Within days, while McKinley still fought for his life, the Polish community in Wilmington held a large public meeting and issued a public statement separating itself from the assassination. One clause of the statement was particularly offensive to the Jews: "Should this miscreant's ancestry lead to the slightest link to prove him to be of Polish lineage, we emphatically declare that he is one in whom the *Russian and Jewish* anarchism is so impressed that he is no longer worthy of being classed a Pole" (emphasis added).[3]

Naturally, the Jews met to discuss the resolution and claimed that it was unfair to accuse Jews simply because Czolgosz was of Jewish parentage. Louis Finger became the spokesman for the Jewish people. His eloquent statement was printed in the *Morning News* on September 12, while President McKinley was still alive.

I desire to impress upon the American nation in general that there is absolutely no connection between Judaism and anarchism. The Jew as a race despises anarchy, as does every other law abiding and liberty loving people. The Jews of this country deplore the attack upon the life of the President as deeply as any other citizens. They were the first to offer prayers for the speedy recovery of the President on Saturday morning last, and it is a great folly to link anarchy with Judaism."[4]

On September 13, when the Jews gathered for services Erev Rosh Hashanah, the night before the new year, President McKinley was still alive, but there was "slight hope for his recovery." At Adas Kodesch, the congregation unanimously adopted a resolution denouncing the attempted assassination of the President as an act tending to subvert all government and authority.[5] The congregants renewed their allegiance to their adopted country and claimed they were people who loved liberty, independence, and God. Morris Levy and J. Harry Gordon cited the patriotism of Jews on the seas and battlefields and their contributions to the stability of the Republic. The president's condition worsened, and he died at 2 A.M. on September 14, Rosh Hashanah.

All merchants were asked to close their stores on the funeral day, Thursday, September 19, and services were held throughout the city.[6] Public buildings were draped in black. Governor John Hunn presided at the memorial service at the Grand Opera House, held under the auspices of the Young Men's Democratic Club and the Young Men's Republican Club. The service attracted so many people that by two o'clock, the doors were closed and thousands were turned away.[7]

Among the services held at religious places of worship was a service at the Adas Kodesch synagogue.[8] J. Harry Gordon read a tribute written by the Reverend T. A. McCurdy. Max Weiner read President McKinley's last speech. Barnet Gluckman, Nathan Barsky, and Rabbis Herman Rezits, Herman Blatt, and A. B. Cohen, also participated in the program.

Traditionally Jews observe a one-year period of mourning for their close relatives. Ten days after McKinley's death, the Jews announced that they would treat the president as one of their own.[9] Therefore, the Hebrew Charity Ball, one of the regular winter features, would not be held out of respect to the memory of President McKinley. Hebrew organizations all over the country had decided to forego their annual dances, and nothing of that sort would be held for one year.[10] The Jews were eager to be accepted as good Americans, even if their compatriots saw them as outsiders.

Unfortunately, some people used the assassination to further their anti-immigration crusade. Representative Metcalf of California proposed to introduce a strong immigration restriction measure at the next session of Congress. He said that no anarchist should be allowed to land on our shores, and that an attack on the life of the president or vice-president should be regarded as treason.[11] The *Every Evening* reported that resolutions to this effect had been adopted by the Merchants' Association of Wilmington.

Instead of its annual ball, the Hebrew Charity Association sponsored a lecture by Rabbi J. Leonard Levy on January 14, 1902.[12] Governor John Hunn, who had opened the 1901 ball, again presided over the evening, which attracted a large crowd and was once again a financial success. The Hebrew Charity Association, which gave charity to all people in need, distributed the funds to the entire community, donating 28 percent of the money raised to non-Jewish causes. The funds were distributed as follows: "Hebrew Charity Association $400; Delaware Hospital $50; Homeopathic Hospital $50; Associated Charities $25; Home for Friendless and Destitute Children $10; Florence Crittendum Home $10; and St. Michael's Day Nursery $10."[13]

RELIGIOUS RIVALRY: ORTHODOX VERSUS ORTHODOX

Ironically, at the same time the general population was singling the Jews out as a separate entity, Wilmington's Jews again disagreed among themselves over religious matters, and a new synagogue was formed. In the month of September, when President McKinley was shot, Morris Chaiken, Morris Kanefsky, Morris Ezrailson, and David Kodesh met to form a new synagogue.[14] On October 13 the group, which had expanded to sixteen members, held a meeting to prepare to incorporate and to elect officers and trustees.[15] Morris Chaiken was elected president, Menashe Goldberg was vice-president, Louis Reches was treasurer, and Morris Kanefsky was elected secretary. Morris Finger, Mandel Hendler, and Frank Nisenbaum were elected as trustees and filed a petition with the recorder of deeds for a new Orthodox synagogue, called in the petition Chesed Shel Ames (later spelled "Emeth") Congregation.[16] In addition to the men named in Chaiken's account, Aaron Holotky, Jonah Levine, Meyer Sklut, Abraham Stromwasser, and Judah Barber were also founding members.[17] Only Frank Nisenbaum and Louis Reches were members of Adas Kodesch at the time Chesed Shel Emeth was formed, so it was not a split from Adas Kodesch.

All the men named as founders were from Russia or Eastern Europe, had modest means of employment, and had arrived in the United States and Wilmington recently. None had been involved in other Jewish organizations. Morris Chaiken left Russia when he was fourteen because of the pogroms.[18] After living in England for at least three years, where he "learned the manners of a gentleman, such as tipping his hat to ladies," Chaiken came to Wilmington alone, without knowing anyone. Shortly after he arrived in Wilmington, Chaiken married Dora Rosen. They had five children in six years; Herman was born in 1898, Louis (or Willie) in 1899, Sophie in 1901, Solomon in 1902, and Isidore in 1904.[19] Chaiken opened a cleaning plant on Fourth and Orange Streets and the family lived at the same place. "Pop worked hard, and the family always needed money in those days, but we ate well and always lived okay," recalled daughter Sophie.[20]

Dora Chaiken's sister Fannie was married to Morris Kanefsky, who was a grocer in 1900.[21] Fannie, Morris, and their two older sons had been born in Russia before they arrived in Wilmington, where Samuel was born at the end of the 1890s.[22] Abraham Stromwasser and his wife Hattie, who was from Galicia, Austria-Hungary, and their infant child boarded with the Kanefskys in 1900.[23] Stromwasser ran a dry goods store at 200 West Second

Street, the home of the two families.[24] Morris Ezrailson, a morocco worker, had just arrived in Wilmington from Russia, where his wife Esther and their infant son Samuel still lived.[25] Morris Finger, brother of Louis, and his wife Rachel, both from Russia, had been married in Wilmington in 1889, but they had lived in Pennsylvania, where their children were born during the 1890s.[26] In 1900, Finger had just returned to Wilmington and was a tailor. Mandel Hendler, from Russia, arrived in Wilmington in the late 1890s after living in Pennsylvania. He had worked in the morocco factory but by 1900 was a rag and iron merchant.[27] Hendler and his wife Sarah had three daughters: Minnie, Fannie, and Beki. Frank Nisenbaum and his wife Dora (who was from Russia) had arrived in Wilmington just before the turn of the century. They had no children. Nisenbaum ran a secondhand merchandise store at 215 West Second.[28] Meyer Sklut, a thirty-year-old tailor, had recently arrived in Wilmington and boarded with Joseph Leopold.[29] Louis Reches and his wife Clara, from Austria-Hungary, lived in Wilmington by 1899, when their daughter Debra was born.[30] Reches was a baker, and he had joined Adas Kodesch in March 1901. Judah Barber, his wife Esther, and oldest daughter Anna were from Russia.[31] During the 1890s, the Barbers' children Ethel, Frena, and Asa were born in Delaware and Pennsylvania. In 1900 they lived at 107 King Street, where Judah ran a notions and dry goods store; Esther also had a cigar store at 103 King. Although these immigrants were very new to Wilmington and faced all the difficulties of beginning life in a new place, they believed it was necessary to form a separate synagogue.

Their precise reasons for wanting a new synagogue have been lost in time, but individuals who remember the early Chesed Shel Emeth agree that there were two major differences—one religious and one social—between Chesed Shel Emeth and Adas Kodesch. First, Chesed Shel Emeth followed the Nusach Sepharad liturgy, while Adas Kodesch followed the Nusach Askenaz liturgy.[32] Developed in Poland and Russia and influenced by the Hasidic movement, Nusach Sepharad was far more emotional than Nusach Askenaz. Its followers recited their prayers with swaying, fervor, and noise, while followers of Nusach Askenaz prayed with more Westernized decorum.[33] Many of Wilmington's newest Jews had grown up in Poland and Russia with the Nusach Sepharad liturgy and wanted to continue that form of observance in their new country. Like other immigrants, the Jews found that reproducing rituals of the Old Country as precisely as possible helped them combat their sense of alienation in a strange land.[34] Second, Chesed had newer, less moneyed people. "Chesed was a small place, they were poor. People at Adas Kodesch had money and influence."[35] Chesed became the working man's shul. It had a different element: the blue-collar workers.[36] Furthermore, at Chesed Shel Emeth, there was no English; the service was all in Hebrew, and the sermon was in Yiddish.[37] Since many of the founders of Chesed were newer to the country, they felt more comfortable speaking Yiddish.[38] Both synagogues were equally Orthodox.[39] At Chesed Shel Emeth, people observed the Shabbat instruction not to carry anything so strictly that worshipers left their talitot and prayer books in shul so that they wouldn't have to carry them. Men tied handkerchiefs to their wrists or necks so they weren't carrying them.[40]

In addition, Chesed Shel Emeth was started because of a problem concerning burials. Unsubstantiated stories suggest that someone was refused burial at Adas Kodesch and this lead to the formation of Chesed Shel Emeth, which means "true loving kindness."[41] Although no specific incident can be documented, the idea of a free burial society was a major factor in the formation of Chesed Shel Emeth. Morris Chaiken titled his history of the synagogue the "History of Hevrah Hesed Shel Emes." (A *hevrah* is a burial society.) In his history, Chaiken implied a problem with burial when he explained, "in the first year they purchased a cemetery because it was necessary to help the poor and the needy."[42] In describing the formation of the synagogue, a later history referred to burial, "whether it was a free burial of a poor fellow Jew in the early days. . . ."[43] In December 1901, shortly after Chesed Shel Emeth was formed, the board of Adas Kodesch voted that "in the case of the death of a stranger, no settlement shall be made without the President and the consent of the Board of Trustees and the Chairman of the Chevra Kadusha, the Burial society," implying there had been a problem earlier.[44]

The atmosphere at Adas Kodesch's board meetings provides further insight into the need for a new synagogue. Despite the fact that one would expect a religious organization to welcome new members, Adas Kodesch had some very strict rules and was less than inviting. Technically, membership was open to men between the ages of twenty and forty-five.[45] However, members were accepted through a rather arcane system that discriminated against many. The individual who wanted to become a member paid "proposition money" so that his name would be presented at a board meeting. Then, a committee visited the candidate and brought back a recommendation for the consideration of the full board. The voting was done by secret ballot using black and white balls, and if three black balls were found, the candidate was rejected—literally "blackballed." Among the many candidates who were rejected in the months just before the formation of Chesed Shel Emeth were Morris Chaiken, Morris Kanefsky, and Judah Barber; the latter was denied membership because he was not in "sound bodily health" as required by the constitution.[46]

Members were routinely dropped because of failure to pay installments on their dues. When someone spoke out of turn at a board meeting, he was fined fifty cents the first time and one dollar, the equivalent of the membership fee, for the second time. After Nathan Altman had a tombstone prepared, the committee agreed no one could erect a tombstone without written permission from the congregation.[47] A heated argument, in which President Joseph Lictenbaum threatened to evict David Topkis from the synagogue because Topkis did not want to purchase a ticket, resulted in President Lictenbaum briefly resigning as president.[48]

There is no question that there was some bitterness between the two synagogues. In December 1901 Adas Kodesch's minutes state, "A committee of the new organization Chesed Chelameas asked to use our building on cemetery. We refused."[49] The extreme disagreement is reminiscent of the Montefiore Society's refusal to give Max Podolsky his $10 two years earlier. To the larger world, the Jews were one group, but despite their unity on some issues, they disagreed strongly on others.

The Chesed Shel Emeth Society was listed as a society, not a "church" like Adas Kodesch, during the entire decade. In 1902 and 1903, it met at 205 West Fourth Street, above Cloud and Pyle upholsterers and across the street from the home of Morris and Dora Chaiken.[50] All of the founding members lived within a block or two of Chesed Shel Emeth and the Chaikens. In 1904, the synagogue moved into Third and Market Streets, which also became the home of the YMHA, and remained there until 1910, when it moved to Third and West Streets. Not until 1915 did Chesed Shel Emeth have its own building.

Although the membership at Chesed Shel Emeth grew during the early years of the century, Adas Kodesch continued to be the larger synagogue. The membership at Adas Kodesch grew from some 75 men in 1900 to about 155 men in 1908.[51] In 1907, Chesed Shel Emeth had about seventy members.[52] A few years after the formation of Chesed Shel Emeth, Morris Chaiken, Morris Kanefsky, Morris Ezrailson, and other Chesed Shel Emeth members did join Adas Kodesch, but they continued to be members of both synagogues.[53]

In 1900, before Chesed Shel Emeth was formed, Adas Kodesch

supervised the Free Hebrew Sunday School. The Sunday school had four teachers, 123 pupils, and met once a week for two hours.[54] In November 1900, Adas Kodesch president David Topkis reported to the board that he had hired a janitor at the cost of $3 for every two weeks, with the understanding that the Sunday School Association should pay half. Several months later the Adas Kodesch board donated $15 to the Free Hebrew Sunday School. These references make it clear that a separate group, the Sunday School Association, and not the board of Adas Kodesch, was running the Sunday school. J. Harry Gordon was principal and vice-president of the Free Hebrew Sunday School.[55] All Jewish youngsters in the city probably continued to attend the Free Hebrew Sunday School after Chesed Shel Emeth was formed. There are no records of Chesed Shel Emeth starting a religious school in the early years of this century.[56] Adas Kodesch also had a separate religious school with sixty-eight students and four classes.[57] In 1904, Adas Kodesch established a permanent Hebrew school, with Rabbi Jacob Abramowitz as both principal and one of the three teachers. Between sixty and one hundred children attended the school.[58] The Hebrew school was established largely through the efforts of Morris Rosenblatt, president of Adas Kodesch, who had worked diligently to establish the school and raise the money.[59]

PERSECUTION IN RUSSIA: RESTRICTING IMMIGRATION TO THE UNITED STATES

The prosperity of the United States attracted unprecedented numbers of immigrants to the country. At the same time, because the persecution of Jews in Russia intensified, increased numbers of Jews sought refuge in the United States.[60] Between 1898 and 1910, the largest number of immigrants to the United States came from Italy, and the second largest number were Jews.[61] As unprecedented numbers of immigrants flocked to the United States, the restrictionists increased their efforts to limit immigration.

William Williams, a well-known restrictionist, became Commissioner of Immigration at the Port of New York in 1902. He told President Theodore Roosevelt that aliens had no inherent right whatsoever to come here and that America ought to exclude all those below a certain physical and economic standard.[62] Williams' definition of public charge category proposed a double standard. People from Southern or Eastern Europe were to be admitted only if their appearance, financial assets in hand, or firm assurance of employment guaranteed their non–public-charge status; newcomers from Scotland and Ireland were to be welcomed regardless of these criteria.[63] William's definition of public charge was accepted by officials in the Department of Commerce and Labor.

The public was aware not only that the tide of immigrants had swelled but also that the place of origin of immigrants had shifted. As early as 1903, newspapers reported that formerly immigrants had come from England, Scotland, Ireland, and Northern Europe, but now the "majority is of different blood and less assimilable."[64] The largest number of immigrants were now from Italy, then Austria-Hungary, then Russia-Finland.

American Jews, many of whom had family members still in Russia, called attention to the plight of the Russian Jews—who suffered from discriminatory laws, anti-Semitic publications, and violent pogroms—and worked to keep the doors of the United States open. In the spring of 1903, the Russian government initiated a pogrom against the Jews in Kishinev. Men and women were slain in the streets and by their own homes; children were torn from the arms of their mothers and ruthlessly killed. The remaining Jewish population of Kishinev, about 37,000 people, was ordered to leave. The response of the American Jewish community was immediate. Within a period of about two months, nearly eighty protest meetings were held in fifty cities from Boston to San Francisco.[65] In Wilmington, a committee for the relief of the sufferers was formed. The committee to receive contributions included Louis Brown, Joseph Lictenbaum, and David Topkis—all Russian by birth.[66] Brown had lived in the United States for at least a decade, Lictenbaum had arrived in Wilmington before his daughter was born in 1890, and Topkis, the eldest son of Rosa and Jacob, had come to the United States in 1882 when he was twelve years old. Brown and Topkis were tailors, Lictenbaum was in the installment business. Each was married and had several children. Like the other early immigrants, they undoubtedly had family and friends still in Russia. In early May, the committee sent its first money for relief of the sufferers. On May 28 the committee sent its second installment of 380 rubles, about $197.[67]

In addition to raising funds, the committee circulated copies of a petition that was to be sent to President Roosevelt urging him to employ the good offices of the United States government with the imperial government of Russia, with the aim of securing more safety to Jews in Russia and making their lives less wretched.[68] The petition argued that the recent massacre of Jews by organized mobs at Kishinev, which was undertaken by the Russian government, and the expulsion of the entire Jewish population of Kishinev could no longer be treated as an internal affair. The United States had to intercede.

Under the auspices of the "local Hebrews," a mass meeting to protest the oppression of the Jews in Russia was held at the Grand Opera House on June 1, 1903. The response from the total community was gratifying and showed that the leaders of Wilmington were people of ideals who were willing to take a stand against wrongdoing outside the United States.[69] The meeting, chaired by Governor John Hunn, attracted a capacity crowd of "Americans and natives of other countries." Among the dignitaries present were Mayor George M. Fisher, Judge George Gray, Bishop Coleman, and members of the City Council. Governor Hunn claimed that the current state of affairs in Russia could only be brought about by fanaticism and ignorance, and he recommended more schoolhouses and better education.

Judge George Gray, a Delaware statesman who had almost run for vice-president of the United States, expressed his outrage eloquently.

I am here to voice what I believe to be the universal sentiment of Christian America, the universal sentiment of American citizenship throughout the length and breadth of this broad land of ours—sentiments of sympathy for the suffering men, women and children who have survived this horror, sympathy with you who are of their race and blood and of protest to be uttered by this great nation, of which we are a part, against the horror and the perfidy and the outrage of the whole matter.[70]

After reciting some of the outrages, Gray emphasized the importance of freedom and dignity. He suggested that if the czar allowed the Jews to live in total freedom, they would be loyal citizens of Russia and would strengthen his empire.

Let them be free and he [the czar] will see statesmanship, philosophy, literature, poetry and all the arts flourish among them and adorn his empire as no other race has ever adorned it. Here in America we know what that race is capable of, and what it has given to humanity and contributed to civilization.[71]

At the end of the meeting, several resolutions were passed and sent to the president and the secretary of state. In addition to resolutions of sympathy, one resolution urged the United States government to use its influence as a friend of the Russian government to stop the persecution that had amazed the civilized world.

The Kishinev pogrom marked a turning point in Jewish emigration from Russia. Before the pogrom, hundreds of dispirited Jewish immigrants returned to the Old World every year. Opinions about emigration were divided, with many thinking that the pogroms would pass.[72] But after the pogrom of 1903, most people agreed that the best solution for the Jewish problem was immigration.[73] Between 1904 and 1908, a total of 672,000 Jews entered the United States, the vast majority from the Russian Empire.[74]

Injustice towards the Jews of Russia did not stop, but increased until the number of pogroms became practically uncountable.[75] In the fall of 1905 over seven hundred communities fell victim to a new wave of pogroms spearheaded by the Black Hundreds.[76] On November 12, 1905, at a meeting of the Hebrew Charity Association, a committee consisting of Morris Levy, Barnet Gluckman, and J. Harry Gordon was appointed to raise money for the relief of massacre victims, both Jewish and Gentile. Over $500 were raised.[77] Rabbis Abramowitz and Rezits, as well as Abraham Tollin, Max Green, and James J. Cohen, were enlisted to help raise the amount to $1000. Shortly after the meeting, the Moses Montefiore Society contributed $100 to the effort.[78]

Once again the broader community assisted the Jews. In an editorial entitled "Help the Jews," the editors of the *Sunday Star* stated that the noble efforts of the Jews of Wilmington to aid their stricken brothers in Russia should command the sympathy and assistance of the general public.[79] The movement was worldwide; if every man gave something, the total would be a grand fund of enormous proportions. In encouraging the assistance of the general public, the editorial pointed out that Jews always are generous in giving to others and cited the money Jews sent to sufferers of the Galveston flood.

In addition to sending money for relief, some Jews wanted to send money for defense. On November 22, 1905 a branch of the Hebrew Defense Bund was organized, with three natives of Russia as its officers: Louis A. Hillersohn, president, Nathan Shtofman, secretary, and Louis Topkis, treasurer. The purpose of the bund was to raise money for the persecuted in Russia so that they could buy arms in order to protect themselves against attacks on their property and lives.[80] Arms were used only for defense and were made available to all who lived in sections of Russia where they were likely to be persecuted, not just to Jews. About sixty members joined the Wilmington branch, enabling the bund to send $60.

Many of Wilmington's Jews had close family members still in Russia. Mrs. Louis Finger was anxiously awaiting additional news from her sister and brother in Odessa. After the massacre, she received a letter saying they had escaped injury by following the advice of the landlord to remain indoors, but she did not know about other family members.[81] Several of the Jews who arrived in Wilmington by the end of the decade, including Harry Cohen and Bernard Glick, had survived the pogroms.[82]

In the midst of all the worry and tragedy, Jews had occasion to rejoice because 1905 marked the 250th anniversary of the settlement of Jews in America, and Jews throughout the country celebrated. In Wilmington, nearly every Jewish family in the city, Orthodox and Reform alike, attended a Thanksgiving Day service at Adas Kodesch on November 30, 1905.[83] The service opened with a prayer by Cantor Abramowitz and the children of the Hebrew Sunday School and included readings by Morris Chaiken (president of Chesed Shel Emeth), Samuel Harris (president of the Moses Montefiore Society), Rabbi Rezits, Rabbi Rabinowitz of New York, Barnet Gluckman, Moses Weil, and J. Harry Gordon. An article in the *Every Evening* noted that history repeats itself: the very reasons why Jews were deserting Russia today caused them three centuries ago to come to America by tens of thousands. These immigrants were an important factor in building this country.[84]

Three days after the Thanksgiving service, Jews throughout the United States held services to honor the Jews recently killed in Russia. All Wilmington merchants were requested to close their stores at 4 P.M. and attend the services at Adas Kodesch.[85]

In Wilmington, a benevolent attitude that recognized the importance of the well-being of all members of the society prevailed. "Every establishment here, public and private, is concerned in the spiritual welfare and material prosperity of every class in the city and State, if not from an altruistic, then from an egoistic point of view."[86]

Despite the positive actions and sentiments expressed in the Wilmington, as more immigrants flooded into the country, public sentiment against newcomers increased. In a 1906 article about immigration, a reporter argued that the United States no longer had the same need of immigrants as it did one hundred or more years ago.[87] He claimed that vacant lands were taken and cities were teeming and overflowing. Therefore, he believed the United States could afford to be particular in its choice of immigrants. The present immigrants were more ignorant than those of forty or more years ago, and the Russian Jews seemed to be, in their individual character, the least desirable of the present large immigration. But even this writer added a qualifier, which turned his article from a nasty harangue into a vision of tolerance.

> The Jew comes from an ancient and great race. Those who are now coming to us from Russia have been oppressed and beaten down by crushing burdens. In kinder American conditions, they may straighten up in a generation or two into a magnificent citizenship.[88]

The subject of immigration was often before Congress. Those who advocated a restrictionist policy did so not to reduce the total volume of immigrants but more importantly to select immigrants. They wanted to eliminate the "new" kind of immigrants while retaining the old.[89] This was the logic of the literacy test, which advocates knew would keep out many of the immigrants from Southern and Eastern Europe without affecting those from Northern or Central Europe.[90] Attempts to limit immigration through a literacy test, which had failed in Congress in 1897, were unsuccessful again in 1903 and 1906–7. Recognizing that the evidence at hand was insufficient to warrant a congressional verdict either for or against a change in immigration policy, the president and Congress agreed to establish a commission to study the situation before making changes.[91] The United States Immigration Commission focused on "the changed character of the immigration movement to the United States in the past twenty five years."[92] In fiscal 1907, 81 percent of immigrants from Europe (including Turkey) were from Austria-Hungary, Bulgaria, Greece, Italy, Montenegro, Poland, Portugal, Romania, Russia, Serbia, Spain, and Turkey; twenty-five years earlier only 13 percent had come from those countries.[93] The commission worked from April 1907 until December 1910. Its report, as we shall see shortly, had dire implications for the future of immigration.

ZIONISM

Some American Jews, recognizing the unbearable quality of life for Jews in Russia and the serious implications of restrictionism, continued to advocate a Jewish homeland in Palestine. In June 1901, Israel Wainer and his son Max attended the Zionist conference in Philadelphia.[94] Among the speakers was Rabbi Stephen Wise, who advocated the establishment of a Zionist newspaper. Five hundred dollars were allocated for the purpose, and each Zionist society was taxed five dollars. A mass meeting of Wilmington's

B'nai Zion was held on July 22, 1901, with Reverend B. Levinthal of Philadelphia, a vice-president of the Zionist Federation, and B. L. Gordon, president of Ohabe Zion Philadelphia. Both Rabbi Rezits and A. B. Cohen spoke about the objectives of Zionism.[95] On January 2, 1902, the Zionists held a third anniversary celebration featuring songs lead by Cantor Herman Blatt and a young Zionist group. In 1904 and 1905, the organization was listed in the city directory under its English name, Daughters of Zion, but then it seems to have become inactive.

During the early years of the twentieth century, American Zionism remained a small, ideological sect, quite unable to become the mass movement that it aspired to be.[96] One reason Zionism did not catch on in America was that it was antipathetic to the whole Jewish migration to America. Hundreds of thousands of people had uprooted themselves from their accustomed life in Eastern Europe and were still struggling to establish themselves in America. They did not want to be told that they had journeyed in the wrong direction.[97]

ASSISTING NEW IMMIGRANTS

While they struggled to earn livelihoods, to assist Jews in Russia, and to further the idea of a Jewish homeland, the Jews worked in numerous organizations to improve life for the new immigrants. The Moses Montefiore Society, B'nai B'rith, and the Hebrew Charity Association, comprised of members who were new to the community as well as members who had been in Wilmington for many years, continued to meet important needs. When the Moses Montefiore Society was organized in 1880, it served religious and social needs. Twenty years later in 1903, the society took a new charter that made it not only a religious but also a social, mutual, beneficial organization.[98] Its name was officially changed to the Moses Montefiore Mutual Beneficial Society. Thirty-three men signed as new charter members. Max Ephraim was the only original founder who signed again in 1903.[99] Perhaps nothing shows the transience of the community more clearly than the fact that nearly all of the 1903 incorporators had come to Wilmington in the last twenty years. Recognizing the need to have a large cemetery, the society amended its charter in 1905 in order to enable it to purchase land outside the city limits.[100] On January 21, 1907, the society purchased land in Lombardy Cemetery, and in 1908 the bodies were moved from the cemetery at Fifth and Hawley Streets to the new cemetery.[101]

During the early part of the century, B'nai B'rith was an active part of District Three and flourished under the presidencies of Louis Topkis, Morris Blumberg, Morris Rosenblatt, and Moses Weil. J. Harry Gordon served as secretary for many years.

The Hebrew Charity Association was incorporated in February 1902 with seventeen signatories: sixteen men and Rosa Topkis, who became the first woman to sign the incorporation papers of any Jewish organization.[102] Fourteen of the incorporators were from Russia and Hungary. Eleven of the incorporators had been part of B'nai B'rith in 1898.

B'nai B'rith and the Hebrew Charity Association were partners in caring for the new immigrants who flooded into the country crowding the large cities of the East and Midwest as conditions in

Community leaders: William Topkis, J. Harry Gordon, James Ginns, and Louis Topkis, 1900s. (Jewish Historical Society of Delaware.)

Russia deteriorated. Over one million Jews arrived in New York between 1881 and 1911, and more than 73 percent stayed there.[103] The physical conditions on New York's Lower East Side, with overcrowded tenements and widespread illness, were appalling.[104] To respond to the growing problems of congestion in the cities, the Industrial Removal Office was founded in 1901 in order to "relocate Jewish immigrants on an individual basis to smaller Jewish communities throughout the United States."[105] The IRO, which operated as a nonprofit employment agency, was centered in New York and used dozens of local committees, usually organized by B'nai B'rith lodges. Between 1903 and 1917, the IRO resettled more than 75,000 people.[106]

Early in 1903, the IRO was working with Wilmington's Jews through J. Harry Gordon, secretary of the B'nai B'rith Lodge and Morris Levy, president of the Hebrew Charity Association. The record of the IRO's Wilmington work is sporadic, but surviving letters illustrate how difficult it was to meet the needs of over one million immigrants when each person had to be treated individually.

In January J. Harry Gordon responded to David Bressler of the IRO that he could place a tailor. "At the request of our Roumanian committee I wish to inform you that we can place a tailor. . . . [T]he party who wants him is a member of this lodge . . . wants a good presser and someone who understands about Ladies tailoring.[107]

In February 1903, Levy wrote to George M. David at the IRO explaining that he had found employment for two men, but after two or three weeks, they had switched from the leather factory to iron and steel. Assuming the men had left Wilmington, Levy wrote with a touch of irony: "They were so thankful to me that they never once came to see me and I can't locate them. Let me know if I can be of further service."[108]

Two days later the IRO apologized for the men's ingratitude. Claiming they couldn't help such occurrences, the IRO begged to send some mechanics as there were a large number of them.

Levy agreed to try to place them and also asked if the IRO had any capmakers. The IRO did not have capmakers but did have a large number of able-bodied laborers, ironworkers, shoemakers, printers, tanners, and glaziers. The New York office was overrun by people who found it utterly impossible to make a living in New York. They were "clamoring for a chance to be sent to some other town where they may be able to be given a chance for respectable self support."[109] By March 6, Levy agreed to take "two men at once and two to follow a week later for morocco factories." He arranged to board them at a "Jewish hotel" at 205 Market, until they procured employment. "We will pay for their board until they get work."[110] At the end of the month, the men had not shown up, and Levy repeated his offer to help.

B'nai B'rith and the Hebrew Charity Association stood firmly behind community members' attempts to bring their relatives. In November 1903, J. Harry Gordon began a series of requests for assistance in bringing relatives of Delaware immigrants to Wilmington. Heinrich Shapiro of Wilmington wanted to bring Marcu Markowitz of Jassy, Romania. Shapiro himself was a new immigrant living with Adolph Frank, but he had sent Markowitz the money for transportation. When the IRO asked for proof of Shapiro's ability to support Markowitz, Gordon wrote a letter explaining "Brother Shapiro is amply able to provide for Markowitz as he has a good job and earns good wages. Also he has a son here doing well. Our lodge will back anything you say in responsibility."[111]

The following day, the IRO wrote back, "he's on his way." Several other Wilmington Jews were successful in bringing relatives to Wilmington in 1904 and 1905. However, the IRO could not be of any assistance in Hungary or Russia.[112] By October 1906, the IRO wrote that it could no longer help because the Jewish Colonization Association had decided to cease assistance in transportation of Romanian immigrants.[113]

In February 1904, the IRO needed placement for a man who was willing to work for a subsistence wage as a clerk in a store. Levy said he could not take a clerk as it was impossible to procure positions. He was ready to accept one man for a tannery. There was no assurance of work, but the Jews of Wilmington would take care of him and surely place him in time.[114]

The man who was sent to Wilmington left almost immediately for Philadelphia, on the advice of his countrymen who were Hungarians. They advised the new man that the Wilmington work was too hard and common laboring for a nice, intelligent man to engage in. He left Wilmington with recommendations to Hungarian bankers and merchants in Philadelphia. Levy claimed he had done everything possible to make it pleasant for the man to remain here, but he wanted to go so Levy transported him to Philadelphia.[115]

In March 1904, Waldman of the IRO told Gordon that he had visited about twelve cities in District 3 of B'nai B'rith and all had agreed to take at least one new immigrant a week. "May you do likewise?[116] Send us a list of the kind you best handle, Waldman wrote. No response has survived.

In July 1904, the IRO wrote to Blumenthal Tannery requesting a position for a man who had been a glazier for seven years. Blumenthal responded immediately: "Send the man, if he's competent, we will give him employment." Within a week Ike Silber was on his way.[117]

Not all Jewish immigrants were eager to leave New York City. In spite of congestion, poverty, and health problems, the ghetto served many constructive functions.[118] It provided the new immigrant with needed friends, countrymen, and relatives who could ease the way into a new society, and could provide help with everyday matters like the law, jobs, and language. The ghetto was a comfortable place to test the heritage they had brought from the Old World against the new reality. Furthermore, New York City provided exceptional possibilities for progress out of the manual classes and many immigrants experienced great occupational mobility.[119] Those Jews who agreed to come to Wilmington were less dependent on a familiar sociocultural community and more willing to strike out on their own.

Continuing its interest in nonsectarian causes, the Hebrew Charity Association actively secured contributions for the Anti-Tuberculosis Society and was singled out for praise by the *Every Evening* newspaper.[120]

By the early years of the twentieth century, Rosa Topkis's loosely organized group of women who had assisted women in confinement at the end of the previous century needed a more formal organization. In 1902, Rosa Topkis called a meeting of all Jewish women in Wilmington to form an organization to care for the sick and needy.[121] Several younger women were put in charge. Mrs. David (Hannah Ray) Topkis was president, Mrs. Hyman (Ida) Kanofsky was vice-president, Mrs. Nathan (Rose) Barsky was secretary.[122] These three women were contemporaries. Hannah Topkis was born in Austria in 1871, Ida Kanofsky was born in Russia in 1869, and Rose Barsky was born in Russia in 1866.[123] Since they each had several children, they understood the difficulty of bearing children in a strange land.[124] After conversations with the rabbi at Adas Kodesch and Rabbi Levinthal of Philadelphia, the women took the name Bichor Cholem, based on the Talmudic concept that "every visitor to a sick person reduces one hundredth part of the sickness."[125] Other women who were involved in the organization in the early years were Mrs. Herman (Rachel) Feinberg, Mrs. Adolph (Bertha) Frank, Mrs. D. M. (Ida) Lurge, Mrs. Louis (Lizzie) Hillersohn, and Mrs. Louis (Sarah) Slonsky, who was the mother of eleven children. After a reorganization in 1904, the organization prospered, growing to forty-two members, with Hannah Ray Topkis as president, in 1907.[126]

Members of the Bichor Cholem Society went house to house with baskets on their arms asking for food, clothing, and supplies for the indigent families.[127] When they went to visit the needy families, the enthusiasm that greeted them was stimulating. Most people were so very, very poor. The Bichor Cholem Society placed all indigent and sick women in local hospitals at $7 a week for two weeks. In addition to helping local families, when there were sufficient funds the Bichor Cholem Society gave all itinerant rabbis and Jewish wayfarers shelter for one night, breakfast, and enough money to reach the next town. The early meetings were conducted in Yiddish, and Rachel Feinberg, an excellent Jewish scholar, wrote up the Yiddish minutes. Since Hannah Ray Topkis was the only one who could read and write English satisfactorily, the early contacts were left to her.[128]

Membership in the organization was open to all married women who had lived in Wilmington for at least six months. Members paid an initiation fee of twenty-five cents and monthly dues of twenty-five cents. Provided there were $100 in the treasury, sick members were given three dollars a week.[129] The Bichor Cholem also contributed to the relief of Kishinev victims, Jewish consumptives on the Hope Farm, and the Denver and Los Angeles Hospitals.[130]

All of the officers of the 1907 organization—Hannah Ray Topkis, Nessie Tiger, Elizabeth Hillersohn, Rose Barsky, and Ida Lurge—and a majority of the members were also part of Adas Kodesch congregation. When the new synagogue was dedicated, the Bichor Cholem Society donated nearly $1000 for the new ark.[131]

As the number of Jews in Wilmington grew, so did the need for a place for cultural, educational, and social activities. In October 1901, at the same time that religious differences led to the formation of Chesed Shel Emeth, Rosa Topkis, mother of David, Louis, William, Charles, Harry, and Sallie, invited several people to her home at 417 King Street to plan a Young Men's Hebrew Association.[132] J. Harry Gordon was elected president, Elias Wetstein vice president, Isaac Finkelstein secretary, and James J. Cohen treasurer. When the YMHA was incorporated in December 1902, Charles, Harry, and William Topkis, Harry Hirsch, Manual Cohen, and Philip Krigstein, as well as the officers listed above, signed the incorporation document.[133] The YMHA's objective was "social and literary purposes and advancing the education of man and for religious purposes generally." By early 1902 the group was comprised of "the best element of the city and was trying to make its organization a big success."[134]

The founders of the YMHA (with the exception of J. Harry Gordon, who was fifty-one) were not yet thirty.[135] In fact, Harry Topkis, Manual Cohen, and Isaac B. Finkelstein were not even twenty. They were all related or acquainted through business. Charles and William Topkis ran Rosa Topkis's dry goods store, James J. Cohen was a barber, and his younger brother Manual Cohen and Elias Wetstein were each in the shoe business. Isaac B. Finkelstein worked at Delaware Notion House, owned by Sam Slessinger. J. Harry Gordon worked for Sam Slessinger's clothing house. Philip Krigstein was a nephew of Rosa Topkis. Harry Hirsch was a clerk for B. G. Goldstein. The group was an Americanized one: Charles and Harry Topkis, J. Harry Gordon, Elias Wetstein, and Isaac B. Finkelstein were all born in the United States. J. Harry Gordon, who was principal of the Free Hebrew Sunday School as well as secretary of B'nai B'rith, treasurer of the Hebrew Charity Association, and a member of both Adas Kodesch and Chesed Shel Emeth, knew all the others and became the guiding leader.[136]

The younger members organized a YMHA juniors, with Nathan Goldstein as president in 1904.[137] At eighteen, the son of Israel and Lizzie Goldstein was the oldest of the group. The juniors continued in 1905 under the leadership of Aaron Finger, son of Louis and Esther Finger, who was only fifteen and led a slate of officers who were fourteen and fifteen and had all been born in the United States.[138] There was also a Ladies' Auxiliary of the YMHA, led in 1904 by president Sarah Korngold, the nineteen-year-old daughter of Morris and Anna and sister of Mrs. James J. Cohen in 1904, and in 1905 by Fannie Faber, the twenty-two-year-old wife of Jacob Faber.[139]

During the first years, the YMHA rented space at Third and Market Streets because there were not adequate facilities in the Adas Kodesch Building, the only building devoted solely to Jewish activities in Wilmington.[140] After holding its meetings in varying places for a few years, the YMHA opened headquarters at Fourth and Shipley Streets, which were formally opened on March 4, 1906.[141] By 1907 the YMHA had fifty-six members, who were a mixture of the community's active adults and many of their sons.[142] The adults passed the concept of contributing to a community and being part of it to their children.

On October 11, 1906, a handful of hard-working men assembled at the YMHA headquarters at Third and King to organize a local branch of the Workmen's Circle of America, an organization

YMHA Outing Club, c. 1906. (Jewish Historical Society of Delaware.)

formed for the "purpose of helping and uniting the working people."[143] The organization brought together Jews who were not particularly religious but shared a common social agenda. "It was like a labor union that wanted to make the world a better place for the working man."[144] Members of Workmen's Circle accepted the long-range goals of the radical leaders, as well as the fact that the Workmen's Circle helped finance the socialist movement.[145] They were dedicated to the principle of equality between the laborer and the employer; to the unity of all working people and their subsequent emancipation. Most of the organizers had been employees at one time, had endured negative experiences and felt great resentment against their treatment and bosses in general.[146] They were now self-employed. Nathan Shtofman, Adolph Silver, Nathan Leopold and Sam Glick were tailors. Harry Evans was a grocer, and Marcus Stiftel was a jeweler. All of the founders except Shtofman had arrived in Wilmington after the turn of the century. In 1907, Nathan Shtofman was president.[147]

Members of the Workmen's Circle were not inclined to follow Jewish religious practices because they felt that religion, which favored the ruling class, had held them down.[148] When Adolph Silver fled Romania to avoid serving in the army, he reacted against his religious background because he didn't want to be tied down by the religious strictures he had grown up with.[149] Benjamin Fineman, who devoted much energy to the Workmen's Circle, "had left religion behind in Europe."[150] Clearly, there was a great divide between the members of Workmen's Circle and the founders of Adas Kodesch and Chesed Shel Emeth.

The Independent Order of Ahawas Israel was organized in New York in 1890, and by 1902 there were 124 lodges with some 121,000 members.[151] A Wilmington branch of an organization called Work of Truth was listed as early as 1902, with Morris Chaiken as president and the other officers the same as the leaders of Chesed Shel Emeth.[152] The overlap in leadership suggests that it was another service organization meeting the same needs but independent because of politics. By 1910, Ahawas Israel had 204 members, and president Max Green was complimented on his last four years of work.[153]

The Jews had different priorities, talents, and interests but because so many of them dedicated themselves to furthering their goals, Wilmington Jews soon had a wide array of organizations serving communal needs. Jews who had been in Wilmington in the 1880s and early 1890s continued to be part of the organizations, but the newer immigrants took on increased responsibilities. Given the tremendous influx of newcomers compared to the sparsity of those who stayed in Wilmington, the new arrivals had tremendous impact on the community. The transition to new leadership was intensified in the middle years of the decade by the deaths of three people: Manual Richenberger, Rosa Topkis, and Nathan Lieberman.

Manual Richenberger, who had lived in Wilmington as early as 1865, died in April 1904. Although he had married a non-Jewish woman and had not remained an active part of the Jewish community, he never renounced his Judaism. After he died at home from a lingering illness, friends and relatives were invited to attend the funeral at his late residence. He was interred at the Montefiore Cemetery according to the rites of the Jewish faith.[154] The *Morning News* remembered Richenberger as the man who put the first enclosure around a baseball park in the city.[155] Richenberger, a German Jew and a founder of the community in Wilmington, had represented a link to the past, a note of continuity.

On March 16, 1905, Rosa Topkis died of meningitis at the home of her son Louis Topkis.[156] Although Rosa had only lived in Wilmington for about a decade, she had been a dynamic agent for change. An enterprising woman, with a strong sense of human compassion and responsibility for those less fortunate, Rosa had organized both the Bichor Cholem Society and the YMHA in order to meet important communal needs. Most importantly, through her words and deeds, Rosa had taught her children that compassion and responsibility had to be translated into action in order to be meaningful and fruitful.[157] Rosa's children—David, Louis, William, Charles, Harry, and Sallie—followed in their mother's footsteps and took important roles in the community in the next decades. In 1918, in honor of their departed mother, the Topkis siblings hired a nurse to visit any Jewish home stricken with disease to offer advice and services free of charge.[158]

With a suddenness that shocked the community, Nathan Lieberman died while conversing with friends at a regular meeting of the Knights of Pythias in February 1906.[159] Lieberman was an outstanding personality who built many of the homes of Wilmington, and later also devoted himself completely to public welfare.[160] Claiming there was no truer or more honest man, the *Sunday Star* recalled that Lieberman once paid the default of the bank official for which he was the surety.[161] Lieberman, who had been the treasurer of the Knights of Pythias from its origin until his death, was recognized as a "mainstay of the organization in its first struggle for existence."[162] One hundred men attended a meeting at Adas Kodesch to make arrangements to attend Nathan Lieberman's funeral, which was held in Philadelphia where he owned a family plot in a large Jewish cemetery.

The Lieberman family had been the social head of Wilmington Jewish society from the 1870s until his death.[163] At the time of his death, Nathan Lieberman had amassed a fortune of nearly one million dollars.[164] He was the last of the original founders of the Jewish community in Wilmington, and his death symbolized the end of the first generation. Although Nathan's daughter Estella and her husband Albert Rothschild remained in Wilmington at least until Rothschild's death in 1923, most of Lieberman's children left Wilmington, and the family ceased to play a central role in community affairs.

ACHIEVING SUCCESS IN A CITY OF OPPORTUNITY

As nearly 650 new Jewish immigrants flocked to Wilmington, they found employment in a variety of areas, branching out even more widely than their predecessors.[165] Given their hard work and ambition, as well as the favorable business climate, several achieved success in a short time.

Max Keil, born in Beicz, Austria in 1878, emigrated to New York when he was about eighteen years old.[166] After a short time as a peddler in Coney Island, Max went to Paterson, New Jersey to work for Zucker and Steiner, a liquor business. He later married Fannie Steiner.[167] Max was not happy with conditions in Paterson because every spring the Passaic River overflowed and the business was flooded out. Hearing about a city called Wilmington between New York and Washington, he decided to try business there. In 1904, Max Keil arrived in Wilmington and became manager of Wilmington Wine and Liquor House at 302 East Fourth Street. Soon Max rented the space from Christopher Pfromer for $720 a year. In addition to selling liquor, he ran the store as a saloon or tavern. Max probably rented rooms as well because he had an innkeeper's license, and by 1906 he and his brother Aaron, who ran the Kentucky Wine and Liquor House on Front and King Streets, were referred to as well-known hotelkeepers.[168] Max brought over all of his siblings—Aaron, Isadore, Samuel, Bertha, Basha, Helen, and Mamie—as well as his mother Gitel. Since they all stayed in Wilmington, the Keil family became one of Wilmington's largest extended families.

Several of the newest immigrants achieved success in the furniture business, which had not been a Jewish enterprise earlier. The

Fanny and Max Keil with their first five children (Leo, David, Bertha, Sam, and Joe) c. 1913. (Jewish Historical Society of Delaware.)

brothers Abraham and Frank Tollin, who had spent much of the 1890s in Pennsylvania, arrived in Wilmington by 1897, when they opened an installment store.[169] By 1900 their store, which sold carpets, furniture, beddings, stoves, household goods, ladies' clothing, and dry goods, was recognized as one of the largest and most popular in the city.[170] Although Abraham and Frank were born in Russia, the *Board of Trade Journal* said the two brothers were born in Germany and had been in the United States for a number of years. The brothers were praised for their business tact and up-to-date ideas. By 1905 Frank had left the business, but Abraham continued to operate Tollin Brothers at 207–209 West Fourth Street.

Morris Altman, who arrived in Wilmington in the late 1890s, was born in St. Petersburg, Russia in the early 1860s.[171] His family lived under ducal protection because they were members of the proud group of Jewish craftsmen whom the czar had brought to St. Petersburg to make his city look like Paris.[172] In the late 1870s, the duke told Altman's father that he could no longer protect the family and he would help the thirteen children settle in countries throughout the world where he had friends. With jewels sewed into his clothes, Altman was sent to Wilmington, home of the duke's friends the du-Ponts. He married Fannie Wolfson, whose father, Bernard, had been the first president of Adas Kodesch. Over the years, Altman listed himself as a clerk in her store or as a furniture maker. He continued to make furniture until 1930, and many Jewish furniture makers had their first experience in the business with him.

Herman (Hyman) Feinberg immigrated to the United States in the 1890s because "it was the thing to do."[173] He settled in Chester, Pennsylvania, where he peddled rugs, blankets, quilts, and ladies' dresses.[174] Herman married Rachel Wolson, and they had five children (Rosa, Samuel, Isaac, Henry, and William) in six-and-a-half years. Isaac, Henry, and William were born in Wilmington.[175] By 1900, Herman Feinberg and Abraham Wolson had opened a store on King Street.[176] A few years later, Herman was in business alone at 616 French Street. By 1908, Herman bought his own store on Second Street, which was the hub of the Jewish community.[177] Herman paid $4500 for the store on Second Street, though he could have bought a store at Sixth and King for less, because he thought Second Street, the center of Jewish life in Wilmington, was a better location. By 1913, he realized this was a mistake and bought a store at 806 King Street in the center of the business district.

Nathan Miller, born on a small farm near Warsaw, Poland in 1884, emigrated to Philadelphia when he was fifteen, joining his brothers.[178] Just after the turn of the century, he came to Wilmington, bought a basket and a small stock of notions, and began peddling from door to door. Within a couple of years, Nathan and his brother Charles had opened a carpet store called Miller Brothers at 607 West Second Street.[179] In 1904, Nathan, Charles, and Samuel ran Miller Brothers, selling furniture and carpets at 231 Market Street, formerly the Boston One Price clothing store. By 1905, when Miller Brothers incorporated, Samuel Slessinger was part of their management.[180] Slessinger, by then a successful and wealthy Jewish leader, most likely helped the brothers financially. The third annual grand opening of Miller's Furniture in 1906 was ushered in by a splendid orchestra rendering popular music, and every visitor was given coupons.[181] Miller Brothers Furniture was one of the first in Wilmington to encourage people to trade in furniture like they traded in cars.[182] By 1909 Sam Slessinger was president of Miller Brothers, Samuel was vice-president, Charles was secretary, and Nathan was treasurer. Miller Brothers became the first furniture company in the area to deliver by truck in 1911.[183] Nathan Miller

The children of Rachel and Herman Feinberg (William, Henry, Isaac, Rosa, and Samuel) c. 1905. (Jewish Historical Society of Delaware.)

married Anna Schultz in 1906 and they had four children, Howard, Richard, Rosalie, and Seymour.

Louis Jacoby, a native of Hungary, came to Wilmington shortly after the turn of the century, about a decade after he had arrived in the United States. He opened a small store with four employees at 224 Market Street in 1902. Business grew rapidly and Jacoby expanded the store to 226 Market Street. After a fire destroyed the entire store, he rebuilt it with a white marble front and handsome plate glass front windows.[184] By 1910 Jacoby's had become a department store with a complete line of all goods, specializing in women's apparel. Jacoby's was known for its fair treatment of all customers. Patrons were always treated with the greatest courtesy and the salespeople were among the most obliging in the city. The firm recognized no favorites, so there was one price for all customers. Louis and his wife Minnie had six children—Sashe, Beatrice, Frances, Harry, Arthur, and Sidney—between 1903 and 1910.

Samuel Greenbaum, born in Austria-Hungary, had come to the United States in the 1880s. He and his wife Sarah arrived in Wilmington by 1898, when their daughter Marion was born.[185] In 1899 Samuel and his wife Sarah ran a women's and men's furnishings store on lower Market Street, and they lived above the store. By 1907 the store was successful enough that the family, which now included sons Joseph and Herman, lived at 1216 Market Street. In 1910 Greenbaum's was a department store that occupied 302–304 Market Street. Greenbaum was successful by remembering the needs of his clientele. In 1910 he advertised: "Of course you know that Easter comes on the 27th of March this year—that is only three weeks away—and means no time to lose. So we have arranged this timely sale."[186] By 1918 the family was successful enough to move to The Boulevard, a prestigious avenue across the Brandywine River.

In the first decade of the 1900s, at least forty Jewish immigrants opened grocery stores.[187] Usually they were small stores that served the tastes of the people in the neighborhood. Harry Cohen, who was a very religious man, opened a grocery store, but he sold no Jewish food in his store: he stocked what the people in his neighborhood wanted.[188] For Jewish food—rye bread, delicatessen, and bagels—people went to Second Street to the Jewish butchers and delicatessen.[189] Wives played a large role in the grocery stores. Benjamin Fineman and his wife Bertha ran a grocery store at 203 West Second Street, next door to their home. Ben, who also worked in the morocco factory, would be up at 6 A.M. and walk to Sixth and King Streets to the wholesalers. He would carry baskets of food back and set up the shop that Bertha ran while he was at the factory.[190] The Finemans did an especially good business on Sundays when many other stores were closed. People considered the grocery store a step up from labor work because at least they were their own bosses. The Jew preferred a situation where his own merit received objective confirmation, and he was not dependent on the goodwill or personal reaction of someone who might happen not to like Jews.[191] Seeking the security that had eluded them in Europe, Russian Jews placed great emphasis on self-employment and independence.[192]

Some immigrants were successful in new areas. Just after the turn of the century, Charles K. Breuer, a native of Hungary, came to Wilmington and opened a cigar factory and store at 724 Market Street.[193] Alexander Hirschman became the manager of the Palace Motion Picture Theatre, the city's first movie theater for black citizens.[194] Hirschman promised by showing the latest and most attractive pictures, his theater would be as fine as any in the city. Daniel S. Laub, a native of Austria, opened the Boston Cloak Store around 1905, after he left New York to get out of the sweatshops. His brother opened a similar store in New Jersey.[195] Solomon Frankfurt, who had been apprenticed as a bookbinder in Yelisavegrad, Russia, fled Russia around 1890 to avoid being drafted and went to New York, where he learned the painting and paperhanging trade by watching others. Shortly after the turn of the century he came to Wilmington and established himself as a paperhanger.[196]

The established Jewish merchants Sam Slessinger, Max Ephraim, David Snellenburg, Reuben Wolters, Louis and Minnie Harris, Sam Harris, and Charles, William, and Louis Topkis enjoyed continued success. In 1904, Louis Topkis became a full partner of Slessinger in the Delaware Notion House. He also took an interest in manufacturing and in 1909 organized the Delmarva Manufacturing Company in Smyrna.[197] William and Charles Topkis continued to run R. Topkis and Company, expanding it so that in 1906 it was the only store in the city to run from Market through to King Street.[198] William Topkis was elected to the board of the Delaware Trust Company in 1911.[199]

Not all Jewish immigrants were self-employed. Wilmington's growing industries continued to provide jobs for many laborers. Morris Markovitz, who was born in Romania in 1882, had been apprenticed to a cabinetmaker when he was about seven years old and had worked for eight or nine years before emigrating to the United States. After living in New York and Philadelphia, Morris and his wife Rose came to Wilmington in 1905 because "we had to go where the work was."[200] As a skilled cabinet worker, Markovitz

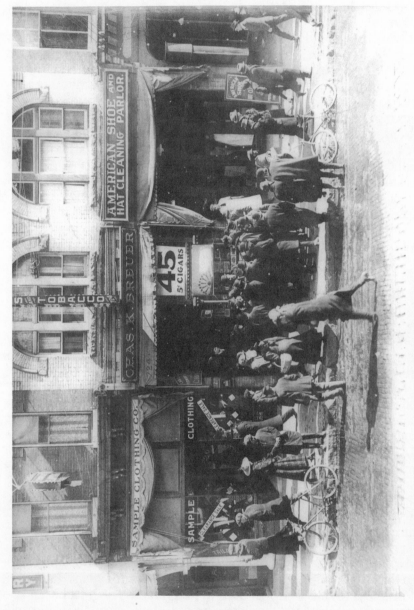

Charles Breuer Cigar Store. (Jewish Historical Society of Delaware.)

found work at both the Pullman Company and the Pennsylvania Railroad.

Jacob Statnekoo, a carpenter and cabinetmaker with "golden hands," could do fine inlay work.[201] After he came to Wilmington from Russia, he found work at both the Pullman Company and the Pennsylvania Railroad. Isaac Milkin was an upholsterer for the Pullman Company; Isaac Sosnoe was a cabinetmaker for Pullman.[202] Most likely some of the other new Jewish immigrants who listed their occupations as laborer also worked for the Pennsylvania Railroad or the Pullman Company.

The morocco business in Wilmington (as well as the United States) expanded tremendously. In 1900, Wilmington had twenty companies involved in the manufacture of glazed kid by tanning.[203] By 1906, hides and skins were the single largest item imported by the United States, and goods manufactured in leather were third in the list of exports. All parts of the world had boots, shoes, and other leather goods made in the United States.[204] At least thirty Jewish immigrants who arrived in the first decade of the twentieth century found their first jobs in the morocco plants. Approximately two-thirds of them only stayed in Wilmington a short time.[205] Of the eleven men who stayed in Wilmington for more than a decade, five men (Bernard Glick, Nathan Hambug, Isidore Redloss, Jacob Schiffer, and Joseph Fried) continued to list morocco worker as their occupation. Charles Stern was a grocer and a powdermaker before returning to morocco work in 1920. Harry Cohen, Harry Evans, and Samuel Berlin opened grocery stores. Louis Briefman peddled tinware. Whether the latter four left the morocco business or had to run stores on the side to supplement income cannot be ascertained, but these newer immigrants followed the same pattern as the morocco workers who had begun in the 1890s.

Richard Patzowsky and David L. Levy achieved great success in the morocco business. Within a year of his retirement from F. Blumenthal and Company in 1900, Richard Patzowsky began construction on his own new morocco company, the New Castle Leather Company, at Eleventh and Poplar Streets.[206] His years of experience with the greatest leather companies in the world enabled him to build the most complete and conveniently arranged leather factory in the world, capable of turning out 12,000 large skins a day.[207] The new company was incorporated with capital of $500,000. Patzowsky was president and had two partners from New York.[208] By 1904 Charles Jellinek, who had been foreman of F. Blumenthal's under Patzowsky, was the foreman of New Castle Leather. With Patzowsky as president, the firm became one of the best glazed-leather manufacturers in the world.[209] The company, which produced a perfect leather, was so successful that by 1909 the company had doubled its equipment and expanded to occupy three city blocks in Wilmington.[210] Its products reached almost every country on the globe. More than one thousand Wilmington citizens were employed by New Castle Leather, and they benefited both mentally and financially.

David L. Levy, who had begun working at F. Blumenthal and Company in 1898, had also risen to a management position. By 1905, he was the secretary and treasurer as well as foreman of a new business called United Leather Company.[211] In 1908, Morris Rees, a Jew who had been a partner of J. Harry Gordon in the piano business, was the president of United Leather, and Levy was still secretary-treasurer.[212]

Other established Jewish immigrants achieved new heights. By September 1901 Moses Weil, an optician, was a finalist for the office of justice of peace. Weil circulated a letter among his German friends asking them to verify that he had been born in the state of Hessen, Germany, because some people intimated that Weil was not German.[213] In 1901 Governor Hunn appointed him magistrate, a government official with jurisdiction in civil matters up to $500 and in minor criminal matters.[214] The Moses Montefiore Society gave an elaborate complimentary dinner to Moses Weil in honor of his becoming a magistrate in February 1902. Max Ephraim, Charles Jellinek, Louis Finger, Morris Levy, J. Harry Gordon, and Moses Levy were in charge of the dinner, which attracted one hundred people.[215] Weil, a "true gentleman of the old school" was one of the most popular magistrates ever; he practiced the Golden Rule and spirit of fair play. He preferred friendship to riches. If service to his fellow man interfered with his business interests, it was the latter that suffered.[216] After his four-year term, Weil went into the insurance business, but he was known for the rest of his long life as Squire Weil. Weil was elected president of the local branch of B'nai B'rith in July 1905.[217]

In the early years of this century, Barnet Gluckman struggled to make a living, earning $16 a week as a cigar maker and a few more dollars a week as a teacher at the Adas Kodesch synagogue and as secretary of Adas Kodesch.[218] He also wrote for newspapers and magazines. At the request of Louis Topkis, Gluckman became involved in Republican politics.[219] His "zeal and devotion" were rewarded in 1909, when a new city magistrate was needed. Louis Topkis, with the support of the Jewish community, put forth Gluckman's name, and Governor Simeon Pennewill appointed him magistrate. "Our lives changed dramatically," recalls Leslie Gluckman. "Dad never again rolled a cigar."[220] He was reappointed continually by every governor until his death in 1934, during his seventh term.[221] His decisions in all cases that came before him were based on the facts, and in every case justice was handed down impartially. His integrity and ability to grasp essential facts resulted in decisions that had never, as far as known, been reversed.[222]

By 1902 Dr. Albert Robin was teaching pathology and bacteriology at Temple University in Philadelphia, in addition to his job at Delaware College's laboratory in Newark. The following year he became Wilmington's city bacteriologist.[223] Dr. Robin's first years in Delaware were tumultuous. Delaware's death rate from tuberculosis, typhoid fever, and malaria was the highest in the country, and Robin believed it was caused by the ignorance of the doctors and the unsanitary conditions of the drinking water.[224] He spoke out and wrote newspaper articles about the bacteria in Delaware's drinking water and the need for a sand filtration plant to purify water.

Many people thought it was an extravagance to engage Dr. Robin, the state chemist, as a bacteriologist, and wrote editorials denouncing Robin. "Why don't that Rooshian go back to where he came from instead of causing us so much trouble."[225] When Robin was called to defend himself in front of the city council, the president rose, held up a glass of clear, sparkling water and said, "Young man, see here; what was good enough for our forefathers to drink should certainly now be good enough for us, especially as we have just spent a million dollars on the installation of the clarification plant."[226] Dr. Robin cleverly answered, "Pity the dead cannot arise to come here and give their testimony," causing an outburst of laughter that offset the antagonism against him. With the assistance of Irénée duPont and Peter Ford, Robin was able to convince the city to build a sand filtration plant.

Although he was busy with public issues, Dr. Robin continued to see private patients. Many of his patients, both rich and poor, suffered from tuberculosis.[227] For the former he could prescribe sunshine, fresh air, and nourishing food. But for the latter, the problem was much more involved. Dr. Robin realized that a sanatorium was indispensable, and he convinced Emily P. Bissell to help him.

When the Robin family moved permanently to Wilmington in April 1903, they had no friends. The fact that they were known to be Jews and unaffiliated with either of the two synagogues made their isolation even worse.[228] Unlike Newark, where the Robins were connected with Delaware College (which later became the University of Delaware) and received the usual courtesy calls from faculty members, in Wilmington the neighbors kept shy of them. Eva Robin speculated that people probably stayed away from her family because at the time Dr. Robin's name was much maligned in the newspapers for having revealed that the water supply was still the cause of the high death rate from typhoid fever. Her other explanation of why the family was ignored demonstrates clearly the differences among the Jewish population.

> The Jews in the community may not have known of our existence and even if they had, they would certainly not have called on us socially as they were of a lowly class, living in the lower section of the city down near the river and eking out a meager livelihood—the women for the most part running small stores while their men worked at trades or in the Pullman shops. Often I would wend my way afoot to the Jewish district to buy such items as cottage cheese, sour cream, pumpernickel, bagels for which we both yearned but could not get in our neighborhood grocery stores.[229]

Many of the Jewish youth continued past grade school for the first time, even though almost all of them had to work after school or on the weekends.[230] The young native-born Jews who had remained in school began to achieve new heights. Aaron Finger, son of Louis and Esther, left school after tenth grade to work as a runner at the DuPont Company.[231] At the same time, he completed a two-year course at Goldey College. In 1908, before law degrees were required for the practice of law, eighteen-year-old Aaron Finger was hired as a legal secretary by Robert H. Richards, who agreed to let young Aaron study law with him.[232] In 1912, after passing examinations at the University of Delaware to qualify for the bar exam, he passed the bar and became the first Delaware-born Jewish lawyer.[233] Joseph Barsky, son of Rosa and Nathan, graduated from Wilmington High School in 1910 and from Jefferson Medical School in 1914. He became the first Delaware-born Jewish doctor.[234] Barsky's classmate Louis Gluckman, son of Fannie and Barnet, went to Goldey College and graduated from the University of Pennsylvania Dental School in 1915, becoming the first Delaware-born Jewish dentist.[235]

Like their brethren in New York and other major cities, Wilmington's Jewish immigrants placed great emphasis on education, which was not only intrinsically valuable but was seen as a key to economic and social success.[236] Jewish students in New York City graduated from high school at a higher rate than other immigrant groups and were taught to exceed their parents' achievements.[237] In contrast, Italian immigrants in New York City were encouraged to leave school in order to assist their families in blue-collar jobs.[238]

During the first decade of the new century, the city of Wilmington prospered and its Jews found employment in a wide variety of endeavors. The center of their business world, shared by other immigrant groups, was downtown Wilmington on Front, Second, King, and Market streets. On Saturday nights, King and Market streets were packed with shoppers and pedestrians.[239] Butchers, hucksters, and fruit dealers had their hands full and made special efforts to help those who preferred to push through the throngs than to wait until Sunday. Many shopped on Saturday night because they could buy cheaper than in the day; others because they were unable to go in the daytime. It was a good-natured crowd and nobody minded if he got pushed or jostled about.[240] All languages, ancient and modern, were heard.[241] Several religious sects preached on the corners.[242] Wilmington was a vibrant, thriving city. Everyone who was willing to work could find a job.

RELIGIOUS RIVALRY: REFORM AND ORTHODOX

After nearly a decade without a formal presence in Wilmington, the Reform Jews became active again. They invited everyone interested in organizing a modern Hebrew congregation to attend a meeting at the YMHA rooms, Fourth and Shipley, on May 27, 1906.[243] Thirty-three men attended the meeting.[244] Seven of them— Nathan Levy, George Baeringer, Morris Levy, Reuben Wolters, Samuel Harris, Samuel Slessinger, and Max Ephraim—had been part of the Reform synagogue Ohabe Shalom in 1895. Nathan Lieberman had died a few months earlier in February 1906, but his son-in-law Albert Rothschild was in attendance. Many of those who attended the meeting had arrived in Wilmington between 1895 and 1906. Their presence gave the Reform-minded Jews the increased numbers needed to organize a synagogue. Nineteen men, more than half of those attending the meeting, were members of Adas Kodesch.[245] None were members of Chesed Shel Emeth.

Although the leaders of the 1895 synagogue participated in the formation of the Temple of Truth, only two, Morris Levy and Nathan Levy, served on the board of directors. Instead, newer community members—those who had not been in Wilmington in 1895 or who had arrived shortly before 1895—made up most of the board, which included Samuel Greenbaum, Abe Bachrach, Nathan Levy, J. Harry Gordon, David L. Levy, Dr. Michael Ostro, Jacob Malis,

Louis Finger, Hyman Kanofsky, Morris K. Blumberg, Dr. Sigmund Werner, and Morris Levy.[246] All of the board members except Nathan Levy and Jacob Malis were also members of Adas Kodesch. Some may have worshipped at Adas Kodesch; others most likely maintained their membership in Adas Kodesch because they wanted to support all Jewish synagogues. As Kate Pizor, sister of Reuben Wolters, explained: "Rube was a member of Adas Kodesch until they built Temple of Truth, but it made no difference to him. He went to all the places where he could worship."[247]

Like their predecessors in 1895, the board members of Temple of Truth represented many different nationalities. J. Harry Gordon and Abe Bachrach were born in the United States; Sam Greenbaum and Sigmund Werner were from Austria; Morris Blumberg and Nathan Levy were from Germany; David Levy was from Hungary; and Louis Finger, Hyman Kanofsky, Morris Levy, and Michael Ostro were from Russia.[248] All had been in the United States for a least a decade, which was a comparatively long time, and had become familiar with life in America. Those who had been in the country longer tended toward Reform. Once again, the *Sunday Star* referred to the Temple of Truth as a congregation of well-known German Israelites even though the members were from a variety of countries.[249] The old qualifier, that "some of Wilmington's best known business men are among its leaders," reminds us that the newspaper continued to associate "German" with success and length of time here.

Most of the board members were self-employed entrepreneurs. Michael Ostro and Sigmund Werner were doctors, and eight men were in business. Blumberg, Greenbaum, and Malis had dry goods stores; Bachrach and Morris Levy sold shoes; J. Harry Gordon was president of Gordon, Rees and Hirsch, which sold pianos and jewelry; Nathan Levy and Hyman Kanofsky were tailors; David L. Levy was in management at United Leather Company; Louis Finger was a letter carrier.[250] A few months after its formation, the *Sunday Star* referred to some of the members as "men who stand high in the business community of this city."[251] The synagogue was incorporated on July 30, 1906.[252]

Perhaps there had not been a profound difference in religiosity between Chesed Shel Emeth and Adas Kodesch, but the service at the new "Americanized Temple of Truth" was different. On Rosh Hashanah 1906, the entire service was done in English and there was nothing in it that could not readily be understood by all."[253] The services, which were held on the third floor of Max Ephraim's clothing store at 504 Market Street, lasted about one hour the first night, and continued in the morning until midday and at night for an hour. Services were also held the second day.[254] Rabbi Jacob Korn, who had lead the Reform synagogue in 1895, returned to Wilmington to serve as the first rabbi.

By November 1906 temple leaders announced their intention to build a "church of their own" in the near future; many friends of the movement had already promised substantial support in raising funds.[255] In January 1907, Temple of Truth leaders were looking for a suitable site on which to build a synagogue and a school.[256] The Reform leaders also announced that the "new organization would teach in English, and the Hebrew language would be eliminated."[257]

In the spring of 1907, the Temple of Truth hired Rabbi Isaac Aaron Rubenstein, who had graduated from Hebrew Union College in 1884, for the following year.[258] Rabbi Rubenstein immediately made his presence felt in the broader community by writing a long letter against prohibition that was reprinted in the *Sunday Star*. According to the rabbi, the remedy for excessive drinking was not prohibition but education. Men had to be free to make the choice and with the correct moral education, they would make the right choice. In favor of freedom, Rubenstein wrote: "in this great liberty-loving country, every man should have an opinion of his own. . . . [H]e cannot afford to be of the non committal type. Give me fish or meat, but not an eel, it is too slippery."[259]

In the spring of 1906, when the Temple of Truth was formed, the Orthodox Adas Kodesch appointed Louis Topkis as chairman of a building committee to collect money for a new building, which would cost about $15,000 (an amount soon increased to $35,000).[260] Members of Adas Kodesch felt that the synagogue was not big enough to accommodate all the people who wanted to worship.[261] Undoubtedly they were hoping to attract members from Chesed Shel Emeth and perhaps to prevent the Temple of Truth from building a synagogue. Just as they had competed for support at the same time a decade earlier, both the Reform and Orthodox synagogues raised money and built new synagogues between 1906 and 1908.

In April 1907, even before the Temple of Truth had selected a site, the contract for the Orthodox synagogue was awarded to C. H. Tindall and Sons, and work on the new synagogue began.[262] The old Zion Lutheran Church was razed in May 1907 in order to make room for the new synagogue.[263] The estimated cost of the new synagogue was $30,000, which was a tremendous amount for these immigrants, as the *Sunday Star* explained:

The members are mostly people of moderate means and they expect to have hard work securing the necessary funds. Therefore they will appeal to Jewish brethren who belong to other congregations as it is believed all members of the faith will take pride in the new building. Many Christians have also expressed desire to help and their contributions are welcome.[264]

For more than a year while the new Adas Kodesch was under construction, synagogue leaders raised funds. On June 16, 1907, when the foundation was poured, the building committee arranged a foundation-laying and brick-selling auction that raised $600.[265] Rabbi Rezits and Rabbi B. L. Levinthal of Philadelphia, chief Orthodox rabbi of the district, both spoke in Hebrew.[266] Rabbi Levinthal expressed his hope that with the erection of this magnificent synagogue, the people would begin to enlarge their moral and religious standing. He said the house would be open to all whether native or foreign.[267]

Two months later on August 18, 1907, the cornerstone laying for Adas Kodesch was a grand occasion witnessed by thousands of people.[268] Members of several Jewish organizations, including the Montefiore Mutual Beneficial Society, Wilmington Lodge B'nai B'rith, Hevrah Chesed Shel Emeth, Ladies' Bichor Cholem Society, YMHA, and the Hebrew Charity Association, marched from Third and Market Streets to the new site at Sixth and French, where the contractors had boarded over the basement and laid out a platform with seats. Four rabbis—Rabbi Rezits of Adas Kodesch, Rabbi Kosut, Rabbi Nathan Brenner of Philadelphia, who spoke in "the Jewish language," and Rabbi Isidore Rosenthal of Lancaster, who spoke in English—participated in the ceremonies.[269] Proclaiming the moment as "the happiest moment of my life," Louis Topkis explained that when the building committee began in June 1906, it did not have one penny. "Tomorrow we must pay $2500 for the first payment and we have it, plus $800." He reminded those assembled that additional funds were still needed.

An auction of articles to be placed in the cornerstone, as well as the tools used in the ceremony, raised significant dollars for the building fund. Daniel Leshem paid $60 for the privilege of laying the mortar, and numerous individuals paid to place the history of their organizations in the copper box that was deposited in the cornerstone.[270] Demonstrating an end of the friction that had divided them, Chesed Shel Emeth presented a hammer, trowel, and silver box to Adas Kodesch. Morris Ezrailson, M. Goldberg, and Joseph Lundy of Chesed Shel Emeth were on the committee.[271]

Laying of the foundation of the Adas Kodesch Synagogue, 1907. (Jewish Historical Society of Delaware.)

Rabbi Rosenthal, a Reform rabbi, gave the main speech of the afternoon. Undoubtedly a Reform rabbi was chosen to make Wilmington's Reform Jews feel comfortable at Adas Kodesch, so they would not build a separate synagogue. Rosenthal began by emphasizing that all Jews were one.

> It is true that in our religious life we have two classes, the Reformed and the Orthodox. I represent the Reformed, you the Orthodox, but after all there is only one Judaism, and the God of that faith has protected you in past ages and protects you today under the stars and stripes of the glorious republic. . . . There is only one kind of Jew in the world, and he is the honest Jew.[272]

Rosenthal urged the immigrants to embrace America and to become good Americans.

> Cherish the name of Roosevelt, be true Americans; it is a country worth your love and loyalty. A bad Jew is a bad American. Let us all be good Americans.[273]

During 1907 and 1908, as work on Adas Kodesch progressed, the committee struggled to raise funds. Louis Topkis initiated a city-wide appeal for funds from prominent business and professional men, many of them Christians.[274] His letter sent in November 1907 had a liberal response. Henry A. duPont, T. Coleman duPont, George Capelle, John R. Marr and Company, and Charles Warner Company were among those who contributed.[275] However, Adas Kodesch's leaders had competition from the new Temple of Truth.

In October 1907, leaders of the Reform Temple of Truth purchased a lot on Washington Street north of Ninth. Nathan Levy lent the congregation $425 to complete the payment of the purchase price.[276] Temple of Truth leaders raised more than $1000 at a ball held at the New Century Club in January 1908.[277] "Nearly all of the young Jewish folks assisted in the affair."[278] The generous contributions of Richard Patzowsky and David L. Levy, both morocco manufacturers, made it possible to erect a building, which cost between $10,000 and 12,000.[279] By April 1908, architectural plans by Jacob Naschold of Philadelphia were finalized and plans had been sent to the contractors.

In May 1908, the newspaper announced that Adas Kodesch would be "entirely finished" by June 1, but funds were still needed.[280] Nathan Miller was chairman of a fundraising bazaar, which sold fine and useful goods donated by many wholesale houses and raised $1000.

On Sunday, May 17, 1908, members of the Temple of Truth held a cornerstone-laying ceremony.[281] Among the dignitaries who gave addresses at the ceremony were Judge George Gray, Chief Justice Charles B. Lore, and Mayor Horace Wilson. Rabbi Joseph Krauskopf of Philadelphia, one of the most distinguished Reform rabbis in the country, and Rabbi Isaac Rubenstein also spoke. About $750 were raised at the ceremony and there were substantial promises to ensure finishing the building.[282] Unlike their brethren at Adas Kodesch, the members of Temple of Truth seemed to raise the money easily. They also built a more modest synagogue for about one third of the cost of Adas Kodesch.

Just three and a half months after the ground breaking, on August 30, 1908, the Temple of Truth was dedicated. Rabbis Rubenstein and Krauskopf led the parade to the new building, Nathan Levy and Ignatz Roth carried the Torahs, and Herman Greenbaum, son of the temple's president Samuel Greenbaum, accompanied by six children, carried the Bible.[283] "Among those in the congregation were a large number of members of other churches and also several pastors of local Methodist churches, and all seemed to be equally proud with the prominent Hebrews of the city to be present on such a pleasant occasion."

In a magnificent dedicatory address, which was praised by a

Temple of Truth, c. 1908. (Jewish Historical Society of Delaware.)

prominent Methodist minister as one of the finest he had ever heard, Rabbi Krauskopf urged the congregants to fight the tide of unbelief so pervasive in the society by having faith in God and continuing their work with faith. "Is your work completed or has it not rather just commenced?" the rabbi asked. He advised the congregants that

> at the present age, the way this unbelief is rolling into our modern society, it is not the size or cost of churches that is needed but the spirit; the religious spirit we need, much more than the religious buildings. In no age have there been more churches and better equipped ones and never a time society has had so little of religious spirit as the present day.[284]

Claiming that people of the present day knew more of politics than of religion and were more in fear of political bosses than of God, the rabbi urged the congregants to instill faith in the members.[285]

Albert Rothschild, chairman of the building committee, presented the building to temple president Samuel Greenbaum. Rothschild's comments gave good insight into the tolerance of Reform Judaism and its emphasis on ethical matters.

> One day many ships left a certain harbour, all bound for the same port. Each ship sailed a somewhat different course and each skipper thought his direction the only and true one. In the end all arrived at their destination in safety bringing the solution as to which had been the real or true course no nearer. . . . This is the case with all religions, we should all live a clean and upright life and ever steer a straight course.[286]

In receiving the building, an exultant Samuel Greenbaum recalled the many obstacles the congregants had overcome and emphasized the founders' desire to establish a religious school where children could receive good moral and religious instruction.[287] Education, which would guarantee the continuation of Judaism, was still primary in the minds of all Jews. Rabbi Rubenstein, David L. Levy, Abe Bachrach, and Morris Levy were among those who participated in the ceremony.[288]

The Temple of Truth was built in several styles, with the Moorish predominating. The front was of Avondale marble, the interior woodwork was of natural cypress.[289] The walls were frescoed. The sanctuary could hold 225 people downstairs and 75 more in the gallery. A unique reading desk had been made by Anton Zelachoski, who worked for David Levy. The carving on the right was of Moses with the ten commandments; on the left, Aaron in his priestly robes.[290] Electricity was installed throughout the building. In September 1908 the *American Israelite* announced that the Temple of

Truth had dedicated the first Jewish house of worship to be erected in Wilmington.[291]

Three weeks later the Adas Kodesch dedicated its new synagogue. The $35,000 cost of the construction made it one of the most valuable church properties in the city.[292] Built in the Moscow style of architecture, with three domes and nine stained glass windows, the synagogue was one of the most artistic religious edifices in Wilmington. The ark, one of the largest in the country, was of Santo Domingo mahogany. The synagogue had eighty-three-foot frontage on Sixth Street and fifty-three-foot frontage on French Street.

The dedication of Adas Kodesch began with a parade of members, led by Neef's Coronet Band, from the temporary quarters on Third and Market Streets to the new synagogue at Sixth and French. A large crowd, including many persons who were not members of the congregation, was waiting. After the opening prayer by Rabbi

Adas Kodesch Synagogue. (Jewish Historical Society of Delaware.)

Rezits, Louis Topkis, chairman of the building committee, auctioned off the privileges of participating in the ceremony. Calling it the "happiest day in the history of the congregation," Topkis recounted the work of the building committee and bestowed great praise on the members of the congregation who by their faithful service and cooperation had made the completion of the synagogue an assured fact. While rejoicing in the success, he reminded those present that funds were still needed to pay off the mortgage. Recognizing that one of the major purposes of a new synagogue was to teach the children to be Jews and to know what Judaism means, Topkis explained:

> Now we have an opportunity to start a daily and Sunday Hebrew school. This must be done at once. Not until you have succeeded to start and maintain a Sunday and daily school can you say that you have done your duty to yourself and to your children.[293]

As the synagogue leaders had hoped all Jews did come together to ensure the success of the synagogue. About 320 individuals subscribed to the Adas Kodesch campaign. Only three individuals contributed more than $200. Two of them, Samuel Slessinger and David L. Levy, were leaders of the new Reform Temple of Truth, and Louis Topkis was the third.[294] Morris Levy, Jacob Malis, Moses Fine, Max Ephraim, and Dr. Michael Ostro were among the other members of Temple of Truth who made contributions to Adas Kodesch. Dr. Michael Ostro was on the board of directors of the Temple of Truth, but he took care of the children at the Adas Kodesch school and was credited with being one of the forces behind the new Adas Kodesch building because he had suggested that conditions at the school were not up to modern sanitary conditions.[295] Some of the founders of Chesed Shel Emeth, notably Frank Nisenbaum, Morris Ezrailson, and Abe Stromwasser subscribed to the campaign for Adas Kodesch.[296]

The Jews did not agree on the right way to practice their religion, but more importantly, like their predecessors, they chose to remain Jewish in the New World. Focusing on the goal of creating Jewish life in America, the Jews were tolerant and supportive of those who practiced Judaism differently than their preferred way.

A Magnificent Citizenship

After building two synagogues, assisting poverty-stricken newcomers to settle in Wilmington, sending money to Russia and Pal-

Dedication of the shacks at Hope Farm, 1909. (Jewish Historical Society of Delaware.)

estine and contributing to general community causes through the Hebrew Charity Association, the Jews might have felt overburdened. But their belief in *tikkun olam*, repairing the world or making the world a more perfect place, meant they wanted to be full partners in the American world. In May 1909, the Hebrew Charity Association became the first private association to play a major role in fighting tuberculosis. Just months after Adas Kodesch and the Temple of Truth were completed, the Jews of Wilmington decided to donate a small facility to house patients to the new state sanatorium at Hope Farm on Newport Gap Pike, about seven miles southeast of Wilmington.[297]

The Hebrew Charity Association formed a special committee with Louis Topkis as chairman, to consider plans for the facility, which was called a shack. At a public meeting on May 30, 1909, Louis Topkis and other members of his committee, J. Harry Gordon, Hyman Kanofsky, Nathan Barsky, and Louis Hillersohn, recommended that instead of building a small shack, costing $200–300, the association should build a larger facility that would be a credit to the organization and of much use to the sanatorium.[298] The proposed building would house twelve patients but could be easily expanded to forty. The total cost of the shack would be about $1,250, and Topkis reported that subscriptions for nearly half were already in hand. "The time to do a thing is now," Mr. Topkis declared. "We want to begin work in ten days, finish the building within a month, and we need the money to make payments to the contractors."

Emily Bissell, who was nationally renowned as the founder of the Christmas Seals to fight tuberculosis, was serving as president of the Anti-Tuberculosis Society. Miss Bissell lauded the Jews for their noble charity work and expressed the hope that other associations in the city and the state would follow the noble example of the Hebrew citizens.[299] She emphasized the importance of the Jewish community donating a shack by explaining that the $15,000 the state had appropriated to the sanatorium could only be used for caring for patients, not for building new facilities. The facility the Jews intended to build would be the best and most up-to-date the society ever had. Following Miss Bissell, Dr. Michael Ostro gave an instructive lecture on tuberculosis, and Dr. Albert Robin urged people to support charity for consumptives because it was a practical charity.

The next day the *Morning News* carried an editorial praising the Jews.

The generosity of the Hebrew association is one that might well be imitated by other organizations and by individuals. The practical character of the gift to the public is one that ought to appeal to everybody. There are no restrictions what ever to to placed upon the use of this new building, and our Hebrew citizens are entitled to the heartiest applause for their thoughtfulness. They have done something that is to stand for years as an evidence of their interest in the public welfare. They have revealed that they are anxious to help the sick to recover, and they have paved the way for the accomplishment of much that is worth while.[300]

The editorial continued with general praise of the Hebrew Charity Association, whose members were broad-minded and thoughtful and did not confine their charitable contributions to narrow limits. In conclusion, "this city is fortunate in having in active operation, such a body of generous and thoughtful men and women."

Four months later, on October 10, 1909, the Hebrew Charity Association's shack and a second shack donated by Nathan Barsky in the name of the great Hebrew philanthropist Baron de Hirsch were dedicated. Among the five hundred people who attended the dedication were Governor Simeon S. Pennewill, Judge Daniel Hastings, General James H. Wilson, Senator William Saulsbury, and Emily Bissell.[301]

In presenting the Hebrew Charity Association's shack, Louis Topkis expressed the hope that the effort of the Jews would bring to the attention of all people, "the absolute necessity for prompt contributions to stop the spread of the great white plague."[302] Topkis spoke about the wish of himself and the community as well as every Hebrew in Wilmington. In spite of the differences among them, the Jews had united for the purpose of helping their American community and were seen as one group by them.

In accepting the building, Governor Simeon S. Pennewill made a laudatory speech, praising the motivation of all the Jews in the state.

We are gathered here today to witness a manifestation of true generosity—an act in which the sordid and selfish elements of human nature have no part, but one in which there is a burning love for humanity. . . . [T]he state of Delaware commends its Hebrew citizens for the noble impulse that actuated the humane feeling that inspired them, the spirit of genuine philanthropy that moved them to make the gift. The people of the State should not forget this act of benevolence.[303]

The Governor expanded his remarks to include praise of all the Jews in the country.

Nor should the country be unmindful of its obligation to the Jew. It was his munificence that helped to equip the caravels of the world seeking Columbus. We find him in New York only forty years after the arrival of the Dutch; in Massachusetts only thirty years later than the Pilgrim Father, helping to lay the foundation of the Republic. We find him in the war of Independence. . . .[304]

The first thirty years of Jewish community life in Wilmington ended in a remarkable fashion. Several prominent Jews sat on a podium with Delaware's dignitaries to receive praise for their communal efforts. Their community, a tiny group of people recently arrived in Wilmington, had managed to transplant themselves to a new land, create a network of synagogues and organizations to meet their needs, and juggle their responsibilities as Jews and Americans. In thirty years, the Jews of Wilmington had made themselves not only acceptable but exemplary. The message seemed clear: in Wilmington, one did not have to choose between being American and being Jewish: one could be both.

6

A Thriving Community—
The 1910s

DURING THE 1920S, PARTICULARLY DURING WORLD WAR I, WILMING-
ton's industries and favorable business conditions brought unprecedented prosperity to the city. The population increased by 26
percent to 110,168 in 1920, and the Jewish population grew to
more than 3.5 percent of the total population.[1] In spite of the fact
that 90 percent of the new Jewish immigrants were from Eastern
Europe and Russia, given the large number of American-born children, the Jewish population became 50 percent American-born.
While some Jews labored in the plants of wartime industries, others became doctors and lawyers. Despite the increased differences
among them, all the Jews continued to work together to assist
those in need.

While Wilmington's Jews succeeded in their work and in their
community standing, the growing national anti-immigration movement grew powerful enough to restrict immigration first through a
literacy test and then through limits in numbers of immigrants. In
Wilmington, which had a large demand for labor, anti-immigration
attitudes were not strong; neither was the anti-Semitism of the
South, so clearly demonstrated in the Leo Frank case.

Wilmington's Jews became part of the dominant culture by participating in Americanization activities, joining the armed forces in
World War I, and using their Jewish organizations to contribute to
the general welfare of the community. At the same time, they continued to attend synagogues and form organizations that preserved
their unique heritage. The Jews achieved an excellent balance between preserving their identity and participating fully in American
society. During the national War Relief Drives of 1917, 1918, and
1920, Wilmington was singled out as an exemplary city, a place
filled with the true American spirit of cooperation between groups.

169

INCREASED OPPORTUNITIES IN A PROSPEROUS CITY

In 1910 Wilmington was a prospering, "first-class" city filled with a spirit of cooperation.[2] With its large supply of skilled labor, Wilmington did not have as many unskilled factory workers as neighboring industrial cities; therefore, tension between laborers and manufacturers was not as intense as in those cities. However, given its proximity to Philadelphia and New York, labor issues in those cities had implications for Wilmington.

In New York City in November 1909, twenty thousand shirtwaist factory workers—girls in their teens and early twenties, nearly two-thirds of whom were Jewish—went on strike to protest sexual discrimination, class exploitation, and "small tyrannies."[3] After several months, the strike resulted in improved working conditions. The strike, which became known as the "uprising of the 20,000," caused an increase in union membership from one hundred to ten thousand, created a sense of pride, and began a mass movement. The shirtwaist strike spread to Philadelphia by December 1909 and lasted seven weeks.[4] When the strike ended, an editorial in the *Wilmington Morning News* expressed its pleasure that the workers had received better pay and shorter working hours and concluded that public sentiment had been with the strikers. Emphasizing the importance of peaceful arbitration, the editorial continued: "it would have been cheaper to have arbitrated the demands before the strike began."[5]

At the end of February, strike fever in Philadelphia spread to the mass transit system and the state militia was needed to quell the violence.[6] A committee of four transit workers from Philadelphia came to Wilmington on March 3, 1910 to solicit financial aid for fellow workmen in Philadelphia.[7] They came with a hand organ and tried to give a performance, but police stopped them. When they mounted one trolley car, Wilmingtonians treated them with scant courtesy and nearly threw them off. Clearly Wilmingtonians had different attitudes than Philadelphians. "Philadelphia workers finding that this city was much different from Philadelphia, left yesterday afternoon on the boat and returned to their own city."[8]

By March 5, between 40,000 and 110,000 Philadelphia union members had gone on a sympathy strike, and every National Guard unit in Pennsylvania was on alert.[9] Among the Philadelphia transit workers' demands was a pay raise from twenty-two cents to twenty-three-and-a-half cents an hour. Wilmington City Railway conductors and motormen earned eighteen-and-a-half cents an hour at the time.[10] When the Philadelphia strike began, Wilmington conductors and motormen were given a raise to twenty cents an hour. Then as the strike fever grew in Philadelphia and spread to New Jersey, Wilmington's transit workers were told they would earn twenty-three cents an hour. When the Philadelphia transit workers' strike finally ended, the unions had won almost every point, and workers were given a raise to twenty-three cents an hour with the promise of an increase to twenty-three-and-a-half cents the following June.[11] Without a strike, violence, or the loss of pay, Wilmington's transit workers had received a greater percentage increase. Wilmington's industrial leaders valued peace and fairness and worked for the advancement of moral, social, and business interests. The anti-strike mentality in Wilmington was also based on the belief that if a worker had a contract for wages and was getting paid, then he had an obligation to keep the contract.[12]

In the midst of violence and disruption in New York City and Philadelphia, Wilmington advertised its advantages in an elaborate, special edition of the *Morning News* called "The Prosperity Issue." Dedicated to showing the potential of Wilmington to those outside the area, the edition claimed Wilmington had an unsurpassed location as a shipping and manufacturing city with excellent water connections, three railways providing access to the north, south, and west, and a good supply of skilled labor.[13] The city had enjoyed wonderful industrial and commercial growth in the past twenty years and had room for one million people. Rich farming land, a good water system, a park system, and the absence of bank failures were other major advantages of Wilmington.

The prosperity issue included a section entitled "This is a Real City of Churches—Congregations of Many Faiths," for which J. Harry Gordon wrote a brief history of the Jewish community. In addition to Adas Kodesch Knesseth Israel with 200 members, Chesed Shel Emeth with 120 members, and the Temple of Truth with its daily and Sunday Hebrew school, the Jewish community had the Moses Montefiore Society, the Hebrew Charity Association, the YMHA, and the Ladies Bichor Cholem Society. Several prominent Jewish businesses, including Jacoby's Department Store, the Snellenburg Store, Miller Brothers Company, New Castle Leather, Greenbaum's, and Max Keil, Popular Wine and Liquor Merchant, advertised in the "Prosperity Edition."

Just as management and labor worked together peacefully, Wilmingtonians from different segments of the society cooperated in other areas. On March 11, 1910 an enthusiastic group of citizens assembled at the New Century Club to learn about the importance of assisting in the Americanization of immigrants. Mayor Spruance presided, and Reverend Cleland of the First United Presbyterian Church emphasized the importance of instructing the hundreds of incoming foreigners in the English language and American ways.[14]

In early February 1910, the Delaware Anti-Tuberculosis Society sponsored an exhibit for the purpose of educating the people most likely to contract the disease. Thousands of people, including many poorer people and young children, flocked to the exhibit each day for more than a week.[15] Dr. Albert Robin gave three talks during the exhibit. Rabbi Moses S. Abels of the Reform Temple of Truth, spoke to a large crowd about the role of "the church" in the fight against tuberculosis. Claiming that it was in the province and duty of the minister to help fight tuberculosis, Rabbi Abels said, "Consumption is the outcome of poverty. The Church must alert people to this. Too long has the church discussed matters of heaven, neglecting things on earth."[16]

As the decade progressed, confidence in Wilmington as a great city increased and business opportunities multiplied. In October 1912, Wilmington celebrated Old Home Week, a public relations extravaganza designed to advertise Wilmington's industrial advantages to the world.[17] Former residents were invited back to Wilmington to witness its progress. Officials claimed Wilmington was "unequaled as a manufacturing city by any of its size in the United States." Fifty-one percent of Wilmington's workers were engaged in manufacturing. Shipbuilding and carriage-making, which had dominated nineteenth-century Wilmington, had decreased, but there had been a rapid expansion in leather tanning and railroad car construction and maintenance.[18] Many of Wilmington's industrial leaders and citizens believed in the reforms embodied in the Progressive movement, including the need to educate immigrants, to improve living conditions, to improve urban life for Americans, to beautify cities, and to help all Americans fulfill their dreams of a decent life.[19] Nearly one-third of Wilmington's electorate voted for the Progressives in 1912.

Many of the Jewish families who arrived in Wilmington in this decade had lived in New York, New Jersey, or Pennsylvania before settling in Delaware.[20] Undoubtedly Wilmington's reputation as a prosperous city with good labor conditions and plenty of jobs influenced their decisions to move to the city. In coming to Wilmington, immigrants from New York left behind the overcrowded, dirty ghetto, but they also left behind New York's unique transitional culture, rich in Yiddish culture and Jewish communalism.[21] Other Jewish immigrants came to Wilmington directly from Europe, often because they had relatives in the city. More than 85 percent of the adult Jewish immigrants who came to Wilmington were from Eastern Europe.[22] Jewish immigrants who came directly to Wilmington, those who had lived in other states, as well as Jews born in America found jobs in Wilmington's industries.

Nineteen-year-old Morris Tomases, who left Romania in 1913 to avoid conscription in the army, came to Wilmington to his uncle Jacob Abramowitz, a shoemaker.[23] Although he was still young, Morris was a skilled cabinetmaker; in Romania he had been denied a secular education, but had been apprenticed at thirteen to a cabinetmaker. He found a job at the Pullman Company, which he liked very much because he could do his cabinet work.

There were enough Jews working at Pullman in 1913 to make Morris feel comfortable. Isaac Sosnoe, who had already been working at Pullman for several years, was a mentor to him. There was no overt anti-Semitism, nothing "like what he had experienced in Romania." In the Old Country, Morris had been brought up in an Orthodox fashion and taught by his grandfather, who was a very learned man. However, the Pullman Company required all employees to work a half-day on Saturdays so Morris worked, then came home, put on clean clothes and went to synagogue. In later years, when he was not required to work on Saturday, Morris observed the Sabbath strictly. Other early immigrants to Wilmington made similar compromises.

At the beginning, when Morris was the newest employee, he would be the first to lose his job, so he would go from Pullman to the other plants: American Car Company, Jackson and Sharp, Harlan and Hollingsworth, and Pusey and Jones. Often he would have to work as a common laborer. At first, Morris had difficulties because he couldn't speak English, but he began going to night school for Americanization classes. By 1927 Morris had become assistant foreman of his division at Pullman. Philip Simon and Jacob Statnekoo were among the other early Jewish immigrants at Pullman.[24] American-born Jews like Marty Flanzer and Esther Cohen also worked at Pullman during World War I.[25]

Sam and Nathan Goldstein, sons of Sarah and Hyman Goldstein, worked for the Pennsylvania Railroad. Like many children born to immigrant parents, Sam and Nathan had to leave school after eighth grade in order to help support the family, which included seven children.[26] In those days, young people were considered adults; they had responsibilities. The boys came home with their pay in envelopes and handed it to their mother who took what she needed for the family and gave them back a few dollars.[27] At the railroad, the Goldsteins worked their way up to the position of engineer—the driver, the top job. The Goldstein family was one of the first families on its block to have a telephone so that the railroad could call the boys to come to work instead of banging on the door as had been the previous custom.

Samuel Green, the third of Rebecca and Max Green's seven children, worked for the Baltimore and Ohio Railroad as a freight agent, a clerical position that was a "big deal" in those days.[28] Sam, who was born in New York, worked for the railroad instead of finishing high school because he had to help support the large family. Although there were not many Jews at the railroad, Samuel, who was outgoing and quick to make friends, was accepted.

Samuel Bell, Joseph Blumenfeld, Benjamin Braxman, George Cramer, Louis Cramer, Max Forman, David Groll, Oscar Groll, Alfred Hartman, and Samuel Sachs were among the other Jews who worked for the railroads.[29]

Joseph Cohen, a Jewish immigrant from Minsk, came to Wilmington with his eldest children, Samuel and Alice, in 1913 because he had connections in Wilmington. His cousin met the family with a horse and wagon at the Pennsylvania Railroad station. Joseph got a job at the leather factory and also peddled handkerchiefs and underwear. The following year he was able to bring his wife, Flora, and children Benjamin, Harry, Morris, Mary, and Bessie.[30]

The Industrial Removal Office in New York continued to work with the Hebrew Charity Association to bring Jews to Wilmington. At the end of 1910, the IRO asked Morris Levy to distribute folders about the work of the IRO to major factories and plants in the area.[31] One of the thirteen companies Levy contacted, the Malleable Iron Company, wrote to the IRO in August 1912 asking for common laborers and also for laborers who were bright and could learn moulding.[32] The company explained, "there are no labor troubles at our plant. Our foundry buildings are of the most modern type, light and nice and warm in winter."[33] At the request of the IRO, Morris Levy instructed his secretary J. Harry Gordon to investigate conditions and to interview some Jewish men employed at Malleable Iron. Gordon reported that the Malleable Iron people needed a lot of laborers and would take five men a week for some time. Laborers were paid sixteen-and-a-half cents an hour and worked fifty-five hours a week, and their principal work was shoveling dirt and helping moulders.[34] Laborers were expected to learn to be moulders, a job for which they could earn higher wages. The company needed strong, healthy men and preferred those who knew some English. No information about whether any Jewish workers went to Wilmington is extant, however, they probably did not. Two years earlier when the Diamond Steel Company had requested laborers for fifteen cents an hour, the IRO had responded, "we have no workers who would be satisfied with fifteen cents an hour. They would consider coming for $12 a week."[35]

World War I brought unprecedented prosperity to Wilmington, expanding not only its munitions industry but shipbuilding and general foundry production as well. As the biggest manufacturer of military powder in the United States, the DuPont Company became the major supplier of powder used by the Allies.[36] The Pennsylvania Railroad had never been busier; the number of persons engaged in leather industry nearly doubled.[37] Although the United States remained officially neutral and did not enter World War I until 1917, the country's industries were used in support of England and France from the beginning of the war.[38]

By the end of 1915, between two and three hundred Jewish men from Philadelphia and New York were employed by the DuPont Company at the Brandywine shop, Lower Hagley Station, and the experimental station.[39] If one boarded the three o'clock car earmarked for Rising Sun, one would see a large number of Jewish workmen leaving for the company shops.[40] At the time, the Jewish immigrants only boarded in Wilmington, but they were expected to settle permanently. The foreigners had only arrived in Wilmington (indeed, in the United States) recently and had foreign characteristics that were very striking.

At least one Jewish woman was not happy about her husband working for an ammunition plant. In October 1916 Benjamin Polack was doing pretty well in Wilmington and asked for assistance from the Hebrew Charity Association to bring his wife and four children from Brooklyn. J. Harry Gordon contacted the IRO, which reported that Polack's wife was opposed to his working in the ammunition factories, and that if he was not able to get work at his trade or any other work, she wanted him to return to New York.[41]

By 1917, the increase in wartime industries had brought even more Jews to Wilmington, so the YMHA offered to hold a seder for all the Jewish men in town who for business reasons could not get home.[42] Before the Jewish New Year in 1918, Rabbi David Swiren of Adas Kodesch spoke with the management of two of the large shipyards, Harlan and Hollingsworth and Pusey and Jones, about allowing men to take off during the holidays. Management was receptive and many shipworkers showed up at services.[43]

The DuPont Company also hired local Jewish boys. Ben Cohen, son of Bessie and Joseph Cohen, was born in Wilmington in 1899. After attending Goldey College, he was hired as a stenographer and typist for Mr. Miller, the supervisor of Plant 3, the Deep Water plant, later known as the Chambers Works.[44] At the time the plant was beginning to work in dyes. After the armistice, Cohen was asked to take a position in South America, but since his mother was a widow, he had to turn it down and resign from the company. Nonetheless, Cohen found the DuPont Company "a beautiful company to work for." During the same years, Izy Rosenblatt worked in a lab, and Ed Bernhardt held a position similar to Ben's in the downtown office.[45]

When Philip Simon, born in Russia in 1898, arrived in Wilmington in April 1914, people from all over the United States were coming to Wilmington for jobs in the leather and shipbuilding factories.[46] Philip came to Wilmington to be with his uncle, Louis Platensky, who had come to Wilmington around 1909 for a job with Pullman.[47] Despite the availability of jobs, Philip's first job was as a peddler. He bought goods from the Delaware Novelty House, put them in a pack on his back, and walked a few miles out to Rockland. People purchased their notions from him because "that way they didn't have to spend a nickel to go in town and didn't have to walk all the way over to Delaware Avenue to the bus."[48] Philip worked briefly for Topkis Underwear Company, but kept changing jobs because "during the war there were so many jobs, you could always find a higher dollar." All the shipbuilders hired Jews. The work "did not require great skill, they showed you once and then you knew." Simon also worked briefly at the Pullman shops in the tin shop using the skills his uncle had taught him.

Philip Simon was a religious young man. He was a member of Chesed Shel Emeth synagogue and its *Hevrah Kadisha,* which prepared the deceased for burial. Still Simon worked on Saturdays. "In the old world no one worked on Saturday, but here everyone did, so I did what everyone else did."[49]

In 1916, when the demand for glazed kid had reached an unprecedented level, New Castle Leather produced 12,000 skins a day.[50] Richard Patzowsky worked conscientiously all the time. In November 1916, at the age of fifty-nine, he died of a nervous breakdown. His career had been one of the most striking of its kind. Starting at the bottom of the leather trade as a helper in a factory, he had become president of a company represented in every principal city of the world.[51] Management passed to his son Frederick. However, within two years, Frederick had left Wilmington and the company became a corporation, run by Patzowsky's former partners Robert Binger and J. Wert Willis.[52]

During the wartime growth of Wilmington, the Jewish population

Samuel Katz's store on Shipley Street, c. 1910.

increased rapidly. Jews were involved in nearly every commercial, industrial, and professional business in the city. "As merchants, they were the greatest."[53] They treated people fairly, tried new ideas, and were always ready to experiment with a new type of business. Many of the Jews who came to Wilmington from neighboring cities entered business.[54]

Braunstein's clothing store opened in Wilmington in 1914, but brothers Harry and Samuel Braunstein had opened stores in Atlantic City and Scranton earlier.[55] Harry Braunstein, born in Russia around 1878, arrived in the United States in 1881 and was naturalized by 1890.[56] When the Wilmington store opened, it had sixteen salespeople.[57] Three years later, the store had expanded to four floors and had sixty-eight employees. Many of the salespeople were from large cities; others represented local talent. Braunstein's offered a variety of clothing and excelled in service. "When service is not provided, the customer has been defrauded," the store advertised. [58] In 1916 Braunstein's opened a millinery and a children's department. No city the size of Wilmington had such a complete store, but the managers were still not satisfied.[59] Many Jews continued to earn a living in the clothing business. In 1916, sixteen of the twenty-nine clothiers listed in the city directory were owned by Jews.[60]

Anna and Abraham Cohen and their children Herman, Bernard, Samuel, Morris, and Hilda arrived in Wilmington from Philadelphia in 1914.[61] Abraham was born in Lithuania in 1880 and left to avoid the army. Anna was from Raseiniae on the border of Poland and Germany. She was very skilled with her hands and earned a large salary for sewing parts on the insides of shirts. Although Abraham had been a baker, in Wilmington he opened a dry goods store at 307 Madison.

Julius and Louise Yalisove opened a dry goods store at 506 King Street around 1916.[62] A few years later Yalisove was in partnership with Samuel Sigmund at the Lace Shop on King Street. The store did well and by 1919 the Yalisoves had moved to The Boulevard.[63] At least twenty five Jewish merchants owned dry goods stores in 1916.[64]

Rubin (Reuben) Balick arrived in New York City from Nikolayev, Ukraine around 1911.[65] He later brought his brother Nathan over, and together they brought the rest of the brothers—Isidor, Samuel, Simon, Louis, and Israel—as well as sister Minnie and their mother, Sadie, to the United States. The brothers were furriers; a couple learned the profession and taught the others when they arrived. "Each one of them did something different, but together they could put together a coat." [66] After some initial success, the business wasn't doing well, and Rubin was anxious to get out of the Lower East Side of New York. A *landsman* (a person from the same town in the Old Country) who lived in Wilmington encouraged Rubin to come to Wilmington so he could get out of the fur business and start his own business.

In 1916 Rubin, the first of the seven Balick brothers to settle in Wilmington, opened a grocery store at 1113 Lombard Street. He would walk to the King Street stores to buy the groceries for his store and would bring home whatever he could carry on his back.[67] Just as the Balick brothers had brought each other in order of birth from the Old World, they assisted one another in moving to Wilmington. Each of the brothers came and opened a grocery store. They formed an "ozy," a private loan association, to which they contributed dues monthly. Whenever a brother needed money, he could borrow from the fund.

The Balick brothers were not the only Jews to choose the grocery business. In 1916, more than seventy Jews ran grocery stores throughout the city.[68] A few of the stores were in the "Jewish downtown area," but most were spread throughout the city. Since people were accustomed to shopping daily in their own neighborhoods, grocery stores were in demand.

There were at least eleven Jewish shoe dealers, sixteen Jewish shoemakers, seventeen Jewish tailors, and several junk dealers in 1916.[69] Of the nineteen secondhand dealers listed in the 1916 city directory, at least eleven were Jewish, and most were on Front Street. The first block of East Front Street, from the Christina River west to the city line, had fifteen businesses, eight of which were Jewish secondhand dealers.[70] Morris Kristol, Chaya Gittel Kristol, and their daughters Sarah and Jenny immigrated to Wilmington in the 1900s and opened a shoe store, and later a clothing store on Front Street. By 1916, Morris was a secondhand dealer. His store eventually became a general store and pawnshop. Chaya's brothers—Hyman, Henry, and Joseph, who all took the surname Cohen—followed the Kristols and opened secondhand shops near the Kristols' store on Front Street.[71] Morris' wife always invited all the relatives for Jewish holidays. For her magnificent Passover seders, she would clear a spacious area of the Front Street store and set up makeshift tables of boards covered with holiday cloths. Over forty guests would celebrate the Exodus from Egypt.[72]

The established merchants flourished. David Snellenburg, who was called Wilmington's most progressive citizen, was always ready to take part in things for the benefit of the city.[73] He continued to tie the future of his store, N. Snellenburg and Company, to the success of Wilmington, and both prospered. In 1913 Snellenburg's advertised the "Do It for Wilmington" spirit. Snellenburg praised the spirit of cooperation, which would make the city great.[74] In 1915, to mark the twentieth anniversary of the founding of his store, David Snellenburg bought the largest ad, six full pages, ever to appear in the *Sunday Star*. He advertised "We believed in Wilmington in 1895 and now when all eyes are on it."[75] David Snellenburg was looked upon as one of the most enterprising merchants in Wilmington. His ad showed confidence in Wilmington and was proof that he believed Wilmington was big enough and live enough to warrant the advertising methods of metropolitan cities. Snellenburg's ads always praised the potential and beauty of Wilmington. Sometimes they took up pages boosting the city and only made reference to his business at the top or bottom.[76]

David Snellenburg's astute business sense led him to continual innovations. In 1913, the store opened a piano department; within a year the new department was so successful that Snellenburg expanded it to a full floor. At the end of 1914, Snellenburg initiated a series of piano concerts on the third floor of his store to familiarize the people with the Delmarva Player Piano.[77] In 1916, the employees of N. Snellenburg formed a minstrel troupe that performed for the benefit of friends and patrons of the store.[78] A souvenir booklet published on the firm's twenty-second anniversary featured an article entitled "Of Wilmington, By Wilmington and For Wilmington," and was called one of the finest pieces of writing ever issued on the city.[79] During the Fourth Liberty Bond drive, every employee of N. Snellenburg bought at least one liberty bond.[80]

About a month after Snellenburg ran his large anniversary ad, Miller Brothers Company signed a contract with the *Sunday Star* to buy five full columns of advertising every week.[81] After ten years in business at Second and Market Street, Nathan Miller decided to buy the store of a retiring furniture dealer, but he needed financing. He met with a committee of five bankers at Wilmington Trust, who were concerned about the World War. The bankers challenged him, "Suppose the world blows up?"[82] Miller responded, "If it blows up, what will you care where your money is?" He got the loan two days later. In March 1916, Miller Brothers bought 904 King Street. The clothing and furnishing business at 213 Market was moved up to Ninth and King.[83] Soon afterwards, Nathan Miller bought his brothers out and became sole owner of the store.[84]

The Topkis brothers and their sister Sallie, who had lived most of their lives in the United States and had been in Wilmington longer than all but a handful of Jews, expanded into new areas. After running the Wholesale Notion House for many years, in 1915 Louis Topkis consolidated the Delmarva Manufacturing Company with Diamond Manufacturing Company to form Topkis Brothers Underwear. The business, which began as a manufacturer of men's underwear, expanded to Philadelphia, New York, Chicago, San Francisco, and Montreal, becoming the second largest of twelve such factories in the U.S. In later years, the company added men's sportswear, pajamas, and robes.[85]

Meanwhile David Topkis, who had earned a living in the early years of the century as a tailor, foresaw the development of the ninth ward of Wilmington and began to buy properties in the area. Between 1908 and 1917, David Topkis acquired about ninety properties.[86] He built at least two hundred homes in the section.[87] David Topkis also built the Arcadia and Strand theaters and the old Topkis Building at Fifth and Market, which later became the home of Wilmington Dry Goods. He designed Adas Kodesch at Sixth and French and the YMHA.[88]

William and Charles Topkis continued to run R. Topkis and Company, which had become a department store, until 1923 when they sold the business.[89] At the same time, the brothers embarked on an exciting new venture, the motion picture business. Movies, which were first shown on a limited scale just before the turn of the century, grew to tremendous importance in the early twentieth century. By 1911, they were the most popular diversion in town; some eight million people attended America's fifteen thousand theaters daily.[90]

In July 1911, William and Charles Topkis and their brother-in-law James Ginns bought St. Paul's Church on Market Street and converted it into the Majestic movie theater.[91] The Topkis brothers had convinced James Ginns, who had become a successful businessman in Coatesville, to return to Wilmington to assist in the new business.[92] Intending to make the theater an attractive architectural addition to the city as well as a quality motion picture house, the new owners added a massive marble marquee, wainscoted the walls of the entrance and balcony with American marble, and used the best cushioned seats, similar to those used in Philadelphia's Forrest theater.[93] In November, during the theater's opening, Charles Topkis announced that the finest pictures would be presented, but that the price of a ticket would still only be five cents. When the Topkis brothers and James Ginns purchased the property, the block was considered one of the poorest on Market Street, but by 1915 it had become one of the best on the west side. Their success in the theater business was attributed to the Topkis' attention to business details, straight dealing with the public, and unlimited faith in Wilmington.[94]

In May 1915, the Topkis-Ginns syndicate, known as the Wilmington Amusement Company, bought the old Clayton House (which had been considered Wilmington's finest hotel for some forty years, prior to the opening of the Hotel duPont) for $150,000, in order to convert it to a first-class movie palace.[95] After $250,000 worth of renovations, the Queen Theater—appropriately named because it had all the beauty associated with royalty—opened in February 1916.[96] Touted as one of the most beautiful theaters in the United States, the Queen was the only theater in the country to use Alaskan marble for ornamentation on the walls of the lobby and ramp. Its two thousand seats, all with unobstructed views of the stage and screen, and one of the best orchestras in the state made the theater an immediate success. One year later, during the theater's anniversary week celebration, the newspaper boasted that the arrangements for safety were so good that the house had been emptied in two and a half minutes. Two ballrooms, the largest and most attractive in the state, had been added on the second and third floors. The rooms were unique because the orchestra played between floors so that the two ballrooms could be used at once. In the lower ballroom, the music appeared to come from the balcony; in the upper ballroom, the music appeared to come from the pit.[97] The theater also had one of the largest and most talented orchestras in the state.

Undated financial statements from the Majestic and the Queen theaters show that the movie industry in Wilmington was extraordinarily successful. One week, the Majestic netted $1755 and the Queen $1676; the following week, the Majestic netted $831 and the Queen $1844; the third week, the Majestic netted $1788 and the Queen $1303.[98]

The Topkis's interest in moving pictures spread beyond Wilmington. Their syndicate owned the Lyric Theatre in Camden, New Jersey, by 1917 when an inefficient manager and cashier allowed a woman with a baby in her arms into the theater causing great confusion.[99] Given his poor health, William Topkis began to spend significant time in California and became involved with Samuel Goldwyn. In 1919, the Goldwyn Picture Corporation announced that William Topkis, a merchant and theatrical producer, H. F. duPont and R. R. M. Carpenter (vice-presidents of the DuPont Company), Eugene G. duPont, W. W. Laird, and George P. Bissell of Laird and Company, Charles Kurtz, vice-president of Wilmington Trust, and others had invested in the Goldwyn Corporation and would be active on the board and directorate. The presence of these investors' financial resources would make the Goldwyn Company "the strongest and most powerful organization of its kind in the United States."[100]

William Topkis worked closely with Samuel Goldwyn for several years. In May 1920, when Goldwyn Pictures Corporation purchased the big Capitol Theater in New York City, Topkis was put on the board along with Eugene duPont.[101] Goldwyn confided his concerns about the company's financial difficulties in a 1921 letter to Topkis. Conditions in New York were even worse than Topkis had led him to believe. Goldwyn felt the hostility of the executive committee and the directors of the studio would not end until they appointed a committee to come out to California and compared the operation to other studios. In an emotional statement to his friend, Goldwyn explained: "it is heart rending to me especially when I know we are producing better quality of pictures for less money than any producing company in this business."[102]

Goldwyn Pictures did not solve its economic problems, and Marcus Loew bought the studio in the 1920s and combined it with Metro to form the Metro-Goldwyn Company. Samuel Goldwyn became an independent producer. If he had not been in such poor health, Topkis would probably have pursued his business with Goldwyn.[103]

In 1914, David Topkis and Benjamin Schwartz opened the Victoria Movie Theater at 834 Market Street.[104] With its walls of stuccoed rose, buff, and old ivory and its one thousand mahogany seats covered in Spanish leather, the theater was praised as one of the finest new movie buildings. The Victoria competed successfully for six years until WSFS took over the property. Ben Schwartz, who was the president of Wilmington and Brandywine Amusement Company, was responsible for the success of the theater. When the Victoria closed in 1920, the *Sunday Star* reporter praised Schwartz's ingenuity, which had "enabled him to rise from a very humble beginning to his present status in business. When he opened the Victoria Theater he was regarded as inviting fickle fortune to toss him upon the shoals of financial failure."[105]

In 1920 David Topkis and Jules H. Rothschild opened the Strand Theater, designed by Topkis, at 2412 Market Street. The house was designed so that none of its nine hundred seats was under the balcony. The general atmosphere was so pleasant that customers returned regularly.[106]

In the month of February 1920, Oscar and James Ginns, who had formed a new partnership with Charles Topkis, announced plans to build a theater next door to Old Town Hall. David Topkis was to design it, based on his studies of the outstanding theaters in the country.[107] This theater, the Arcadia, opened in 1921.

While the Topkis brothers expanded in the moving picture business, other Jews found new areas of employment. Sophie Ostro, wife of Michael, became the first female Jewish doctor in Delaware in 1911.[108] Jennie Greenstein, the oldest daughter of Albert and Amelia Greenstein, born in Wilmington around 1892, became the first Jewish public school teacher by 1913.[109] Two years later, Sarah (Sadie) Topkis, daughter of Ray and David Topkis, became a teacher.[110] Louis Rosenblatt, who had apprenticed at Harlan and Hollingworth shipyard before becoming a furniture dealer, joined the Equitable Life Assurance Company in 1914. Within a short time, Rosenblatt would write over a million dollars of insurance policies a year, and was therefore a member of the successful and restricted million-dollar club.[111] Later he became president of the Mutual Savings and Loan Association. Ralph Saltzman, who had been a salesman at Miller Brothers, became private secretary to Mayor James F. Price.[112] Samuel Knopf, a 1912 graduate of Delaware College, was appointed chief assistant to the state engineer.[113] Increasingly, Jews in the younger generation, who had stayed in school, found white-collar jobs in business or the professions. Although Wilmington's second generation came of age later than New York's second generation because Jews arrived in Wilmington later, Wilmington's Jews followed a pattern similar to the Jews of New York City, where 70 percent of Jews who stayed in school vaulted into the white-collar world within a decade of leaving school.[114]

Not only did the Jews expand into new businesses, they also became more visible in the professions. Wilmington's three established Jewish doctors, Albert Robin, Michael Ostro, and Sigmund Werner, were joined by several younger physicians. Samuel Zion, David Rossman, and Jacob Keyser graduated from the Medico Chirurgical College in Philadelphia in 1912 and came to Wilmington shortly thereafter.[115] David Rossman, born in Philadelphia in 1889, received his Delaware certification in December 1912 and opened a general practice on South Heald Street. He was accepted for membership in the Medical Society of New Castle County in October 1914.[116] Sam Zion, born in 1890, practiced for one year after graduation in Philadelphia and then came to Wilmington and opened a general practice at 2230 Market Street.[117] Jacob Keyser, born in Russia in 1885, opened a practice at 2000 Washington Street by 1916.[118] In 1920, when elected to the Medical Society,

Keyser had been an anesthesiologist and pathologist at Delaware Hospital for two years. Mark B. Holzman, another graduate of Medico Chirurgical medical school, came to Wilmington by 1915.

Joseph Barsky, the first Jewish boy born in Wilmington to go to medical school, graduated from Jefferson Medical College in Philadelphia on June 6, 1914 and received his state certification a few weeks later.[119] After interning at Delaware Hospital as an assistant to Dr. Robin, at Mt. Sinai Dispensary, and at the Hope Farm Sanitarium, Dr. Barsky opened a general practice at West Ninth Street.[120]

The first Jewish dentists also arrived in Wilmington at this time. Abraham Goberman, a native of Russia who had graduated from Baltimore Dental School, married Sylvia Levy, daughter of Nathan Levy, in 1914, and opened a dental office at Fourth and Market Streets.[121] Isadore Kreshtool—a native of Russia and Goberman's classmate and good friend from dental school—married Goberman's sister Bertha and settled in Wilmington shortly afterwards.[122] Both men had grown up in New York, but recognized Wilmington as a city with opportunities. Louis Gluckman graduated from the University of Pennsylvania Dental School in 1915 and opened a Wilmington office in September 1915.[123] Morris Greenstein was a dentist by 1920.[124]

In 1915, the Jewish doctors and dentists joined together to assist the community through a medical clinic known as the Mount Sinai Dispensary, which was comprised mainly of Jewish doctors.[125] Dr. Albert Robin, who was the impetus for forming the clinic, and Michael Ostro were consulting physicians in general medicine along with Edwin Bird and D. F. Wonder.[126] Samuel Zion headed the clinic in general medicine; Jacob Keyser led the clinic for surgery; David Rossman headed the clinic on children's diseases; David Davitch led the genitourinary clinic; and Mark B. Holzman directed the ear, nose, and throat department. Doctors I. K. Kreshtool, Lewis, and Goberman were in the dental department of the dispensary. Louis Gluckman and Robert Davis would join the dental staff as soon as they took the state examinations.[127] One of the new features of the clinic was the Children's Registration Bureau, which enabled mothers to know the physical standing of their babies. A few months after its establishment, two hundred of the four hundred patients who had been treated at the dispensary were non-Jews.[128] By December, the clinic saw an average of forty-five cases a week.[129]

In the spirit of being good Americans, three members of the executive committee of Mt. Sinai Dispensary (Dr. Albert Robin, J.

Harry Gordon, and Joseph Wintner) appeared before the Board of Education in September 1915 to offer the services of the dispensary's dental clinic to all schoolchildren in the city.[130] By October, arrangements had been made for all schoolchildren to have their teeth examined and cured at the dispensary free of charge.[131] After about five years, the Mount Sinai Dispensary went out of existence because its functions were taken over by the city and state.[132]

While the newer doctors were establishing their practices, Dr. Albert Robin remained a central presence in Wilmington medical circles. In December 1911, he became editor of the Medical Society of Delaware's journal, one of the oldest state medical journals in the country.[133] He often wrote articles about tuberculosis, which he believed was curable if treated in the early stages. In one article, Dr. Robin defended the use of heroin to treat patients, claiming that use over a short time did not make people addicts. After four years, Robin resigned as editor, saying he had not received assistance, cooperation, or encouragement from members of the profession, but he continued to write and lecture about tuberculosis. Dr. Robin served as the medical director of the tuberculosis sanitarium from 1910 to 1920 and was executive secretary of the Delaware Tuberculosis Commission from 1920 to 1922.[134]

Dr. Robin played a central role in the formation of the Wilmington General Hospital, originally known as the Physicians and Surgeons Hospital. Wilmington had two hospitals, the Homeopathic and the Delaware hospitals, but Robin felt they were out of reach because Jewish doctors were not welcome to practice there.[135] Robin interested several members of the duPont family in contributing funds to the hospital and persuaded Mrs. E. I duPont to buy property for the expansion of the hospital.[136] In the 1920s Robin became a prime factor in the $500,000 campaign to erect a new institution at South Broom and Chestnut Streets.[137]

Soon after Aaron Finger became an attorney in 1912, his extraordinary abilities were recognized, and in 1916 he was made a deputy city judge.[138] A man of great character, Aaron Finger resigned as deputy judge in 1918 in order to join the military, even though he could have been excused because of his official status.[139] After the war, in January 1920, Finger was appointed as chief deputy attorney general, a position he held through 1923 when he resigned to resume private practice.[140]

In 1914 Emile Topkis, son of David and Hannah Ray Topkis, was admitted to the bar.[141] The day after Topkis's admission, Morris Levy, who was "by far the outstanding representative of Jewish affairs in Delaware," came to Emile to ask him to prepare a lease.

Emile Topkis saw Levy's gesture as a typical act of kindness, since he believed Levy had no need for the lease.[142] By 1918 Emile was in practice with Townsend and Topkis.

Victor Barsky, son of Rosa and Nathan, was admitted to the bar in 1918.[143] Evangeline Barsky, sister of Victor and Joseph, became one of Delaware's first two women attorneys in 1923, after the Delaware constitution was amended to provide that no citizen should be disqualified from holding office by virtue of sex.[144] S. Lester Levy was admitted to the bar in 1920 and Joseph Handler in 1921.[145] Although there were only six Jewish attorneys in Delaware by 1923, the Jews had at least broken the barrier and would be able to enter the profession in greater numbers.

The younger generation continued to pursue education. By 1916, there were nine Jewish young men at Delaware College and two Jewish women at Women's College.[146] A number of Jewish Wilmingtonians chose Delaware College because Newark was only twelve miles away, and they could live at home while attending college.[147]

The Jewish community included a broad range of people. There were "greenhorns" who had just arrived in the United States, immigrants who had lived in other parts of the United States before coming here, older immigrants who had lived in Wilmington for most of their adult lives, and an increasing number of American-born citizens. Approximately 25 percent of the adult men and women who came to Wilmington in the 1910s or reached eighteen years of age in this decade were American-born. In addition, a growing number of children were born in America. The American-born Jewish youth, who were educated in this country, had very different attitudes than their parents. America was not foreign, it was the only country they knew. Like the American-born children of all immigrants who attended public schools, they were influenced by an authority other than their parents, and they felt a separation from the older generations of their families.[148] They "wore their nativity like a badge that marked their superiority over their immigrant elders . . . and became mediators between the culture of the home and the culture of the wider society."[149]

As their economic diversity increased, the Jews began to spread out geographically. The newest immigrants lived on Front Street, a world of secondhand shops. The center of the community was Second Street between Orange and Tatnall. In 1916, there were twenty-nine Jewish businesses on Second Street between Shipley and Tatnall Streets.[150] There one would find kosher butchers, delicatessens, bakeries, and produce stores, as well as many dry goods and clothing stores. But the more established Jews, along with middle-class WASPs and the Irish, began to move north over the Brandywine into the ninth ward.[151] By 1925 nearly as many Jews lived in the ninth ward as downtown.[152] Most Jews still came downtown to shop, particularly on Saturday nights. Shopping on Second Street was as much a social event as a retail activity. "That's where you'd hear all the gossip."[153]

RESTRICTING IMMIGRATION

While the Jews of Wilmington did well in a city of prosperity, the future of immigration to the United States was threatened by a growing anti-immigration movement. The report issued by the United States Immigration Commission in 1911 was devastating to those who favored open immigration. In unequivocal terms, the committee recommended "restriction as demanded by economic, moral and social considerations."[154] The commission unanimously approved several basic principles that changed the nature of immigration in this country: the most desirable immigrants were those whose assimilation would not be too difficult; economic or business concerns should be the primary basis for admission to the country; and the slow expansion of industry was preferable to a rapid expansion.[155]

After naming specific classes of immigrants to be restricted, the commission suggested that if Congress agreed with its findings, it could use several methods to restrict immigration. The first and "most feasible single method of restricting immigration" was exclusion of those unable to read or write in some language.[156] Limitation of the number of each race arriving each year to a certain percent of the average of that race arriving during a given period of years, the exclusion of unskilled laborers unaccompanied by wives or families, limitation of the number of immigrants arriving annually at any port, and an increase in the head tax were among the other recommended methods to restrict legislation. Jewish leadership had opposed these methods.[157]

When the commission was first established in 1907, there had been great hope that it would provide a body of verified and indisputable facts that would supply the groundwork for future action.[158] Unfortunately, the Dillingham Commission was not impartial or scientific.[159] It began by taking for granted the conclusion it aimed to prove: that the new immigrants were inferior. No public hearings were held, no witnesses were cross-examined. The summary of reports did not give all the information in the reports, and senators and congressmen did not have time to review all the volumes of the report.[160] For example, the body of the report concluded that the most apparent cause of illiteracy in Europe as elsewhere was poverty. The economic status of a people had a decided effect upon literacy. The commission's investigators abroad recognized that inability to read was predicated on environmental rather than racial deficiencies and predicted steady improvement in the future. However, the summary omitted this optimistic discussion and instead made the sweeping statement that the high rate of illiteracy among new immigrants was due to inherent racial tendencies.[161] Similarly, the report simply said that there was a higher degree of illiteracy among immigrants of recent years than those of old. It completely disregarded the fact that earlier immigrants had lived in the United States much longer, and therefore had learned to speak English.[162] Furthermore, the majority endorsed the literacy test as the most feasible means of limiting immigration, even though many of the nation's most respected educators—including the presidents of Harvard University, University of Chicago, Notre Dame, Georgetown, Cornell, and Boston University—submitted letters testifying that existing legislation was sufficient and that educational tests should not be applied at the moment of entrance but at the moment of naturalization.[163] As William Bennett stated in his minority report, "the educational test proposed is a selective test for which no logical argument can be based in the report."[164] Unfortunately, the minority report did not hold much influence.

Once the immigration commission had established the need to restrict immigration, change was inevitable. In 1912 the Department of Labor, with responsibility for immigration matters, was created and was another step in the "inexorable march to restrictionism."[165]

In 1913 both houses of Congress passed the Dillingham Burnett bill, which recommended a literacy test as part of the immigration process, but President William Howard Taft vetoed the bill, calling the literacy test undemocratic.[166] He claimed the literacy test, which would lock the doors against aliens who could not read some language or dialect, was not a good test of a person's merits because it judged a person based on the opportunity to acquire reading and writing. Taft recognized that frequently immigrants coming to our shores were striving to free themselves from the conditions under which they had been compelled to live and which deprived them of an opportunity to learn to read and write. As soon as the president's veto message was read, Senator Henry A. duPont of Winterthur,

Delaware endorsed the president's view, saying he disapproved of the literacy clause in the bill and would therefore vote to sustain the President's veto.[167] He told the Senate

> Some years ago I had the opportunity to examine the muster rolls of the continental line of the Revolutionary Army, and I discovered that in many companies, as high as 75 or 80 percent of the soldiers were illiterates or foreigners—were they good enough to risk their lives in assisting to attain our independence, it seems to me that the same class of men are now good enough to assist in the development of this great country by their labor on the farms, in the mines, and in every other department where labor is so much needed.[168]

The next day, the Senate overrode the President's veto by an overwhelming majority of 72 yeas, 18 nays, and 5 abstentions. Senator Henry A. duPont opposed overriding the veto, but Senator Henry A. Richardson voted with the majority to override the veto.[169] When the House of Representatives voted, Delaware's representative William Heald voted with the majority to override the veto, but since the bill did not receive two-thirds of the vote, it failed.[170]

The *Wilmington Morning News* opposed the literacy requirements, calling a literacy test a "fallacious means of providing for the exclusion of agitators." The pressure for a literacy requirement was coming from those who opposed what was happening in industrial life.[171] It was not the ignorant foreigner who was responsible for the mischief, but rather it was the men who led them—men who could meet any kind of literacy test that a government might think of using, and the sooner this truth was appreciated, the sooner would Americans who defended the present institutions realize that the proper method of opposing the forces of industrial destruction was by means of education.[172]

In the next session of Congress, both the Senate and House again considered and passed an immigration bill. At the end of January 1915, President Woodrow Wilson used his first veto against the bill. Like Presidents Cleveland and Taft, he felt the proposed bill would radically change the policy of this country. In the President's opinion, the bill would

> all but close entirely the gates of asylum which have always been open to those who could find nowhere else the right and opportunity of constitutional agitations for what they conceived to be the natural and inalienable right of men; and it excludes those to whom the opportunities of elementary education have been denied without regard to their character, their purposes, or their natural capacity. [173]

On February 4, 1915 the House of Representatives voted on overriding the President's veto. Representative Franklin Brockson of Clayton, Delaware voted with the majority to override the veto. The vote fell just short of two-thirds, so the veto was not overridden.[174]

Ironically, as Congress debated limiting immigration, there was a sharp decrease in the number of immigrants to the United States because of World War I. In the twelve months before July 1, 1914, there had been 1,211,480 immigrants to the country; in the twelve months before July 1, 1915, only 300,000.[175] Predictions were that numbers would stay down because of the war.

In January 1917, the House and the Senate again passed an immigration bill with a literacy test requirement. The test excluded all aliens over sixteen who could not read English or some other language, including Hebrew or Yiddish. Jewish organizations had deluged the White House and Congress with memorials against it.[176]

When Congress passed the literacy bill, immigration, as important as it was, could hardly have been President Wilson's top priority. Europe was engaged in a brutal war, and Wilson wanted the United States to end its isolationist policy. His speech of January 22, recommending that the United States enter a World Peace League, caused great debate throughout the country. In spite of his preoccupation with the war, President Wilson swiftly vetoed the immigration bill on January 29 because of the literacy test, which he believed was based on the unfair principle that an immigrant should be punished for the lack of opportunity in his native country.

> I cannot rid myself of the conviction that the literacy test constitutes a radical change in the policy of the nation which is not justified in principle. It is not a test of character, quality or personal fitness but would operate as a penalty for lack of opportunity in the country from which the alien seeking admission came. The opportunity to gain education is in many cases one of the chief opportunities sought by immigrants to the U.S. and our experience has not been that illiterate immigrants are undesirable. Tests of quality and of purpose cannot be objected to on principle, but tests of opportunity surely may be.[177]

The Jewish people, fearful that the literacy test would pass, had managed to include a provision exempting those aliens who wanted to enter the United States to avoid religious persecution from the literacy requirement. Claiming that those who pushed the exemption provision had no incorrect motives, Wilson said he could not accept the provision because it would place an unfair burden on United States officials to pass judgment on foreign governments and would raise serious questions of international justice.[178]

Days later, on February 1, as President Wilson responded harshly to the German announcement of unrestricted submarine warfare, the House overrode the President's veto by a vote of 287 yeas, 106 nays, 3 present, and 37 abstentions.[179] Representative Thomas Miller of Wilmington was one of the three people who voted present. Party lines were ignored: Democrats, Republicans, and Progressives were equally divided in their desire to override the President.[180]

Siding with President Wilson the *Wilmington Morning News* expressed the belief that passing the bill with the literacy test would be wrong because the test was meritorious and thousands of persons who have become good citizens would have been excluded by it. Furthermore, the editorial believed in the need for immigrants.

It would be more unfortunate at the present time than ever before if this bill becomes a law, for this country will need immigrants. The bill would cause an even greater shortage of labor than at present. Also few "undesirables" would be prevented from landing on our shores by such a test.[181]

On February 5, 1917 the Senate also overrode the veto by a vote of 62–19, and the bill became law. Delaware senators Willard Saulsbury and Henry A. duPont were among the nineteen senators who upheld the Presidential veto and opposed the immigration bill.[182]

Comments of Senator Ellison D. Smith from South Carolina, chairman of the immigration committee, revealed the ugly truth: more than a literacy test had been at stake. Smith spoke in crude, exclusionary terms when he said " the present state of international affairs emphasized the necessity for a pure, homogeneous American people such as the bill was intended to protect."[183] In his statement, Smith spoke of the clear-cut expression of the American people of two principles, economic and political:

[R]esources yet to be developed should be regarded as the patrimony of *real* Americans and not to be exploited for those who have had no part in the great struggle to bring us to our present state of wealth and education. (emphasis added)

[T]he influx of adult foreigners without the *heredity* influence of spirit of our government jeopardizes the stability of the country.[184]

The *Wilmington Morning News* admitted that the great support for the immigration measure was a clear indication that the sentiment of the country favored it, though the nation needed workers. However, in its opinion, the labor market was short, and the labor supply was likely to become scarcer.[185] Believing the vote was wrong, the newspaper said, "Perhaps in the not distant future, it will be realized that a serious mistake has been made."[186] The immigration law of 1917 dramatically changed the character of the United States and sent a negative message to the immigrants already here and to foreigners hoping to emigrate.

ANTI-SEMITISM

In the midst of the Congressional attempts to restrict immigration through a literacy test, anti-Semitism in the United States took a dangerous turn in the Leo Frank case. Between 1913 and 1915, Leo Frank was convicted of murder and then lynched by an angry Georgia mob.

Frank, a Jew born in Texas in 1884 but raised in New York, had moved to Atlanta in 1907 to become superintendent of his uncle Moses Frank's pencil factory.[187] A businessman of good reputation, Frank married into a wealthy, established Atlanta Jewish family, became active in the Jewish community, and in 1912 was elected president of the Atlanta Lodge of B'nai B'rith.[188] On Confederate Memorial Day, April 26, 1913, a fourteen-year-old factory employee, Mary Phagan, was brutally murdered in the basement of the pencil factory. Frank, who had been the only one in the factory for many hours with Phagan during the holiday, was held as the prime suspect. Despite the fact that the statements of the factory sweeper, Jim Conley, raised considerable doubt, Frank was indicted in May.[189] His thirty-day trial was held before a cheering, menacing crowd that often murmured "Hang the Jew." With inconclusive evidence, based largely on the testimony of Jim Conley, Frank was convicted of the crime. For two years, Frank remained in jail while attorneys and activists throughout the country tried to get him a new trial. The Georgia Supreme Court upheld the decision, denying an appeal for a new trial.[190] The Federal District Court also denied a new trial but expressed some doubt about Frank's guilt.[191] The U.S. Supreme Court claimed it had no jurisdiction over the case and refused to hear it. With the appeals process exhausted, Governor Slaton commuted Frank's sentence to life imprisonment. In June 1915, he was moved to a state prison farm in Milledgeville.

On August 17, 1915, a band of twenty-five men removed Frank from the state prison, drove him nearly one hundred miles to Marietta, Mary Phagan's hometown, and hung him from a tree. The ease with which the mob carried out its lynching, the lack of obstacles, and the absence of cooperation in finding the guilty parties raised suspicions that the endeavor was sanctioned.[192]

National leaders as well as Georgia officials condemned the lynching. In Delaware, the newspaper blamed the hatred and prejudice in the South for the event, implying it couldn't possibly happen in the North. "Not surprising at all to those who have lived in the south and are familiar with certain classes of its people is the shocking fate of Leo Frank who was brutally lynched by a small body of well organized clansmen."[193] The Wilmington editorial suggested that Governor Slaton should have pardoned Frank so he could have left the state where he was obviously unsafe. Georgia will suffer the wrath and scorn of fair-minded people, the editorial predicted.[194]

In the days immediately after the lynching, Governor Slaton announced that he preferred lynching to hanging by judicial mistake. One attacked the soul of civilization: the other merely the body. The governor felt that Frank was innocent and remarked: "when the people find out the truth of the Frank case their condemnation of me will turn to approval, and they will know I saved the state from a stain that never could have been eradicated."[195]

Years later, the reason for the governor's assurance became public knowledge. Jim Conley, the black janitor, had confessed his own guilt to his attorney. Governor Slaton had heard that Conley's attorney suspected his guilt or knew about the confession when he commuted the death sentence to life imprisonment.[196] Years later, on his deathbed, the black janitor, the star witness against Frank, publicly confessed his guilt.

Fear of the immigrant and the Southerner's fear of industrialism created an atmosphere that fed anti-Semitism. While Wilmington's Jewish immigrants knew they lived in a more tolerant city, where anti-Semitism never reached such heights, the treatment of Leo Frank was a brutal reminder of the unpopularity of Jews in some parts of the country.[197]

RELIGIOUS RIVALRY: A NEW ALTERNATIVE

In Wilmington's welcoming environment, the Jews expressed their religious beliefs openly, but given the freedom of life in America, they had to define positions relative to religious observance. Throughout the decade the Jews chose between two Orthodox synagogues, Adas Kodesch and Chesed Shel Emeth, and the reform Temple of Truth. In 1922, the choice expanded to include a Conservative synagogue, Beth Shalom.

Chesed Shel Emeth continued to attract many of the more recently arrived families who were not as Americanized, felt most comfortable with other newcomers, and earned a modest living.[198] During the first decade of its existence, Chesed Shel Emeth had met in different buildings. In 1912, while the synagogue rented space on the third floor of Freihofer Bakery at Eighth and Orange streets, President Isaac Weinstein appointed a building committee, which consisted of Morris Chaiken (chairman), Max Green, Fred Flanzer, Morris Braiger, Morris Feldman, Julius Glantz, Abraham Hirshman, Solomon Moore, Simon Spire, Morris Ezrailson, Jonah Levine, and Ben Muderick.[199] Shortly after its appointment, the committee purchased 229 Shipley Street and hired E. W. Hance as an architect.

Nearly all of the members of the committee were born in Russia. With the exception of Morris Chaiken, most had come to Wilmington after the turn of the century. Some, such as Ben Muderick, had just arrived. President Isaac Weinstein and his wife, Jennie, came to Wilmington from Russia in 1905. After working as a peddler and a salesman, Isaac opened a shop, selling secondhand goods. Several other committee members were tailors, junk dealers, and secondhand clothing merchants.

On June 21, 1914, at the beginning of World War I, Chesed Shel Emeth celebrated the laying of the cornerstone for its new synagogue on Shipley Street below Third.[200] Reverend Hillel Sbritsky, the rabbi of Chesed Shel Emeth, led the opening prayer. Sbritsky, who was from Yelisavetrad, Russia, lived in New York and Pennsylvania before moving to Wilmington to be with his sister , Mrs. Solomon (Mary) Frankfurt.[201] He remained as the rabbi of Chesed Shel Emeth until at least 1923 or 1924.[202] By 1921 Rabbi Isaac Schub was also at Chesed Shel Emeth as a cantor or rabbi.[203]

Despite the differences among Jews, the larger world continued to look at all Jews as one group. At the cornerstone ceremony, Mayor Howell complimented the congregation, and all Jews for their participation in American life: "they represent one of the very best classes of people who in all public movements give their heartiest cooperation and in work among themselves never ask for outside help."[204]

Reverend Maliansky, who was "well known among the Hebrews in all parts of the country," addressed those assembled "in their own tongue" and emphasized the importance of the United States

Chesed Shel Emeth. (Jewish Historical Society of Delaware.)

to the Jews.[205] Unlike other immigrant groups, the Jewish immigrant had no land to go back to, so he labored hard to make a name for himself in this country. It was the "duty of every good Jew to uphold the synagogue as well as the American government." Maliansky advised mothers to stick to the old customs and to instill into the hearts of the new generation the things that were taught them in their childhood. In concluding, the rabbi thanked "old Israel for the learning given to the Jews and young Uncle Sam for the training they would receive."[206]

Even the Orthodox rabbi saw his job as helping the Jew accommodate religion and the new country. In Wilmington, neither Orthodox synagogue was strict enough to advocate separation from the general society.

Eight months later, on February 21, 1915, over two thousand people attended the dedication of Chesed Shel Emeth, which was arranged by Morris Chaiken.[207] As in the earlier synagogue dedications, representatives of numerous Jewish organizations joined in the festivities, which began with a procession from Adas Kodesch at Sixth and French to the new synagogue at Third and

Shipley. Harry Kety, Samuel Warawitz, Michael Drucker, Abraham Sklut, Jacob Strauss, Isaac Weiner of Delaware City, I. Geller, and Hyman Cohen had purchased the privilege of carrying the Torahs in the procession.[208] Following the custom of the day, people paid for the privilege of various formalities. Mrs. Louis Topkis, who along with her husband was a leader of Adas Kodesch, paid the highest amount of the day, $175, for the privilege of turning on the Ner Tamid, the eternal light. The opening prayer was given by Rabbi Rezits of Adas Kodesch, who praised the United States, the president, and his cabinet for remaining neutral in the war raging through Europe. Rabbi Rezits spoke about how good it felt to be in America and not among the millions that were rendering destruction unto one another.[209] The Ladies' Bichor Cholem Society donated the ark where the Torahs were kept. The presence of so many people and the participation of representatives of all the organizations indicates that the unpleasantness surrounding the founding of the synagogue fourteen years earlier had disappeared. As more newcomers arrived in Wilmington during the decade, Chesed Shel Emeth grew; by 1927, the synagogue had some 225 members.[210]

Adas Kodesch continued to be the largest Orthodox synagogue. Most people considered it the anchor of the community.[211] In 1917, the attendance at the daily Hebrew school had increased to over one hundred pupils. Harry Greenblatt and Harry Blum were in charge of the school, which taught Yiddish and Hebrew. In addition to attending classes every afternoon Monday to Thursday, the children conducted special Friday evening and Saturday morning services in the basement.[212] The children were taught the importance of Zionism. Theodore Herzl's picture hung on the wall of the cheder, just like the picture of George Washington in school.[213] Since the children went to cheder every afternoon, they could not participate in sports at public school.[214] The daily Hebrew school supervised the Hebrew Sunday School, which taught Bible, Hebrew, history, and legends and attracted between one hundred and two hundred children on Sunday afternoons.[215]

Rabbi Rezits continued as the reader of the synagogue, but apparently the congregants also wanted a fully ordained rabbi. In November 1915, Rabbi Max Hoffman of Brooklyn came to Wilmington as the rabbi of Adas Kodesch and the principal of the Hebrew School, but he only stayed two months before returning to New York.[216] In late 1917, Adas Kodesch hired Rabbi David Swiren, who remained at Adas Kodesch until January 1921, along with Rabbi Rezits.[217] Rabbi Swiren, who was born in Lithuania, had a rabbinical degree from Russia, but he had also studied in rabbinical colleges of this country.[218] He was a member of the United Orthodox Rabbis Association and had served as rabbi of the Montefiore Congregation in Philadelphia.[219] Although he was already a young man when he arrived in the United States, he mastered English and spoke with only a slight accent.[220] A learned and studious man, the rabbi was author of several books published in Hebrew, English, and Yiddish and liked to combine Jewish and secular learning. After Rabbi Swiren's departure, Rabbi Solomon Margoline served as rabbi with Rabbi Rezits until the arrival of Rabbi Samuel Berliant in 1929.[221]

Many of Wilmington's more established businessmen continued to lead the Adas Kodesch congregation. Louis Topkis, Abe Tollin, Charles Schagrin, and Hyman Kanofsky served as presidents between 1910 and 1917.[222] All of them had come to Wilmington before the turn of the century and had been successful in business. Topkis manufactured underwear, Schagrin had begun a millinery store, Kanofsky had been a tailor but by 1916 he was in real estate and insurance, and Tollin ran a furniture store.

The ladies of the congregation organized a sisterhood in 1918 and began to work with all the women's organizations in the city on patriotic work.[223] Mrs. David Swiren was the first president; Mrs. Harry (Eva) Kaufman, Mrs. Charles (Frances) Schagrin, and Mrs. Louis (Sarah) Slonsky served as officers.[224]

A majority of Adas Kodesch's members at this time kept kosher.[225] In the free world of America, it was difficult for some youngsters to understand the need for keeping kosher. Bill Frank, born in New York City in 1905, came to Wilmington when he was five or six because his mother had remarried. Her new husband, the Wilmington jeweler David M. Lurge, was a very religious man. He had a seat right next to the *bima* at Adas Kodesch and his home was "101 percent kosher."[226] One day when Bill was about twelve years old, after observing the kosher rules strictly for several years and never even eating in a restaurant, Bill decided he had to have a piece of lemon meringue pie from the New York Restaurant. He took ten cents that he had saved, snuck into the restaurant and bought the coveted piece of pie. Bill planned to hurry back to his house and eat the pie on the third floor. About halfway through the alleyway near his home, he became terrified by the thought that God was going to come down and strike him in the alleyway. Looking around to make sure that no one was there, he gobbled down the whole piece of pie. "It was terrific. From that day until this day, I love lemon meringue pie," Bill remembered more than seventy years later.[227]

There were several kosher butchers on Second Street, and a *sho-*

chet to kill the chickens in a kosher fashion. One of the jobs of many young people was taking the live chickens to the shochet. Bill Frank's mother would go into the backyard, grab a chicken, and tie its legs. She would hand Bill the chicken and a quarter for the *shochet*. After saying a prayer, the *shochet* killed the chicken in one stroke to save it from suffering and drained the blood, a ritual young Bill could never make himself watch. Then he'd wrap the chicken in newspaper. "At that time, that's all I thought newspapers were for, wrapping chickens," joked the veteran reporter and columnist, who later worked for the *News Journal* for sixty years.[228] On his way home, Bill would notice the legs of the chicken still moving. "It would scare the hell out of me."

In a world where Jews were trying to balance their religious beliefs with the need to succeed in America, religious practices could lead to contradictions that were particularly difficult for young people to understand. Although D. M. Lurge was a very religious man, he did not attend services every morning. However, after Bill Frank's bar mitzvah, Mr. Lurge required him to go to synagogue every morning, and then come home and show his stepfather the strap marks from the tefellim to prove that he had been at services.[229] But on Saturday, the holiest day of the week, Bill was excused from services because he had a job at Geller's on King Street as a hawker, the person who stood outside the store persuading customers to come in. Bill worked from early morning until ten at night to earn fifty cents. Even Mr. Lurge kept his shop open on Sabbath. To Lurge, working on the Sabbath was a compromise that was necessary for survival. But when some Jews began keeping their stores open on the High Holidays for a similar reason, Lurge thought that was terrible. Everyone searched for the right way; everyone made different compromises.

The Temple of Truth, which had been formed in 1906 to meet the needs of Reform Jews, had four different rabbis during its first four years of existence, and four more during the next twelve years. The instability in leadership was caused by the difficulty of defining a religious agenda. When the Temple of Truth was established in 1906, it was the only alternative to Orthodoxy, but not all those who opposed Orthodoxy wanted the same thing. For many years, Temple of Truth fluctuated between Reform and Conservative ideas. The synagogue's first two rabbis, Jacob Korn and Isaac Aaron Rubenstein (a graduate of Hebrew Union College), were Reform leaders.[230] The fourth rabbi, Moses Abels, had graduated from Columbia University and the Jewish Theological Seminary, a school for rabbis in the historical or Conservative movement.[231] Despite his Conservative training, Rabbi Abels introduced the confirmation service, which was a Reform ceremony, frowned upon by the more Orthodox as an imitation of Christianity.[232] A man of broad views and scholarly attainments, Abels was active in numerous Progressive organizations in the general community, including the Social Service Club and the Juvenile Court Association.[233] His concern for the welfare of all Jews in Wilmington, made him "the rabbi of all the Jews in Wilmington."[234] In 1911 Rabbi Abels organized the first Jewish federation (or *kehillah*) to unify all Jewish organizations. Unfortunately, the *kehillah* disappeared shortly after his departure.[235] Rabbi Abels believed in the importance of Jews coming together for social purposes and worked closely with the YMHA, actually stimulating its redevelopment. In 1912, Abels left Temple of Truth and within a few years was the rabbi at a Reform synagogue in Altoona, Pennsylvania.[236]

Rabbi Emanuel Schreiber succeeded Abels. Born in Leipnik, Moravia, Schreiber had received his rabbinical training from schools in Berlin and Hungary and had received his rabbinical training from Abraham Geiger, the giant of Reform Judaism. [237] In a book about Geiger, Schreiber described his teacher as the greatest Reform rabbi of the nineteenth century, who led the way in the idea of "living development" in Judaism.[238] "One of the most remarkable personalities that ever honored the Temple," Schreiber was a noted scholar, thinker, and writer who gained the respect and goodwill of the entire community.[239] His sermons on the social problems of the day attracted many non-Jews to the Temple, and he often spoke at civic events. When the Wilmington community introduced the idea of bringing working people and merchants together through a Capital and Labor Parade on Labor Day, Schreiber wrote a letter to the newspaper praising the idea, and Wilmington for originating it. During Rabbi Schreiber's tenure in 1913, Temple of Truth affiliated itself with the Union of Hebrew Congregations, the central organization of the reform movement.[240]

In 1915, when Rabbi Schreiber left Temple of Truth, he was replaced by Rabbi Samuel Rabinowitz, a native of Ohio and a graduate of Haverford College and the Jewish Theological Seminary. Rabinowitz represented the more traditional element of the historical school, and the temple took a turn towards Conservative Judaism. Confronting the dilemma of being American and Jewish in a sermon in April 1916, Rabinowitz argued for the retention of more rituals. He claimed Jews had not taken advantage of religious liberty in America. Instead of using freedom, many Jews, through fear of mockery or a false idea of what Americanism means, had dropped a number of Jewish observances. Rabinowitz believed the Jews should develop all that was good in Judaism. By being loyal Jews they would also be true Americans.[241]

During Rabbi Rabinowitz's tenure, the temple stopped using the Reform Union Prayerbook and returned to the Szold-Jastrow Prayerbook, a more Conservative prayerbook.[242] The rabbi conducted Hebrew classes, which were well attended.[243] Under Rabinowitz's direction, Temple of Truth celebrated two days of Rosh Hashanah, a custom that had been abolished by the Reform movement.[244] At the same time, the temple followed the nontraditional idea of ending services for the summer. On June 22, 1917 Rabbi Rabinowtiz sermonized about thoughts that should be in people's minds during the coming summer months.[245]

Members of the Temple of Truth were the more Americanized Jews in the community. A significant percentage of the members had been born in the United States, and many of those born in Russia had lived in the United States for many years.[246] The members were self-employed people, including dentists, doctors, and real estate agents. None were factory workers or laborers. Several of the members of Temple of Truth had belonged to Adas Kodesch or Chesed Shel Emeth earlier.[247] Many Jews continued to belong to several synagogues because they wanted to ensure the survival of Judaism, no matter what its form. Esther Topkis Potts, daughter of William Topkis, explained: "My father felt that the practice of Judaism was important whatever guise it took, and hence he supported both Adas Kodesch and Beth Emeth financially and with personal attendance and dedication."[248] In many cases, the children of people who had been members of Adas Kodesch joined Temple of Truth.

The presidents of Temple of Truth were long-term residents of Wilmington who were well-established economically. Max Ephraim, who served as president in 1914, had arrived in Wilmington in the 1880s. David Snellenburg, president in 1912–1913 and 1919, had been in Wilmington since 1895. Charles Topkis (president 1916–17) and Aaron Finger (president 1921–22) were born in the United States. All were held in high regard by the entire community. Abraham Goberman, a dentist who was born in Russia, became president in 1922, a decade after he arrived in Wilmington.

By 1921 when Aaron Finger became president of Temple of Truth, the differences between the members who preferred Reform and those who wanted a more Conservative approach had become serious. In May 1921 Finger wrote to Cyrus Adler at the Jewish Theological Seminary and Dropsie College to inform him that

Samuel Rabinowitz had resigned, and Finger wanted assistance in securing a new rabbi. Finger described the congregation's desires in a curious fashion:

> the congregation desires a rabbi whose views are of the sort usually termed conservative but preferably one with orthodox leanings. Perhaps it would be more nearly accurate to say that the congregation wants a modern orthodox rabbi.[249]

The friction at the synagogue was clear. Although Rabinowitz had served the temple with distinction for six years, longer than any previous rabbi, Finger believed that the rabbi should be relieved of his responsibilities after confirmation in June, rather than in September as the rabbi had dated his resignation. While he was president of Temple of Truth, Charles Topkis, through the family business of Wilmington Stores Company, had generously lent the congregation money to deal with its deficit. Suddenly in June, after the announcement of Rabinowitz' retirement, Topkis asked for immediate repayment.[250]

In his correspondence with potential candidates that summer, Finger referred to Temple of Truth as a Conservative synagogue. Rabbi Moses Baroway, who was trained at the Conservative Jewish Theological Seminary, agreed to become the new rabbi in August, 1921. Under Baroway's leadership, a regular Jewish school was organized.[251] However, the strife between those who wanted a Reform synagogue and those who wanted a Conservative synagogue reached new heights.

Dr. Abraham Goberman was elected president of Temple of Truth in May 1922.[252] On June 1, he sent a letter to all members urging them to come to a meeting to decide the policy of whether to be a Reform, Conservative, or modern Orthodox house of worship. Calling the meeting, the most important legislation to be determined since the organization of the temple, Goberman assured the members that the board would carry out the wishes of the majority of members.[253]

The results are clear, though there was no public description of the June 5 meeting. In July, Temple of Truth began inviting different rabbis to conduct Friday evening services. Rabbi Baroway resigned in August and Rabbi Lee Levinger, an author and chaplain, who worked at the 92nd Street YMHA in New York, was hired as the new rabbi.[254] Levinger had been trained at the Reform Hebrew Union College.

Less than a week after the Temple of Truth meeting, on June 11, several of the more Conservative group, including Mr. and Mrs. Aaron Finger, Mr. and Mrs. Charles Breuer, Mr. and Mrs. Max Breuer, Mr. and Mrs. Manual Cohen, Mr. and Mrs. Jacob Faber, Mr. and Mrs. Daniel Laub, Mr. and Mrs. Aaron Levitt, Mr. and Mrs. Max Keil, Mr. and Mrs. David Roth, and Mr. and Mrs. Charles Schagrin met at the Faber's home to plan a new synagogue.[255] They wanted to form a synagogue that would perpetuate the traditions and ceremonies of the Jewish people and their faith with due regard to the time and conditions.[256] In other words, they believed in the historical or Conservative school and wanted to make more changes than the Orthodox were willing to make, but fewer changes than the Reform group. Before the split, the Reform wanted no one to wear a hat in synagogue, but some men wanted to wear hats.[257] The more Reform element wanted a Sunday School one day a week, while the more conservative people wanted a Hebrew school several days a week.[258] By July, the Conservative group had selected the name Congregation Beth Shalom to demonstrate the desire for a peaceful community. They incorporated and purchased the Eastburn property, a large house at the northeast corner of 18th and Washington Streets, for use as a synagogue.[259] Aaron Finger was the first president, Charles W. Schagrin was vice-president, Jacob Faber was financial secretary, Joseph Handler was recording secretary, and Max Keil was treasurer.[260]

The new synagogue brought together members of Temple of Truth and Adas Kodesch who wanted a Conservative approach. The officers of Beth Shalom included two younger men: Aaron Finger, a thirty-two-year-old attorney, and Joseph Handler (Hendler), a twenty-one-year-old attorney who had recently been admitted to the Delaware bar.[261] Both of their fathers, Louis Finger and Samuel Hendler, had been long-term members of Adas Kodesch but had also attended the organizational meeting of the Temple of Truth in 1906. Louis Finger was actually on the first board of Temple of Truth at the same time he was a member of Adas Kodesch. The other three officers—Jacob Faber, one of Wilmington's earliest Jewish residents, Charles Schagrin, and Max Keil, who had come to Wilmington around the turn of the century—had been members of Adas Kodesch for many years. Jacob Faber had attended the 1906 organizational meeting at Temple of Truth. At least thirteen of Beth Shalom's new members were members of Adas Kodesch in 1920. Many might have been members of Adas Kodesch in the spirit of supporting the largest synagogue in town in order to help Judaism flourish, and were most likely also members of Temple of Truth.[262] Several other younger men, including Leo Keil (son of

Max), Sidney Schagrin (son of Charles), Matt Finger (another son of Louis), and Paul Handler (son of Samuel), joined the new Conservative synagogue. The young people were looking for new answers.

In the fall of 1922, Congregation Beth Shalom established voluntary dues of "not less than twenty five dollars a year," and affiliated with the United Synagogue of America.[263] The first rabbi of Beth Shalom was Rabbi Moses Abels, the popular rabbi who had served Temple of Truth a decade earlier.

With no public mention of a dispute over religious observance, the *Sunday Star* reported that the new temple was started principally for geographic motives, in the interest of the Jewish people on the north side of the city and in the Washington Heights section.[264] Geography was, of course, a factor in the founding of the new synagogue, since Beth Shalom was the first synagogue in the area north of the city, to which Jews were moving. But the *Sunday Star* column was written by Jews who didn't want to share their disputes in the newspapers and therefore did not discuss other reasons for the synagogue's formation.

Once the more Conservative members withdrew from Temple of Truth, the temple moved rapidly to a liberal interpretation. It was agreed that hats need not be worn.[265] The celebration of the second day of holidays was eliminated. [266] The reformers at the Temple of Truth wanted to follow liberal Judaism, which insisted that "to be vital, Judaism must be living, and that each generation must be left free to add its share to the growing life of the whole."[267]

Orthodox, Conservative, and Reform Jews saw things very differently. Each believed its form of religious expression was the best. Despite their differences, they shared a belief in the need to preserve Judaism. They wanted to be both Jewish and American. In the United States, they chose freely how to express their religion.

ASSISTING NEW IMMIGRANTS

Given their desire to help those in need become self-supporting, Wilmington's Jews formed several loan associations. The Hebrew Charity Association had a loan committee, which in 1910 was led by three Russian immigrants (Albert Greenstein, Louis A. Hillersohn, and Morris Chaiken) who had only been in Wilmington a decade themselves.[268] Offering loans with very low interest rates, the Hebrew Loan Association started a lot of people in business, recalled Molly Cohen Sklut. "You could borrow one hundred dollars, which was enough to start a business in those days, and repay one hundred and six."[269]

In 1912, twelve men, including Nathan Miller, Max Keil, Louis Rosenblatt, and Samuel Sachs, began the Home Building and Loan Association to assist struggling new immigrants. Each of the twelve men, many of whom were recent immigrants themselves, paid $5 and agreed to pay $5 a month into a fund that could provide loans to those in need. Nathan Miller had always dreamed of owning his own home, and he thought such an association would help others accomplish the same.[270] J. Harry Gordon, who had been working for Miller Brothers, began working for the new loan association and remained there for the rest of his life.[271] The Home Building and Loan came to be known as one of the leading institutions of its kind in the state.[272] By 1956, it had 2,063 stockholders and assets of more than $4 million.[273] Workmen's Circle also had a loan association; members would buy shares and be eligible for loans.[274] James J. Cohen was president of the Commercial Loan Association, which had begun the year before, in 1916. [275] These loan associations, like those started by Jews throughout the country, became important factors in the upward mobility of Jewish immigrants; before 1925, only one bank in all of the Northeast extended credit to Jews, and 85 percent of the Jewish population was too poor to supply the collateral necessary to qualify for bank loans.[276] In Delaware, banks did not lend people money for mortgages until the 1920s.[277]

As the news of Wilmington's prosperity spread and immigrants' lives in large neighboring cities worsened, Jewish immigrants flocked to Wilmington and the Hebrew Charity Association was increasingly busy. In 1914, the Hebrew Charity Association gave $2,364 to the needy, an amount that "ranked high among the charities distributed among the poor, considering the size of the Jewish population."[278] The association's distributions helped to make self-supporting families who would no longer need charity. The following year a similar amount was donated in general relief, loans, meals, groceries, and medical needs.[279] Predicting an influx of immigrants to find employment in the prosperous city, Morris Levy and J. Harry Gordon asked for increased support.[280]

In 1916, more than 976 human beings passed through the Hebrew Charity Association's offices requesting work, financial aid, legal or medical aid, and assistance with problems from sickness to runaway children.[281] Many immigrants were sent by employment bureaus of others cities and told work was plentiful in Wilmington. Superintendent J. Harry Gordon reported that he had been able to find employment for many, and he had helped men bring their families here by advancing them money, that in every instance had been repaid. The Jewish doctors had rendered a great deal of service, in many cases serving without pay.[282] In addition to assisting people in Delaware, the Hebrew Charity Association sent about $400 a month to European war victims.[283]

The Hebrew Charity Association had received income from dues of more than 1,200 members, proceeds from the annual ball, repaid loans, and wages.[284] Expressing his hope that every Jewish member of the community would contribute according to his ability, Gordon said the community should be divided into "two classes, those who give and those who receive."[285] The association needed to raise a large fund for use after the war, and all were urged to increase their contributions.[286]

The Hebrew Charity Association of Middletown began as a part of the Wilmington group, but by 1912 it had become an independent organization with Joseph Berkman as president. Berkman was re-elected president in 1917. Solomon Rosenberg was vice-president, Abraham Fogel was secretary, and Sam Burstan was treasurer. Although Middletown was a small town, the association had expended $5000 there in nine years. A large part of the money had gone to members of the Hope Farm for consumptives.[287]

The Hebrew Charity Association had tremendous stability. Morris Levy, "who was recognized for his charitable work by the state," served as its president for twenty years from its founding until his death in 1920.[288] Under his leadership, the Hebrew Charity Association continued to cooperate closely with the Industrial Removal Office. Many of the cases involved bringing the families of men who had come alone to Wilmington. In February 1914 the IRO wrote to Morris Levy inquiring if it was wise to send the family of a man who had only been in Wilmington for two weeks.[289] Gordon visited the man and reported that though the man had established himself as a shoemaker and was highly recommended by his friends, the Hebrew Charity Association could not take any of the expense for a person who had just arrived. Gordon advised the IRO that they could pay for sending the family if they thought the man was deserving.[290]

Ten days later, in an angry tone Gordon told the IRO they should not have sent the family while refusing to send their furniture. Under such conditions the family would have been better off in New York.[291] Officials of the IRO were surprised that the family was in Wilmington because after discovering that the wife had withheld facts, they had denied her application.[292] Two weeks later, Gordon wrote to the IRO saying the man seemed to be getting along, and the Hebrew Charity Association would lend the man the money to have his furniture sent.[293] Two years later, in a letter discussing another case, Gordon reported that the shoemaker had made a great success, he was earning a good living and saving some money, to such an extent that he had two properties valued at $3200, not all paid as yet.[294]

Abe Goldstein worked in Wilmington in 1916 while his wife and four children remained in New York. Goldstein approached the Hebrew Charity Association to lend him the money to bring his family. Harry Gordon inquired about Goldstein's reputation.[295] "Thoroughly trustworthy and deserving assistance," the IRO answered.[296] By the end of May, the family was in Wilmington and happy. The Hebrew Charity Association had lent the family $62, of which Goldstein had already repaid twenty.[297]

In 1918, an immigrant who had defaulted on an earlier loan from the Hebrew Charity Association requested assistance to bring his family from New York. The Hebrew Charity Association was not inclined to give him any assistance because he made $30 a week and had never repaid the earlier loan.[298]

The Industrial Removal Office referred some of the Hebrew Charity Association's cases to other sources. When Gordon requested assistance in locating an immigrant who had come to Wilmington in March 1919 with his wife and four children and abandoned them in June, the IRO told Gordon to communicate with the National Desertion Bureau in New York.[299] Several Wilmington families wanted to bring relatives from Poland and Romania who would pay their expenses, but the IRO referred Gordon to HIAS, the Hebrew Sheltering and Immigrant Aid society.[300]

As the members of the Jewish community grew older, their needs changed. By 1914, the need for a home for older people was clear, and the Ladies' Bichor Cholem Society, which had been started to assist pregnant women and to care for the sick and needy, decided it wanted to own a building in order to care for the aged and indigent as well as to provide shelter for wayfarers passing through the city.[301] The society changed its charter to enable it to buy property in 1914, and purchased 211 West Street, formerly a hospital, for $6,500 in 1916.[302] While the society made plans for renovation, the building was rented out to help pay the mortgage.[303] During World War I, members of the Bichor Cholem Society put their plans for renovation on hold and gave freely of their services and time for the drives of the Red Cross, Liberty Loans, and the Jewish War Relief.[304] Women volunteered at the Red Cross making bandages and knitting for men in uniform; they also knit and sewed garments for refugees in Europe.[305]

In 1919 a campaign was held to finance the renovation, which was expected to cost about $7,000.[306] The ladies of the Bichor Cholem Society planned to use the home to care for the aged as well as to house a maternity clinic. Since little money could be paid by the individuals who were served, the society hoped to establish an endowment.[307]

The renovated home on West Street was dedicated on June 13, 1920.[308] A bazaar, held at the home every afternoon and evening from June 14 through June 17, raised funds for the maintenance of the institution.[309] One of the most interested people at the dedication was Sadie Levy, the first aged person to live at the home.[310] In order to emphasize the nonsectarian character of their philanthropic work, the Bichor Cholem Society turned over a large plot of ground adjoining their property as a playground for all the children of the neighborhood.[311] The home was also used as a refuge for traveling people. When a very religious person came to town, he was taken to the Bichor Cholem home. Poor people who didn't have money for food were also given meals at the home.[312]

The Bichor Cholem Society benefited from the stability in its leadership. Many founding members continued their involvement. Esther Finkelstein, Anne Ostro, and Nessie Tiger signed the 1914 paper to permit the society to buy land.[313] Mrs. Max (Rosie) Breuer, Mrs. Max (Fannie) Keil, Mrs. Herman (Rachel) Feinberg, and Mrs. Charles (Frances) Schagrin were among the presidents between 1912 and 1920.

In 1916, Mrs. Nathan (Clara) Shtofman, Mrs. Simon (Ida) Album, and Mrs. M. Badershefsky, who were part of Chesed Shel Emeth, organized a women's organization, the Moshev Zekenim, that supplied many of the same needs as the Bichor Cholem but was affiliated with Chesed Shel Emeth.[314] The Moshev Zekenim had over 150 members within a year.[315] Although there was considerable rivalry between the two groups, a month after the Bichor Cholem opened the doors to its new home, it combined with the ladies Moshev Zekenvim.[316] The two organizations, which had similar purposes and often duplicated work, hoped more could be accomplished by working together. The new society was known as the Bichor Cholem–Moshev Zekenim.[317]

The YMHA's new home at Third and King Streets above Samuel Greenbaum's store was formally opened on September 28, 1913.[318] Rabbi Moses Abels, who had helped reinvigorate the YMHA during his tenure at Temple of Truth, spoke about the YMHA's important role in preserving the Jewish soul in a land of freedom by bringing Jewish people together in harmony.[319] In Rabbi Abels's opinion, without the persecution of previous centuries, Jews were losing their Jewish soul. Associations like the YMHA would allow them to rediscover the ideals of Judaism.[320] In 1913, Sallie Topkis Ginns organized a YWHA so that the Jewish girls of the community would have a place to meet and hold social gatherings.[321] Seventy-five women joined the new organization. Jennie Greenstein was the first president, and Rosalie Hillersohn was the secretary.[322]

In its new home, the YMHA had a full schedule of sports and social activities that were initiated by a fall reception each year. Dances for holidays and for the benefit of organizations, as well as public meetings like the one sponsored by the Congressional Union for Women's Suffrage, were held at the YMHA.[323] By 1916 the YMHA even had a Boy Scout troop, Troop 28.[324] In addition to housing activities sponsored by the YMHA, the new building was the regular meeting place for several Jewish organizations including the Hebrew Charity Association, Lodge 470 of B'nai B'rith, Delaware Lodge 140 of B'rith Sholem, Diamond State Lodge B'rith Abraham, Merchants Mutual Association, Workmen's Circle, Wilmington Lodge No. 269 of the Progressive Order, and the Young Women's Hebrew Association.[325]

The presidents of the YMHA—Harry Topkis, Aaron Finger, Jacob Rosenblatt, William Topkis, Dr. Albert Robin, and Louis Topkis—were leaders of the community who had either lived in Wilmington for many years or had been born here. In 1917 when William Topkis was president of the YMHA, J. N. Sokohl was hired as the first professional director.[326] When Sokohl resigned in July 1917, he had started ten new clubs and increased growth tremendously.[327] Abram Becker was the next director, but he resigned in 1918 to enlist in the army.[328] Harry Levi had a brief tenure, because he tragically died of influenza during the epidemic of 1918.[329] Philip Heimlich served as executive from fall 1918 until November 1920. A. D. G. Cohn served less than one year, and Samuel Saretsky was hired in September 1921 and remained until the summer of 1923.[330]

During World War I, YMHA members dedicated themselves to support of the government and the war effort.[331] Discussions about the war, lectures, classes in Americanization, and activities to benefit the soldiers became regular parts of the YMHA program.[332] The proceeds from a minstrel show and dance held during the summer of 1918 were used to send money belts and *simleage* books to the Y boys overseas.[333] On soldiers' nights, held every Thursday night, members would entertain soldiers by reading, talking, and hosting dances. Even the Blue Bird Club of eleven- to fourteen-year-old girls engaged in Red Cross work. During the 1918–19 season, the recently organized Jewish Welfare Board began conducting its work at the YMHA.

The postwar YMHA became a vehicle for dealing with the entire family on a cultural and religious level.[334] There was an emphasis on education for all ages. By the fall of 1919, four classes were initiated: Hebrew, Sabbath School Teaching, English to Foreigners, and Show Card Writing and Math. Hebrew was the most popular class, but the latter appealed to those eager to improve their business skills.[335]

Leaders visualized the YMHA as a Jewish center from which all community activities would radiate, a place where all Jews regardless of religious, political, or other differences would have an opportunity to gather in a spirit of friendship. In their view, the YMHA would

> instill broad mindness, tolerance and a sense of community spirit; bridge the gap between parent and child; train in ideals of Judaism and Americanism; help remove race prejudice; help remove Jewish youth from the noxious influence and temptations surrounding him, and instill higher ideals.[336]

As the number of native-born Americans increased, the importance of preserving Jewish identity took on new dimensions. Many of the young people seemed indifferent to Judaism. There was a gap between parents and children.[337] The YMHA, which dealt with young people, was in a position to effect change, but first it had to become a club of the whole community.[338]

By 1919, when President William Topkis appointed a committee to lay the groundwork for a building campaign, the need for a new home was clear. For a few years, nothing happened. Then, early in 1922, acting on Judge Aaron Finger's suggestion, delegates from every Jewish organization met and agreed to start a Jewish community center.[339] Even the girls of the YWHA transferred their memberships to the Jewish community center in recognition of the fact that the new center considered women an important part of the center and had numerous programs for them.[340] Working together under the General Jewish Committee, which had been developed during the war relief drives, the community held a bazaar in May 1922. Rarely has a community effort reached the idealistic heights of the 1922 bazaar. With their slogan "The Bigger we make the

Bazaar, the Bigger we make Wilmington," chairman David Snellenburg and co-chair Mrs. Albert Robin rallied the support of the entire Jewish community. Organizations and individuals contributed liberally because of the determination to make the occasion the outstanding event of the city and state.[341]

Urging the entire community to assist the Jews, the *Morning News* noted

> The Jewish residents of Wilmington have always been prominent in every movement undertaken here for the improvement of this city or for the uplifting of the town's civic interest, but this will be the first time they have ever made a direct appeal to the citizens at large for something that was for their own special and direct benefit in this city.[342]

David Snellenburg emphasized that the Jews wanted to take a more prominent place in the development of the city's welfare and to do so they needed proper facilities.[343] The building would service not only spiritual and recreational needs, but civic values in interpreting the true meaning of America and American institutions to its members.[344] The Jewish community center would preserve the Jewish moral inheritance for the Wilmington community.[345]

After four record-breaking days (May 22–25, 1922), which attracted some 27,000 people, the bazaar raised enough money to meet the entire indebtedness of the YMHA and to set aside a fair sum for a building fund.[346] By not permitting games of chance, the committee sacrificed huge profits, but won the admiration and respect of the community.[347] Profits in hand, the community met to organize a Jewish community center on June 29, 1922.[348] The constitution of the new Jewish community center was passed and with its establishment, the YMHA became extinct.[349] The small boys' club of 1901 had evolved into a broad-based agency that would address the needs of all Jews from those who needed help with English or math, to those who were wrestling with the complexity of preserving their Jewish identity while becoming American.

The Workmen's Circle continued to assist working men, by helping them achieve what was most important to them: better wages. By 1916 the Workmen's Circle had grown to a membership of nearly 130 and was considered one of the most essential assets of the Jewish community.[350] In 1916, shortly after the Bichor Cholem Society purchased its house, the organization bought a house at 223 Shipley Street, which it planned to renovate as a home for the agency.[351] On the twelfth anniversary of the Workmen's Circle, Samuel Cannon gave a speech about the similarities in the fundamentals of Americanism and Judaism.

Workmen's Circle, 1914. (Jewish Historical Society of Delaware.)

In 1916 in New York, Workmen's Circle began secular schools that were the most ambitious of the schools started by those interested in the Yiddish secular movement.[352] Two years later, Wilmington's Workmen's Circle contributed the first $400 towards an educational fund to establish a Jewish forum where authoritative scholars would discuss Jewish, national, and world problems in an unbiased manner. The fund also provided money for night courses in civics and citizenship. Samuel Cannon, organizer of the fund, had graduated from the University of Delaware (formerly Delaware College) in 1918 as an adult, after immigrating to Wilmington and establishing himself in business.[353] Cannon served as secretary of Workmen's Circle for many years. Education was of central importance to Workmen's Circle members. During the 1920s, Workmen's Circle ran a school that taught Yiddish and constantly exposed children to lectures.[354] However, like other fraternal organizations, the Workmen's Circle also had old age homes, insurance benefits, and regional and national meetings.

By 1913 the Moses Montefiore Society, the oldest Jewish organization in Wilmington, was concerned primarily with burial. The society maintained two cemeteries at Fifth and Hawley Streets and a plot in the Lombardy cemetery.[355]

The Apex Club, which was open to all Jews sixteen to twenty-five years of age of good moral character, had over one hundred members in 1916. The club, which met at 504 Market Street, had assisted the Chesed Shel Emeth building fund, the war relief efforts, and the Hebrew Charity Association.[356]

Jewish fraternal organizations flourished in the United States, and by the early 1900s there were thousands of Jewish societies scattered through the world. They offered financial benefits and cheap insurance as well as serving as social centers.[357] Wilmington's Jews formed branches of many of these national organizations. For several years Wilmington had two B'nai B'rith lodges, but by 1917 the Maimonedes Lodge had merged with the original lodge 470.[358] Wilmingtonians also formed a Delaware Lodge of B'rith Sholem, Diamond State Lodge of B'rith Abraham, and a Wilmington Lodge of Progressive Order of the West.

Mrs. James Ginns, Mrs. Herman Feinberg, and Mrs. Henry Harris sent a letter to every Jewish home asking the women to attend a mass meeting of great importance at the Queen Theater on June 9, 1918. "This matter is of such vital interest to all women of our community that you are urged to attend. It should be your duty to put everything else aside and be present for it is expected that this meeting will make history of which you will be proud."[359]

The women formed a Delaware branch of the National Council of Jewish Women, whose purpose was to unify the work of Jewish women throughout the country and to organize them in the most effective way, ministering to patriotic, social, educational, civic, and philanthropic endeavors. Sallie Ginns, who had always been interested in community activities, was motivated by her belief that "we owe a debt to the community in which we live."[360] In her opinion, women articulated and understood social problems better than men.[361] At the beginning, the council joined in various patriotic activities related to the war effort, such as helping the Red Cross roll bandages, raising dollars to help defray Red Cross expenses, and working for the Council of Defense.[362] By 1920, when Sallie Ginns was elected president, the National Council was raising funds for its newly established kindergarten.

As early as 1911, Rabbi Abels had organized a Jewish federation, or *kehillah,* with representatives of every Jewish organization for the purpose of unifying communal work and securing a building as a home for Jewish activities.[363] New York's Jews attempted to organize a *kehillah* between 1908 and 1922 in order to unify all Jews and show them they were one people with a common history and common hopes.[364] Like New York's experiment, the Wilmington federation failed largely because immigrants were most interested in the purposes of their individual organizations and didn't want to accept the authority of a central organization. Wilmington's *kehillah* lost its president and motivating factor when Rabbi Abels left Wilmington.

Several years later, during the War Relief Drive of 1917, Chairman David Snellenburg organized a general committee with representatives from all Jewish organizations.[365] The general committee achieved such excellent results that it decided to constitute itself as a permanent entity, with David Snellenburg as its first president.[366] The General Jewish Committee helped the community run efficiently by registering all public functions thereby avoiding duplication and promoting harmony among the constituent organizations. It also regulated all community appeals from transients so that no one could ask assistance from members of the Jewish community without its approval.[367]

Whether the organizations offered outright assistance, such as the Hebrew Charity Association and the Bichor Cholem, or guidance to newly arrived immigrants in adjusting to life in America, they all helped Jews accommodate to life in the United States. At the same time the organizations served as a comfortable way for Jews to socialize.[368] Over the years the Hebrew Charity Association, the Bichor Cholem Society, and the YMHA modified their purposes to meet the needs of the people in the community. Their ability to change in order to meet real needs was a key to their success.

ZIONISM

Prior to World War I, Zionism was shunned by wealthy, assimilated Jews, and derived what little support it had from Yiddish-speaking intellectuals.[369] The lack of anti-Semitism and the economic opportunities available in America made many see the United States as the new Zion. For others, the hardships of life in the ghetto left little time for dreams.[370] But the war years marked a critical period for American Jewish attitudes to Zionism. In 1917, after the Russian Revolution and the entrance of the United States into the war, the terrible living conditions of the Jews in Eastern Europe and Palestine became apparent to the entire world.[371] Furthermore, Louis Brandeis, who had become the leader of the American Zionist movement, emphasized the compatibility of Americanism and Zionism, which shared the same beliefs in democracy and social justice.[372] In addition, the increasing power of the anti-immigration movement in the United States caused fear among the Jews that unlimited numbers of their brethren would not be able to continue to come to the United States and made the need for a Jewish homeland even stronger.

On November 2, 1917, Arthur James Balfour wrote to Lord Rothschild to announce British sympathy for a Jewish homeland in Palestine.

His Majesty's Government view with favor the establishment in Palestine of a national home for the Jewish people, and will use their best endeavors to facilitate the achievement of this object, it being clearly understood that nothing shall be done which may prejudice the civil and religious rights of existing non-Jewish communities in Palestine, or the rights and political status enjoyed by Jews in any other country.[373]

The British attitude was seconded by Italy, France, and other allies, including the United States. The Pope promised to be a good neighbor.[374] The Balfour Declaration was hailed as the greatest event in nineteen centuries of Jewish history.

On December 2, 1917 Wilmington's Jews held a demonstration at the YMHA to celebrate the Balfour Declaration and to prepare for the tasks that would follow.[375] Charles A. Cowen, a member of the executive committee of the American Zionist Organization, explained the meaning of the declaration. Those present unanimously expressed their profound gratitude and deep joy and resolved to pledge their lives for the work of the consummation of Zionist ideas. They sang the Jewish national anthem, "Hatikvah." Harry Greenblatt, of the Hebrew School of Adas Kodesch, was secretary of Delaware's Zionist society.

During 1917 and 1918, the Wilmington Zionist Society grew rapidly, and by November 1918, it had about two hundred members. Louis Topkis was president, Morris Chaiken was vice-president, Harry Greenblatt was secretary, and Mrs. Louis Slonsky was treasurer.[376] The organization's goal was to enlist every Jew in Wilmington in the cause of Zionism.

In April 1920 the principal Allied Powers of the League of Nations decided that the mandate for Palestine should be assigned to Great Britain, in keeping with the spirit of the Balfour Declaration.[377] In May the Zionist Organization of America urged "all Zionists to gather and proclaim the great event."[378] Adas Kodesch and Chesed Shel Emeth held special services and Wilmington's ZOA held a celebratory picnic in Shellpot Park.[379] Several prominent Wilmington Jews, including Mrs. Aaron (Anna) Finger, Simon (Solomon) Margoline, Louis Topkis, William Topkis, Harry Eisenman, and Barnet Gluckman, attended a special conference in New York.[380]

In 1917 Delaware Jews had elected William Topkis as Delaware's delegate to the first American Jewish Congress, which was formed to secure civil and political rights for Jewish communities in reconstructed postwar Europe.[381] By the time the Congress met in December 1918, the Zionists had convinced the Congress to press for a Jewish national homeland in Palestine for those who wanted to leave Europe. [382] After attending the Congress, William Topkis became increasingly active in national Zionist affairs. In 1922, he decided that in order to understand what was really going on in Palestine, he would have to spend several months there. Topkis went to Palestine in 1923 in order to set up the first American Information Bureau.[383] While in Palestine Topkis wrote the script, directed, and was the catalyst for the production of *Palestine Awakening,* the first film made to interest Jews in immigration to Palestine.[384] The film, which was shot by the Israeli filmmaker Yaacov Ben Dov, was also known as *A Tour of Palestine in 5683* and *Bloomberg in Eretz Yisrael.*

BECOMING AMERICAN

At the same time they participated in organizations to aid the Jews in the United States, Russia, and Palestine, the Jews were active in Americanization programs, which intensified in 1915. Some 3400 immigrants arrived in Wilmington between 1911 and 1914, more immigrants than in any previous three-year period.[385] The presence of so many newcomers, in addition to the 5,170 new immigrants from the decade before, made education and Americanization efforts essential.[386] Foreign-born illiterates were the natural prey of designing and scheming foreigners and natives.[387] According to the census of 1910, 21.3 percent of foreign-born immigrants were illiterate as compared to 0.7 percent of the native-born population.[388] Wilmington's leaders wanted to bring immigrants into the mainstream and the Jews, eager to become part of their new country, participated in the efforts.

In accepting the need for Americanization efforts, Wilmington's Jews showed that they understood the need for biculturalism and did not fear becoming part of the dominant society. Many traditional Jews, like those on the Lower East Side of New York City, resisted Americanization activities because they feared that plunging even tentatively into the Gentile culture would lead them to religious apostasy.[389] They also doubted that a government might really provide free schooling for benevolent motives.

In 1915 the federal government encouraged cities to hold Independence Day celebrations that would inculcate the American idea in the minds and hearts of those who had come to America to improve their conditions.[390] Wilmington held an Americanization Day to welcome those immigrants who had become citizens in the previous year and to discuss the meaning of American citizenship.[391] In explaining the duties and responsibilities of American citizenship, Mayor James Price said the ideal citizen was activated by concern for other citizens and subjugated self-interest to the good of the whole.[392] Among the approximately eighty new citizens who were special guests at the ceremony and concert, at least sixteen were Jewish.[393] The *Morning News* praised the Jews as an example of a group that had rapidly adopted the American idea.

We wish that all foreigners in this country would have the feeling for it and the appreciation of it that some men who have come to Delaware from Russia—Russian Jews—have. They know what this country is as compared with the nation they left, and so knowing it does not take them long to get the American idea.[394]

In an article about the meaning of America to the immigrant, Barnet Gluckman referred to the Declaration of Independence as "the most holy of holies of human documents, next only to the Bible."[395] The Declaration's assertion that "all men are created free and equal and are therefore entitled to life, liberty and the pursuit of happiness" was the real human heart and soul of America. Because America was being built on justice, equality, and brotherly love, the patriarchs of America would receive the brain and brawn of the whole world. America would be able to count on all foreign- and native-born to defend the institutions of America with every drop of blood and with wealth.[396]

Wilmington joined 250 cities in a national effort to further Americanization by opening a night school to assist foreign candidates for citizenship, operated jointly by the Bureau of Education and the Department of Labor, in 1915.[397] The Bureau of Naturalization gave the names of all aliens who had filed an intent of citizenship to the schools on a monthly basis. Mayor Price appointed a committee of immigrants, including Louis Topkis representing the Jews, to secure attendance at the classes.[398] In describing the night-school effort, the *Morning News* stated that the German and Hebrew societies had been interested and active in the "learn English" campaigns, even though most of the representatives of those races already spoke English. The German and Jewish people were complimented for their adaptation to life in America: "their organizations are so well known and so prominently associated with the life of the city that they no longer suggest the adjective 'foreign.' "[399]

Urging the foreigners to attend night school, learn English, and prepare for naturalization, an editorial in the *Sunday Star* explained that only by becoming American could foreigners gain their share of American prosperity and liberty.[400] If they remained isolated among people of their race, they only partly gained the blessings of American life.

By February 1916 many of the non-English-speaking youths were going to night school at the #4 School on Washington Street or at the #1 School at Sixth and French. They were learning English rapidly, as well as civics.[401] In the fall of 1916 the nationwide campaign of citizen preparedness was begun again through the Bureau of Naturalization, working with public schools in 650 cities.[402]

Pierre duPont called a conference of the chief executives of Delaware industries employing foreign-born laborers, to enlist their aid in Americanization efforts in 1918.[403] Dupont believed that the foreign-born had contributed greatly to the development of Delaware but had not been made part of the state. Americanization, the genuine assimilation of the foreign-born into the society and citizenship, was a matter of first importance to the American government.

During the fall of 1918, nearly two hundred people attended six weeks of classes to prepare them to teach in the night school for foreigners. By 1919, more than one thousand Wilmingtonians were attending twenty-eight night schools in Wilmington, which was better than the attendance in many other cities.[404] The Americanization program received earnest cooperation from the Jews of Wilmington. Rabbi Swiren composed a circular that he sent to every Jewish home in Wilmington, urging participation. At a meeting at the YMHA in February 1919, Rabbis Swiren and Rabinowitz discussed the advantages of learning English and becoming a citizen.[405]

In addition to participating fully in the Americanization programs, the Jews used their communal organizations to help American causes. From its inception, the Hebrew Charity Association contributed annually to the general community. The Mount Sinai Dispensary offered free dental services to children. During World War I members of the Bichor Cholem gave freely of their services and time for the drives of the Red Cross, Liberty Loans, and the Jewish War Relief. Women worked at the Red Cross making bandages and knitting for men in uniform.[406] The YMHA held Americanization classes and served as headquarters for the Jewish Welfare Board.

Wilmington's Jews demonstrated their dedication to the United States by participating fully in all branches of the armed services during World War I. Nationwide, approximately 200,000 Jews were in the armed forces of the United States, and nearly 40,000 were volunteers.[407] In Delaware, at least 113 young Jewish men joined the armed services.[408] Approximately 20 percent of them had been born in Russia.[409] As Barnet Gluckman had predicted a few years earlier, the immigrants were willing to give everything to the country that offered them life, liberty, and the pursuit of happiness.

Max Wainer, born in Russia around 1887, was brought to Wilmington as a young child in 1890. One of the first Jewish graduates of Wilmington High, Max yearned to be a soldier, but since it was impossible for him to go to West Point, he enlisted as a private and worked his way up.[410] In the fall of 1918, Major Max Wainer wrote to Harry Topkis from Europe expressing his pride in being a Wilmingtonian: "you know I owe everything I am to dear Wilmington, and as I gradually climb up the ladder, I hope to add to our city's reputation, and I feel confident all the soldiers she has sent over here will do the same."[411] By December 1918, Wainer had been made a colonel and was the subject of a story in the *Saturday Evening Post*.[412]

Joseph Braiger, born in Russia in 1902, had arrived in Wilmington around 1904 with his family. As soon as the United States entered the war, Joseph enlisted with the army. He was sent home when the army realized he was only fourteen-and-a-half. Braiger later enlisted in the cavalry.[413]

In June 1917, when Delaware held a day for young men to register, thirty-one young Jews came out in the first ward alone.[414] George Slonsky, oldest son of Sarah and Louis Slonsky, received the distinction of being the first Jewish youth to be called up for training camp.[415] A 1913 graduate of Wilmington High, Slonsky was reported to be in good spirits and happily ready to respond to the call of the country.[416]

When the United States entered World War I, Mark B. Holzman was the first physician to volunteer his services to Delaware.[417] Although he did not leave with the State Rifle Range until September, Holzman had gradually given up his private practice in order to assist the regiment.[418] Joseph Barsky entered the Army Medical Corps in 1917 and went overseas with the American Expeditionary Force. In 1918, Barsky became a captain.[419] Doctors Abram Halprin, Louis Levinson, A. J. Gross, and Samuel Zion and dentists Louis Gluckman and Morris Greenstein also served in the war.[420]

Two brothers from Middletown, Delaware, Rupert and Jack Burstan, served with distinction. Rupert was the first Delaware Jew appointed to the U.S. Naval Academy.[421] He invented the machine gun and became a second lieutenant in the U.S. Marine Corps. Jack Burstan, a doctor, found his brother dying in France.

Samuel Green, who worked for the Baltimore and Ohio Railroad, joined the 39th Engineers Division. His unit ran the railroad and communications systems for moving the troops around.[422] Green believed so strongly that "he owed service to his country" that he fought again in World War II, even though he was an older man with two sons in the armed services.

The four Feinberg brothers, Samuel, Isaac, Henry, and William— sons of Rachel and Herman Feinberg—all volunteered for the armed services.[423] Samuel was with the Delaware Pioneers, Isaac and William served in the navy, and Henry was in the marines.

In September 1917, a Jewish Welfare Board was organized for the purpose of caring for the physical and moral welfare of soldiers.[424] Several community leaders who were too old for active service, including J. Harry Gordon, Philip Heimlich, Nathan Miller, and David Snellenburg, volunteered for the Jewish Welfare

Board.[425] Dr. Albert Robin was a member of the Exemption Board.[426] David Snellenburg was a member of the State Council of Defense and Chairman of Community Labor Board No.1, which was charged with the responsibility of keeping production of items vital to the war effort at maximum level.[427]

WAR RELIEF EFFORTS

At the outbreak of World War I in 1914, more than nine-and-a-half million Jews, 73 percent of the estimated thirteen million Jews in the world, lived in the belligerent countries, including some three-and-a-half million in Poland, one-and-a-half million in Russia, and two million in Galicia.[428] With each country struggling and applying all of its resources to military matters, the only Jews who could help those in the belligerent countries were the Jews in the United States.[429]

The first call for help came from Palestine in 1914. Thousands of Jews who had depended on contributions from Jews in the war-torn countries, were in distress and needed some $50,000 to save them from starvation. The American Jewish Committee sent $25,000 and said other groups would send the rest. When appeals from every belligerent country followed, American Jews realized that united action on their part was necessary. On October 25, 1914 representatives of forty Jewish organizations formed the American Jewish Relief Committee. Louis Marshall was elected president, Cyrus Sulzberger secretary, and Felix M. Warburg treasurer. By the end of 1916, the American Jewish Relief Committee had joined with the Central Relief Committee and the People's Relief Committee to form the Joint Distribution Committee, which had raised more than $4,750,000 for the relief of war sufferers.[430] The fact that so many Jewish immigrants had left Europe recently and had close family still there made the concern for people in the war-torn area intense and personal.

In September 1915, Louis Topkis was elected chairman of a local drive to raise funds for the relief of war sufferers.[431] From September through December, a few mass meetings and a general subscription drive were held, but despite the generosity of some individuals, only about $500 was raised.[432]

In January 1916, Louis Topkis organized a meeting of the presidents and vice-presidents of every Jewish organization to plan a relief drive for 1916. He was very frank about Wilmington's unsatisfactory participation thus far.

The spirit of relieving our brethren did not yet seem to have grasped the Jewish public of this city. They seem to be entirely indifferent to this matter. The City of York, Pennsylvania with a Jewish population similar to Wilmington has pledged itself to raise $18,000 this year. Other cities Wilmington's size have done great things while Wilmington Jews are still in the background.[433]

President Wilson, always a sincere friend of American Jews, proclaimed January 27, 1916 a day for all, regardless of race or creed, to contribute toward the relief of the Jews in war-torn countries.[434] Morris Levy was state committee chairman; Louis Topkis was local chairman. Sallie Topkis Ginns was in charge of tag day. The effort raised $3,600. People in New Castle, Lewes, Middletown, Dover, Bridgeville, and Milford contributed to the campaign.[435] Elated with their results, the leaders thanked the press for its courtesy in printing articles about the drive.[436]

By 1917, the national Jewish War Relief effort had become more tightly organized, and the national goal was $10 million. Julius Rosenwald, the founder of Sears, Roebuck and Company, then serving as chairman of the National Council of Defense, offered to contribute $1 million if the Jews of the United States would contribute $9 million.[437] Wilmington was assigned a goal of $18,000. David Snellenburg was chair of the drive, which included a mass meeting and a weeklong bazaar. The centerpiece of the campaign was the mass meeting on June 3, 1917 at the Queen Theater, owned by the Topkis-Ginns Corporation. Rabbi Stephen Wise, a nationally renowned leader of Reform Jewry, was the featured speaker, along with Judge George Gray, Mayor Price, David Snellenburg, and Rabbi Sam Rabinowitz of the Temple of Truth. Rabbi Wise related pitiful stories of life in Poland, which had been fought over four times in two years. Urging the Jews to contributed generously, Wise said "It is as if we Jews who have come here to this country had been blessed by God with plenty now to help those who have been deprived of their all by the ruthlessness of the German world."[438]

Wise told those gathered that Christian friends of Wilmington Jews had subscribed $15,000 to the fund, and it was the duty of Wilmington Jews to do as well or better on behalf of their own brethren. An additional $20,000 was quickly raised.

After its opening event Wilmington had raised more than $35,000, double its goal. New York leadership congratulated Wilmington and assigned a new goal of $45,000. The weeklong charity bazaar, which had a different Jewish organization in charge every evening, opened on June 11. Each night of the campaign brought large crowds.

The General Charity Bazaar Committee

CHAS. TOPKIS • NATHAN MILLER • ABE TOPKIS

MRS. ABE FISCHER • RALPH SALTZMAN • EDWARD S. CANNON • MRS. JAMES N. GINNS

LOUIS TOPKIS • DAVID SNELLENBURG • DR. S.A. RABINOWITZ

NATHAN E. LEOPOLD • MORRIS LEVY • BARNET GLUCKMAN

HARRY KETY • MORRIS SHTOFFMAN • DR. L.D. GLUCKMAN • NATHAN REISSMAN

JOSEPH BERMAN • ABE FISCHER • JAMES N. GINNS

David Snellenburg, President   Morris Levy, Treasurer.   Ralph Saltzman, Secretary

General Charity Bazaar committee, 1917. (Jewish Historical Society of Delaware.)

On the evening of June 14, hundreds of Jews and Gentiles mingled in one happy family, all intent upon lending a helping hand for the relief of war sufferers in foreign lands. Josiah Marvel, a prominent attorney born in Sussex County who in 1918 was president of the Wilmington Associated Charities, described the pride he felt in his own ancestry (which he could trace back many generations) in order to give an interesting tribute to the Jew.

> If we feel pride of ancestry, how much more reason have you people for feeling proud of your ancestry which goes back many centuries. . . . Hundreds of your race have not only done much for themselves but have accomplished greater things for the world.[439]

On the evening of June 16, a Friday evening, Secretary of State Everett C. Johnson spoke about the greatness of the Jews, claiming "The more Jews in Delaware the nearer we become a Christian state." After citing examples of Jews throughout history, Johnson claimed

> We love the Jew in Delaware. The Jews are one nationality that sees visions and backs them up with actions. . . . The Jew has played a very important part in making Wilmington what it is today. . . . If we of another creed had some of the virtues the Jew is endowed with, it would be far better for this nation today.[440]

The bazaar raised $6,000, approximately $1,000 each night. The fact that 10 percent of the money raised went to the Red Cross created interest among many local residents.[441] Since the campaign had been so successful, the committee agreed that an additional 5 percent of the proceeds would go to the war campaign fund.[442]

In thanking the community, chairman David Snellenburg explained that by surpassing its first $18,000 goal and being on the brink of reaching its $45,000 goal, Wilmington was on the honor roll of forty-two cities, out of a total of 1,500 cities engaged in relief work. In fact, Wilmington was at the head of this honor roll of cities that had met their first goal and were within reach of their second goal.[443] David Snellenburg praised the general community, which had shown broadminded generosity in contributing liberally to a cause that was primarily a Jewish cause. "Once again Wilmington has shown it is bigger than any one cause," he claimed. According to Jacob Billinkopf, executive director of the National War Relief Campaign, "the per capita contribution of Wilmington exceeded that of any city in the country."[444]

David Snellenburg and Louis Topkis were both members of the

American Jewish Relief Committee that developed national campaign plans.[445] In November 1917, Louis Topkis was elected to the executive committee of the American Jewish Relief Committee. His election was seen as a testimony to the work he had done in the last three years and as recognition that Delaware was a state worthy of representation on the national executive board.[446] National leadership designated the week of December 3–10, 1917 as Julius Rosenwald Week, for the collection of all gifts pledged in the spring campaign. During the week in Wilmington, chaired by David Snellenburg, T. Coleman duPont gave an additional $3000 to the campaign.[447] The Jews of the United States were successful, and Julius Rosenwald wrote a check for $1 million.

In 1918 the American Jewish Relief Committee established a national goal of $30 million to assist the eight million Jews in the war zone. Since America had entered the war and the magnitude of needs was fully understood, the Jewish War Relief committee realized it couldn't raise such sums alone, and it chose Wilmington for an experiment to appeal to non-Jews for contributions.[448] Wilmington was a good place for a test of general support for several reasons. Wilmington's record of per capita giving to the recent campaigns of the Red Cross, Liberty Loan Bonds, Knights of Columbus, Young Men's Christian Society, as well as to the 1917 Jewish War Relief Campaign, was outstanding.[449] During the latter campaign, Wilmington's Jews had received great support and endorsement from the broader community. The Jews had been very active in the Liberty Loan campaign and according to John S. Rossell, chairman of that campaign, had even suggested the campaign's slogan, "A bond in every home."[450] The Jewish community had been the first to contribute liberally to the Hope Farm facility for treatment of tuberculosis patients. David Snellenburg had made the first contribution to the campaign of the Young Men's Christian Association after an appeal by Dr. John Mott.[451] Furthermore, the Jews of Delaware had built strong ties with the broader community. Louis Topkis, who was very active in Republican politics, was an ally of Coleman duPont.[452] William Topkis was a director of the Delaware Trust Company, owned by William duPont. Dr. Albert Robin was Irénée duPont's doctor and friend. In addition, Senator Saulsbury knew Julius Rosenwald, then chair of the National Council of Defense.[453]

Delaware was asked to raise $75,000, "an amount beyond any possibility of attainment" by Jews alone.[454] David Snellenburg was chairman of a broad-based committee representing the total community. At their first meeting on May 6, 1918, the workers agreed that all campaign expenses would be paid with private money so that 100 percent of every dollar could go to the drive. The campaign was scheduled for one week, May 11 to May 18, 1918.

The opening dinner, held at the Hotel duPont on Saturday evening, May 11, 1918, attracted three hundred prominent Jews and non-Jews. It became a legend in Delaware because of the spirit of cooperation and brotherhood (epitomized by Pierre S. duPont, chairman of the Dupont Company), that "united all Wilmingtonians, without the prejudice of race or creed, in the cause of humanity," and set an example for the country.[455] According to the *Sunday Star,* it was the "greatest event that ever transpired here on a single evening." Or more correctly, it was "one of the greatest events of its kind that have ever taken place at anytime in the history of the nation."[456]

Among the prominent Delawareans at the dinner, in addition to Pierre duPont, were Senator Willard J. Saulsbury, then president pro tem of the United States Senate, and industrialists John Raskob, William Coyne, and John S. Rossell. Some prominent Delawareans who could not attend the dinner, like Lammot duPont and Governor John G. Townsend, sent letters of sympathy for the cause, which were printed in the newspaper.

Dr. Nathan Krass of New York was the featured speaker. Pierre duPont, Julius Rosenwald, Reverend John Connelly, Reverend Charles Candee, and David Snellenburg also made brief speeches. When David Snellenburg introduced Pierre S. duPont as the man responsible for halting the German drive on Paris at Marne, a reference to duPont gunpowder, there was a long ovation. DuPont opened his remarks with the revelation that he was part Jewish.

> Mr. Snellenburg has introduced me as somewhat of an outsider, but I think that I am as much entitled to be here as he is. I have a special reason for being here as I have one eighth of Jewish blood in my veins. My grandfather was a Jew, and I therefore consider it my special duty, not only privilege, to join in raising these funds. Now raising of the funds is simple. We will simply go after the amount until we get it.[457]

Mr. duPont claimed the right thing for financiers to do was to subscribe the whole fund of $75,000, which he was willing to do as he was so sure it would be raised.[458] He suggested that the Jews themselves should be able to raise $75,000 and should ask the non-Jews to raise a similar amount. The crowd rose to its feet for several minutes of cheers and applause. Julius Rosenwald thanked Mr. duPont for his "most generous offer made in the most generous way."

He expressed his belief that the Delaware Jewish community "would see to it that Mr. duPont would not have to bear the burden, but that they will sail upon the work with ever more vigor and enthusiasm and once again put Delaware on the map as the model state for the other states to follow."[459]

After a stirring address by Dr. Krauss about the unparalleled miseries to which the Jews had been subjected during the war, not only by the enemy but from the governments under which they lived, donors began announcing their gifts. Mr. and Mrs. David Snellenburg, Mr. and Mrs. Louis Topkis, Mr. and Mrs. Charles Topkis, Mr. and Mrs. William Topkis and Mr. and Mrs. James Ginns contributed $2,500 each.[460] Pierre duPont contributed $10,000; Alfred I. duPont and William Coyne contributed $5,000 each. During the evening, $43,800, more than half of the goal, was pledged. The editorial in the *Sunday Morning Star* the next morning called the mass meeting

> a wonderful exposition of the new spirit of unanimity and brotherhood that permeates our country and which finds even greater expression in Wilmington than elsewhere. . . . The hearts of our people are open to the needs of humanity everywhere, and in succoring the helpless, neither race nor creed interposes a barrier to our gift.[461]

On Sunday evening, Jews and non-Jews attended the mass meeting at the Queen Theater.[462] Senator Saulsbury praised the Jews for their philanthropic work, which he had first become acquainted with several years ago in the Hope Farm campaign, in which the most substantial gifts for the tuberculosis facility were from the Jewish citizens. Senator Saulsbury asked

> What is money but the power to do good with? What's the use of having money if these things are going on in Europe and if they might be going on in America? If the races that inhabit Europe are to be allowed to starve, what is the future of the human race to be?[463]

Julius Rosenwald spoke briefly praising the unity of ideals of all races and creeds as the "finest example of Americanism I have ever met with." An additional $7,000–8,000 was subscribed at the mass meeting.[464] In two days, $50,000, or two-thirds of the goal, had been raised.

Each day for the following week, a campaign event was held, and the total of the campaign was reported on the front page of the *Morning News*. On Wednesday, May 15, the paper announced that

$70,600 was in hand, and the goal had been increased to $100,000. Julius Rosenwald sent a telegram of congratulations.

If Wilmington succeeds in raising $100,000 it will be the greatest achievement of the entire Jewish War Relief effort. Wilmington has more fine citizens to the square inch than any other city I know of. My heartiest congratulations on what you have accomplished.[465]

Following Pierre duPont's leadership, many duPont family members and other members of the general community contributed to the campaign. By Friday morning, $101,000 was raised and the committee expected to raise $125,000. The frenzied spirit of success reached everyone. A female employee of R. Topkis and Company asked if a one dollar contribution was acceptable. Upon being told yes, she gathered $60 from her fellow employees. Harry Kety collected $39 by walking through the King Street Market, gathering gifts of a dollar or two from nearly every farmer.[466]

The Jewish Sabbath begins on Friday evening; however, on Thursday, May 16 the newspaper announced that services at Adas Kodesch and Temple of Truth would begin fifteen minutes early Friday evening so that workers could attend the Friday event.

On Saturday evening a Jewish Community Holiday culminated the week. David Snellenburg asked all Jewish merchants to close their stores by 9 P.M. so they could attend the celebration. The entire city was proud of the campaign results. "Certainly the splendid results of this campaign should call forth rejoicing not only by our Jewish fellow citizens but by the people in general, for the city is very proud of the success of the campaign."[467] The campaign was about to close at $110,000 when John Raskob, a vice-president of the DuPont company, announced that Mr. Pierre duPont and he would contribute the amount necessary to reach the total of $125,000. "Unity of understanding and conviction will always lead to unified and strengthened achievement," Raskob explained.[468]

In his closing remarks, David Snellenburg said that the spirit shown in Wilmington's campaign had not been exemplified in any of the 1,400 cities where the campaign was taking place. Praising Wilmington as a unique place, Snellenburg said, "We believe it is a distinction which belongs to Wilmington to do better than other cities. We believe if we will have faith in Wilmington people, that we can be the best city in the whole world."[469]

Wilmington's brilliant success affected the entire country.[470] The cause that had seemed hopeless quickened with confidence and energy. Telegrams and letters, heralding the Wilmington marvel, were rushed to all pivotal points. The Jewish War Relief Campaign swept the country with its new conquering slogan, "This is not only a Jewish movement—It is a Human Movement."

Wilmington became known as "the model city of charity and good will."[471] In the report of the American Jewish Relief Committee for the year 1918, Jacob Billinkopf credited Wilmington with being the place the campaigns became "not merely sectarian but humanitarian."[472]

It was in Wilmington that Senator Willard Saulsbury expressed the new spirit when he said, "This is not only a Jewish movement; it is a human movement. It will clothe when clothing is needed and feed when feeding is necessary; it will go wherever the cry of humanity calls it. It is of human beings, for human beings and by human beings."[473]

Wilmington was held in such high regard that the New York committee decided "not to burden Wilmington with a quota for the 1920 campaign, for which the national goal was thirty five million dollars."[474] Under the leadership of chairman Nathan Miller, the community once again planned a nonsectarian campaign, which would last for one week, March 20 to March 27, 1920. Retired Federal Judge George Gray was honorary chairman of the campaign, David Snellenburg was vice-chair, Rabbi Samuel Rabinowitz was secretary, Louis Topkis was treasurer, and David C. Aspril was assistant treasurer.[475] Delaware's senators L. Heisler Ball and Josiah O. Wolcott, Congressman Caleb R. Layton, Governor John G. Townsend Jr., and Right Reverend John J. Managhan, Bishop of Delaware, were among the dignitaries who served on the fourteen-member advisory committee.[476]

The campaign opened with a dinner at the Hotel duPont on Saturday, March 20. Louis Marshall, head of the American Jewish Relief Campaign who had represented the Jews at the Versailles conference, was the principal speaker. Judge George Gray, Congressman Caleb Layton, Mayor William G. Taylor, John S. Rossell, Henry P. Scott, Dr. Charles L. Candee, and Reverend Connelly addressed the crowd, and most praised the Jews and the record of their race in America.[477] Judge Gray called the Jews "a remarkable race that never has lost its identity in two thousand years." Governor Townsend sent a telegram that said "No call for help appeals to me more strongly than this campaign. After all you have done as citizens of this State and Nation, I am sure Delaware will respond to the call made by your kin and race."[478]

Louis Marshall delivered a magnificent appeal for aid on behalf of the sufferers abroad. The Jews had suffered most terribly because they were confined to the Russian Pale by the edict of the former czars. Being in the very battleground of the contending armies, they suffered from the cruelties of both sides.[479] Marshall praised Delaware and the Jews of Delaware.

> I feel the testimonial of the worth of the Jews of Delaware given tonight is an indication of the respect the Jewish community of Delaware deserves. Delaware was the first of all the States that gave to us of the American Jewish Relief Committee the encouragement that the contributions were non-sectarian. When word came to us that this State had arisen non-Jew and Jew together, it was as a balsam upon a sore wound. Tonight we have a repetition of that same spectacle of brotherhood.[480]

After Marshall's excellent address, $65,000 was raised in sixty minutes with the spontaneous generosity that had become characteristic of Wilmington's war relief drives.

In an editorial about the campaign the *Wilmington Morning News* emphasized the nonsectarian nature of the campaign.

> It is needless to say that those in active charge of this good work will be assisted by persons of all religious faiths. The suffering of the great war, the devastation and heart rending that the titanic conflict caused broke down all religious lines and Americans citizens worked as one for the benefit of humanity.[481]

During the remainder of the week, team captains reported their progress at large festive gatherings. On Monday evening, it was reported that Pierre S. duPont had donated $10,000. Nine-year-old Edward Schwatko had contributed five cents after approaching Dr. Louis Gluckman to inquire if they would take a "small gift to help those poor Jewish kids over there."[482]

By Tuesday evening, the campaign had taken a great leap forward and $93,371 was in hand.[483] Chairman Nathan Miller warned workers not to diminish their efforts because they had been so successful thus far. On Thursday night the campaign had reached $110,000 and was gaining momentum. The committee decided to extend the campaign until Monday because workers throughout the state wanted to make appeals at the churches on Sunday morning.[484]

On Saturday evening, at the meeting for captains and workers, the air sizzled with the enthusiasm that comes from knowing one has done something really good for someone else. The campaign reached a total of $122,500.[485] Louis Leshem, a barber, received a standing ovation when he told his story about Eugene duPont.

I was pondering how to start my subscriptions when Mr. duPont walked into the shop for a shave. . . . While I was shaving him, I asked him to contribute to the campaign. Dupont quickly answered "I guess I can help you some on that. About how much do you think I ought to give, Louis?"

"As much as you think is right, Mr. duPont."

"Will a thousand dollars be all right?" he asked.

I nearly fainted. Mr. duPont got the finest shave I ever gave.[486]

Nearly three hundred workers from Wilmington and towns throughout the state attended the final meeting of the campaign on Monday, March 29. One of the great surprises of the campaign was that $10,000 had been raised in the cities and towns of the state under the chairmanship of Morris Levy. A total of $152,348 was raised, and the celebration reached such heights that the "workers cheered themselves hoarse."[487]

Nathan Miller thanked the public and the press for their most generous support. He attributed the campaign's success to "the public and humanitarian spirit of noble Delaware. Race, religion and creed were forgotten by our fellow citizens who gave to the utmost of their means and personal service to bring to a successful conclusion this most worthy cause."[488]

The success of Wilmington's Jewish community culminated in the War Relief Drives. For a brief moment in time, the city of Wilmington and its Jewish community were the center of national admiration. Wilmington, which encouraged its Jews to be Jewish and American, was an ideal American city.

THE COMMUNITY OF 1920–1921

The Wilmington Jewish community, which was praised throughout the country, had grown enough to be a more visible presence than the Jewish community of 1879. With approximately four thousand people, the Jewish community now accounted for between 3.5 and 4 percent of the population of Wilmington.[489] It comprised some 24 percent of the foreign-born population.[490] The entire city was more "foreign" than it had been in 1879 because in addition to the foreign-born population, which now accounted for about 15 percent of the total population, another 23 percent of the population had foreign parentage or mixed parentage.[491]

The Jewish community, largely a mixture of Jews born in America and Eastern European immigrants, was both more American and more foreign than the community of 1879. About 21 percent of the Jewish adults were American-born.[492] In addition, children under eighteen years of age, who accounted for nearly half of the Jewish population, were largely born in America, so the Jewish population was between 50 and 60 percent American-born.[493] The issue facing American-born Jews was how to combine their Americanism and their Jewishness. They did not have to become American, as the earlier immigrants did, nor did they have to prove that they were worthy of being American.

But the Jewish community was also more foreign than the community of 1879 because some 65 percent of the adult population and nearly 40 percent of the total population was Eastern European.[494] Very few new Jewish immigrants to Wilmington were from Germany or Western Europe; most of those who were here had arrived before the turn of the century. Many of the immigrants from Eastern Europe had been in Wilmington for many years and served as role models to the newer immigrants much the way the Germans had helped the East Europeans earlier. For the new immigrants becoming American was still a primary issue. The American-born and immigrant populations had different priorities, which inevitably challenged the unity of the community.

By 1920 the community was an established entity with some history of its own. A core of people had been in the city since before the turn of the century.[495] There were established leaders and traditions. Even the relative newcomers had been in Wilmington longer than the transients who stayed in Wilmington only briefly before the turn of the century.

The community was still youthful. About 65 percent of the adults were in their twenties and thirties.[496] Some 15 percent were fifty or older.[497]

No longer could the community be described as a collection of clothiers and retailers. The Jews of 1920 had branched out into industries, business, and the professions, and they continued to explore new areas. When Prohibition began, Max Keil, a successful liquor merchant, entered the automobile business along with his son Leo and his brothers, Isadore and Samuel.[498] Keil Motor Company expanded into air conditioning, television, furniture, and jewelry.[499] Leo Blumberg became a professor of electrical engineering at the University of Delaware. Charles Belfint became an accountant with the DuPont Company. Louis Grossman opened an electrical supply store, Joseph Berman founded a realty company, Bill Frank went to work for the *Wilmington Morning News,* Sol Polotsky wrote obituaries for the *Sunday Morning Star,* and Joe Green was elected to city council. On an individual basis, Jews seemed to be able to enter any field.

More young people continued on to the university, because education was seen as the route to success. About a dozen Jewish boys, including Herman Cohen, Charles Levy, Harry Reitzes, Al Simon, Max Sline, and Hyman Yanowitz, graduated from Wilmington High in 1922 and went to the University of Delaware.[500] As Jews, they were not permitted to join any of the five fraternities so popular on campus. Furthermore, the university had a rule limiting the number of fraternities to five. The boys decided to protest the injustice of the system. In 1924, they lobbied the university's board members one-on-one and were successful in convincing the board members to allow a sixth fraternity, Sigma Tau Phi, on campus. Nathan Miller gave the fraternity the money to buy a house.[501] Although the result allowed the boys to enjoy fraternity life, it also clearly separated the Jewish boys from the rest of the students. Undoubtedly, such separation was disturbing to the young people, particularly to American-born Jews.

Outwardly, the Wilmington Jewish community of 1920 was more advanced than the earlier communities. It had run nationally acclaimed War Relief Drives and offered a wide range of communal services. Despite its success in accommodating to life in Delaware, the Jewish community of 1920 differed dramatically from earlier communities in one fundamental aspect. The commitment to remain Jewish, always the foundation of the community, was not as firm as it had been earlier. The weakening of the commitment to observe Judaism and voluntarily be part of a community that provided assistance to other Jews and the broader community was partly a result of the changing attitudes in America.

7

End of an Era

AFTER WORLD WAR I, SEVERAL FACTORS, INCLUDING THE ALLEGED connection of Jews and Bolshevism, Henry Ford's publication of *The Protocols of the Elders of Zion,* and the immigration laws of 1921 and 1924, completely changed the climate of America. Few Jews doubted that they were witnessing an intensification of anti-Semitism.[1] As people who had experienced persecution throughout their history and knew the story of the Jews of Spain, who had been expelled after living in harmony with the Christians and Moslems for centuries, Jews were particularly sensitive to signs of their being unwelcome.

In many circles, the Jews were linked to political radicalism, specifically to the Bolshevik Revolution in Russia.[2] Some people claimed that Bolshevism was a purely Jewish movement and part of a plan by an international group of Jews to control the world.[3] In the United States, a group of anti-Semitic publicists led by George A. Simons, a minister who had witnessed the revolution firsthand, alleged that the men who made the revolution in Russia were overwhelmingly apostate Jews, and that in the United States nineteen out of twenty communists were Jewish.[4] According to the Wilmington *Morning News,* there was little danger of anarchists or Bolsheviks. "The entire matter of anarchists and Bolsheviki has been grossly exaggerated. Extreme radical sentiment is almost negligible in the United States."[5]

During the war, a typewritten document entitled "The Protocols of the Elders of Zion" clandestinely circulated in Europe. The document depicted Jews and Freemasons trying for centuries to produce revolution and anarchy in order to obtain control of the world. The original Protocols had been published in Russia in 1905 by a little-known supporter of czarism, Serge Nilus, who claimed they were absolutely truthful and had been delivered to him in 1901.[6] By 1919 the Protocols were being circulated in the highest levels of government in Washington.[7]

234

In May 1920, the *Dearborn Independent,* a newspaper owned and controlled by Henry Ford, published an article entitled "The International Jew: The World's Problem," and shortly afterwards, began serializing the *Protocols of the Elders of Zion.*[8] Despite protests from presidents Taft and Wilson heading a group of 119 distinguished Americans, and from the Federal Council of Churches, Ford continued publishing the *Protocols* for seven years.[9] The anti-Semitic tirades alleged that the Jews had a worldwide conspiracy to control the world and used their ideas to corrupt collective opinion, control finance, sponsor revolution, and exercise power.[10]

Finally, in July 1927, after being sued for libel, Ford apologized for the articles and ceased publication, but the damage had been done. As the country's foremost industrial magnate, with vast sums of money at his disposal, Ford had made the *Protocols* world famous.[11] The ideas affected attitudes that influenced public policy.[12] Undoubtedly, Ford's campaign reviling Jews contributed to a latent attitude of anti-Semitism that is difficult to measure because it remains concealed.[13]

During the 1920s, the restrictionists, who had attempted to limit immigration for several decades, achieved their goals. The struggle over immigration, which had ceased during the war when all immigration essentially stopped, was revived. However, there was a new climate in America and the debate was different. Aware of the fact that they were not immune from international crises, Americans were suddenly afraid of the number of unassimilated immigrants in their midst who could prove disloyal to the United States.[14] A new spirit of 100 percent Americanism "demanded an unprecedented national solidarity: loyalty and social conformity became virtually synonymous."[15] The question was no longer about the desirability of restrictions on immigration but simply about the degree and kind of restrictions.

In January 1921 Congress debated the Johnson bill, which proposed prohibiting immigration for one year. Proponents of the bill claimed that without such a bill, millions of aliens would flood the United States increasing unemployment and creating economic chaos.[16]

T. Coleman duPont, who was serving as chair of the Interracial Council, spoke against the immigration bill before Congress. He had no fear that the United States would be flooded with undesirable immigrants.[17] During the entire fiscal year ending June 30, 1920, fewer than ten thousand males had arrived in the United States. In fact, the outflow of immigrants was greater than the inflow. Dupont believed that the proposed immigration bill would keep out able-bodied unskilled laborers. He believed that the present business slump was temporary, and limiting immigrant labor might cause a shortage when manufacturing returned to normal conditions. Dupont also referred to limiting immigration as a campaign of hostility and insult toward the foreign-born that made Americanization futile.

The Wilmington *Morning News* praised General duPont for "piercing the fog and confusion." The newspaper agreed that able-bodied unskilled workmen were producers of wealth and therefore essential to the country's prosperity. A hostile attitude to foreigners didn't win their hearts or make them good Americans.[18]

Even the *Dover State News* favored admitting immigrants, although its angle was slightly different. According to this paper, farmers needed workers. Because the population of cities in America exceeded that of the country for the first time, all new immigrants should be required to work three to five years on a farm.[19]

By the time the Senate concluded its hearings on the Johnson bill at the end of January 1921, it had rejected the idea of prohibiting immigration and was working on a percentage formula.

In May 1921, both the Senate and the House passed a bill that limited European immigration to 3 percent of the number of foreign-born of each nationality present in the United States at the time of the census of 1910. The effect of the law was to hold transatlantic immigration to a maximum of 350,000 and assign most of the total to northwestern Europe. Thus, ethnic affiliation became the main determinant for admission to the United States.[20] The bill, which reflected the mood of the country, passed both houses with large majorities.[21] Delaware's Senator Josiah Wolcott voted yes, and Senator L. Heisler Ball did not vote.[22] Congressman Caleb Layton voted yes.[23] President Harding approved the bill, and it became law.

In 1924, a more restrictive law, proposing that the annual quota of any nationality be 2 percent of the number of foreign-born individuals of such nationality resident in the United States as determined by the census of 1890, came before Congress. The conference report on the bill was presented to the Senate and the House on May 15, 1924 and passed both houses with large majorities.[24] Both Senators L. Heisler Ball and Thomas F. Bayard voted with the majority, as did Congressman William H. Boyce. [25] After President Calvin Coolidge signed the bill, the flow of immigration from Eastern and Southern Europe was severely curtailed. The combined quota of Poland, Russia, Romania, and the Baltic countries, which before World War I furnished about 100,000 Jewish immigrants annually, was now fixed at 9,443.[26]

The end of mass immigration was devastating to Jewish unity. Once the influx of immigrants ended, the unifying theme of the Jewish community was gone. The need to help each other succeed in America had been foremost in the minds of the Jews in our story. In spite of their differences, the Jews remained publicly unified because it was good for all of them. But the new immigration laws clearly told the Jews they were less desirable than other people. Their bretheren were prohibited from entering the country. Despite all of their efforts to assist immigrants so that they would not be a burden on the society, the Jews had failed to keep the doors open.

As fewer immigrants arrived in the country, an important source of knowledge about Jewish life disappeared. The shtetl Jews with their traditional beliefs and lifestyles had reinvigorated the Jews of America much the way the German Jews had influenced the Sephardic Jews. Gradually, as fewer immigrants arrived, the reality of life in the Old Country became more remote. Without close personal connections and intimate knowledge of the hardships borne by relatives in the Old World, the Jews in America cared less about the needs of Jews in Europe and more about themselves. Their emphasis shifted to doing well in this country, which meant being as American as possible.

By the 1920s, the message, sometimes blatant but often just below the surface, was "if you want to get ahead, be more American and less Jewish." For young people, particularly those born in America, there was a temptation to downplay their Jewish side. For some, the next logical question would become, why be separate at all? If being Jewish was such a disadvantage, why not just emphasize the American qualities? In other words, some Jews no longer wanted to maintain a balance between being Jewish and American.

In this new climate, with all its uncertainties, Wilmington's Jews found it more difficult to overcome the usual disagreements between factions in their community. The split between the Reform and Conservative synagogues in 1922, in spite of the name Beth Shalom to signify peace, was anything but peaceful, and caused bitter feelings that were still prevalent twenty years later. Rabbi Herbert Drooz, who began serving Temple Beth Emeth in the 1940s, noted "The bitterness was still sharply present when I came to Wilmington twenty one years later."[27]

Although the YMHA had been converted into a Jewish community center after the successful bazaar in 1922, the center effort met with failure at the moment it was needed to help young Jews answer the identity question. The acrimony caused by the Temple of Truth—Beth Shalom split eliminated Aaron Finger and other leaders of the community center movement from the effort. Samuel Saretsky, the dynamic director, resigned in the summer of 1923. Louis Topkis, the president of the center, was on an extended European vacation. The level of activity at the Jewish Community Center decreased tremendously. Throughout 1923 and 1924, fewer and fewer activities were held at the deteriorating old YMHA building. Activities that had been held at the YMHA were dispersed throughout the community in synagogue buildings. The Temple of Truth, Adas Kodesch, and Chesed Shel Emeth each built new annexes for their schools and other activities.[28]

In 1925, Wilmington and "Jews the world over" sustained a great loss when William Topkis died.[29] Topkis was an outstanding example of the Jew who understood how to become American and remain Jewish.

> The career of William Topkis closed yesterday by his untimely death might well be an inspiration to success for every young American. . . . He quickly assimilated the essential qualities of Americanism and became a prominent and successful figure, not alone in the business life of the community but in every civic betterment project as well. . . . [I]n recent years he was ardently interested in the transformation of Palestine into a homeland for oppressed Jews of the Old World.[30]

Topkis's death symbolized the end of the era of balance.

By 1929, when the Jewish Welfare Board was called in to Wilmington to study the Jewish community, the magnificent community, which had been the epitome of the successful balance of Jewishness and Americanism, no longer existed. The General Jewish Committee, which brought all Jews together was practically nonexistent.[31] The Jewish Welfare Board reported "There are serious factional divisions which have operated to check community progress. . . . Differences between individuals and groups obtain in all communities, but Wilmington is extreme."[32]

The Jewish community, which had stood as a symbol of what could be achieved through the cooperation of Jews and the broader community, had become a fragmented collection of Jewish synagogues and organizations with no common purpose.

Afterword

Between 1879 and 1920, the Jews in Wilmington were success-ful because they were able to preserve their heritage and at the same time become American. By accepting some compromises, they found that they could balance the demands of being Jewish and American. Through values taught in Judaism, they became exemplary citizens, who worked closely with the broader community to achieve goals.

Beginning in the 1920s, the balance of the early community was lost. Gradually, the majority of Jews born in America emphasized their American identity and minimized their Jewishness. At the end of the twentieth century, with more than 90 percent of American Jews born in the United States, the understanding of what it means to be American is much greater than the understanding of what it means to be Jewish. Today we might most aptly describe the challenge facing the Jewish community with the phrase, "Becoming Jewish: Remaining American." In a reverse of the original situation, today's American Jews must probe the meaning of being Jewish and strive to recapture Jewish values in their lives, recognizing that they can be actively Jewish and still be good Americans. Regaining the balance is essential to the survival of Judaism in America and the strengthening of America.

The model of a religious or ethnic community supplying core values to its members who then interact with the larger society is one that should be encouraged in the United States because it strengthens the society. The United States offers a governing system, and as such it cannot provide the spiritual perspective or philosophical dimension needed by most people. The Declaration of Independence asserts the simple yet revolutionary concept that all men are created equal and that they are endowed by their Creator with certain inalienable rights, among them life, liberty, and the pursuit of happiness. But it does so in order to explain why the colonies had to break from the British crown and establish a new government. In other words, the Declaration of Independence focuses on establishing a new government in order to guarantee basic civil rights. The Constitution of the United States provides a form of government meant to "ensure a more perfect union with justice, domestic tranquility, common defense, general welfare and the blessings of liberty." It provides a way for civil rights to be guaranteed. Both of the founding documents assume Americans should have their liberty in order to fulfill their individual desires, but neither document defines those individual desires and beliefs. A governing system should not answer such questions, and the new United States government certainly did not intend to do so. The first amendment to the Constitution specifically says, "Congress shall make no law respecting an establishment of religion or prohibiting the free exercise thereof." The American system leaves people free to define their spiritual or philosophical side outside of the governing system. If more Americans exercised that freedom, we could lessen the materialism and violence that plague American society at the end of the twentieth century.

Compromise is fundamental to the American way of life. By living in America, we have accepted the basic premise that we believe in a just society where all individuals have basic rights. There is no place in such a society for fanaticism. No one group can provide answers for all the people. Each group accepts its right to assert ideas with the understanding that other groups have equal rights, and that all expressions must be within American law. The unique strength of the United States is its ability to accept the coexistence of people with different beliefs under one government. America is strongest when all citizens understand their origins and enrich the society with their perspectives.

The Jewish community of 1879–1920 was not monolithic. Synagogues and organizations competed for support. Each faction found its own way to fulfill the precept of remaining Jewish, and each believed its purpose was the most significant one. Nevertheless, the Jews managed to cooperate on the larger efforts, assistance to immigrants and the needy in Europe, that required broad-based support. Therefore, they achieved enormous success. Once they could no longer agree on their primary function of assisting new immigrants, they were left with disagreements about religious observance, and a diminished capacity to accomplish their goals.

At the end of the twentieth century, the Wilmington Jewish community, like its predecessor, and like Jewish communities throughout the United States, has a plethora of synagogues and organizations, each believing it represents the key component of Judaism. But unlike the community in our story, Jews today cannot agree on one overriding purpose. Decreasing numbers of Jews identify with a specific branch of Judaism, and numerous Jews construct their Jewish identity around philanthropy, Israelism, political liberalism, social justice, and anti-Semitism.[1] At this critical moment, there is no agreement on the overall meaning of a Jewish community. Even more significantly, there is no widespread agreement that the community should be united. Such lack of unity threatens to transform the influential American Jewish community into a collection of ineffective interest groups.

The Jews in our story came from different countries and had diverse backgrounds, but because the outside world treated them as a separate group they understood very well that they were a minority and that their only hope for success was through united action. At the end of the twentieth century, with more than 90 percent of American Jews born in the United States, Jews are far more homogeneous than those in the earlier community, but our interests in different aspects of Jewishness make us more diverse than ever. Since the majority of the general community sees Jews as part of the establishment, not as outsiders, external pressure no longer brings the diverse factions together. As our study of Wilmington's first Jewish community teaches us, tiny minorities need the power of numbers to accomplish their goals. Therefore, while Jewish groups continue to pursue individual aspects of Jewishness which they feel are most significant, they must also be ready to transcend their differences in order to promote the cornerstones of a Jewish community: preservation of a valuable religious heritage, assistance to those in need, and enhancement of Jewish peoplehood.

The story of Wilmington's Jewish community is the story of people's accomplishments. Events don't just occur; they depend on individuals to make them happen. The early Jews struggled to earn livings under circumstances much harder than most of us face today. They raised large families without most of the time-saving devices of our technological age. But they managed to find time to establish communal institutions that they felt were important to themselves and others. They did not wait for the government to create an agency, or for someone to pay them to do a job. Individuals took responsibility for bringing their values into the society. Each of us has an individual life, but each of us is also part of a community. We must dedicate a portion of our time and energy to the communal life if we expect to live in a supportive community that meets real needs.

Appendix

These lists (based on information from census, birth, death and marriage records as well as interviews and newspapers) include Jews twenty years of age and older who lived in Wilmington. Some individuals who might have been Jewish but who do not appear in any records that prove their religion are not included. Several people mentioned in the chapter on the 1910s were born after 1900; therefore, they do not appear on the lists of the 1910s. Sources sometimes used Jewish first names that were anglicized later and spelled individuals' names in different ways. I selected the most frequently used names and spelling. Men often remarried after their first wife died. In the column of wife's name, the woman is the wife at the time of arrival or the first wife if the man married after his arrival. Women who were single or widows are included in the first column, head of household. However, given the importance of marriage in the immigrant culture and the absence of primary sources to document women's religions, there are not many single adult women in the lists. When naming country of origin, immigrants often told the census taker one country in the first census and a different country twenty years later. I used the earliest response unless I knew it was incorrect. Often people answered Poland-Russia or Russia-Poland which I interpret as meaning they considered Poland a part of Russia. Others answered Austria-Germany as if it were one entity. The people in the lists changed occupations often. Many remained in their first occupations for less than a year. By using the first occupations, the lists illustrate clearly the nature of the early Jewish community. People who arrived at the beginning or end of a decade may be listed in the proximate decade.

Adult Jews in Wilmington in 1879-80

Name	Wife's name	Birthplace (m)	Birthplace (f)	First occupation
Arnold, Adolph		Germany		clothing salesman
Bishof, Ferdinand	Harriet	Prussia	France	optician
Cohen, Aaron	Rose	Germany	New York	tailor
Cohen, Samuel		Russia		clothier
De Wolf, Jacob	Isaacs, Fanny	Liverpool, England	London, England	clothier
Fellheimer, Louis	Liebman, Emma			clothier
Fellheimer, Marx	Yeisenberg, Ellen	Germany	Pennsylvania	clothier
Fischer, Julius	Nogler, Sarah		Massachusetts	clothier

Continued on next page

243

Adult Jews in Wilmington in 1879-80, Continued

Name	Wife's name	Birthplace (m)	Birthplace (f)	First occupation
Hocheimer, Sam	Caroline	Holland	Germany	dry goods
Isaacs, Isaac		England		retired
Israel, Aaron				cigarmaker
Italie, Charles	Nogler, Dora	Denmark or Netherlands	United States	optician
Jacobs, George	Amelia	England	England	clothier
Jacobs, Lewis				salesman
Kahn, Gershon		Maryland		clothier
Kahn, Mayer		Maryland		clothier
Kerns, Samuel	Charolette	New York	New Jersey	coach builder
Levi, Samuel		Germany		clothing salesman
Lieberman, Nathan	Arnold, Rosa	Bavaria, Germany	Wurtemberg, Germany	clothier
Meyers, Meyer	Wiles, Selena	Bavaria, Germany	Switzerland	clothier
Nogler, Samuel		Germany		clothier
Richenberger, Manual	Margaret	Bavaria, Germany	Delaware	clothing salesman
Rosenblatt, Barney	Rachel	Poland	Bavaria	hairdresser
Row, Bernard	Sophia	Bavaria, Germany	Bavaria, Germany	clothier
Row, Issac		Delaware		clothing clerk
Saphir, Leon	Henrietta	Austria	Bavaria, Germany	clothier
Sondheimer, Kaufman	Stern, Barbara	Bavaria, Germany	Bavaria, Germany	clothier
Wolfson, Bernard	Mina	Russia	Germany	clothier

244

Adult Jews Who Arrived in Wilmington in the 1880s

Name	Wife's name	Birthplace (m)	Birthplace (f)	First occupation
Abramson, David	Koerpol, Johanna	Hungary	Hungary	peddler
Abramson, Max	Jelnick, Bertha	Hungary	Tamesware, Hungary	tailor
Adelman, Abraham	Berlin, Tula	Russia	Russia	carpenter
Album, Simon	Glick, Ida	Russia	Russia-Poland	tailor
Anfenger, Cody	(single)	Germany		real estate
Barsky, Nathan	Ostrosky, Rosa	Russia	Russia	peddler
Belin, Henry				
Bischoff, John				shoemaker
Blass, Jacob				tailor
Blumberg, Morris	Block, Gertrude	Russia	Wurtemberg, Germany	salesman
Brofsky, Louis	Rachel	Russia	Russia	peddler
Brown, Louis	Katie	Russia	Russia	laborer
Cabe, Julius		Germany		clerk
Cabe, M.				clothier
Cohen, Charles				watchmaker
Cohen, Harry	Weinstein, Sophie	Russia	Russia	tailor
Cohen, Morris	Sarah	Russia		dry goods
Cohen, Philip	Minsker, Esther	Russia	Russia	peddler
Cohen, Simon	Dollstein, Annie	Russia	Russia	tinware

Continued on next page

Adult Jews Who Arrived in Wilmington in the 1880s, Continued

Name	Wife's name	Birthplace (m)	Birthplace (f)	First occupation
Cooper, Isaac		Russia		clothier
Cooper, Jacob	Broydman, Rachel	Russia	Russia	grocer
Dannenbohr, Max	Fridmann, Ellen	Russia	Russia	laborer
Dentret, Isidor	Cohen, Sarah	Hungary	Magmeaan, Hungary	shoemaker
Dolphman, Jacob	(single)	Russia		clothier
Ephraim, Max	Reichert, Rebecca	New York	London, England	clothier
Eskin, Jacob		Russia		
Faber, Jacob	Price, Fannie	Hungary	New York	dry goods
Faber, Morris	Rosenback, Regina	Hungary	Hungary	rabbi, teacher
Faber, Simon		Hungary	Hungary	salesman
Feldman, Isaac				tailor
Fellheimer, Simon				cigars
Field, Jonas	(single)	Pennsylvania		manager
Fineman, Abraham	Leschem, Sarah	Russia	Russia	merchant
Fineman, Benjamin	Freidelberg, Bertha	Lithuania	Russia	
Finger, Arthur	(single)			laborer
Finger, Louis	Tartakovsky, Esther	Russia	Russia	peddler
Finger, Morris	Sabilovsky, Rachel	Borditeur, Russia	Russia	tailor
Fink, Jacob	Albert, Elizabeth	Germany	Germany	foreman
Fisher, Benjamin	Kline, Jennie or Anna	Hungary	Magyar, Hungary	peddler

246

Name	Spouse			Occupation
Fogal, Herman	Julia	Austria	Hungary	clothier
Freedly, Solomon				
Freedman, Moses				
Friedman, Solomon		Russia-Poland		picture frames
Friedman, Wolf L.	Rubenstein, Rosa			picture frames
Geist, Aaron				clothing clerk
Geist, Max				clothier
Gluck, Sam	Weiss, Rosa	Hungary	Hungary	baker
Gluckman, Barnet	Harris, Fannie	Russia	Russia	cigarmaker
Gold, Louis	(single)			laborer
Goldberg, Micha	Emma	Hungary	Hungary	merchant
Goldstein, Bernard G.	Yetta	Poland-Russia	Germany	laborer
Goldstein, Herman	Gelman, Sarah	Russia	Russia	clothier
Goldstein, Isaac	Leshem, Rachel	Russia	Russia	printer
Gordon, Simon		Russia		
Grossman, Solomon	Mary	Russia	Russia	shoemaker
Hamburger, Henry I.				clothier
Handleman, Benjamin		Poland-Russia	Poland-Russia	picture frames
Harris, Aaron	Ida	Russia	Russia	clothier
Harris, Louis	Hannah	Russia		clothier
Harris, Samuel	Pick, Minnie	Russia	New York	clothier
Hart, Henry or Harry	Fannie			clothier
Hindin, Baer	Newman, Sarah	Russia	Russia	painter

Continued on next page

Adult Jews Who Arrived in Wilmington in the 1880s, Continued

Name	Wife's name	Birthplace (m)	Birthplace (f)	First occupation
Hurshman, Jacob				shoemaker
Hurshman, Joseph				shoes
Hurshman, Nathan				shoemaker
Jacobs, Harry	Mary	Pennsylvania		cigarmaker
Jasofosky, Alexander			New York	painter
Kaufman, Henry	Kline, Katie	Germany	Germany	musician
Klein, Julius	Fredericka			salesman
Klein, Philip				house furnishings
Kleinberg, Isaac				salesman
Kline, Aaron		Pennsylvania		cabinetmaker
Korn, James	(single)			peddler
Korngold, Morris	Reich, Anna	Austria	Austria	tailor
Lang, Harry	Steiner, Julia	Germany	Germany	
Lebowz, Hiram				baker
Leshem, Daniel	Fannie	Russia	Russia	pocketbook maker
Leshem, Morris	Sidell, Dora	Russia	Russia	pocketbook maker
Levi, H.	Henrietta			clothier
Levi, Louis				clothing salesman
Levin, Wolf	Sarah	Russia	Russia	
Levy, Joseph	Bernisky, Bertha	Russia	Russia	blacksmith

248

Levy, Morris	Jette	Germany	Germany	peddler
Levy, Samuel	Rubin, Hannah	Temecronoke, Russia	Russia	clothier
Lichenstein, Jacob	Amelia, Bertha			shoes
Lichenstein, Max	Turner, Elizabeth	New York	Pennsylvania	merchant
Lictenbaum, Joseph	Dora	Russia	Austria	installments
Livingston, Morris	(single)			shoes
Livingston, Nathan				manager
Livingstone, Ed.				peddler
Lockman, Levi				tailor
Lockyer, William	Isabella	Germany		tailor
Lurge, David M.	Bomgarty, Ida	Russia	Germany	watchmaker
Mann, Samuel				clothier
Mann, Solomon				
Max, Abram				cabinetmaker
Mex, David		Russia		cabinetmaker
Miller, Harry	Levy, Rosalie	Russia	Russia	cabinetmaker
Miller, Isaac	Annie	Russia	Germany	butcher
Miller, Morris	Friedman, Betta	Germany	Russia	peddler
Mitchell, Sam	Bash, Freda	Russia	New York	millinery store
Mitzberg, Isaac		Germany		
Moses, Morrison E.		Russia		
Nonky, Marcus	Lipshitz, Maria	Tomowish, Russia	Tomowish, Russia	clothier
Openlander, Charles	Louisa	Germany	Germany	tailor

Continued on next page

249

Adult Jews Who Arrived in Wilmington in the 1880s, Continued

Name	Wife's name	Birthplace (m)	Birthplace (f)	First occupation
Pick, Frederick				peddler
Pinder, Solomon				builder
Pizor, Charles				bottler
Pizor, Harry	Wolters, Mary	England	Pennsylvania	clothier
Pizor, Joseph	Wolters, Kate	Illinois	Pennsylvania	bottler
Pizor, S.				secondhand goods
Podolsky, Gidel	Cramer, Minnie	Russia	Russia	cabinetmaker
Podolsky, Max	Golotki, Bessie	Russia	Russia	peddler
Powdermaker, Abraham	Picard, Claire	England	Pennsylvania	butcher
Powdermaker, Emanuel				butcher
Raphael, R.				watchmaker
Reisman, Emanuel	Abramson, Mina	Hungary	Hungary	peddler
Reisman, Morris	Wineberger, Annie	Hungary	Hungary	peddler
Rezits, Herman	Lebenson, Lena	Russia	Russia	rabbi
Rosenberg, Simon		Prussia, Germany		rabbi
Rosenblatt, Benjamin	Fanowitz, Lena	Wolkomig, Russia	Tomowish, Russia	carpenter
Rosenbloom, Jacob				shoemaker
Roth, Adolph		Hungary		shoemaker
Roth, Ignatz	Fischer, Rosie	Hungary	Hungary	peddler
Rysman, Joseph	Emma	Austria	Austria	shoemaker

Sack, Jacob				tailor
Samuelson, Hyman		Russia		junk dealer
Schaller, Andrew	Miller, Emilie	Germany	Delaware	baker
Schindler, Jacob	Henrietta	Germany	Germany	machinist
Schlager, Martin	Lowenstein, Lena	Austria	Prussia	boots
Schneider, Frank				clothier
Schneider, Isaac				tailor
Schnurman, Abraham				upholsterer
Schwartz, Morris		Russia		carpenter
Scoffsky, Charles				peddler
Shapiry, Nathan	Rosenthal, Ann	Russia	Russia	butcher
Siegel, Charles		Hungary		salesman
Singer, Isadore		Russia		shoes
Sklut, Philip (Fiva)				installments
Slessinger, Sam	Frumen, Fanny	Hungary	Hungary	carpenter
Slomonson, Morris	Singer, Lena	Russia	Russia	tailor
Smith, Abraham	Dishler, Rosalie	England		traveler
Taenenbaum, Marcus	Friedman, Ellet.			
Topkis, Jacob	Avrach, Rosa	Russia	Russia	clothier
Tucker, Peter	Anna	Poland-Russia	Poland-Russia	hats
Wachtel, M.				clerk
Wachtel, S.				clothier
Wainer, Israel	Rebecca	Russia	Russia	

Continued on next page

251

Adult Jews Who Arrived in Wilmington in the 1880s, Continued

Name	Wife's name	Birthplace (m)	Birthplace (f)	First occupation
Weichselbaum, Leo				clothing salesman
Weil, Moses	Goldberg, Lena	Germany		optician
Weiss, Harry		Hungary		
Wirtshafter, Joseph				baker
Wolters, Abe S.		Pennsylvania		clothier
Wolters, Otto				clothier
Wolters, Reuben	Stern, Rebecca	Pennsylvania	Pennsylvania	clothier
Wolters, Wolf		Netherlands	Neustadt, Germany	clothier

Adult Jews Who Arrived in Wilmington in the 1890s
(or reached the age of 20 in the 1890s)

Name	Wife's name	Birthplace (m)	Birthplace (f)	First occupation
Ackerman, Harry	Lang, Lizzie	Russia	Russia	merchant
Adelman, Marcus	Lichtenbaum, Sarah	Russia	Pennsylvania	installment manager
Altman, Morris	Wolfson, Fannie	Russia	Russia	canvasser
Altman, Nathan	Dora	Russia	Russia	installments
Amerman, Bernard	Lena	Russia		installments
Amerman, Henry	Minnie	Russia	Russia	installments
Amerman, Philip		Russia		clerk
April, Charles	Mary S.	Delaware	United States	shoestore manager
Bachrach, Abe	Weinberg, Lena	Maryland	Maryland	showcase maker
Bader, Joseph	Goldstein, Rae			shoes
Baer, Louis	Levi, Sarah	Maryland	Germany	clothier
Baeringer, Solomon	Wolters, Julia	New York	Pennsylvania	cigars
Barber, Judah	Esther	Russia	Russia	machinist
Barsey, Samuel	Feenstein, Pauline	Russia	Russia	clothier
Bash, William	Koppman, Rebecca			hardware
Berger, Benjamin	Rachel	Germany	Germany	morocco finisher
Berger, Louis				tailor
Berger, Michael	Corbine, Bertha	Germany	Germany	grocer
Berger, Samuel A.	Greenback, Lizzie	Russia	Russia	

Continued on next page

Adult Jews Who Arrived in Wilmington in the 1890s
(or reached the age of 20 in the 1890s), Continued

Name	Wife's name	Birthplace (m)	Birthplace (f)	First occupation
Berger, William	Mary	Russia	Russia	cigars
Berkovitz, Bernard	Sarah	Hungary	Hungary	morocco worker
Berkowitz, Louis	Gross, Anna	Hungary	Hungary	morocco worker
Berkwitz, Albert	Rosenback, Sallie	Austria	Austria	morocco worker
Berkwitz, Samuel	Hirshout, Annie	Germany	Germany	morocco worker
Berman, Barareth	Matilda			notions
Berman, David				barber
Berman, Solomon	Jennie			clothing
Blumberg, Isaac	Schwartz, Matel			
Brachler, Nathan	Eva	Russia	Russia	morocco worker
Briefman, Meyer		Russia		morocco worker
Brodsky, Jacob	Goldberg, Dora	Russia	Russia	morocco shaver
Brown, Louis	Mary	Russia	Russia	tailor
Bryer, Sam	Ida	Russia	Russia	
Chaiken, Morris	Rosen, Dora	Russia	Russia	dyer
Chertok, Meyer	Fogel, Histie	Russia	Russia	cigar merchant
Cohen, Abraham B.	Goldstein, Jeanette	Russia	Russia	teacher of Hebrew
Cohen, Benjamin	Rosenstein, Cecilia	Germany	Germany	tailor
Cohen, David		New York		laborer

Name		Origin	Origin	Occupation
Cohen James J.		Russia	Austria	barber
Cohen, Joseph	Korngold, Jennie	Russia	Russia	capmaker
Cohen, Julius,	Fruman, Bessie	Russia	Russia	grocer
Cohen, Max	Kramer, Pauline			clothier
Cohen, Robert				barber
Cohen, Rosa				clothier
Cohen, Samuel	Mary	Russia-Poland	Poland-Russia	shoemaker
Cohen, Samuel	Bessie			morocco worker
Cohen, Wolf	Rebecca	Russia	Russia	peddler
Cohn, James				laborer
Cohn, John				laborer
Cohn, Michael	Ann			laborer
Cramar, Jacob	Goldberg, Fannie	Russia	Russia	bottler
Cramar, Manual	Fannie	Russia	Russia	morocco worker
Cramar, Rebecca		Russia	Russia	
Danberg, Frank	Binder, Minnie	Poland-Russia	Russia	barber
Dannenberg, Albert	Lazofski, Annie	Russia	Russia	shoemaker
Deitch, Max	Galucki, Mary	Germany	Germany	clothier
Eckstein, Joseph				shoemaker
Engelstein, David				tailor
Ezrailson, Morris	Cosse, Esther	Russia	Russia	morocco worker
Feinberg, Abraham	Shoenfeld, Betsie	Russia	Russia	furniture
Feinberg, Herman (Hyman)	Wolson, Rachel	Russia	Russia	peddler

Continued on next page

255

Adult Jews Who Arrived in Wilmington in the 1890s
(or reached the age of 20 in the 1890s), Continued

Name	Wife's name	Birthplace (m)	Birthplace (f)	First occupation
Feinberg, Herman	Wolson, Rachel	Russia	Russia	peddler
Fine, Moses	Rachel	Russia	Russia	clothing manager
Finkelstein, David	Baer, Esther	Russia	Germany	tailor
Fisher, Harry	Handleman, Rosa	Russia	Russia	restaurant worker
Fisher, Isaac	Louisa	Maryland	Texas	ice dealer
Fisher, Joseph	Minnie	Germany	Germany	shoemaker
Fogel, Abraham		Russia		clothing salesman
Frank, Adolph	Silverman, Bertha	Romania	Romania	dry goods
Fridman, Joseph	Carie	Russia	Russia	tanner
Fried, Joseph	(single)	Hungary		morocco dresser
Friedman, David	Keel, Hannah	Germany	Russia	shoemaker
Friedman, Isaac	Sarah			morocco finisher
Friedman, Jacob	Goedernord, Sarah	Russia		morocco dresser
Friedman, Jacob	Fleischer, Hattie	Russia	Russia	hat maker
Friedman, Max	(single)	Romania		barber
Friedman, Morris	Wootford, Katie	Russia	Russia	morocco worker
Friedman, Morris	Bessie	Russia	Russia	shoemaker
Friedman, Nathan	Miller, Rachel	Russia	Russia	carpenter
Friedman, Tsvick	Heiskorm, Luirg	Russia	Russia	laborer

256

Name	Spouse	New York	Maryland	Occupation
Gardner, David	Baer, Theresa			men's goods
Geitelman, Meyer				grocer
Gluckman, Frederick	Francis			carpenter
Gold, Max	Saltman, Lena	Russia	Russia	dry goods
Goldberg, Levi	Haber, Rosa	Romania	Romania	hat and cap maker
Goldberg, Morris	Megalsky, Esther	Russia	Russia	merchant
Golden, Max	Mary	Russia	Russia	laborer
Goldstein, Barney	Rebecca	Germany	Germany	morocco worker
Goldstein, David	Yetta	Austria-Hungary	Germany	peddler
Goldstein, Israel	Leah	Russia	Russia	shoemaker
Goldstein, Jacob	Greenwald, Bessie	Russia	Russia	baker
Goldstein, Max		Poland	Russia	speculator
Goldstein, Meyer	Goodman, Catherine	Russia	Russia	
Goldstein, Morris	Lena	Russia	Russia	
Goodlevege, Jacob	Slisewski, Sarah	Russia		shoemaker
Goodman, David	Rose	Russia		cigarmaker
Gordon, J. Harry	(single)	Georgia		clothing-store manager
Goudiss, Alex. E		Russia		
Green, Isadore				
Greenbaum, Abraham				dry goods
Greenbaum, Israel				dry goods salesman
Greenbaum, Joseph				dry goods salesman
Greenbaum, Samuel	Reich, Sarah	Austria-Germany	Austria	clothier

Continued on next page

Adult Jews Who Arrived in Wilmington in the 1890s
(or reached the age of 20 in the 1890s), Continued

Name	Wife's name	Birthplace (m)	Birthplace (f)	First occupation
Greenberg, Isaac		Russia	Russia	morocco finisher
Greenstein, Albert	Gilman, Amelia	Austria	Austria	puddler
Groll, Morris	Greenberg, Annie			tailor
Gross, Morris	Sarah	Poland-Russia	Poland-Russia	laborer
Grossman, Harry				morocco glazer
Handleman, Thomas	Fisher, Mollie	Poland		morocco worker
Hankin, Sam	Rosie	Russia	Russia	salesman
Harkovitz, Harry				boots, shoes, dry goods
Hendler, Michael	Parnitz, Sarah	Russia		morocco worker
Hendler, Sam	Goveskie, Sallie	Europe	Europe	morocco dresser
Hillersohn, Louis	Ostro, Elizabeth	Russia	Russia	cigar merchant
Hinden, Abraham	Holotkin, Sarah (Lena)	Russia	Russia	barber
Hirsch, Harry	Mary			shoe store clerk
Hirschbaum, Henry	(single)	Hungary		morocco stoker
Hirschman, Nathan	Ida	Russia	Russia	laborer in iron mill
Hirshberg, Harry	Wolk, Mary	Russia	Russia	clothier
Hirshout, Abraham	Wildman, Mary	Austria	Austria	morocco worker
Hirshout, Albert	Mollie	Austria	Austria	morocco worker
Hirshout, Harry	Fisher, Annie	Austria	Austria	laborer

258

Hirshout, Louis	Rosa	Germany or Austria	Germany	china and crockery
Hockstein, Nathan	Shopierd, Annie	Russia	Russia	shoemaker
Holodky, Aaron	Lena	Russia	Russia	
Holodky, Louis	Aetie, Mollie	Russia	Russia	fruit dealer
Holodky, Morris	Bessie	Russia	Russia	produce
Holotky, Aaron				
Horowitz, Louis				morocco worker
Indian, Abe				
Jacobs, Benjamin	Jennie	Germany	Russia	butcher
Jacobs, Maurice L. (Morris)	Margaret	Russia	Canada	clothing salesman
Jacobsen, Albert	Aldina			owner, Freie Press
Jacobsen, Julius				manager, Freie Press
Jacobsen, William	Greenstein, Lina	Hungary	Hungary	merchant
Jacobwitz, Meyer	Minnie	Austria-Hungary	Hungary	tailor
Jellinek, Charles	Ellen	Hungary	Austria	morocco worker
Jellinek, Emanual	Mary			morocco foreman
Joseph, Michael				peddler
Kanefsky, Morris	Fannie	Russia	Russia	grocer
Kanofsky, Hyman	Ida (Fannie)	Russia	Russia	tailor
Kasdin, Samuel	Brenner, Olgie	Russia	Russia	cigarmaker
Klein, Alex	Matilde	Indiana	Pennsylvania	clothier
Knopf, Jacob	Augusta	Austria	Austria	
Kodash, Joseph	Rebecca			baker

Continued on next page

Adult Jews Who Arrived in Wilmington in the 1890s
(or reached the age of 20 in the 1890s), Continued

Name	Wife's name	Birthplace (m)	Birthplace (f)	First occupation
Kodesh, David				rabbi
Kohn, Adolph				morocco shaver
Korn, Jacob				clerk
Kramer, Julius				tailor
Krechevsky, Issac	Brofsky, Jennie	Russia	Russia	kosher butcher
Kyle, Emma				barber
Leopold, Jacob	Zoberklut, Tillie	Russia	Russia	barber
Leopold, Judi		Russia		barber
Leopold, Sam		Russia		barber
Leshem, Charles		Russia		barber
Leshem, David		Russia		barber
Leshem, Jacob	Annie	Russia		barber
Leshem, Joseph		Russia		barber
Leshem, Louis	Hinden, Esther	Russia	Russia	barber
Leshem, Philip		Russia		pool and billiards
Levi, Jessie B.	Solomon, Bertha	Pennsylvania		clerk
Levin, Meik	Rothstein, Henny	Russia	Russia	peddler
Levin, Michael	Anna	Russia		peddler
Levine, Harry	Kocrynski, Lena	Russia	Russia	hatter

260

Name				Occupation
Levine, Jonah				railroad worker
Levitski, Marian	Mary			morocco
Levy, Abraham	Wolberg, Matilda	Washington, D.C.	Maryland	merchant
Levy, David L.	Julia	Hungary	Hungary	morocco assorter
Levy, Morris	Stern, Leah	Russia	Pennsylvania	shoe store owner
Levy, Moses	Conselbaum, Sarah	Russia	Russia	
Levy, Nathan	Nash, Ettie	Prussia, Germany	Germany	clothing-store manager
Levy, Reuben	Shapiro, Rifka	Russia		shoemaker
Levy, Solomon	Levy, Kate			
Lieberwitz, Sarah				notions
Lipkin, Jacob	Polinsky, Mary	Russia	Russia	morocco worker
Markowich, Maurice	(single)	Russia		laborer
Miller, Harry	Friedman, Lena	Germany	Russia	tailor
Miller, Reuben	Ida	Russia	Russia	clothier
Millman, Jacob	Katie	Russia	Russia	morocco shaver
Moskovitz, Harry				
Muscovitch, Morris	Altmann, Anna	Germany	Germany	morocco dresser
Nisenbaum, Frank	Dora	Russia	Russia	secondhand dealer
Olacki, Aaron	Mollie	Russia	Russia	
Orenstein, Harry	Gussie	Russia	Russia	grocer
Orenstein, Isaac	Jennie	Russia		grocer
Orenstein, Plumm				grocer
Ostro, Michael	Sophie	Russia		drugstore clerk

Continued on next page

261

Adult Jews Who Arrived in Wilmington in the 1890s
(or reached the age of 20 in the 1890s), Continued

Name	Wife's name	Birthplace (m)	Birthplace (f)	First occupation
Ostrow, Jacob		Ukraine, Russia		clothing salesman
Ostrow, Joseph				cigars
Patzowsky, Richard	(widower)	Austria		morocco worker
Press, Jacob				
Price, Lazarus	Sarah	Poland-Russia	Poland-Russia	clothier
Price, Samuel Robert	Satinsky, Fannie	England	Russia	clothier
Rappaport, Max	Kramer, Mary	Austria	New York	rabbi
Raw, Lipman	Katie	Russia	Russia	furniture and carpets
Reches, Louis	Aron, Clara	Austria	Austria	baker
Reisman, Joseph	Emma	Magyar, Hungary	Magyar, Hungary	shoemaker
Roos, Levy	Liren	Russia	Russia	
Rosen, Alexander	Lena	Germany	Russia	furniture
Rosenbaum, Meyer	Lena	Russia	Russia	shoemaker
Rosenbaum, Shim	Lime	Germany	Germany	laborer
Rosenberg, Joseph	Dobecke, Lime	Russia	Russia	shoes
Rosenberg, Louis	Aarons, Mary	Germany	Pennsylvania	tailor
Rosenberg, Meyer				shoes
Rosenblatt, Joseph				railroad car builder
Rosenblatt, Morris	Rebecca (Jane)	Russia	Russia	canvasser

Rosenthal, Abraham	Morris, Kate	Russia	Russia	morocco worker
Rosenthal, Peter	Katie	Hungary	Hungary	shoemaker
Rosenthal, Phillip	Saltzberg, Lena	Poland	Poland	shoemaker
Rosenzweig, Michael	Hirshout, Mary	Germany	Germany	capmaker
Roth, David	Rachael	Russia	Russia	grocer
Rothstein, Herman	Weinstein, Fannie	Russia	Russia	watchmaker
Sacks, Benjamin	Hannah	Germany	Germany	grocer
Salinger, Joseph	Annie	Russia	Russia	lodgings
Schafer, Max	Gertrude	Austria	Russia	clothier
Schagrin, Abe	Schwartz, Frances	Austria	Hungary	clothier
Schagrin, Charles	Pearl		Austria	milliner
Schless, Jacob				jeweler
Schless, Maurice				
Schless, Sam	Berger, Julia	Russia	Austria	jeweler
Schwartz, Max	Tillie	Germany	Germany	morocco shaver
Schwartz, Moris	Welby, Mary	Russia	Russia	laborer
Schwartz, Morris	Julia	Russia	Bohemia	morocco worker
Shafer, Max	Annie	Russia	Russia	clothier
Shapiro, Adlai	Annie	Russia	Poland-Russia	shoes
Shapiro, Jacob	Esther	Russia	Romania	clothier
Shapiro, Jacob	Annie	Russia	Russia	clothier
Shapiro, Max	Ermie	Russia	Russia	morocco worker
Shapiro, Simon	Siegel, Tennie		Russia	carpenter

Continued on next page

Adult Jews Who Arrived in Wilmington in the 1890s
(or reached the age of 20 in the 1890s), Continued

Name	Wife's name	Birthplace (m)	Birthplace (f)	First occupation
Shar, David	Lena	Russia	Russia	cap maker
Shlomsky, Pessah				installments
Shtofman, Nathan	Clara	Russia	Russia	tailor
Sigle, Isaac	Bessie	Russia	Russia	fruit dealer
Silberger, Abraham	Sarah			
Silberger, Morris	Levy, Lena	Russia	Russia	morocco worker
Silverman, Nathan	Anna			cantor and shochet
Silverman, Solomon	Bertha	Russia	Russia	clothier
Singer, Jacob	Rosa	Russia	Russia	cabinetmaker
Sklut, Joseph	Rachel	Russia	Russia	shoemaker
Sklut, Joseph	Esther	Russia	Russia	
Sklut, Louis	Annie	Russia	Russia	clothier
Sklut, Meyer	Fanny	Russia		tailor
Sklutt, Louis	Rosie	Russia	Russia	laborer
Slonsky, Louis	Sarah	Russia	Poland-Russia	merchant
Snellenburg, Albert	(single)	Germany		clothing salesman
Snellenburg, David	Amberg, Jeanette H.	Germany		clothing-store manager
Snellenburg, Julius	(single)	Germany		clothing salesman
Sobel, Abraham	Lilly, Cecilia	Russia	Russia	tailor

Sobl, Simon	Jenne	Russia	Russia	laborer
Spire, Simon	Esther	Ukraine, Russia	Russia	furniture
Statnekoo, Morris	Kaufman, Bertha	Germany	Germany	carpenter
Stern, Samson	(single)	Germany		furniture-store
Stern, Samuel	Leah	Germany	Germany	house furnishings
Stone, Morris	Salinger, Hattie	Austria or Galicia	Russia	clothier
Stromwasser, Abraham	Clark, Mollie	Germany	Germany	laborer
Swinger, Herman	Sarah	Russia	Russia	tailor
Tampolsky, Phillip	Weitzman, Fannie	Russia	Romania	cigars and tobacco
Teitleman, Morris				
Tiger, Nessie				
Tollin, Abraham	Bessie	Russia	Russia	furniture merchant
Tollin, Frank	Ida	Russia	Russia	furniture merchant
Topkis, David	Tiger, Hannah Ray	Russia	Austria	tailor
Topkis, Louis	Krigstein, Esther	Russia	Russia	clothing store manager
Topkis, William	Ginns, Vitelia	Russia	Russia	dry goods clerk
Tuff, Simon	Sarah	Russia	Romania	grocer
Warawitz, Samuel	Hirshout, Annie	Austria	Austria	grocer
Wasserman, Morris	Lime	Russia	Russia	shoemaker
Weinberg, Abram	Theresa	Germany	Germany	
Weinberger, David	Katie	Austria	Austria	morocco finisher
Weiner, Julius	Katie	Austria	Austria	morocco assorter
Weiss, Max	Moiskoinvitsh, Mary	Germany	Germany	shoemaker

Continued on next page

Adult Jews Who Arrived in Wilmington in the 1890s
(or reached the age of 20 in the 1890s), Continued

Name	Wife's name	Birthplace (m)	Birthplace (f)	First occupation
Werner, Sigmund	(single)	Austria		doctor
Wetstein, Elias	(single)	Pennsylvania		shoe salesman
Wolfman, Allen	Rosenfeld, Boicca	Russia	Russia	laborer
Wolfman, Louis	Rosa	Russia	Russia	cabinetmaker
Wolson, Abraham	Larrie		Russia-Poland	furniture
Zucker, Gerson	Rae	Austria		tailor

266

Adult Jews Who Arrived in Wilmington in the 1900s (or reached the age of 20 in the 1900s)

Name	Wife's name	Birthplace (m)	Birthplace (f)	First occupation
Abels, Moses, S.		Russia		rabbi
Abramowitz, Jacob	Sarah	Romania	Romania	shoemaker
Ackerman, Benjamin	Fanny	Russia	Russia	car-shop merchant
Adelman, William	Rebecca	Russia	Russia	
Adels, Frank	Rebecca	Romania	Romania	clothier
Alper, Nathan	Renick, Rebecca	Russia	Russia	morocco stoker
Alterman, Harry	Cecilia	Russia	Russia	
Ammerman, William		Russia		
Arsht, Moses	Osenhandler, Bessie	Russia	Russia	paperhanger
Bank, Harry	Yalfshitz, Dora	Russia	Russia	meat dealer
Bank, William	Melchior, Rosie	Russia	Russia	meat dealer
Barsky, Israel	(single)	Russia		
Beadicouski, Bergie	Rosie	Russia	Russia	jewelry salesman
Beckstein, Morris	Lena	Russia	Russia	
Benstock, Robert	Rosa			
Berdichevsky, Mayer	Rosie	Russia	Russia	shoemaker
Berger, Hyman	Rose			morocco stainer
Berkowitz, Maurice	Sali	Hungary	Hungary	home furnishings shoe merchant

Continued on next page

Adult Jews Who Arrived In Wilmington in the 1900s
(or reached the age of 20 in the 1900s), Continued

Name	Wife's name	Birthplace (m)	Birthplace (f)	First occupation
Berlin, Joseph	Dimenstein, Minnie	Russia	Russia	shoemaker
Berlin, Max		Russia	Russia	morocco worker
Berlin, Samuel	Caplin, Lillie	Russia	Russia	
Berman, Jacob	DuBose, Goldie	Russia	Russia	grocer
Berman, Joseph	Brodsky, Florence	Russia	Russia	tailor
Berman, Louis	Greenwalt, Sarah	Russia	Russia	
Bernhardt, Rosie	(widow)	Austria	Austria	
Bernstein, Isidor	Slomsky, Rebecca	Russia	Russia	tailor
Bernstein, Morris	Goldstein, Fannie	Russia	Russia	
Bernstine, Levy	Pauline			
Bilfant, Barney	Annie	Russia	Russia	installment house
Binder, Morris	Podolsky, Sarah	Russia	Russia	peddler
Blatman, Morris	Mollie	Russia	Russia	gun shop proprietor
Blatt, Herman				cantor
Blyberg, Myer	Gasser, Esther	Austria	Austria	fruit dealer
Bogdonoff, Maurice	Minnie	Russia	Russia	tinsmith
Bragui, Nathan	Jennie	Russia	Russia	shipbuilder
Braiger, Morris	Gradys, Bessie	Russia	Russia	blacksmith
Braunstein, Ozias	Rebecca	Russia	Russia	tailor

268

Breuer, Charles K.	Gold, Miriam	Hungary	Hungary	cigar merchant
Breuer, Max	Wintner, Rosie	Hungary	Hungary	cigar store
Briefman, Harry	Lena	Washington, D. C.	Hungary	morocco shaver
Briefman, Louis		Russia	Russia	morocco worker
Brofsky, Isik		United States	United States	
Brofsky, Lena				
Brofsky, William				
Bronstein, Harry		United States	United States	jeweler
Brouda, Samuel	Rebecca	Hungary	Hungary	carpenter
Brown, Abe	Eva	Russia	Russia	
Brown, Michael	Rose	Russia	Russia	
Caney, Abraham	Ploener, Eva	Russia	Russia	confectionary merchant
Caney, David	Annie	Russia	Russia	carpenter
Caney, Louis	Esther	Russia	Russia	tailor
Cannon, Samuel	Matilda	Russia	Russia	tailor
Caplan, Albert	Podolsky, Jessie	Pennsylvania	Delaware	dry goods
Caplan, Philip	Barofsky, Rebecca	Russia	Russia	milk dealer
Cherbakot, Max	Golda	Russia	Russia	junk dealer
Closic, Joseph	Fannie	Russia	Russia	tinsmith
Cobin, Taube				
Cohen, Aaron Samuel	Mary	Delaware	Delaware	driver
Cohen, Benjamin	Boriski, Jennie	Russia	Russia	tinsmith
Cohen, David	Tiraspolsky, Chie	Russia	Russia	meat dealer

Continued on next page

Adult Jews Who Arrived In Wilmington in the 1900s
(or reached the age of 20 in the 1900s), Continued

Name	Wife's name	Birthplace (m)	Birthplace (f)	First occupation
Cohen, David	Esther	Russia	Russia	morocco worker
Cohen, Harry	Harwitz, Yeddie	Russia	Russia	
Cohen, Herman	Ann	Pennsylvania		store manager
Cohen, Hyman	Jennie	Russia	Russia	
Cohen, Israel	Bessie	Russia	Russia	tinsmith
Cohen, J.	Basha, M.	Russia	Russia	shoemaker
Cohen, Joseph	Schwartz, Esther	Russia	Pennsylvania	furniture dealer
Cohen, Joseph	Fogel, Minnie	Russia	Russia	rabbi
Cohen, Julius	Ida	Russia	New York	clerk
Cohen, Manual	Finkelstein, Lena	Russia	Russia	
Cohen, Max	Jessie	Russia	Russia	peddler
Cohen, Nathan	Rachel	Russia	Russia	carpenter
Cohen, Samuel	Rebecca	Russia	Delaware	
Davis, Max	Margaret	Pennsylvania	Russia	
Dektor, Charles W.	Rebecca	Russia	Hungary	grocer
Dennis, Joseph	Symolomia, Rosa	Hungary	Russia	grocer
Drucker, Michael	Bessie	Russia		
Drukker, Anna				
Drukker, Isaac	Catharine P.			

DuBois, David	Esther	Pennsylvania	Pennsylvania	gas fixtures
Eckstein, William	Hildebrand, Louise	Russia	Russia	salesman
Eisenman, Harry	Winocur, Mollie	Russia	Russia	merchant
Eisenman, Israel	Sklutt, Bessie	South Dakota	Delaware	grocer
Eisenman, Samuel	Elizabeth M	Russia	Russia	eggs
Ephraim, Jay	Mollie	Romania	Russia	coppersmith
Ettingoff, Harry	Rebecca	Russia	Russia	dry goods
Euster, Joseph	Maris, Minnie	Russia	Pennsylvania	morocco worker
Evans, Harry	Cohen, Fannie	Russia	Russia	fruit
Feinberg, Isadore	Goldie	Russia	Russia	furniture
Feinberg, Peter	Sarah	Hungary	Russia	grocer
Feinberg, Simon	Lena	Russia	Hungary	morocco worker
Feldman, Jacob	Szaksi, Lena	Delaware	Russia	tailor
Feldman, Morris	Esther		Hungary	railroad clerk
Ficher, Jacob	Bertha		Russia	
Finger, Matt				
Finkelstein, Isaac B.	Statnekoo, Clara	New York	Russia	stock boy
Finkelstein, Keffie		Pennsylvania		capmaker
Finklestein, Max		Romania		morocco
Fischer, Jacob		Delaware		clerk
Fischer, Manual		Delaware		morocco worker
Fischer, Nicolas		Hungary		grocer
Flait, Morris	Barber, Annie	Russia	Russia	

Continued on next page

Adult Jews Who Arrived In Wilmington in the 1900s
(or reached the age of 20 in the 1900s), Continued

Name	Wife's name	Birthplace (m)	Birthplace (f)	First occupation
Flanzer, Frederic	Fannen, Annie	Austria-Germany	Austria-Germany	milkman
Fogal, Ike (Isaac)		Delaware		
Frankel, Emanuel		Hungary		
Frankel, Morris	Sheingold, Sarah	Russia-Poland	Russia-Poland	fruit dealer
Frankfurt, Solomon	Spritzky, Mary	Russia	Russia	painter
Freedman, Harry	Stern, Rosa	Russia	Russia	shoemaker
Freedman, Jacob	Sarah	Russia	New Jersey	
Freeland, Morris	Zarona	Hungary	Hungary	tinsmith
Freeman, Harry		Russia	Russia	tailor
Freeman, Morris	Annie	Russia	Russia	tailor
Freid, Joseph	Lena	Hungary	Hungary	morocco worker
Freid, Max	Annie	New York	Washington D.C.	morocco shaver
Friedlander, Morris	(single)	Hungary		shoemaker
Ginsburg, David	Katz, Fannie	Russia	Russia	salesman
Glantz, Julius	Zutz, Marria	Russia	Russia	tailor
Glick, Bernard	Renick, Sadie	Russia	Russia	morocco worker
Glick, Samuel	(single)	Hungary		
Gold, Michael	Sarah	Russia	Russia	rabbi
Goldberg, Aaron	Ausman, Annie	Romania	Russia	shoe merchant

272

Name	Place	Occupation
Goldberg, Abraham	Russia-Poland	milk and grains
Goldberg, Al	Rosie	Russia-Poland	salesman
Goldberg, Harry	Anna		manager
Goldberg, Louis	Kahan, Fannie	Romania	Russia	grocer
Goldberg, Morris	Fanny	Russia	Russia	morocco worker
Goldenberg, Samuel	Shorr, Mary	Hungary	Hungary	stenographer
Goldstein, Elizabeth			Russia	gents furnishings
Goldstein, Isaac	Rose	Russia	Russia	salesman cigars
Goldstein, Nathan	Lillian	Russia	Pennsylvania	shoes
Goldstein, Philip	Braunstein, Fannie	Delaware	New York	saleslady
Goldstein, Rose			Russia	milk dealer
Goldstein, Samuel	Aron, Sadie	Austria-Germany	Austria	shoemaker
Goodlevege, Daniel	Goldie	Russia-Poland	Russia-Poland	shoemaker
Goodlevege, Morris	Ester	Russia-Poland		tailor
Goodman, Charles	Rosa	Hungary	Hungary	tailor
Goodman, Harry	Volinsky, Gussie	Russia	Russia	pipefitter
Green, Abraham	Anna	Russia	Russia	
Green, Louis		Pennsylvania		tailor
Green, Max	Rebecca	Austria	Hungary	shoemaker
Greenberg, Morris	Levy, Minnie	Russia	Russia	paperhanger
Greenblatt, Harry		Russia		paperhanger
Greenblatt, Isidor (Ezy)	Kutljaw, Sima	Russia	Russia	conductor
Greenstein, Maurice	Adeleman, Rosa	Hungary	Russia	

Continued on next page

273

Adult Jews Who Arrived In Wilmington in the 1900s
(or reached the age of 20 in the 1900s), Continued

Name	Wife's name	Birthplace (m)	Birthplace (f)	First occupation
Grossman, Isaac	(single)	Hungary		shoemaker
Grossman, Jacob	Sarah	Russia		
Grossman, Jacob	Ida	Pennsylvania	Pennsylvania	tin roofer
Grossman, Reuben	Elizabeth	Russia	Russia	hardware store
Groth, David	Mary	Austria	Austria	
Halotkin, Charles				morocco seasoner
Hambug, Nathan	Rose	Austria	Austria	salesman
Hankin, Aaron				salesman
Hankin, William				
Harbor, Joseph		Austria		grocery salesman
Harris, Henry	Wolf, Carolyn	New York	Massachusetts	pawnbroker
Harwitz, Joseph	Clara	Russia		grocer
Haylor, Isidore		Austria		
Herman, Jacob	Rosie	Russia	Russia	mattress maker
Hirschbaum, Alexander,				
Hirshblond, Benjamin F.				salesman
Hirshman, Alexander	Clara	Germany	Germany	theatrical business
Hirshoff, Isidore	Pauline	Russia-Poland	Russia-Poland	woodworker
Holodsky, Isaac	Lena			printer

274

Holzer, John			
Horsch, Harry			
Horwitz, Samuel	Ginsberg, Annie	Russia	barber
Hurwitz, Louis	Bertha		morocco worker
Hychka, Charles	Mary	Galicia	railroad hostler
Jacobs, Max	Rachel	Russia	carpenter
Jacobson, Benjamin			
Jacobson, John	Anna		
Jacoby, Louis	Stand, Minnie	Hungary	dry goods
Jaffe, Meyer	Annie	Russia	laborer
Josilowitz, B.			
Kaane, Charles	Hattie	Russia	shoemaker
Kates, Harry			
Katz, Samuel	Palatnik, Mary	Russia	capmaker
Kaufman, Harry	Handleman, Eva	Russia	
Kazlowsky, Morris	Grossman, Annie	New York	optician
Keil, Aaron	Jennie	Austria	
Keil, Max	Steiner, Fannie	Austria	saloon proprieter
Keller, Philip	Rose		clothier
Kety, Harry	Mamie		grocer
Kiensburg, Samuel	Ida	Austria	morocco colorer
Kingsberg, Joseph	Lena	Austria-Poland	morocco stoker
Klein, Louis	Julia	Hungary	morocco worker

Continued on next page

275

Adult Jews Who Arrived In Wilmington in the 1900s
(or reached the age of 20 in the 1900s), Continued

Name	Wife's name	Birthplace (m)	Birthplace (f)	First occupation
Kline, Philip	Ella	Russia-Poland	Russia-Poland	shoemaker
Kominsky, Hyman	Ida	Russia	Russia	
Konsburg, Samuel	Ida	Austria	Austria	student
Korngold, Louis		Delaware		tailor
Korngold, Max				
Korngold, Sarah			Pennsylvania	rabbi
Kossuth, Philip				plumber
Kovin, Abram	Jennie	Russia	Russia	barber
Kraft, Harry	Bessie			
Kramer, Isaac	Eva			
Kramer, Samuel	Bernstine, Sophia	Russia	Russia	druggist
Kretsch, Louis	Litcher, Lizzie			morocco worker
Krichevsky, Maurice	Sarah			grocer
Kriciewsky, Louis	Lena			
Krigstein, Philip				
Kristol, Morris	Gittel, Chaya (Ida)	Russia	Russia	secondhand shoes
Kron, Herman	Fannie			grocer
Kyle, William F	Ada			blacksmith
Landau, Joseph				

Lang, Anna				
Laub, Daniel S.	Rosenblum, Tillie	Austria-Germany	Pennsylvania	cloaks
Leibowitz, David	Soloman, Rebecca	Romania	Romania	grocer
Leipshin, Leib	Jennie			clothing
Leopold, Nathan	Minnie	Russia	Russia	tailor
Lepson, Samuel				
Levin, Aaron				
Levin, Abraham	Somna	Russia	Russia	shoemaker
Levin, Max	Annie	Russia	Russia	secondhand clothing
Levine, Samuel	Matilda	Russia	Russia	tailor supplies
Levinsky, Bernard	Kron, Bertha	Russia	New York	dry goods
Levy, Bernard	Finkelstein, Ray	Russia	New York	
Levy, Jacob				
Levy, Max	Silverman, Florence			
Levy, Simon	Cartun, Gitty			
Liberman, Samuel	Sarah	Austria	Russia	
Lichtenbaum, Adolph	Genolinsky, Dora	Russia	Russia	morocco worker
Lichtenbaum, Bernard				salesman
Lincoln, Anna				teacher
Lippinsky, William	Clara	Russia-Poland		
Lipson, Lewis	Laura	Russia	Russia	clothier
Litcher, Albert		Russia		
Litcher, Samuel	Elizabeth	Russia	Russia	grocer

Continued on next page

277

Adult Jews Who Arrived In Wilmington in the 1900s
(or reached the age of 20 in the 1900s), Continued

Name	Wife's name	Birthplace (m)	Birthplace (f)	First occupation
Livingston, Ann				shoes
Luchter, Emil	Ray	Austria	Austria	store manager
Lundy, Joseph	Briezuan, Lina	Poland-Russia	Washington, D. C.	meats
Lutwin, Abraham	Rosie	Russia	Russia	morocco stoker
Marcowitz, Michael	Lebensohn, Sarah	Russia or Romania	Russia	tailor
Marcowitz, Mike	Sara	Romania	Russia	tailor
Margolin, Sam	Bertha			furniture
Markizon, Isidore				
Markowitz, Morris	Rose	Romania	Russia	carpenter
Markowitz, Moses	Mollie	Romania	Romania	butcher
Melis, Jacob				
Milkin, Isaac	Fannie	Russia	Russia	upholster
Miller, Charles	Cecilia	Russia	Russia	furniture store
Miller, David	Anna	Russia	Russia	lodging
Miller, Morris	Catharine			manager
Miller, Nathan	Schultz, Anna	Europe		furniture clerk
Miller, Samuel	Cille			milk
Morris, Charles				
Moskowitz, Bernard	Fannie	Romania	Romania	clothing salesman

Name				Occupation
Nast, Sarah				
Notion, Joseph				
Ostro, Hirsch	Annie	Russia		cigar manufacturer
Ostrolski, Stanislaw	Mary	New York	New York	
Patzowsky, Amelia				
Patzowsky, Ferdinand	Lillian		Hungary	morocco worker
Peskoff, Louis		Lithuania		cabinetmaker
Plain, Harry	Sophie	Russia	Russia	car shop
Platensky, Louis	Anna			roofer
Platnick, Peter	Hannah	Russia		
Ploener, Harry	Bessie	Russia	Russia	junk dealer
Plotnek, Louis	Helen	Russia	Russia	tinsmith
Podolsky, Charles	Anna	Russia		barber
Podolsky, Isaac		Russia		barber
Price, Harry	Caroline	Delaware		painter
Putzkur, John	Hannah	Russia	Russia	grocer
Rabinowitz, Joseph	Grossman, Beckie	Russia	Russia	tin roofer
Rachwell, Harry	Dora	Russia	Russia	morocco stoker
Raphaelson, Israel	Anna	Germany	Germany	junk dealer
Rapkin, Frank	Goldie	Russia-Poland	Russia-Poland	auto accessories
Rapperport, Isaac	Rebecca	Germany	Germany	
Reches, Frank (Fishel)	Fanny	Austria	Austria	language teacher
Redloss, Isadore	Rachel	Russia-Poland	Russia-Poland	morocco-shop laborer

279

Continued on next page

Adult Jews Who Arrived In Wilmington in the 1900s
(or reached the age of 20 in the 1900s), Continued

Name	Wife's name	Birthplace (m)	Birthplace (f)	First occupation
Rees, Morris	Isabella	Hungary	Hungary	jeweler
Reinstein, Leon	Mary	Pennsylvania	England	
Reisman, Jacob	Addie	Russia	Russia	jeweler
Rezits, Samuel	Lilly	Delaware		cigars
Rezits, Sam	Tillia	Romania	Romania	
Rich, Barney		Russia		candy-store salesman
Robin, Albert	Rosmunson, Eva	Ukraine, Russia	Russia	doctor
Robinson, Samuel	Ida	Russia	Russia	
Rosbrow, Charlie	Rosie	Russia	Russia	bottler
Rosbrow, John	Pauline	Palestine	Palestine	hotel manager
Rosen, Hymen	Rebecca	Russia	Russia	junk dealer
Rosen, Jacob	Anna	Russia		tailor shop
Rosen, Morris		Russia		morocco worker
Rosenbaum, Herman				accountant
Rosenbaum, Marcus				
Rosenblach, Louis	Mary	New York	New Jersey	
Rosenblatt, Benjamin	Anna	New York	Pennsylvania	
Rosenblatt, Louis	Knopf, Ray	Pennsylvania	New York	installment house
Rosevich, Herman	Martha	Russia	Russia	tailor

Rosin, Louis	Wolfman, Baila	Russia	Russia	salesman
Roth, John		Delaware	Delaware	saleswoman
Roth, Lena				baths
Rothman, David	Rebecca			
Rothschild, Albert	Lieberman, Estella	Germany	Delaware	clothier
Rothstein, Abraham	Dora	Russia	Russia	shoe store
Rothstein, Louis		Russia		
Rothstein, Michael	Rubin, Fannie	Russia		clerk
Ruben, Morris	Silkind, Annie	Russia	Russia	rabbi
Rubenstein, Isaac Aaron				
Rubenstein, Joseph				
Rubenstein, Samuel				
Rubin, Max	Sarah			teacher
Sablosky, Benjamin	Fannie			theater manager
Sachs, Samuel	Rose	Romania		
Saks, Albert				
Saltzman, Harry	Elli	Russia	Russia	millener
Samuels, Jacob	Sarah	Russia	Russia	shoemaker
Satinsky, William				
Sayers, Abraham	Katie	Russia	Russia	tailor
Sayers, William	Annie	Austria	Hungary	tailor
Schaffer, David	Hillwerth, Goldie			fur dealer
Schaul, Phillip	Levy, Amelia			

Continued on next page

Adult Jews Who Arrived In Wilmington in the 1900s
(or reached the age of 20 in the 1900s), Continued

Name	**Wife's name**	**Birthplace (m)**	**Birthplace (f)**	**First occupation**
Schchansky, Louis	Bernhardt, Katie	Russia	New York	dry goods
Schendelman, Max	Ethel	Russia	Russia	merchant tailor
Scher, David N.	Rebecca	Hungary		grocer
Schiffer, Jacob	Frieberger, Lena	Austria	Hungary	morocco foreman
Schimmel, Max	Keil, Bertha	Austria-Germany	Austria-Germany	clothing salesman
Schlanger, Nathan	Annie	Germany	Austria	
Schlesinger, Rudolph	Mary	Austria	Austria	liquor retailer
Schraml, John	Sarah	Russia	Russia	merchant
Schwartz, Benjamin J.	Jennie	Russia	Russia	grocer
Schwartz, David	Levy, Stella N.	Varanno	New York	grocer
Schwartz, Harry	Sophia	Russia	Russia	
Schwartz, Louis	Schwartz, Klara	Austria	Austria	
Schwartz, Max	Samowitz, Yetta	Pennsylvania	Hungary	millenery
Schwartz, Morris	Sarah	Russia	Pennsylvania	
Segal, Max	Dinah			grocer
Shapiro, Henry		Russia		carpenter
Shar, William	Bertha	Russia	Russia	grocer
Shore, Harry	Kate	Russia	Russia	shoemaker
Shul, Abe				

282

Silker, Abe	Sophie	Russia	Russia	tailor
Silker, Joseph	Krichevsky, Annie	Russia	Russia	grocer
Sillinger, Harris				student
Silver, Abe	Isolovitch, Sophia	Russia	Russia	tailor
Silver, Adolph	Adella	Romania	Austria	tailor
Silverstein, Joseph	Markovitch, Fannie	Romania	Romania	tailor
Silverstein, Max	Emma	Russia	Russia	morocco worker
Simmon, Ellis	Lena	Russia	Russia	furniture
Simon, Harry	Leopold, Jennie	Russia	Russia	picture dealer
Singer, Morris	Sarah	Russia	Russia	shoemaker
Sklut, Abraham	Sklut, Debra	Russia	Russia	butcher
Sklut, Isaac	Dora	Russia	Russia	dealer in hides
Sklut, James	Etta (Esther)	Russia	Russia	furniture dealer
Sklut, Michael	Frances			tailor
Sklut, Rachel	(widow)			
Sklut, Zalman			Russia	peddler
Slomonson, Julius		Delaware		
Slomsky, Philip	Annie	Russia	Russia	clothing merchant
Snellenburg, Carl	Laura			clothing
Solomon, Morris	Rose	Hungary	Hungary	merchant
Sortman, Isaac	Linda	Russia	Delaware	tea and coffee merchant
Sosnoe, Isaac	Bella	Russia	Russia	cabinetmaker
Spegler, Sigmond	Esther	Romania	Romania	grocer

Continued on next page

283

Adult Jews Who Arrived In Wilmington in the 1900s
(or reached the age of 20 in the 1900s), Continued

Name	Wife's name	Birthplace (m)	Birthplace (f)	First occupation
Spigler, Harry	Henrietta	Romania	England	laborer
Spirer, Henry	Thine	Austria	Romania	carpenter
Statnekoo, Jacob	Zutz, Sarah	Russia	Russia	cabinet maker
Statnekoo, Nathan	Ray	Russia-Poland	Russia	carpenter
Stein, David	Freid, Dora	Hungary	New York	morocco worker
Stern, Charles	Lena	Russia	Russia	morocco stoker
Sternberg, Joel	Yampolsky, Fannie	Austria	Russia	
Stiftel, Marcus				jeweler
Straus, Morris	Lurie, Sarah	Russia	Russia	carpenter
Sugarman, Wolf	Jennie	Russia-Poland	Russia-Poland	grocer
Sund, Albert	Debbie			inspector
Swartz, Abraham	(single)	Austria		grocery
Swartz, B.				
Tannen, Morris	Annie	Austria	Austria	tobacco store
Tilman, Isidore		Austria		
Tolchinosky, Morris	Jennie	Russia	Russia	shoemaker
Tollin, Harry	Jennie	Russia	Russia	frame maker
Topkis, Charles	Rothschild, Edna	Pennsylvania	New York	dry goods clerk
Topkis, Harry	Kanofsky, Ray	Delaware		dry goods clerk

Unfried, Eva				
Unfried, Oscar	Marguerite			clerk
Unfried, Russell				
Vernowitz, Frank	Katherine	Russia-Poland	Russia	grocer
Vettemsky, Lewis	Becky			tinsmith
Victor, Samuel				salesman
Wachman, Max	Annie	Russia	Russia	tile worker
Wainer, Max	Beckie			
Waldman, Hyman	Anna	Russia	Russia	clothing
Warowitz, Morris	Destocwich, Mollie	Austria	Austria	
Weiner, Max	Whittecher, Rebecca	Russia	Russia	grocer
Weinstein, Isaac	Oldenberg, Jennie	Russia	Russia	peddler
Weinstine, Myer	Zucreman, Fannie	Russia	Russia	shoemaker
Weinstock, Bernard	Filen, Jennie	Russia	Russia	grocer
Weinstock, David	Bertha	Russia	Russia	grocer
Whitaker, David	Elizabeth	Russia	Russia	grocer
White, Raymond	Dorothy			jeweler
Wineberg, Abraham			Hungary	morocco worker
Winkler, Jacob	Sarah			dyer
Winocur, Hyman	Bernstein, Fannie	Russia	Russia	grocer
Wintner, George	Nellie		Hungary	tobacco
Wishneff, Louis	Clara			dry goods

Continued on next page

Adult Jews Who Arrived In Wilmington in the 1900s
(or reached the age of 20 in the 1900s), Continued

Name	Wife's name	Birthplace (m)	Birthplace (f)	First occupation
Wolf, Harry	Mildred (Mabel)		New York	laborer
Wolfman, Benjamin	Helen	Russia	Delaware	men's furnishings
Wolson, Samuel	Rose	Russia	Russia	installment house
Wolters, Samuel	Leva	Pennsylvania	Maryland	hat merchant
Zamorski, Tony	Julia	Austria	Prussia	
Zutz, Clara	(widow)		Russia	
Zutz, Max	Tillie	Russia	Russia	tailor

Adult Jews Who Arrived in Wilmington in the 1910s
(or reached the age of 20 in the 1910s)

Name	Wife's name	Birthplace (m)	Birthplace (f)	First occupation
Aaron, Maurice	Sarah	Russia	Russia	baker
Abramow, Charles E.	Fannie			cigar store
Abramow, Nathan	Rosie			
Abramson, Sarah			Delaware	
Album, Mollie			Delaware	
Album, Morris		Delaware		laborer
Album, Rosie			Delaware	
Alcoff, Samuel		Russia		car shop upholsterer
Allainer, Samuel	Rebecca			grocer
Allman, David	Ezrailson, Reba			meats
Allman, Sam	Goldenberg, Nancy	Russia	Delaware	dry goods
Aranoff, Joseph A.	Sophia			rabbi
Arieff, Nathan	Anna	Russia	Russia	laborer
Arnoff, Morris	Minnie	Russia	Russia	foreman
Aronstein, Abraham	Dora	Russia	Russia	shoemaker
Astrin, Harry				clerk
Astrin, Morris				men's furnishings
Astrin, Saul				men's furnishings

Continued on next page

Adult Jews Who Arrived in Wilmington in the 1910s
(or reached the age of 20 in the 1910s), Continued

Name	Wife's name	Birthplace (m)	Birthplace (f)	First occupation
Atkinson, David	Annie R.			machinist
Bachman, Frank				carpenter
Backstein, Morris	Backstein, Lena			
Bader, Benjamin	Clara	Russia	Russia	grocer
Baer, Irving		Delaware		rubber factory clerk
Balick, Isidore	Rubenstein, Sadie	Russia		grocer
Balick, Joseph	Sternman, Ida	Russia		grocer
Balick, Nathan	Goldberg, Yetta	Russia		grocer
Balick, Rubin (Reuben)	Klein, Jennie	Russia		grocer
Barber, Israel		Maryland		
Barnett, Herman		Russia		
Barsky, Evangeline			Delaware	lawyer
Barsky, Isidore	Mary	Russia		grocer
Barsky, Jennie			Russia	saleslady
Barsky, Joseph	Snellenberg, Helene	Delaware		doctor
Barsky, Victor		Delaware		lawyer
Batinsky, Louis	Rebecca	Russia	Russia	
Beck, Bessie				
Becker, Abram				Y.M.H.A. director

Name				Occupation
Becker, Samuel	Sarah	Russia	Russia	shoemaker
Begel, Herman		Russia		
Begel, Joseph		Russia		
Begel, Simon		Russia	Russia	clothier
Belfer, Benjamin	Gerber, Rebecca			
Belkin, Arthur				
Bell, Iggi	Sophie	Russia	Russia	merchant
Bell, Ralph	Jaspan, Gertrude	Russia	Pennsylvania	grocer
Bell, Samuel		Russia		clothier
Bender, Morris A.	Sarah			railroad laborer
Bendheim, Carrie Strauss	(widow)		New York	meat cutter
Bendheim, Lillian			Pennsylvania	
Bendheim, Louis				
Bendheim, Milton	Esther	Pennsylvania		shoes
Berdit, Max	Sarah	Russia	Russia	shoes
Berger, Edward	Ana			junk dealer
Berger, Maurice		Pennsylvania		
Berger, Nathan	Sarah	Austria	Austria	installment collector
Bergerhoffer, Nathan				
Berkman, Samuel				
Berkowitz, Rubin	Mary	Russia	Russia	shoemaker
Berman, Abraham	Lena	Russia	Austria	grocer
Berman, Abraham	Rosie			mattress

Continued on next page

Adult Jews Who Arrived in Wilmington in the 1910s
(or reached the age of 20 in the 1910s), Continued

Name	Wife's name	Birthplace (m)	Birthplace (f)	First occupation
Berman, Joseph	Mary	Russia	Russia	furniture
Berman, Simon	Fannie			carpenter
Bernhardt, Ed	Nellie	New York		stenographer
Bernstein, Meyer	Cotton, Rosie	Russia	Russia	tailor
Bernstein, Nathan	Minnie	Russia	Russia	fruit salesman
Betansky, Clara	(widow)			confectioner
Betansky, Jack	Rose		Russia	tinsmith
Betansky, Louis	Rebecca	Russia	Russia	furniture company
Bierman, Harry	Stella	Russia		
Binder, Harry P	Anna		Russia	boat captain
Binder, Morris	Sara	Russia		upholstery
Birnbaum, Benjamin	Rose			grocer
Bloom, Abraham	Sarah	Russia	Russia	lodgings
Bloom, Annie	(widow)		Russia	teacher
Blum, Harry (Henry)		New York		clothing salesman
Blumberg, Lena	Baum, Julia	Delaware	Delaware	clerk
Blumberg, Leo	Rose	Russia	New York	salesman
Blumberg, Samuel	Ida	Romania	Lithuania	railroad worker
Blumenfeld, Joseph				

290

Name				
Bobb, Morris		Russia	Russia	newsdealer
Borew, Benjamin	Esther	Russia	Russia	manager
Borish, Jacob	Jennie	Russia	Russia	grocer
Braderman, Philip	Rebecca			grocer
Braiger, Ruben	Bessie			
Brand, John H.	Swartz, Theresa	Massachusetts	Maryland	furniture
Braunstein, George	Goldstein, Anna	Russia	Delaware	clothier
Braunstein, Harry	Rebecca	Russia	Pennsylvania	clothier
Braunstein, Maurice	Ethel	Delaware	Delaware	
Braunstein, Morris		New York	Russia	grocer
Braunstein, Samuel		Russia	Russia	clothier
Braverman, Kalman	Rose	Russia	Delaware	insurance agent
Braxman, Benjamin	Elizabeth	Pennsylvania	Austria	tinsmith
Breskman, Reuben	Reba	Hungary	Pennsylvania	auto accesories
Breuer, William	Edith	Pennsylvania	Russia	druggist
Briefman, Martin	Ida	New York	Delaware	confectioner
Briefman, Samuel		Russia	New York	salesman
Brodinsky, Eli		Russia	Russia	peddler
Brodsky, Harry	Rose	Russia		notions
Brodsky, Morris				
Brofsky, Mary				
Bromberg, Isadore	Rose			
Bronfin, Jacob	Levy, Florence	Russia		storekeeper

Continued on next page

Adult Jews Who Arrived in Wilmington in the 1910s
(or reached the age of 20 in the 1910s), Continued

Name	Wife's name	Birthplace (m)	Birthplace (f)	First occupation
Brown, Alek		Delaware		
Brown, Baer				
Brown, Charles		Delaware		
Brown, Jacob		Delaware		upholsterer
Buchler, Bela	Dora	Russia	Russia	installments
Budin, Louis	Ida	Pennsylvania	New York	drug store
Bunin, Albert	Weinstock, Jessie	Russia		barber
Caney, Benjamin		Russia		tailor
Caney, Joseph	Annie	Russia	Russia	
Cannon, Edward Selman		White Russia		newspaper reporter
Chaby, Abraham S.	Bess			convenience store
Chaiken, Herman		Delaware		
Chaiken, Louis		Delaware		cleaner
Chaiken, Robert	Lena	Russia	Russia	men's furnishings
Chambers, Alfred	Pauline	Russia	Russia	carpenter
Chard, Jacob	Mary	Russia	Russia	auto supplies
Chavin, Max				
Chavin, Sid				
Cherrin, Benjamin	Lena	Russia	Russia	grocer

292

Name		Birthplace	Birthplace	Occupation
Chesler, Sam	Sara			grocer
Citrenbaum, David				pharmacy
Citrenbaum, James				pharmacy
Citrenbaum, Morris				pharmacy
Cluetish, Myer	Anna	Hungary	Hungary	shoestore
Cohen, Abe	Ida	Russia	Russia	truck driver
Cohen, Abraham	Anna	Russia	Russia	dry goods merchant
Cohen, Ben		Delaware		stenographer
Cohen, Benjamin	Rosie	Russia-Poland	Russia-Poland	morocco worker
Cohen, David A.	Frances	New York		cloaks
Cohen, Harry A.	Freda	Russia	Russia	merchant
Cohen, Henry	Freda			shoes
Cohen, Jake	Ella	Russia	Russia	
Cohen, Joel	Fannie			
Cohen, Joseph	Flora	Russia	Russia	real estate agent
Cohen, Joseph	Clara	Russia	Russia	morocco
Cohen, Louis	Becky	Russia	Russia	grocer
Cohen, Percy	Rosie	Russia	Russia	presser
Cohn, A.D.G.				bakery employee
Cohn, Max	Pauline	Russia	Russia	Y.M.H.A. director
Colton, Edward	Rebecca	Russia	Russia	shipyard laborer
Cooper, Max	Anna	Russia	Russia	tailor
Corbin, Dora			Russia	merchant

Continued on next page

293

Adult Jews Who Arrived in Wilmington in the 1910s
(or reached the age of 20 in the 1910s), Continued

Name	Wife's name	Birthplace (m)	Birthplace (f)	First occupation
Corbin, Philip	Rosie	Russia	Austria	grocer
Coverman, Benjamin	Jeanette			furs
Cramer, George	Finkel, Pearl	Delaware	Pennsylvania	clerk
Cramer, Louis		Delaware		railroad bookkeeper
Cuttler, Meyer	Esther			tailor
Davis, David	Esther			shoes
Davitch, David				doctor
Dektor, Abraham	Mollie			notions
Dorzensky, Morris		Russia		
Drucker, Morris	Alice	Russia	Russia	confectioner
Drucker, Samuel	Clara			teacher
Dubin, Oscar		Russia	Russia	grocer
Dworkin, Isador	Cohen, Alice			driver
Eisenhandler, Edward	Gershenfeld, Lena		Pennsylvania	eggs and butter
Eisenman, Morris	Millie			painter
Emmetts, Louis	Minnie	Russia	Russia	
Epstein, Harry	Sarah	Russia	Russia	grocer
Epstein, Morris	Annie			salesman
Euster, William		Romania		

294

Name	Spouse	Birthplace	Birthplace	Occupation
Evans, Alvy R.				
Faulbaum, Morris	Helen	Russia	Russia	candy-store
Feinberg, Henry		Pennsylvania		salesman
Feinberg, Isaac		Delaware		garage manager
Feinberg, Samuel	Sarah			
Feinberg, William	Levenstein, Mary	Delaware	New York	salesman
Feingold, Nathan	Minnie	Austria	Austria	dry goods
Feldman, Louis	Augusta (Gussie)	Russia	Russia	merchant
Feldman, Sam	Rose	Russia	Russia	grocer
Field, Benjamin				grocer
Fielder, Harry	Carrie			
Fieldstone, Jennie	(widow)			
Fine, Moses	Sophia	Russia	Russia	cigars
Fine, Sam	Nellie	Russia	Russia	dry goods
Finesmith, Louis	Sarah	Russia	Massachusetts	clothing-store manager
Finesmith, William	Sosnov, Esther	Russia	Russia	dry goods
Finger, Aaron	Breskman, Anna	Delaware	Russia	plumber
Finger, Samuel		Delaware	Pennsylvania	lawyer
Fink, Benjamin B	Elsie	Romania		
Fink, Harry	Anna		Russia	auto supplies
Finkel, Bernhard	Harris, Hildreth	Russia		
Finklestein, Max		Romania		capmaker
Finkley, Henry	Edith	Russia	Pennsylvania	window trimmer

Continued on next page

Adult Jews Who Arrived in Wilmington in the 1910s
(or reached the age of 20 in the 1910s), Continued

Name	Wife's name	Birthplace (m)	Birthplace (f)	First occupation
Fischer, Abraham	Bessie	Pennsylvania	Pennsylvania	merchant
Fisher, David	Baruch, Florence	United States		railroad laborer
Fisher, David		Russia		
Fisher, Harry	Rose	Russia	Russia	grocer
Fisher, Hyman	Sara	Russia	Russia	morocco foreman
Fishman, Isidore	Rose	Romania	Russia	paperhanger
Fishman, Louis	Ida	Russia	Russia	bakery
Fogelmann, Abe	Eva			
Fogle, Esther				clerk
Fogle, Herman				confectioner
Forman, David	Yetta	Russia	Russia	storekeeper
Forman, Jacob	Catherine	Russia	Russia	grocer
Forman, Morris	Rosie	Russia	Russia	painter
Foxtow, Joseph		Russia		paperhanger
Frank, Barney		Russia		clerk
Frankel, Lewis	Marie		New York	
Frankfurt, Emma		New York		
Frankfurt, Isadore				
Frankfurt, Nathan		Russia		

Name		Origin	Origin	Occupation
Freed, Joseph	Tillie		Russia-Poland	theater musician
Freedman, Lewis	Sarah	Russia-Poland		clerk
Friedman, Fannie		Pennsylvania		railroad telephone
Friedman, Sam				
Frielick, Israel	Bertha	Russia	Russia	grocer
Garfinkel, William	Carrie	Romania	England	confectioner
Geller, Aaron	Dora	Russia	Russia	dry goods merchant
Geller, Harry	Dora			
Geller, Isaac	Minnie	Russia	Russia	grocer
Geller, Max				
Geller, Solomon	Anna	Austria	Russia	morocco worker
Gerber, Sarah			Russia	underwear factory
Ginns, Abel	Sarah	Russia	Russia	
Ginns, James	Topkis, Sallie	Russia	Russia	moving picture owner
Ginns, Oscar		Russia		moving picture owner
Glass, Jacob				
Glazar, Joseph	Zutz, Anna			tailor
Gluck, Bella			Delaware	operator
Gluck, Bertha			Delaware	saleslady
Gluck, David	Tillie	Delaware	Russia	baker
Gluck, Jacob	Sadie			shipworker
Gluck, Sadie		Delaware	Delaware	saleslady
Gluckman, Arthur				stenographer

Continued on next page

Adult Jews Who Arrived in Wilmington in the 1910s
(or reached the age of 20 in the 1910s), Continued

Name	Wife's name	Birthplace (m)	Birthplace (f)	First occupation
Gluckman, Harvey		Delaware		dentist
Gluckman, Louis	Goldye	New York	New York	dentist
Goberman, Abraham	Levy, Sylvia Nash	Russia	Russia	grocer
Gold, Hyman	Molly	Russia	Russia	
Gold, Louis	Katie	England	Russia	grocer
Goldberg, Harry	Sarah	Russia	Russia	grocery salesman
Goldberg, Joseph	Bessie	Russia	Russia	merchant
Goldberger, David	Sadie			soft drinks store
Goldberger, Isadore	Sadie	Austria	Austria	laborer
Golden, Israel	Mayerowitz, Gussie	Russia	Romania	
Golden, Max	Gussie	Russia	Russia	shipyard inspector
Goldenberg, Aaron	Anna	Russia	Russia	clothing salesman
Golder, Samuel	Tolchinsky, Bessie	Delaware	Russia	shipyard tinsmith
Goldin, Harry	Eva	Russia	Russia	
Goldman, Annie	(widow)			
Goldman, Israel	Sarah	Pennsylvania	New York	tobacco merchant
Goldstein, Abraham	Rebecca	Russia	Russia	car shop tinsmith
Goldstein, Abraham	Rose	Russia	Russia	tailor
Goldstein, Barney		Delaware		

298

Goldstein, Charles W.	Lillian	Russia	Russia	shoe
Goldstein, Harry	Esther	Russia	Austria	furniture finisher
Goldstein, Joseph	Ida	Romania	Romania	carpenter
Goldstein, Joseph		Delaware		plumber
Goldstein, Nathan	Rebecca	Russia	Russia	carpenter
Goldstein, Nathan		Poland		shoemaker
Goldstein, Nathan		Delaware		railroad engineer
Goldstein, Paul		Romania		upholsterer
Goldstein, Sam		Delaware		railroad
Goldstein, Samuel	Rebecca	Romania	Romania	clerk
Golin, Louis	Selma	Ukraine, Russia	Russia	
Goodlevege, Goldie	(widow)	Russia-Poland	Russia-Poland	grocer
Goodman, Nathan	Lena	Russia	Russia	musician
Goodman, William	Russell, Ann	Delaware		jewelry store manager
Gordon, Abraham	Goldsmith, Lottie	New York	Pennsylvania	blacksmith
Gordon, Harry	Sophia	Russia	Russia	
Gordon, Harry	Dora	Russia	Russia	car shop pipefitter
Gordon, Jacob	Clara	Russia	Russia	
Gordon, Samuel	Rose	Russia	Russia	
Grant, Theo	Celia			waists
Green, Joe	Solomon, Bertha	United States		photographer
Green, Samuel	Goldsmith, Julia	Pennsylvania	Pennsylvania	shoes
Green, Samuel	Elizabeth	New York	Delaware	railroad clerk

Continued on next page

Adult Jews Who Arrived in Wilmington in the 1910s
(or reached the age of 20 in the 1910s), Continued

Name	Wife's name	Birthplace (m)	Birthplace (f)	First occupation
Greenbaum, Joseph		Delaware		dry goods
Greenberg, Harry		Russia		cigars
Greenberg, Jake		Russia		tailor
Greenberg, Louis	Tillie	Russia	Russia	tailor
Greenspan, Morris	Blanche			
Greenstein, Abe	Gertie	Russia	Russia	grocer
Greenstein, Benjamin	Wolfman, Anna	Delaware	New Jersey	newspaper reporter
Greenstein, Jennie			Delaware	teacher
Greenstein, Joseph	Rebecca	Russia	New York	grocer
Greenstein, Morris	Snellenburg, Norma	Delaware	Delaware	dentist
Greenwald, Isaac	Helen	Pennsylvania		salesman
Greenwald, Michael	Bessie			grocer
Groll, Harry		Pennsylvania		musician
Gross, Andrew J.	Wilson, Pearl	Pennsylvania	Maryland	doctor
Gross, B. T.				
Gross, Elmer				doctor
Gross, Samuel	Jennie	Russia	Pennsylvania	grocer
Grossman, Benjamin				teacher
Grossman, Louis	Fannie	Pennsylvania	Austria	clerk

300

Name				Occupation
Grossman, Louis J.	Dorothy	Russia	Russia	electrical contractor
Grudnofsky, George		Russia	Russia	grocer
Gudless, Louis	Ida	Russia	Russia	tailor
Guttman, Samuel		Austria		electrician
Haber, Jacob	Cara	Romania	Romania	grocer
Haber, Samuel	Sophie	Romania	Romania	dry goods
Halprin, Abram		Russia		doctor
Handleman, Israel		Delaware		
Handleman, Sarah				
Handler, Paul		Delaware		
Harbor, Harry	Tonie	Austria	Austria	bakery salesman
Harbor, Joseph	Reba	Austria		grocery salesman
Hart, Gabriel		Austria		furniture
Hart, Harry				shipbuilder
Hartman, Alfred	Sylvia	Russia	New York	railroad laborer
Harwitz, Edward		Pennsylvania		
Harwitz, Louis	Sarah	Russia	Romania	grocer
Heimlich, Philip	Mary	New York	New York	Y.M.H.A. director
Heisler, Joseph				morocco worker
Heisler, Morris				laborer
Hellman, Wolf				cigars
Henick, Morris	Rendlich, Sadie	Russia	Russia	paperhanger
Hiller, Samuel				assistant store manager

301

Continued on next page

Adult Jews Who Arrived in Wilmington in the 1910s
(or reached the age of 20 in the 1910s), Continued

Name	Wife's name	Birthplace (m)	Birthplace (f)	First occupation
Hillersohn, Rosalie			Pennsylvania	teacher
Hirsch, John Martin		Pennsylvania		grocer
Hirshman, Abraham	Ethel	Austria	Delaware	grocer
Hirshout, Harry	Gussie	Austria		morocco
Hirshout, Sam	Anna			tailor
Hochstein, Louis				rabbi
Hoffman, Max				milk inspector
Hollett, David		Delaware		doctor
Holzman, Mark B.				merchant
Honey, Max	Leibowitz, Reba			
Horwitz, Abraham	Lena	Russia	Russia	real estate salesman
Husman, Harry	Mollie			
Isaac, Louis				livestock dealer
Izenman, Samuel	Elizabeth	Russia	Russia	egg store inspector
Jacobovitz, Abe	Sarah	Poland	Russia	home furnishings
Jacobs, Samuel	Pauline	Russia	Russia	auto salesman
Jacoby, Harry	Martha	Pennsylvania	Hungary	auto salesman
Jacoby, Samuel	Marie	Austria-Germany	Austria-Germany	grocer
Jaffee, Abraham		Russia		

Name			Occupation
Janofsky, Isadore		Russia	morocco employer
Jasper, Charles		Russia	grocer
Jasper, Isaac			grocer
Jasper, Louie	Russia	Russia	grocer
Jasper, Samuel			
Edith			
Sophia			
Rosie			
Jennie			
Juresco, Julius	Romania		grocer
Kahn, Max		Pennsylvania	merchant
Kate			
Budin, Lillian			
Kanofsky, Joseph	Pennsylvania	Russia	grocer
Sadie			
Kanofsky, Pincus	Pennsylvania		real estate
Madeline			
Karden, David	Russia		real estate
Mollie			
Karp, Bernard		Pennsylvania	clothier
Rose			
Karp, Morris	Pennsylvania		flour and seed store
Catherine			
Kates, Samuel			delicatessen
Sarah			
Katz, Joseph	Russia	Russia	dry goods
Anne			
Katz, Louis	Austria	Austria	
Yetta			
Katz, Max	Russia	Russia	bottler
Bessie			
Katz, Rebecca		Pennsylvania	school teacher
Katz, Sadie		Pennsylvania	dry goods clerk
Kaufman, Samuel	Austria	Austria	grocer
Pauline			
Keil, Isadore	Austria	Russia	clerk in liquor store
Goodman, Sadie			
Keil, Leo	New Jersey		auto salesman
Keil, Sam	Austria	Pennsylvania	auto salesman
Anna			
Kelrick, Reub	Russia	Hungary	merchant
Rose			

Continued on next page

Adult Jews Who Arrived in Wilmington in the 1910s
(or reached the age of 20 in the 1910s), Continued

Name	Wife's name	Birthplace (m)	Birthplace (f)	First occupation
Keyser, Harry	Riebman, Ida	Pennsylvania	Pennsylvania	Rialto Theater manager
Keyser, Jacob	Topkis, Sarah	Russia	Pennsylvania	doctor
Kirschner, Samuel	Lena			grocer
Kirshner, Harry	Rachel	Austria	Austria	grocer
Klein, Harry L.	Freda			
Klein, Ignatz	Rosie			morocco worker
Klein, Israel	Lizzie	Russia	Russia	grocer
Klein, Samuel A.	Katherine	Romania	Russia	furniture store collector
Knopf, Joseph	Cohen, Fannie	New York		cashier
Knopf, Samuel	Millman, Eva	New York	Pennsylvania	civil engineer
Kohn, Max	Lillian	Russia	Russia	grocer
Kohn, Samuel	Rebecca	Russia	Russia	
Koppel, Alex				
Koppel, Samuel	Sophie	Russia	Russia	window cleaning
Kovner, Morris	Ida			grocer
Kraft, Morris	Miller, Minerva			
Krauss, Sam				
Kreshtool, Isadore	Bertha	Russia	Russia	dentist
Krigstein, Isaac	Rose	Russia	Russia	fruit merchant

Name				Occupation
Krigstein, Morris				scrap iron
Kroll, Joseph	Stella			shipworker
Krouse, Israel				clothing clerk
Kruger, Abraham	Miller, Edna	Russia	Russia	salesman
Kruger, Morris	Heilig, Anna	Russia	Austria	dry good
Kurfirst, Israel	Anna	Russia	Russia	automobile repair shop
Kushner, Samuel	Clara	Russia	Russia	merchant
Landen, Max	Rose		Delaware	grocer
Lang, Grace				
Lang, Leslie		Delaware	Delaware	salesman
Lang, Marie			Delaware	clerk
Lang, Stella				clerk
Lefkow, Louis	Esther	Russia	Russia	painter
Lehrer, Benjamin	Bessie	Austria	Austria	dyer
Leibowitz, Jacob	Jennie	Romania	Russia	commission merchant
Leibowitz, Morris	Brown, Lillian	Russia	Delaware	commission merchant
Leichter, Emil	Rachel			
Leshem, Albert (Abe)		Delaware		
Leshem, Max				
Leshem, Morris		Delaware		
Leshem, Philip	Kravitz, Dorothy	Delaware	Pennsylvania	stenographer
Leshem, Tillie			Pennsylvania	
Lesner, Max	Ida	Austria	Romania	dry goods salesman

Continued on next page

305

Adult Jews Who Arrived in Wilmington in the 1910s
(or reached the age of 20 in the 1910s), Continued

Name	Wife's name	Birthplace (m)	Birthplace (f)	First occupation
Leven, Simon				barber
Levenberg, David	Frank, Pauline	Russia	Austria	paperhanger
Levenkron, Samuel	Jennie			butter and eggs
Levey, Michael	Anna	New York	New York	Y.M.H.A. director
Levi, Harry				cigars
Levin, Benjamin				cigars
Levin, Jacob	Mollie	Russia	Russia	ship carpenter
Levin, Louis	Eva	Russia	Austria	shoemaker
Levin, Max	Rosie	Russia-Poland	Lithuania	
Levin, Morris		Delaware		
Levin, Samuel	Matilda	Russia-Poland	Russia-Pol and	cigar merchant
Levin, William	Minnie			clothing store manager
Levine, Samuel	Reba	Russia	Pennsylvania	car shop cabinetmaker
Levinsky, Lewis	Deborah			tailor
Levitetz, Louis	Rose	Russia	Galicia	jeweler
Leviton, Simon	Ethel	Russia	Russia	grocer
Levitt, Aaron	Clara	Lithuania	Lithuania	jeweler
Levitt, David	Pearl	Russia	Russia	truck driver
Levy, Abraham	Holodky, Annie	Russia	Delaware	salesman

306

Levy, Alfred			Delaware	store manager
Levy, Lester	Madeline	New York	Russia	lawyer
Levy, Regina	Kesser, Reba	Russia		
Lewis, Benjamin	Sarah	New York		salesman
Lewis, Isaac				salesman
Lewis, Jacob J.	Anna	Russia	Pennsylvania	grocer
Lewis, Moses	Fannie	Russia	Russia	railroad laborer
Lichtenbaum, Jacob				
Lincoln, Abraham	Mary	Delaware	Russia	shipyard laborer
Lipson, Abe	Rose	Russia	Russia	tailor
Lipson, Samuel	Mamie	Russia	Russia	hardware
Lisakoff, Meyer	Clara	Russia	Russia	dry goods
Locoshefsky, Morris	Esther	Russia	Russia	salesman
London, Harry	Mary	Russia	Russia	fruit dealer
London, Mike (Myer)	Sarah	Russia	England	paperhanger
Louis, Leslie	Sarah	Virginia	Pennsylvania	electrician
Lovinger, Rudolph	Bessie	Hungary	Russia	waiter
Lundy, Morris	Jennie	Russia	Delaware	butcher
Lurge, Nettie				
Main, Charles				painter, grainer, glazier
Maisel, Joseph	(widow)	Russia		carpenter
Maisel, Sarah			Russia	confectioner
Mann, Abraham	Swartz, Lillian	Maryland	Maryland	furniture

Continued on next page

Adult Jews Who Arrived in Wilmington in the 1910s
(or reached the age of 20 in the 1910s), Continued

Name	Wife's name	Birthplace (m)	Birthplace (f)	First occupation
Mansky, Samuel	Yetta	Prussia	Prussia	confectioner
Margolin, Solomon	Fanny	Russia	Russia	delicatessen
Maritz, Isaac				
Markel, Adolph	Levy, Minnie	Austria	New York	jeweler
Markowitz, Samuel	Esther	Russia	Pennsylvania	paperhanger, painter
Markowitz, Samuel	Beatrice	Romania		dry goods merchant
Matt, Charles	Annie	Russia	Russia	storekeeper
Matt, Harry	Esther	Russia	Russia	furniture
Mattes, Joseph	Orensky, Kate	New York	Russia	gunpowder maker
Mazer, Samuel	Katherine			grocer
Meirovitz, Morris	Sarah	Romania	Romania	tailor
Meltz, Isidore	Hettie	Russia-Poland	Russia-Poland	grocer
Miller, Ben				clerk, auto shop
Miller, Carl	Rose	Russia	Russia	grocer
Miller, Harry	Carrie	Russia	Russia	grocer
Miller, Joseph	Minkin, Fannie	Galicia	Galicia	grocer
Miller, Meyer	Bessie	Pennsylvania	Russia	salesman
Miller, Samuel	Rose	Russia	Russia	hide dealer
Milman, Bertha			Delaware	milk dealer

308

Millman, Louis		Delaware		insurance agent
Minden, Israel	Jennie	Russia	Russia	salesman
Moerinsky, Harry	Annie	Russia	Russia	candy-store merchant
Mogilevsky, Hyman	Anna			grocer
Moranz, Max	Rebecca	Russia	Russia	paperhanger
Morganstein, Abraham	Sadie		Russia	
Morris, Alan				egg candler
Morris, David	Marian			
Morris, Joseph	Rose	Pennsylvania	Russia	grocer
Moses, Harry	Bella	Russia	Russia	railroad metalworker
Moses, Lewis	Sarah	Russia		auto mechanic
Moss, John	Lang, Bertha	New York	Delaware	barber supply merchant
Muderick, Benjamin	Klopit, Edith	Russia	Russia	shoe store
Myers, Fannie				domestic
Nadell, Max		Austria		clerk soft drinks
Naimen, Louis	Minnie			grocer
Naman, Joseph				junk dealer
Nathans, Samuel	Sarah	Russia	Russia	grocer
Nehkin, Morris	Anna	Russia	Austria	morocco worker
Newman, Joseph				
Newstadt, Louis	Minnie	Russia	Russia	contractor, painter
Noskow, Jacob	Ida	Russia	Russia	grocer
Novik, Michael	Esther	Russia	Russia	junk dealer

Continued on next page

Adult Jews Who Arrived in Wilmington in the 1910s
(or reached the age of 20 in the 1910s), Continued

Name	Wife's name	Birthplace (m)	Birthplace (f)	First occupation
Okonow, Herman	Helig, Celia	Russia	Russia	notions, dry goods
Olowte, Herman	Krichevsky, Goldie	Romania	Delaware	grocery clerk
Orenstein, Archie		New Jersey		doctor
Orenstein, Lillian			Delaware	
Paiken, Max	Mary	Russia	Russia	grocer
Paston, Abe	Rose	Russia	Russia	railroad laborer
Pearl, Albert	Anna	Russia	Delaware	insurance agent
Pearlman, Maurice	Anna	Russia	Russia	capmaker
Pearlman, Morris	Pearl	Russia	Russia	laborer
Pearlstein, Abraham	Rebecca	Russia	Russia	dry goods
Peck, Max	Ida	Russia	Pennsylvania	men's clothier
Perlman, Samuel		Romania		
Pinkus, Michael	Minnie	Russia	Russia	railroad tinsmith
Pizor, Marion		Delaware	Delaware	stenographer
Pizor, Morris C.	Rose	Delaware	Delaware	railroad engineer
Plaff, Samuel	Rose	Russia	Russia	grocer
Platensky, David				
Pledkin, David	Fannie	Russia	Russia	rabbi
Ploener, David	Kravitz, Lillian	Russia		bottler

Name		Birthplace	Birthplace	Occupation
Ploff, Samuel	Rose	Russia	Russia	grocer
Plum, Louis	Cecilia	Russia	Hungary	morocco worker
Poch, Alexander		Pennsylvania		
Podolsky, Abraham	Ida	Russia	Russia	laborer
Podolsky, Morris	Sophia	Delaware	Pennsylvania	auto supply
Podolsky, Rebecca			Delaware	
Podolsky, Samuel	Sophie	Russia	Russia	grocer
Podolsky, Sophia			Pennsylvania	
Pogach, Harry	Sarah	Russia	Austria	hardware
Pogach, Sarah	(widow)			rooming house
Poland, Myer	Emma	Russia	Russia	jeweler
Polotsky, Isaac	Helen			tailor
Polotsky, Isaac (Ike)	Goldberg, Yetta	Russia	Russia	grocer
Price, Samuel	Bertie	Russia		policeman
Prober, John	Libbie	Russia		
Protigal, Jacob	Lena	Russia	Delaware	junk dealer
Rabinowitz, Sam J.				rabbi
Rachlin, Daniel	Hilda			clothier
Rachlin, Samuel				newspaper reporter
Radolansky, Maurice	Rose	Russia	Russia	paperhanger
Raphaelson, Louis	Krigstein, Esther	Pennsylvania	Russia	scrap metal
Redlus, Edward	Hannah			egg chandler
Reissman, Augustus		Delaware		clerk

Continued on next page

Adult Jews Who Arrived in Wilmington in the 1910s
(or reached the age of 20 in the 1910s), Continued

Name	Wife's name	Birthplace (m)	Birthplace (f)	First occupation
Reissman, Charles		Delaware		stenographer
Reissman, Nathan		Delaware		clothing salesman
Rezits, Anna			Delaware	grocer
Rezits, Frank	Mary	Romania	Romania	shoemaker
Rezits, Morris	Anna	Russia	Russia	morocco finisher
Rhine, Edward	Elizabeth	Hungary	Hungary	
Rice, David				
Ring, Hyman				
Rissman, Jacob	Anna	Russia	Russia	grocer
Roll, Max	Bessie			merchant
Rose, Adolph	Annie	Russia	England	morocco worker
Rose, Earl	Elizabeth			
Rose, John	Lillian	Pennsylvania	Pennsylvania	jeweler
Rosen, Joseph	Rebecca			
Rosenbaum, Daniel				clerk
Rosenbaum, Jacob				merchant
Rosenbaum, Max	Rose	Russia	Russia	tailor
Rosenberg, Morris	Freida		Russia	tailor
Rosenberg, Simon	Ida	Russia	Russia	tailor

Rosenblatt, Isadore		Pennsylvania		bookkeeper
Rosenblatt, Jacob	Freida	Pennsylvania		
Rosenblatt, Lena			Delaware	salesman
Rosenblum, Aaron			Pennsylvania	butter and eggs
Rosenfeld, Saul				
Rosenthal, Herbert,	Hand, Lottie	Delaware		
Rosenvich, Reuben	Annie	Poland	Russia	morocco worker
Rosevich, Isadore	Sarah	Russia	Pennsylvania	tailor
Rosin, Harry	Rose	Russia	Russia	
Rosin, Louis	Bessie			
Rossman, David	Bertha	Pennsylvania	Delaware	paperhanger
Rothberger, David	Backie	Germany	Russia	doctor
Rothman, Charles	Bertha	New York	Pennsylvania	grocer
Rothman, Joseph	Sally	Hungary	Hungary	factory superintendent
Rothman, Samuel	Yetta		Russia	bottler
Rothman, Yetta	(widow)		Russia	
Rothschild, Jules	Coplan, Mary		Virginia	theater manager
Rothstein, Annie			Delaware	
Rothstein, Michael	Rose	Russia	Russia	hand express clerk
Rothstein, Morris	Dora	Russia	Russia	shoes
Rubenstein, Morris	Mary	Russia	Galicia	blacksmith
Rubenstein, Morris	Marie	Galicia		window cleaner
Rubin, Joseph	Anna	Russia	Russia	shipyard laborer

Continued on next page

Adult Jews Who Arrived in Wilmington in the 1910s
(or reached the age of 20 in the 1910s), Continued

Name	Wife's name	Birthplace (m)	Birthplace (f)	First occupation
Rubin, Louis	Mollie	Poland	Poland	wallpaper
Rubin, Morris	Anna			grocer
Rudman, Cecilia			Russia	dressmaker
Rudnick, Benjamin	Sklar, Mimmie			butcher
Rudnick, Fredrick	Lena	Russia	Russia	cattle dealer
Sachs, Raphael	Jennie	Romania	Romania	grocer
Sackler, Jacob	Eliza			grocer
Salinger, G.				
Salinger, Harris		Pennsylvania	Pennsylvania	
Salinger, Ida				cigarmaker
Salinger, Jacob		Delaware		
Salinger, Rose				
Salkind, Nathan	Rosa	Russia	Russia	butcher
Saltzman, Ralph	Reva	Pennsylvania	Delaware	broker
Saltzman, Robert		Pennsylvania		
Salus, Morris	Pauline	Russia	Russia	paperhanger
Samonisky, Harris	Mina	Delaware	Virginia	newspaper, sports editor
Sayer, Isaac		Pennsylvania		textile worker
Sbritsky, Emma			New York	factory bookkeeper

314

Surname, Given name				Occupation
Sbritsky, Hillel (Louis)	Sadie	Russia	Russia	rabbi
Schafer, Abe S.	Lena			dyer
Schaffer, Samuel	Sarah			meats
Schagrin, Sidney		Delaware		doctor
Schendelman, Jacob	Yedda	Russia	Russia	grocer
Schendelman, Louis	Sadie	Russia	Russia	grocer
Schendelman, Morris		New York		hosemaker
Schichler, Albert	Bella	Austria	Poland	grocer
Schiechter, Samuel	Esther	Austria	Austria	grocer
Schimmel, Anna			New York	
Schimmel, Louis		New York		grocer
Schimmel, Moses	Rose	Austria	Austria	grocer
Schimmel, Sidney		New York		chauffeur, taxi driver
Schoenberg, Charles	Annie			grocer
Schoenberg, Israel	Anna	Russia	England	furniture salesman
Schoenberg, Morris	Fannie	Russia	Russia	butcher
Schoenfeld, Hyman	Esther	Russia	Russia	confectioner
Schorr, Leopold	Newman, Cecilia	Hungary	Hungary	commercial studio
Schreiber, Emanuel		Moravia		rabbi
Schub, Isaac J.		Russia	Russia	rabbi
Schutt, Isaac	Frances			
Schutzman, Isadore	Goldman, Ida	Austria	Pennsylvania	window cleaner
Schwartz, George	Julie			window cleaner

Continued on next page

Adult Jews Who Arrived in Wilmington in the 1910s
(or reached the age of 20 in the 1910s), Continued

Name	Wife's name	Birthplace (m)	Birthplace (f)	First occupation
Schwartz, Jennie	(widow)		Russia	tailor
Schwartz, Myer	Mary	Poland	Poland	merchant
Schwartz, Nathan		Austria	Austria	investment company
Schwartz, Samuel				window cleaner
Seftel, Louis	Freda	Galicia	Galicia	saleslady
Segal, Bessie			Pennsylvania	clerk, steamboat company
Segal, Clara			Pennsylvania	railroad fireman
Segal, Harry		Pennsylvania		paperhanger
Segal, Lewis		Pennsylvania		blacksmith
Seltzer, Sol	Annie	Romania	Russia	paperhanger
Shaff, Morris				window trimmer
Shames, Harry	Florence	Russia	Russia	tailor
Shapiro, Abraham	Leona	Delaware	Connecticut	dry goods merchant
Shapiro, Harry	Ida	Russia	Russia	grocer
Shapiro, Harry	Mary	Russia	Russia	
Shapiro, Harry S.	Rebecca	Pennsylvania	Russia	salesman
Shapiro, Isaac		Delaware		cigars
Shapiro, Itze	Miller, Goldie	Delaware		
Shapiro, Morris	Sarah	Pennsylvania	Russia	

Sherbokow, Max	Hilda	Russia	Russia	furniture
Sherby, Louis	Pastor, Rose	Russia	Pennsylvania	sheet metal laborer
Shiffer, Jacob				
Shiller, David	Mary	Russia	Russia	barber
Shlein, Morris	Jennie	Austria	Russia	grocer
Shtofman, Jacob	Mary	Delaware	Pennsylvania	clothier
Shtofman, Morris	Eva	Russia	Russia	
Shtofman, Norman		Delaware		
Shtofman, William		Pennsylvania		clothing salesman
Shumer, Isadore	Goldie	Russia	Russia	powder maker
Sigmund, Samuel	Koffler, Rose	Russia	Romania	lace merchant
Silver, Daniel	Ida			tire shop
Silver, Harry				
Silver, Nathan				
Silverman, Benjamin	Bessie			
Silverstein, Joseph	Dora			confectioner
Simon, Louis	Sadie	Russia	Russia	grocer
Simon, Philip	Polsky, Jennie	Russia		peddler
Simon, William	Sarah			laborer, machinist
Sklar, Rubin	Pauline	Russia	Russia	grocer
Sklut, Abraham		Delaware		hide buyer
Sklut, Jacob	Esther	Russia	Russia	junk dealer
Sklut, Michael	Bessie			

Continued on next page

317

Adult Jews Who Arrived in Wilmington in the 1910s
(or reached the age of 20 in the 1910s), Continued

Name	Wife's name	Birthplace (m)	Birthplace (f)	First occupation
Sklut, Morris		Delaware		hides
Sloan, Harry	Borish, Anna	Russia	Russia	merchant
Slonsky, George		Delaware	Delaware	
Slonsky, Mollie				
Slonsky, Norman	Emma	Delaware		grocer
Slovin, Samuel	Rebecca	Russia	Russia	laborer, Pullman
Slutsky, Benjamin	Anna			hardware store
Smith, David	Dora	Russia	Russia	stockman
Smolen, Joseph	Bessie	Russia	Russia	assistant store manager
Smookler, Henry	Rebecca	Russia	Pennsylvania	clothier
Snellenburg, Carl				
Snellenburg, Ervin	Schwartz, Anna	Delaware	Delaware	
Snellenburg, Helene				
Snyder, Louis	Mary	Russia	Russia	tailor
Sokohl, J.N.				Y.M.H.A. director
Sollander, Joseph	Fannie	Austria	Pennsylvania	merchant
Sommers, Eugene	Eva			clerk
Spain, Abraham	Pauline			variety store
Spiegel, Abraham	Anna	Russia	Russia	

318

Surname, Name	First name	Origin	Origin	Occupation
Spiegel, Nathan	Leah	Russia	Pennsylvania	grocer
Spigel, Samuel	Annie	Austria	Austria	shoe store
Spiller, Frank	Elizabeth	Russia	Russia	tailor
Spiller, Israel	Ida	Russia	Russia	tailor
Spire, Max (Meyer)				watchmaker
Spiro, David	Ida	Russia	Russia	jeweler
Spiro, James	Risa			
Stein, Morris	Esther	Austria	Austria	paper hanger
Stein, Myer		Russia		shipyard laborer
Steinberg, Samuel	Ida	Russia	Russia	meats
Stone, Joseph	Dora	Pennsylvania	Russia	shoes
Stone, Leslie		Delaware		
Straus, Isidore	Sarah			paperhanger
Stretzky, Benjamin	Edna	Russia	Russia	grocer
Stuffmiller, Morris	Jennie	Galicia	Galicia	grocer
Sund, Leonard				laborer
Swartz, Joseph		Russia		tinsmith, car shop
Swartzman, Morris	Sarah	Russia	Russia	eggs and butter
Swasky, Solomon	Eva	Russia	Austria	bartender
Swinger, Jacob	Mamie	Delaware	Austria	grocery manager
Swinger, Kath				clerk at Woolworth's
Swinger, Louis		Delaware		grocery clerk
Swiren, David				rabbi

Continued on next page

Adult Jews Who Arrived in Wilmington in the 1910s
(or reached the age of 20 in the 1910s), Continued

Name	Wife's name	Birthplace (m)	Birthplace (f)	First occupation
Tamarchin, David	Rose			grocer
Tampolsky, Abraham		England		
Tampolsky, Bessie			England	
Tampolsky, Thomas		Delaware		grocer
Tannen, Harry	Anna	Russia	Russia	wholesale confectioner
Tannen, Louis	Sadie			whoesale confectioner
Tannen, Samuel	Lena			grocer
Tanzer, Morris	Gussie			
Tappman, Isaac				
Teitelbaum, Max	Lena	Hungary	Hungary	grocer
Thompson, Jacob	Catherine	Russia	Russia	grocer
Tidus, Max	Rose	Russia	Russia	shoes
Tollin, Joseph		Delaware		
Tollin, Louis		Pennsylvania		
Tomases, Benjamin	Atha			
Tomases, Morris	Maisel, Nettie	Romania	Russia	cabinetmaker
Tonik, Benjamin	Sylvia	Pennsylvania		grocer
Topkis, Abe	Braunschweiger, Adeline	Pennsylvania		
Topkis, David	Schwartz, Marion	Delaware		

320

Topkis, Emile	Segal, Hannah	New Jersey	Delaware	lawyer
Topkis, Hannah			Delaware	
Topkis, Sarah				
Topkis, Victor	Cohn, Sallie	Delaware		
Tubman, John	Casnia	Russia	Russia	tinsmith, carshop
Tuck, James G.	Eva			merchant
Tucker, John	Jenny			morocco worker
Tucker, Morris	Ida	Russia	Russia	
Tuckerman, Theodore	Abramson, Sarah		Romania	clothier
Tuff, Frank		Russia	Russia	presser
Tuff, Joseph		Pennsylvania		
Tullbovitz, Louis	Anna	Russia	Russia	tailor
Tupp, Harry	Rose			store decorator
Tyankow, George		Galicia		
Uman, Max	Mary	Russia	Russia	merchant
Ungar, Henry	Schwartz, Regina			candy store salesman
Unger, Louis	Belle			foreman
Usher, Harry	Fannie	Russia	Russia	
Vitansky, Abe	Ada	Russia	Russia	railroad metalworker
Vittes, Herman	Fanny	Austria	Austria	automobile repair shop
Wahl, Julius	Belle			shipping clerk
Wainer, Louis	Korngold, Dora	Delaware	Delaware	
Wapner, Gabriel	Fannie	Russia	Russia	dry goods

Continued on next page

Adult Jews Who Arrived in Wilmington in the 1910s
(or reached the age of 20 in the 1910s), Continued

Name	Wife's name	Birthplace (m)	Birthplace (f)	First occupation
Wasserman, Isidore	Pauline	New York	Hungary	railroad brakeman
Waterman, Lester	Viola			merchant hats
Watstein, Harry		Russia		morocco worker
Wax, Louis	Keil, Helen		Austria	meats
Waxman, David	Fannie (Frances)	Russia	Russia	grocer
Waxman, Frank	Clara	Russia	Turkey	grocer
Weiman, Joseph	Rebecca	Russia	Russia	notions merchant
Weinberger, Helen			Delaware	stenographer
Weiner, Jacob	Rosa	Russia	Russia	tailor
Weiner, Judas	Rebecca	Russia	Russia	laborer in car shop
Weinstein, Jacob	Fannie	Russia	Hungary	shoe store salesman
Weinstein, Jacob		Russia		railroad clerk
Weinstock, Sol				auto
Weintraub, Benjamin	Katie	Russia	Russia-Poland	fish merchant
Weintraub, Max	Mary	Austria	Austria	grocer
Weyman, Lewis	Sophie	Russia	Delaware	carpenter
Wheeler, Samuel				shipper
Whitaker, Harry				
White, Isaac	Rose	Russia	Russia	real estate agent

Name				
Willer, Harris	Fannie	Russia	Russia	tailor
Willprove, Jacob	Anna	Russia	Russia	merchant
Winkler, Louis	Anna			
Wintner, Joseph				doctor
Wise, John	Anna	Hungary	Hungary	storekeeper
Yalisove, Julius	Louise	Romania	New York	lace merchant
Yanowitz, Harry	Rose	Russia	Russia	grocer
Yaros, Abraham	Rebecca	Russia	Russia	baker
Yarowsky, Benjamin				dentist
Yarus, Abe		Russia		baker
Yasen, Alexander	Julia	Russia	New York	merchant
Yellner Harry	Mamie			grocer
Yelner, Morris H.	Annie	Russia	Russia	grocer
Yucht, Louis				salesman
Zelkind, Jacob	Rosie	Russia	Russia	railroad machinist
Zerkow, Joseph	Jennie	Romania	Romania	laborer
Zinman, Max	Sarah	Russia	Russia	butter and eggs
Zion, Samuel	Jeanette			druggist
Zogratt, Hyman	Jennie			grocer
Zucker, Bertha				
Zucker, Rose	Mary	Russia	Pennsylvania	stenographer
Zutz, David			Russia	cleaning and dying
Zutz, Esther			Russia	tailor

Continued on next page

Adult Jews Who Arrived in Wilmington in the 1910s
(or reached the age of 20 in the 1910s), Continued

Name	**Wife's name**	**Birthplace (m)**	**Birthplace (f)**	**First occupation**
Zutz, Harry		Russia	Russia	shipyard worker
Zutz, Samuel	Cecilia	Russia	Russia	tailor
Zutz, Sarah	(widow)			

Notes

PREFACE

1. During the same time span, the United States' Jewish population increased from 250,000 to 3,600,000. Abraham Karp, *Haven and Home* (New York: Schocken, 1983), 374–75, reprinted in Gerald Sorin, *A Time for Building: The Third Migration 1880–1920,* vol. 3 of *The Jewish People in America,* ed. Henry L. Feingold (Baltimore: Johns Hopkins University Press, 1992), 7.

INTRODUCTION

1. M. David Geffen, "Delaware Jewry: The Formative Years 1872–1889," *Delaware History,* 16, no. 4 (Fall-Winter 1975): 271.

2. Delaware Public Archives, Walter Wharton, *Land Warrants of New Castle County, 1670,* Jacob Fiana Land Sale, p. 5, 5A . The document is the first absolute proof of Jewish background. Isaac Israel and Benjamin Cardoso, fur traders in 1655, are sometimes mentioned as the first Jews to step foot in Delaware. However, research by Emile Topkis at the Archives of the Jewish Historical Society of Delaware questions the Judaism of these men.

3. Toni Young, "Establishing Judaism in Delaware," in *Delaware and the Jews* (Delaware, Jewish Historical Society of Delaware, 1979), 19–21.

4. Geffen, "Delaware Jewry," 272. Dr. Geffen's article is the source of information about all immigrants in this paragraph.

5. Young, "Establishing Judaism in Delaware," 20.

6. Sorin, *A Time for Building,* 5. See also Gerald Sorin, *Tradition Transformed: The Jewish Experience in America* (Baltimore: Johns Hopkins University Press, 1997), 24.

7. Carol E. Hoffecker, *Wilmington, Delaware: Portrait of an Industrial City 1830–1910* (University of Virginia for Eleutherian Mills-Hagley Foundation, 1974), 4–15.

8. Ibid., 20, 27.

9. Carol E. Hoffecker, "Four Generations of Jewish Life in Delaware," in *Delaware and the Jews,* 38.

10. Hasia Diner, *A Time for Gathering: The Second Migration 1820–1880,* vol. 2 of *The Jewish People in America,* ed. Henry L. Feingold (Baltimore and London: Johns Hopkins University Press, American Jewish Historical Society, 1992), 73.

11. Hoffecker, *Wilmington, Delaware,* 28.

12. Yda Schreuder, "Wilmington's Immigrant Settlement: 1880–1920," *Delaware History,* 23, no. 2 (Fall-Winter 1988): 140–142. In 1880, the population of

Wilmington was 42,478, of whom 36,804 were native-born and 5,674 were foreign-born. See also *Compendium of the Tenth Census 1880* (Washington, D.C.: Government Printing Office, 1883), 453. In 1900 Wilmington's population was 76,508, of whom 66,030 were native-born and 10,478 were foreign-born. See also *Compendium of the Twelfth Census 1900* (Washington, D.C.: Government Printing Office, 1902), 102,105.

13. Hoffecker, *Wilmington, Delaware,* 115.

14. *Compendium of the Tenth Census 1880,* 546. In 1880, New York's total population was 1,206,299 and its foreign-born population was 478,670; Baltimore's population was 332,313 and its foreign-born population 56,136; Philadelphia's population was 847,170 and its foreign-born population 204,335.

15. Schreuder, "Wilmington's Immigrant Settlement," 143.

16. Ibid., 142, figure 22.

17. Ibid., 142–43.

18. Hoffecker, *Wilmington, Delaware,* 117.

19. Schreuder, "Wilmington's Immigrant Settlement," 155.

20. Hoffecker, *Wilmington, Delaware,* 116.

21. Emil J. Abeles, "The German Element in Wilmington 1850–1914," (Master's thesis, University of Delaware, 1948), 12–13.

22. *Harkness Magazine,* 2, no. 5, (September 1873): 351.

23. Carol E. Hoffecker, *Delaware: A Bicentennial History* (New York: Norton, 1977), 112.

24. *Compendium Tenth Census 1880,* 2 and 412. The Delaware population in 1880 was 146,608 of whom 9,468 were foreign-born.

25. Ibid., 464.

26. Jacob Marcus, *Memoirs of American Jews 1775–1865* (Philadelphia: Jewish Publication Society of America, 1955), 1:10.

27. Diner, *A Time for Gathering,* 56.

28. Sorin, *A Time for Building,* 5; Sorin, *Tradition Transformed,* 26.

29. Diner, *A Time for Gathering,* 233.

30. Bertram Wallace Korn, "1655–1901" in *Seventy Five Years of Continuity and Change* (Philadelphia: 75th Anniversary Supplement of Federation of Jewish Agencies, 1976); Murray Friedman, ed., *Jewish Life in Philadelphia 1830–1940* (Philadelphia: ISHI Publications, 1983), 2.

31. *Gopskill's Philadelphia City Directory* (Philadelphia: James Gopskill, 1875) and Edwin Wolf II and Maxwell Whiteman, *The History of the Jews of Philadelphia from Colonial Times to the Age of Jackson* (Philadelphia: Jewish Publication Society of America, 1957), 32, 115.

32. Information on Philadelphia is from: Wolf and Whiteman, *History of the Jews of Philadelphia;* Friedman, *Jewish Life in Philadelphia;* Henry Samuel Morais, *The Jews of Philadelphia: Their History from the Earliest Settlements to the Present Time* (Philadelphia: Levytype Company, 1894); Jonathan D. Sarna, *JPS The Americanization of Jewish Culture 1888–1988* (Philadelphia: The Jewish Publication Society, 1989); and Murray Friedman, *When Philadelphia was the Capitol of Jewish America* (Philadelphia: Balch Institute Press; London and Toronto: Associated University Presses, 1990).

33. Jonathan Sarna, "The Making of an American Jewish Culture," in Friedman, *When Philadelphia was the Capitol,* 145, 153; Jonathan Sarna, *JPS The Americanization of Jewish Culture,* 16–17; The Philadelphia Group: The Making of an American Jewish Community, Conference, 12–13 November 1990.

34. Sarna, "The Making of an American Jewish Culture," 145. Most impor-

tant members of the group were lay people who were not especially eager to turn over leadership entirely to rabbis. Their organization foreshowed the dominance of lay leaders in communal structures.

35. *Encyclopaedia Judaica* (Jerusalem: Macmillan, Keter Publishing House, 1971), s.v. "Philadelphia" says "At a defining moment in American Jewish life, the 1880's through the 1920's Philadelphia may well lay claim to having been the Jewish capital of the United States." Daniel Elazar in Proceedings of Symposium, "The Philadelphia Group: The Making of an American Jewish Community," 2; Friedman, *When Philadelphia was the Capitol*, 9.

36. *Encyclopaedia Judaica*, s.v. "Baltimore." See also Isaac M. Fein, *The Making of an American Jewish Community: The History of Baltimore Jewry from 1773 to 1920* (Philadelphia: Jewish Publication Society of America, 1971), 77. Fein quotes Lesser saying that Jews in Baltimore were perhaps greater in number than Philadelphia, at least not much smaller.

37. Fein, *The Making of an American Jewish Community*, 43–49, 54–58. The synagogue had been organized a decade earlier.

38. Michael A. Meyer, *Response to Modernity: A History of the Reform Movement in Judaism* (New York and Oxford: Oxford University Press, 1988), 236.

39. Fein, *The Making of an American Jewish Community*, 90, 117–18, 183–84. For many years before the Pittsburgh Platform of 1885, Szold was considered by the Reformers as one of them.

40. Ibid., 120.

41. Ibid., 120. Szold's prayer book was later modified by Rabbi Morris Jastrow and became known as Minhag Jastrow.

42. Ibid., 74, 68–70.

43. Ibid., 194. *Encyclopedia Judaica*, s.v. "Baltimore."

44. *Encyclopedia Judaica*, s.v. "Trenton."

45. Young, "Establishing Judaism in Delaware," 29; *Delaware Gazette*, 21 September 1866, and *Delaware Republican*, 6 September 1869.

46. Diner, *A Time for Gathering*, 115.

47. Ibid., 115.

48. Ibid., 123.

49. Meyer, *Response to Modernity*, 228.

50. Ibid., 231.

51. Ibid., 235.

52. Leon Jick, *The Americanization of the Synagogue 1820–1870* (Hanover, N.H.: University Press of New England, 1976), 182, 190–191.

53. Ibid., 183.

54. Ibid., 57.

55. Meyer, *Response to Modernity*, 261–62; Naomi Cohen, *Encounter with Emancipation: The German Jews in the United States 1830–1914* (Philadelphia: Jewish Publication Society of America, 1984), 171. Cohen says the religious census of 1890 revealed that Reform had outdistanced its opponents in membership and synagogue property.

56. Ibid., 235.

57. Diner, *A Time for Gathering*, 14, 15.

58. Ibid.

59. Ibid., 22.

60. Diner, *A Time for Gathering*, 118; Meyer, *Response to Modernity*, 257–60.

61. Meyer, *Response to Modernity*, 252.

62. Cohen, *Encounter with Emancipation*, 58,

63. Michael A. Meyer, "German-Jewish Identity in Nineteenth Century America," in *The American Jewish Experience,* ed. Jonathan D. Sarna (New York and London: Holmes & Meier, 1986), 53.

64. By 1870 more than fifty congregations had adopted *Minhag America;* four years later it was one hundred, making *Minhag America* the most widely used prayerbook in America during the 1870s. Michael A. Meyer, *Response to Modernity,* 255.

65. Meyer, "German-Jewish Identity," 56.

66. Ibid., 58.

67. Daniel Jonah Goldhagen, *Hitler's Willing Executioners: Ordinary Germans and the Holocaust* (New York: Alfred A. Knopf, 1996), 55, 58–59.

68. Meyer, "German Jewish Identity," 58, 59.

69. Ibid., 58.

70. Oscar and Mary F. Handlin, "A Century of Jewish Immigration to the United States," in *American Jewish Yearbook 1948–49* (Philadelphia: Jewish Publication Society of America, 1949), 34–35; Naomi Cohen, *Encounter with Emancipation,* 125. Long before rabbis came to the United States, lay people often provided for their own needs

71. Handlin and Handlin, "A Century of Jewish Immigration to the United States," 34–35.

72. Oscar Handlin, *The Uprooted* (Boston: Little, Brown, 1952), 152–53.

73. Jick, *The Americanization of the Synagogue,* 20.

74. Ibid.,109.

75. Diner, *A Time for Gathering,* 87.

76. Today, Reform synagogues and many Conservative synagogues count women towards the *minyan.*

77. Arthur Hertzberg, *The Jews in America* (New York: Simon and Schuster, 1989), 110.

78. Ibid., 110.

79. Cohen, *Encounter with Emancipation,* 129–30.

80. Ibid., 147–48.

81. Joakim Isaacs, "Ulysses S. Grant and the Jews," in Sarna, *The American Jewish Experience,* 62.

82. Ibid., 63.

83. Ibid., 64.

84. Ibid., 71.

85. Cohen, *Encounter with Emancipation,* 251–22.

86. Eric L. Goldstein, "Different Blood Flows in Our Veins: Race and Jewish Self-Definition in Late Nineteenth Century America," *American Jewish History* 85, no. 1, (March 1997): 30.

87. Ibid., 31, from Jick, *The Americanization of the Synagogue 1820–1870,* 173.

88. Goldstein, "Different Blood," 30–37.

89. Cohen, *Encounter with Emancipation,* 266–78.

90. Handlin, *The Uprooted,* 236.

91. Ibid., 245.

92. Information in this section is from Young, "Establishing Judaism in Delaware," 22–35.

93. *Every Evening,* 16 October 1872.

94. *Every Evening,* 5 November 1872

95. Geffen, "Delaware Jewry," 275, 280.

96. Archives of the Jewish Historical Society of Delaware (hereafter JHSD), Emile Topkis Collection, (hereafter ETC), Box I, Carrie Row's letter to Emile Topkis.

CHAPTER 2: IN THE BEGINNING

1. *Every Evening*, 27 September 1879.

2. The author has compiled this estimate using census records; birth, death, and marriage records; and city directories. It includes only those people definitely known to be Jewish. The notes of Emile Topkis at the Jewish Historical Society of Delaware have been a tremendous assistance.

3. Diner, *A Time for Gathering*, 179.

4. *Every Evening*, 27 September 1879.

5. Ibid.

6. Ibid.

7. *Wilmington Gazette*, 29 September 1879.

8. *Every Evening*, 29 September 1879.

9. Moshe Davis, *American and the Holy Land: With Eyes Toward Zion* (Westport, Conn.: Praeger, 1995), 111–12.

10. Bertram W. Korn, "A Preliminary Checklist of American Jewish Institutions and Organizations Named in Honor of Sir Moses Montefiore" in Moshe Davis, *America and the Holy Land.*

11. *Every Evening*, 29 September 1879, and *Wilmington Gazette*, 29 September 1879.

12. Information on Lieberman is from Wilmington City Directories, 1860s–1905 (hereafter WCD plus year.) United States Bureau of the Census, Tenth Census of the United States, 1880, Manuscript Returns for Delaware and Twelfth Census of the United States, 1900, Manuscript Returns for Delaware (hereafter Census plus year). Archives of JHSD, Biographical and Historical Information on 17th, 18th and 19th Century Jews and ETC, Box 1, Clarence Lipper, interview by Emile Topkis, 1 November 1954; Delaware Public Archives, Rosa Lieberman's will, 1908; Fannie Lieberman's birth record, 2 October 1884.

13. Richard Edwards ed., *Industries of Delaware: A Historical and Descriptive Review* (Wilmington: Richard Edwards, 1880), 76.

14. *Sunday Morning Star*, 24 October 1926.

15. Ibid.

16. JHSD, ETC, Box 3, Emile Topkis' notes on *Morning Herald*, 20 April 1878.

17. Edwards, *Industries of Delaware*, 76.

18. Diner, *A Time for Gathering*, 196.

19. Information on Jacob DeWolf is from WCD 1860s–1880s; Census 1880; Archives of JHSD, ETC Box 2, letters from Estella Hoffman, 1955; interview with Sally DeWolf, 1955; Delaware Public Archives, birth records, Sophie DeWolf, 18 October 1885 and Albert DeWolf, 3 October 1882.

20. *Harkness Magazine*, June 1873.

21. ETC, Sally De Wolf interview, 1955.

22. ETC, Estella Hoffman's letter to Emile Topkis, 28 February 1955.

23. Tefellim are small leather boxes containing pieces of parchment with

selections from the Bible, with leather straps attached. During prayer, traditional Jews wear tefellim on their arms to symbolize their devotion to God.

24. ETC, Hoffman letters to Emile Topkis, 28 February 1955 and 19 April 1955.

25. WCD 1860s–1896; Census 1880; ETC, letter from Monroe Sondheimer, 1955.

26. WCD 1860s–1891; Census 1880; Delaware Public Records, birth record, Rachel Meyers, 2 March 1882.

27. *Delaware's Industries: An Historical and Industrial Review* (Philadelphia: Keighton Printing House, 1891), 90.

28. ETC, notes on *Sunday Star*, 12 August 1883.

29. WCD 1878–1883; Census 1880; Young, "Establishing Judaism in Delaware," 33.

30. John Higham, *Send These to Me: Jews and Other Immigrants in Urban America* (New York: Athenaeum, 1975), 34.

31. ETC Box 3, notes on *Every Evening,* 17 February 1879.

32. *Every Evening,* 19 February 1880.

33. *Every Evening,* 14 February 1880.

34. *Every Evening*, 24 April 1883 and *Morning News*, 25 April 1883.

35. WCD 1870s–1889; Census 1880; *Delaware State Journal*, 11 November 1880; Delaware Public Archives, George Jacobs's death certificate, 18 July 1888

36. *Sunday Star*, 22 July 1888.

37. Emile Topkis, who studied Delaware Jewish history in the 1950s, suggests that George Jacobs might have been related to the Jacobs of Sussex County of the 1700s.

38. WCD 1878.

39. ETC, Box 3, notes on *Delaware Gazette*, 7 March 1878.

40. WCD 1870s–1885; Census 1880.

41. WCD 1879; Census 1880; JHSD, ETC, Bertie Fellheimer, interview by Topkis, 1955 ; obituary of Marx Fellheimer 21 September 1883.

42. ETC, Bertie Fellheimer, interview by Emile Topkis, 1955.

43. WCD 1880–81; Census 1880; ETC, notes on *Morning Herald*, 12 December 1878.

44. WCD 1870s; Census 1880.

45. WCD 1870s; Census 1880.

46. ETC, Box I, notes on Row Family: WCD 1860s–1880s; Census 1880.

47. ETC Box I, notes on letter from Monroe Sondheimer.

48. *Morning News,* 22 September 1880.

49. WCD, 1880–81, Ferris Brothers, Wilmington, Delaware, 1879,

50. Diner, *A Time for Gathering,* 79, 82.

51. Irving Howe, *World of Our Fathers* (Simon and Schuster, New York, 1976), 154.

52. Ibid., 155.

53. Census 1880.

54. Cohen, *Encounter with Emancipation,* 13; Sorin, *Tradition Transformed,* 21.

55. Cohen, *Encounter with Emancipation,* 14.

56. Information on age is from census records and records at the Hall of Records.

57. Census 1880.

58. Census 1880; ETC Box 3, notes on Row family.

59. WCD 1879–80; Edwards, *Industries of Delaware*, 95.

60. ETC, notes on 1900 directory.

61. Bernard D. Weinryb, *"The German Jewish Immigrants to America,"* in *Jews from Germany in the United States* (New York: Farrar, Straus and Cudahy Inc, 1955), 126.

62. Abeles, "The German Element in Wilmington," 9–12.

63. For an analysis of the importance of religion in the lives of new immigrants, see Handlin, *The Uprooted,* Chapter five.

64. *Every Evening,* 7 February 1880.

65. *Wilmington Daily Gazette*, 14 February 1880.

66. Diner, *A Time for Gathering*, 152; Lloyd P. Gartner, *Jewish Education in the United States: A Documentary History* (New York: Teachers College Press, Columbia University, 1969), 7–9.

67. Gartner, *Jewish Education*, 7–9.

68. Diner, *A Time for Gathering*, 134; Gartner, *Jewish Education,* 9.

69. Diner, *A Time for Gathering,* 222.

70. *Every Evening* 16 February 1880.

71. Geffen, "Delaware Jewry," 281–2.

72. *Wilmington Daily News,* 25 March 1880.

73. *Every Evening*, 7 February 1880 and 27 February 1880.

74. Diner, *A Time for Gathering*, 104.

75. Geffen, " Delaware Jewry," 282.

76. Toni Young, *The Grand Experience: A History of the Grand Opera House* (New York: American Life Foundation, 1976), 131.

77. *Every Evening,* 27 February 1880.

78. Ibid.

79. *Every Evening*, 20 March 1880. For a detailed description of the event, see Geffen, "Delaware Jewry," 284–86.

80. ETC, Mrs. Bendheim interview by Emile Topkis.

81. Joseph Hoffman, interviewed by the author, 1979.

82. *Every Evening*, 31 August 1880; Geffen, "Delaware Jewry," 286.

83. *Every Evening*, 24 November 1880.

Chapter 3: With Increased Diversity—The 1880s

1. *Every Evening*, 18 January 1883.

2. JHSD, History of Moses Montefiore Mutual Beneficial Society, 1927.

3. Handlin, *The Uprooted,* 155.

4. ETC, Box 2, Joe Martin interview by Emile Topkis.

5. JHSD, Montefiore Mutual Benefit Society Collection, Act to Incorporate the Montefiore Mutual Benefit Society, 24 February 1883.

6. JHSD. The names are listed in a booklet on the Moses Montefiore Society, 1883 . The 1927 history, referred to above, lists the child, Jacob Jacobs, rather than his father George.

7. *Every Evening*, 3 February 1883.

8. Information on the Pizor-Wolters family is from WCD 1879–1890; obituary of Reuben Wolters, *Sunday Star*, 29 December 1918; obituary of Wolf Wolters, *Morning News,* 10 January 1913; ETC, Kate Pizor, interview by Emile Topkis, 1954.

9. ETC, Kate Pizor interview by Emile Topkis, 1954.

10. Information on Julius Cabe is from WCD 1879–1885; JHSD, Rabbi David Geffen Collection, news clippings, *Every Evening,* 1 January 1883 and *Morning News,* 17 January 1884.

11. Information on Harris is from WCD 1880s–1890s; ETC, notes from Leslie and Louis Gluckman and Sallie Topkis Ginns interview; Recorder of Deeds 1884; obituary of Aaron Harris, *Every Evening,* 6 April 1895.

12. Information on the Manns is from WCD 1880–1886; ETC; and *Sunday Star,* 23 August 1885 .

13. *American Jewish Yearbook 5664, 1903–1904* (Philadelphia: Jewish Publication Society of America, 1903), 53.

14. Information on Rabbi Faber is from Delaware Public Archives, Dover— birth record, Fanny Faber 23 January 1882 and Harry Faber 15 September 1883, death certificate, Regina Faber 1885; WCD 1879–1888; ETC, Mrs. Bendheim interview.

15. Information on Jacob and Simon Faber is from WCD 1880s; ETC, miscellaneous notes; and obituary, Jacob Faber *Journal Every Evening,* 4 September 1951. The younger Fabers were either cousins or nephews.

16. WCD 1880s; ETC, letter from Samuel Abramson; Delaware Public Archives, birth records of Gidor Abramson, 26 June 1884, Jakeup Fisher, 9 June 1884, Stella Schlesinger, 19 October 1884.

17. Gerald Sorin, *A Time for Building,* chap. one; Gerald Sorin, *Tradition Transformed,* 34–39.

18. David Berger, ed., *The Legacy of Jewish Migration: 1881 and Its Impact* (New York: Brooklyn College Press, 1983); Sorin, *A Time for Building,* chap. 1, particularly p. 32.

19. *Every Evening,* 27 February 1882.

20. *Every Evening,* 2 March 1882.

21. *Sunday Star,* 5 March 1882

22. Ibid.

23. *Every Evening,* 13 July 1882.

24. *Delaware Industries: An Historical and Industrial Review,* p. 224.

25. ETC, Clarence Lipper interview by Emile Topkis, 12 October 1954.

26. *Morning News,* 23 March 1883. Although Lieberman did not list his occupation as real estate in the city directories, in the 1900 census he did name real estate as his occupation.

27. New Castle County, Recorder of Deeds, Direct Deed Index, 1873–1897.

28. ETC, notes on newspaper 27 March 1888.

29. ETC, letter from Lieberman's grandson, Clarence Lipper, 12 November, 1954.

30. *Every Evening,* 5 June 1883.

31. Delaware Public Archives, birth record of George Washington Levy, 22 February 1883.

32. ETC, notes of Emile Topkis. They lived at 101 Shipley in 1885 (WCD).

33. JHSD, Jechebet Roos, interview by Yetta Chaiken.

34. David, Louis, William, and Sallie were born before the family arrived in America; Charles was born in Pennsylvania days after their arrival. Sallie Ginns recalled that her father took charge of the burial of a baby of Nathan Lieberman. A son of the Lieberman's died in 1883. A daughter died in 1886.

35. ETC, Sallie Ginns, interview by Emile Topkis, 13 August 1955.

36. Ibid.

37. ETC, note on his handwritten excerpts from WCD, 1895.

38. HIAS, Index of People resettled 1884–1945, microfilm, Balch Institute, Philadelphia PA. Chana came to meet her husband. In 1913 the association was involved in resettling new immigrants outside of Philadelphia.

39. Delaware Public Archives, return of a marriage, Taenenbaum and Friedman, 15 December 1885.

40. *Morning News*, 6 February 1885.

41. Hasia Diner, "Like the Antelope and the Badger," in *Tradition Renewed: A History of the Jewish Theological Seminary,* ed. Jack Wertheimer (New York: Jewish Theological Seminary of America, 1997), 1: 10.

42. JHSD, Adas Kodesch Collection, "History of Adas Kodesch" by Barnet Gluckman, 1908, p. 23. Oscar Handlin, in *The Uprooted*, suggests that immigrants suffered from loneliness and isolation and brought their religious ways with them as a support system, a way of holding on to tradition in a strange land. See particularly chapters four and five.

43. The names are given in *The Jewish Messenger,* 58, no. 8 (21 August 1885), at JHSD. Other information is from Wilmington City Directories.

44. JHSD, Geffen Collection, *Jewish Messenger* (21 August 1885). Shorter accounts of the opening were given by local newspapers found in ETC: *Every Evening,* 17 August 1885; *Sunday Star,* 16 August 1885; and *Morning News,* 17 August 1885. See also Geffen, "Delaware Jewry," 291–92; Bill Frank, "A Day to Remember," in Adas Kodesch Shel Emeth 90th Anniversary Edition, 1975.

45. Reverend Sabato Morais, "An Address: Delivered on the Feast of Pentecost" (Philadelphia , Collins Printer, 1869, 5629), 3.

46. Oscar Handlin, *Adventure in Freedom: Three Hundred Years of Jewish Life in America* (New York: McGraw-Hill, 1954), 112; Diner, "Like the Antelope and the Badger," 6–7.

47. Moshe Davis, *The Emergence of Conservative Judaism: The Historical School in Nineteenth Century America* (Philadelphia: Jewish Publication Society of America, 1963), 13–19.

48. Ibid.

49. Henry L. Feingold, *Zion in America: The Jewish Experience from Colonial Times to the Present* (New York: Hippocrene Books, 1964), 182.

50. Davis, *The Emergence of Conservative Judaism*, 17–19; Diner, "Like the Antelope and the Badger," 3.

51. JHSD; Geffen Collection, *Jewish Messenger,* 21 August 1885. At the time, many Americans believed Jews could not be good American citizens because they were always thinking of the Holy Land. See Moshe Davis, *American and the Holy Land* (Westport, Conn.: Praeger, 1995), 118.

52. *Jewish Messenger,* 21 August 1885.

53. Henry Morais, *The Jews of Philadelphia,* 84, 86. Caro later became a Reform rabbi in Milwaukee. See Louis J. Swichkow and Lloyd P. Gartner, *The History of the Jews of Milwaukee* (Philadelphia: Jewish Publication Society of America, 1963), 185–87, 200–201.

54. Geffen, "Delaware Jewry," 291. See also *Every Evening,* 13 August 1885.

55. *Wilmington Morning News,* 11 September 1885

56. ETC, notes on *Sunday Star,* 19 July 1885; *Every Evening,* 18 July 1885; *Wilmington Morning News,* 18 July 1885.

57. ETC, notes on *Morning News,* 15 May 1886.

58. *Every Evening,* 28 September 1886.

59. *American Jewish Yearbook 5664, 1903–04* (Philadelphia: Jewish Publication Society of America, 1903), 90. Despite the fact that the *Yearbook* cites his

rabbinical degree, it refers to Rezits as a cantor. Rabbi David Geffen and Rabbi Leonard Gewirtz say that Rezits was not a real rabbi, although the congregants thought of him as a rabbi because he was their leader. In later years, ordained rabbis were brought to Adas Kodesch with Rabbi Rezits. See also Emile Topkis's notes on *Wilmington Morning News,* 7 September 1930. According to Emile Topkis's interview with Benjamin Fineman in ETC, Israel Wainer, who was the most religious Jew in Wilmington at the time, brought Rabbi Rezits to Wilmington.

60. ETC, Box 1, Emile Topkis's notes.

61. Delaware Public Archives, return of a marriage, Barnett Gluckman and Fannie Harris, 12 December 1887. Rabbi Rezits officiated and Bernard Wolfson witnessed several other marriages between March 1887 and August 1888. If Harris was very religious, he may have objected to a rabbi who wasn't a "real" rabbi performing the ceremony.

62. Gluckman, "History of Adas Kodesch," 29.

63. *Evening Journal,* 5 September 1888.

64. Ibid.

65. Ibid.

66. Gluckman, "History of Adas Kodesch," 25.

67. Ibid., 29.

68. John Higham, *Send These to Me: Jews and Other Immigrants in Urban America* (New York: Atheneum, 1975), chapter two, particularly 30–38.

69. Handlin, *The Uprooted,* 236–37.

70. Higham, *Send These To Me,* 38; for additional information, 30–37.

71. Howe, *World of Our Fathers,* 50–51.

72. Higham, *Send These to Me,* 38.

73. *Laws of the State of Delaware,* Volume 17, 1883, 74.

74. Ibid., 75.

75. Higham, *Send These to Me,* 32.

76. *Sunday Star,* 4 February 1883.

77. Handlin and Handlin, "A Century of Jewish Immigration," 65.

78. See JHSD, Bill Frank Collection, for additional information. Also tape of Bill Frank's 1975 lecture.

79. Charles Callan Tansill, *The Foreign Policy of Thomas E. Bayard, 1885–1897* (New York: Fordham University Press, 1940), xx.

80. The events that had occurred in April and May 1885 were reviewed in detail in the *Morning News,* 15 December 1885. Also Tansill, *The Foreign Policy of Thomas E. Bayard,* xxi–xxiii

81. *Morning News,* 15 December 1885; Tansill, *Foreign Policy of Thomas E. Bayard,* xxiii.

82. Letter, Secretary Bayard to Baron Schaeffer May 18, 1880, quoted in Tansill, *Foreign Policy of Thomas E. Bayard,* xxiii.

83. JHSD, Bill Frank Collection, Bill Frank notes.

84. Edward Spencer, *An Outline of Public Life and Services of Thomas F. Bayard* (New York: D. Appleton & Co. 1880), 47.

85. Reported in *Wilmington Morning News,* 2 May 1885.

86. *Wilmington Morning News,* editorial, 7 May 1885.

87. Ibid.

88. Tansill, *The Foreign Policy of Thomas E. Bayard,* xxx.

89. ETC Box I, Letter from Carl L. Lokke at National Archives, 31 January 1958.

90. Oscar and Mary F. Handlin, "The Acquisition of Political and Social

Rights by Jews in the United States," *American Jewish Yearbook, 1955*, vol. 56 (Philadelphia and New York: American Jewish Committee and Jewish Publication Society, 1955), 60.

91. Ibid., 60, Cohen, *Encounter with Emancipation*, chapter two, specifically pr. 65 and 81.

92. *Every Evening*, 1 October 1889. Sam and Rosa Gluck are from Hungary in the census of 1900, Germany in census of 1910, and the widowed Rosa lists Germany in the 1920 census.

93. *Every Evening*, 1 October 1889.

94. Laws of Delaware, 1874 Revised Code, 782.

95. Handlin and Handlin, "The Acquisition of Political and Social Rights," 61.

96. *Every Evening*, 9 September 1889 through 11 September 1889.

97. ETC, Sallie Topkis Ginns interview.

98. *Every Evening*, 9 September 1889.

99. *Every Evening*, 15 February 1890. See also JHSD, Bill Frank Collection.

100. *Every Evening*, 15 February 1890.

101. *Every Evening*, 24 September 1890 says 500. This estimate is consistent with the *Evening Journal*, 5 September 1888 estimate of 400 and with the 1894 estimate of 150 families in *History of Wilmington, Commercial, Social and Religious Growth of the City During the Past Century* (Wilmington: Every Evening, 1894), 153. Extensive research on birth, death, and marriage records as well as directories leads me to accept the estimate. I have identified a minimum of 141 adult Jewish males and a minimum of 87 married women. It is reasonable to estimate that at least half, probably more, of the population were people under the age of twenty.

102. *Compendium of the Eleventh Census 1890, Part III*, (Washington, D.C.: Government Printing Office, 1897), 12.

103. In 1890, the foreign-born population was 9,099. (*Compendium 1890*, 12)—less than 15% of the total.

104. Data on country of origin is from census records, birth, death, and marriage records. Information includes country of origin for 95 of the 141 Jewish men and for 70 of the 87 Jewish women here in 1890.

105. Marx's son Louis ran the clothing shop on Market Street for several years with his mother Ellen; however, at the end of the decade, he moved to Richmond, Virginia with his wife, Emma, and Ellen returned to Philadelphia. Another son, Samuel, who ran a cigar store in Wilmington, left by the end of decade.

106. Meyer Meyers was opening stores elsewhere and about to leave Wilmington.

107. Sorin, *Tradition Transformed*, 33.

108. Data on date of arrival is available for 133 of the 141 Jewish men; about 81 arrived between 1888–1890.

109. Naturalization records, Historical Society of Delaware.

110. Data on age is from birth, marriage, death, and census records and includes estimates on 80 men and 76 women.

111. Bernard Row, who at 72 was the oldest Jew in Wilmington was no longer a practicing Jew; Wolf Wolters worked in Wilmington but lived in Philadelphia.

112. *Wilmington Business Directory 1890*, 594.

113. Thomas Kessner, *The Golden Door: Italian and Jewish Immigrant Mobility in New York City 1880–1915* (New York: Oxford University Press, 1977), 37, 61–62, 198.

114. Ibid., 63.

115. Data on occupations is from WCD 1880s, birth, marriage, death, and census records.

116. Diner, *A Time for Gathering*, 66, 67.

117. Kessner, *The Golden Door*, 60.

118. The Laws of Delaware, 1887–89, Vol. 18, 762–763. The 1874 law had lumped retailers and peddlers together with no definition of terms. *Revised Statutes of the State of Delaware 1874* (Wilmington: James Webb, n.d.), 368–71.

119. Laws, 1887, 763.

120. *Sunday Star,* 15 January 1888.

121. ETC, Kate Pizor, interview by Emile Topkis, 1954.

122. ETC Box 1, notes on obituary of Wolters, 31 December 1918; conversation with Kate Pizor.

123. *Every Evening*, 15 June 1889; *Every Evening,* 17 July 1889.

124. ETC, notes on *Every Evening* , 23 July 1888.

125. ETC, notes on *Every Evening*, 4 October 1889.

126. ETC, notes on *Every Evening*, 5 February 1890.

127. Geffen, "Delaware Jewry," 296; *Evening Journal,* 9 September 1889.

128. *Morning News,* 27 December 1888.

129. Emphasis added.

130. Jonathan D. Sarna, ed., *The American Jewish Experience*, 118.

131. Ibid.

Chapter 4: Taking Care of Their Own—The 1890s

1. *Every Evening*, 1 January 1890.

2. *History of Wilmington* (Wilmington: Compiled by the Every Evening and F.T. Smiley and Company, 1894), introduction.

3. *History of Wilmington*, 38; A. J. Clement, *Wilmington, Delaware: Its Productive Industries and Commercial and Maritime Advances* (Wilmington: Delaware Printing Company, 1888), 38.

4. Dr. Carol Hoffecker, conversation with the author, July 1997.

5. *Sunday Star*, 26 February 1893.

6. Information on Richard Patzowsky is from Census 1910; Hall of Records, will 1916; obituary, *Morning News,* 27 November 1916; *Morning News*, 4 August 1900; *Sunday Star,* 26 February 1893; and Eleutherian Mills Hagley Foundation, Collection of New Castle Leather Company.

7. ETC Box 2, conversation with Michael Ostro, 29 July 1955.

8. ETC, notes on *Sunday Star,* 25 March 1894.

9. *Sunday Star*, 7 February 1897.

10. *Sunday Star*, 20 December 1893.

11. Delaware Public Archives, birth of Rosa Hendlar, 20 August 1893.

12. WCD 1893–95. Benjamin Fischer had come to Wilmington from Hungary in 1884. After struggling to make a living as a peddler, he moved to Philadelphia for a few years and then returned to Wilmington and became a morocco worker for a short time.

13. Sometimes laborers had stores on the side, so Hendler and Fischer may still have worked in morocco. Information on early morocco workers is from WCD 1892–1900; Delaware Public Archives, birth of Lizzie Handler, 15 February 1893; birth of Rosa Muskywiseh, 27 January 1894. Not all of these Jewish morocco employees came to Wilmington for morocco work. Morris Muscovitch was a cigar

maker in 1894 when he lived on the 800 block of Reed Street near Blumenthal employees Isaac Greenberg and Sam Hendler. The following year, Mucovitch also worked for Blumenthal's.

14. WCD 1895–1900.

15. JHSD, "Twentieth Century Jews," Matthew Hirshout paper.

16. WCD 1900–1914 and census records.

17. Ida Fineman Goldman, interview by author, July 1989; Ed Glick, interview by author, January 12, 1997.

18. *Wilmington Morning News*, 4 August 1900.

19. *Morning News*, 4 August 1900

20. Information is from WCD 1893–96.

21. *Delaware Industries: An Historical and Industrial Review*, 46.

22. Information on Gidel Podolsky is from Census 1900, 1910, 1920; probate of Gidel Podolsky, 11 June 1937; probate of Fannie Podolsky, 1899; WCD 1880s–1920.

23. WCD 1890.

24. New Castle County, Recorder of Deeds, Direct Deed Index, 1893, "Podolsky."

25. JHSD, Oral History Collection, I. B. Finkelstein, interview by Bill Frank.

26. Ibid.

27. HIAS, Index of People Resettled 1884–1915, Balch Institute, Philadelphia, Pennsylvania.

28. WCD, 1893–1900.

29. Delaware Public Archives, birth record of Nellie Berger, 1900

30. Martin Berger, interview by the author, November 1996.

31. Ibid.

32. Census 1900.

33. Birth record, Millie and Ethel Gold, 26 September 1903; WCD 1898.

34. Census 1900 and 1910.

35. Census 1900; Delaware Public Archives, will of Louis Wolfman, 25 January 1929.

36. Based on census records and city directories, 10 of the 19 were from Eastern Europe.

37. Kessner, *The Golden Door,* 50.

38. Ibid., 61.

39. Ibid., 50.

40. Ibid., 60.

41. *Morning News*, 12 February 1891.

42. *Laws of the State of Delaware, Revised Code 1893*. Produce peddlers no longer needed a bond and their costs were reduced to $25 for one horse, and $35 for two horses.

43. *Morning News*, 1 March 1895. The peddlars were David Grodefsky, David Winezirge, and Samuel Feldstern.

44. *Morning News*, 25 June 1891. Delaware Public Archives, birth records, Lillie Cohen, 5 November 1887; Alexander Cohen, 10 November 1893; and William Cohen, 27 May 1895.

45. JHSD, Geffen, Rabbi David Geffen's notes on *Every Evening*, 5 November 1894.

46. JHSD, "Twentieth Century Jews," Michael Ostro obituary, 9 October 1964.

47. WCD 1891–1900. The only year he is not listed is 1896. In 1898 the name

changes to Ostro. Since he was still listed, perhaps he continued to assist Dr. Downes.

48. JHSD; *Wilmington Morning News*, 30 December 1899.

49. WCD 1900.

50. Arthur W. Hafner, ed., *Directory of Deceased American Physicians 1804–1929* (Chicago: American Medical Association, 1993), s.v. "Werner," 1652.

51. JHSD, Albert Robin Collection, Eva Robin, biography of Albert Robin, Emile Topkis's notes.

52. Ibid. At the time, the school was known as Delaware College.

53. Ibid.

54. *Sunday Star*, 17 January 1892.

55. Ibid.

56. Handlin, *The Uprooted*, 16–18. Handlin describes the attachment of most peasants to the land. See also Kessner, *The Golden Door,* 37–38.

57. Information on Gluckman is from *Reform Advocate*. Delaware Public Archives, return of marriage, Barnet Gluckman and Fannie Harris, 12 December 1887; return of will, Barnet Gluckman, 16 March 1934; birth record of Fannie Gluckman, 22 September 1890; and Albert 1903; Census 1900, 1910 and 1920; *Delaware Industries,* 111–12; JHSD, Biographical and Historical Information on Seventeenth, Eighteenth and Nineteenth Century Jews.

58. JHSD, "Twentieth Century Jews," Gluckman, Leslie H. Gluckman, "Memoirs of Wilmington at the Turn of the Century."

59. *Delaware Industries,* 111.

60. Ibid., 79.

61. JHSD, Gluckman, "History of Adas Kodesch," in *Programme Dedication of the Adas Kodesch Synagogue,* 20 September 1908, 29.

62. Census 1920. Delaware Public Archives, will, Moses Weil, July 26, 1932; JHSD, Seventeenth, Eighteenth and Nineteenth Century Jews; obituary, *Every Evening,* 26 January 1932; *Every Evening,* 27 February 1892; *Delaware Industries,* 103–4.

63. JHSD, Information on Seventeenth–Nineteenth Century Jews.

64. *Delaware Industries,* 90. Only five stores mentioned in the book were run by Jews.

65. *Every Evening,* 20 September 1890.

66. *Sunday Star,* 14 August 1892.

67. WCD 1900–1905.

68. WCD 1890.

69. WCD 1900; Louis Harris and Sybil Keil Harris, interview by the author, 8 December 1996.

70. WCD 1895–1900.

71. *Sunday Star,* 23 October 1892.

72. Information on the Hamburgers is from WCD 1888–1900 and ETC.

73. Information on Mitchell & Bash, JHSD, Bessie Grant, interview by Emile Topkis, 6 December 1955; *Morning News,* 12 March 1897; *Sunday Star,* 6 February 1898; WCD 1890–1900.

74. *Sunday Star,* 17 January 1897.

75. ETC, notes on *Sunday Star,* 11 October 1896.

76. ETC, notes on 24 January 1897.

77. ETC, Bessie Grant interview, 6 December 1955.

78. *Sunday Star,* 16 December 1894. Additional information on Slessinger is from Hall of Records, birth record, Stella, 19 October 1884; Census 1900 and 1910. Name is spelled Slessinger in both census records.

79. *Sunday Star*, 3 April 1898.

80. *Board of Trade Journal,* Wilmington Delaware, June 1900, 49.

81. Background on Jacob is in ETC Box 3, research notes on Delaware Jewish History, notebook, 177.

82. ETC, notes on *Sunday Star*, 16 October 1892.

83. Ibid. According to his grandson, Emile Topkis, Jacob Topkis was not as erudite as one might expect from one who could speak seven languages. He could speak English, Polish, Hungarian, and Slovakian, but he couldn't read or write any of them. He could read and understand Hebrew. He could read, write, and speak Yiddish and Russian.

84. Leon A. Harris, *Merchant Princes: An Intimate History of Jewish Families Who Built Great Department Stores* (New York: Harper & Row, 1979), 113–14.

85. Ad in *Every Evening*, 19 September 1895.

86. New Castle County Recorder of Deeds, Direct Deed Index, 1873–1897.

87. Samuel Rachlin, "A History of the Jews of Wilmington," in *Reform Advocate*, (Chicago: Bloch & Newman, 1916), 7.

88. *Every Evening*, 19 September 1895.

89. *Sunday Star*, 27 March 1898.

90. *Morning News*, 10 June 1899.

91. JHSD, Gluckman, " History of Adas Kodesch," 29. The group paid $60 down and continued to pay $50 a month until December 1893, when it made the final payment.

92. ETC, notes on *Every Evening*, 15 September 1890.

93. The reference is to talit, a prayer shawl worn on the shoulders by observant Jews and wrapped over the head by some groups. The *Every Evening* mistakenly used the word "tulas."

94. ETC, notes on the *Every Evening* 15 September 1890.

95. ETC, notes.

96. Gluckman, "History of Adas Kodesch," 29.

97. Ibid.

98. JHSD, Adas Kodesch Shel Emeth Collection, undated news article pasted on a piece of paper. I have used Bill Frank's attribution of it to 1893. No reference to this school is made in later histories.

99. Information on Isaac Goldstein is from Delaware Public Archives, Marriage Bond, 2 July 1886; birth record, Anna Goldstyne, 21 September 1889; Lillie, 1 December 1895; Bessie, 28 April 1902; Census 1900, 1910, and 1920; JHSD.

100. Census 1900 and 1910, in which he appears as Gluck.

101. Gluckman, "History of Adas Kodesch," 33. This school may have been the same one as the one just discussed. J. Harry Gordon, who arrived in Wilmington from Georgia around 1890, wrote the entry about Delaware in the *Encyclopedia Judaica,* 1906 edition, and in it he says that the free Hebrew Sunday School dated from January 1, 1896. Harry Bluestone, *A Historical Review of A Century of Jewish Education in Delaware* (Wilmington: Jewish Historical Society of Delaware, 1976), 5, repeats the 1896 date.

102. J. Harry Gordon, "The Sunday School," in *Programme of Dedication,* 71, 72.

103. *Morning News,* 15 February 1899. Bluestone, "A Historical Review of Jewish Education," 6.

104. Handlin, *The Uprooted*, 222.

105. Ibid., 218.

106. JHSD, I. B. Finkelstein, interviewed by Bill Frank.

107. Ibid.

108. *Evening Journal*, 1 March 1895; *Morning News*, 1 March 1895.

109. Ibid.

110. *Evening Journal*, 1 March 1895.

111. Ibid.

112. *Evening Journal*, 4 March 1895.

113. *American Israelite* 41, no. 50 (1895):3.

114. *Jewish Messenger* 77, no.17 (26 April 1895): 3.

115. According to the *Evening Journal*, David Abramson was president, Solomon Baeringer secretary, and Morris Levy treasurer. Nathan Levy, Samuel Slessinger, Nathan Barsky, and Joseph Lictenbaum were also members. The *Jewish Messenger* named Nathan Lieberman as president, and Max Ephraim as chairman of the board of trustees. The March 31, 1895 deed recording the incorporation of Oheb Shalom lists Jacob Schless, Abraham Greenbaum, Max Ephraim, Samuel Harris, David Abramson, and Moses Weil as trustees.

116. Information on Nathan Levy is from Census 1900 and 1920; ETC, Hall of Records, probate record of Solomon Levy.

117. Census 1910.

118. Information on Morris Levy is from census 1900, 1910, 1920, Delaware Public Archives, birth of Bertha, 28 October 1891 and Silba, 22 March 1895; ETC Box 2, obituary, 22 October 1954.

119. Handlin, *The Uprooted*, 126.

120. *Evening Journal*, 4 March 1895.

121. Bernard Wolfson had left Wilmington after 1892, but he remained an honorary president of the synagogue. Gluckman, "History of Adas Kodesch," 35.

122. *Morning News*, 20 September 1895.

123. *Sunday Star*, 15 September 1895.

124. *Every Evening*, 28 September 1895.

125. Ibid.

126. JHSD, Biographical and Historical Information on Twentieth Century Jews. During the 1895–96 school year, Lester Levy received a certificate of honor for punctual attendance at the school. J. Korn was superintendent and Rose Schless was Levy's teacher.

127. *Evening Journal*, 27 September 1897.

128. Ibid.

129. *Evening Journal*, 28 September 1897.

130. *Sunday Star*, 26 September 1897.

131. Gluckman, "History of Adas Kodesch," 31.

132. Ibid.

133. Ibid., 31–33.

134. The description of the dedication is in *Morning News*, 5 August 1898. The paper erroneously stated "The new Adas Kodesch building at Sixth and French was the first dedication of a Jewish synagogue that ever took place in this city." As Emile Topkis states in his notes (ETC), this is an obvious error that ignored Ohab Shalom in 1880 and Adas Kodesch in 1885. Topkis suggests that it might mean the first building totally devoted to synagogue purposes. He notes there were other dedications, but they were in an otherwise commercial building.

135. Handlin, *The Uprooted*, 158, explains that parades were enormously popular among immigrants because they enabled the group to display solidarity before the whole world and enabled the individual immigrant to demonstrate that he was part of a whole.

136. Cohen, "Encounter With Emancipation," 283.

137. Rabbi Elihu Schagrin, "The Jews of Delaware," in H. Clay Reed, *Delaware: A History of the First State* (New York: Lewis Historical Publishing Company, 1947), 2:620.

138. David Garber paid $5 for the privilege of placing the cover on the first scroll, Morris Levy paid $10 for covering the second scroll, and Meyer Geitelman paid $10 for placing a cover on third scroll.

139. Gluckman, "History of Adas Kodesch," 35.

140. Author's estimate based on data from census, birth, death, and marriage records.

141. Ibid. Birthplace is known for about 222 men and 180 women. The largest number of men (about 145), and the largest number of women (about 113), came from Russia. Because the overwhelming number of Eastern European immigrants were from Russia, the tendency among the general public was to refer to all immigrants from Eastern Europe as Russians.

142. Sorin, *Tradition Transformed*, 43.

143. ETC, notes on *Every Evening* 28 April 1891.

144. *Every Evening*, 19 October 1891.

145. ETC, notes on *Every Evening*, 25 February 1892.

146. WCD 1890–1900.

147. Census 1910 and 1920; Mollye Sklut, interview by the author, July 1989.

148. Ibid.

149. Ibid. Bessie's marriage certificate lists the Skluts' address, 104 W. Second.

150. Dr. Charles Levy, interview by the author, 21 March 1991.

151. Ibid.

152. Ibid. Sons Burt and Leon were born in Delaware. JHSD, Samuel Herman Bronfin's Levy Family Genealogy .

153. ETC, Benjamin Fineman interview by Emile Topkis, September 1954; Ida Goldman, interview by the author, July 1989. Abraham had been brought over by an older brother, Simon, who lived in Philadelphia.

154. Ibid.

155. Ida Goldman, interview by the author, July 1989.

156. ETC Box 1, letter from Kate Wolters Pizor to Emile Topkis.

157. Ibid.

158. Mollye Sklut, interview by the author.

159. ETC, Miscellaneous Notes, letter from Sam Abramson to Emile Topkis, 27 October 1954. Later Abramson went to Far Rockaway, New York.

160. Kessner, *The Golden Door*, 94.

161. Gluckman, "History of Adas Kodesch," 29.

162. *Every Evening*, 16 January 1890.

163. *Sunday Star*, 2 February 1896; *Every Evening,* 31 January 1896. Among those on the committee of arrangements were Nathan Levy, Solomon Baeringer, S. Schless, and William Bash. The reception committee included the familiar names Moses Weil, Sam Harris, Reuben Wolters, Nathan Levy, and Morris Levy.

164. *Sunday Star,* 24 January 1897; *Every Evening*, 28 January 1897.

165. Sorin, *Tradition Transformed*, 37.

166. Ibid., 78.

167. In the 1890s Wilmington lost three more founders—Aaron Harris died, and Kaufman Sondheimer and Bernard Wolfson left Wilmington.

168. *Every Evening*, 11 February 1892.

169. Information on Louis Finger is from author's conversations with Aaron

Finger's son Louis Finger; Delaware Public Archives, return of a marriage, 10 March 1888; birth record, Aaron Finger, 25 May 1890, probate of Louis, 1909; Census 1900; JHSD.

170. Delaware Public Archives, marriage license, 15 July 1891; return of marriage, 19 July 1891; birth record, Benjamin, 26 August 1893, Moses, 22 December 1895; probate, 7 November 1914; Census 1910.

171. Census 1910; WCD 1891.

172. Author's estimate. Of the 187 women in Wilmington in 1900 and known to have children, 105 had five or more.

173. Fifty-four of the women who bore five or more children experienced the death of at least one.

174. JHSD, Sallie Ginns's handwritten history of Jews in Delaware, 11; ETC, notes on conversation with Mrs. David T. Topkis, 4 January 1955.

175. ETC, research notes on specific Delaware Jews and institutions; conversation with Sallie Topkis Ginns, "Recollections of my Father and Mother," 2–5.

176. JHSD, Sallie Topkis Ginns, history of Jews in Delaware, 12.

177. Sallie Topkis Ginns, "Recollections of my Father and Mother," 2.

178. She also understood the trauma of losing a child, because although she had six living children, she had borne four others who did not live.

179. ETC, conversation with Mrs. David T. Topkis, 1955.

180. Census 1900, with David and Hannah Ray Topkis.

181. Census 1900, Davis Finklestein.

182. *Sunday Star,* 30 January 1898. Morris Levy, president of the Montefiore Society, and his wife led the grand march.

183. *Sunday Star,* 13 March 1898; *Every Evening,* 14 March 1898.

184. *Sunday Star,* 17 April 1898; *Every Evening,* 18 April 1898.

185. *Sunday Star,* 20 March 1898.

186. JHSD, History of B'nai B'rith, 1907, in Adas Kodesch cornerstone. The meeting was actually held on December 25, a free day for Jews.

187. *Sunday Star,* 8 January 1899. Most likely the Podolsky case is the "matter" referred to in the 1927 history of the Hebrew Charity Association, quoting Morris Levy: "by reason of certain matters arising during the past four weeks, it would be expedient to organize a charity organization."

188. *Morning News,* 2 January 1899, front page.

189. *Morning News,* 9 February 1899, and 19 January 1900.

190. Harry Bluestone, *Jewish Family Service of Delaware: A Historical Review 1899–1965,* (Wilmington: N.p., 1966), 6–7.

191. *Morning News,* 2, 3, and 6 February 1899.

192. *Morning News,* 9 February 1899. Nathan Lieberman had chaired a committee that asked the bishop to officiate at the ball.

193. Ibid.

194. Bluestone, *Jewish Family Service,* 9; ETC, notes on *Morning News,* 26 April 1899.

195. *Sunday Star,* 19 March 1899.

196. Higham, *Send These to Me,* 40.

197. Esther Panitz, "The Polarity of American Jewish Attitudes Toward Immigration," *American Jewish Historical Quarterly* 53 no. 2 (December 1963): 103–4, and Panitz, "In Defense of the Jewish Immigrant," *American Jewish Historical Quarterly* 55, no. 1 (September 1965). Higham *(Send These to Me)* explains that because the restrictionists couldn't agree on one plan and there was still confidence in the idea that new immigrants would assimilate into America, not too many changes were made in the 1890s.

198. *Reports of the Immigration Commission, Abstracts of Reprints of the Immigration Commission* (New York: ARNO and The New York Times, 1970), 571.

199. Panitz, "In Defense of the Jewish Immigrant," 58–59.

200. Ibid., 59–74. See also Panitz, "Polarity of American Jewish Attitudes," 103–4, 127.

201. Ibid., 59.

202. Handlin, *The Uprooted*, 257.

203. Higham, *Send These to Me*, 41.

204. Ibid., 42.

205. *Congressional Record*, 54th Cong., 2d sess., 1897, vol. 29, pt. I and II: 1677.

206. *Morning News*, 10 February 1897.

207. *Morning News*, 17 February 1897.

208. *Congressional Record*, 54th Cong., 2d sess., 1897, vol. 29, pt. I and II: 1937–1938. *New York Times*, 18 February 1897.

209. *Morning News*, 18 February 1897.

210. *New York Times*, 3 March 1897.

211. *Morning News*, 3 March 1897.

212. *Immigration Report*, volume 2, 574.

213. Panitz, "In Defense of the Immigrant," 76.

214. John A. Munroe, *History of Delaware* (Newark: University of Delaware Press, 1979), 169.

215. *Debates and Proceedings of the Constitutional Convention of the State of Delaware*, reported by Charles G. Guyer and Edmond C. Hardesty Esq. (Dover, Del.: Supreme Court of Delaware, 1958), 1:348.

216. *Debates of Constitutional Convention*, Volume 2, 1046–50.

217. Women's suffrage was the subject of a front-page story and an editorial in *Every Evening*, 17 February 1897.

218. Justice Randy J. Holland, editor-in-chief, and Harvey Rubenstein, editor, *The Delaware Constitution of 1897* (Wilmington: Delaware Bar Association, 1997), 62–64.

219. *Morning News*, 20 February 1897.

220. Melvin I. Urofsky, "Zionism: An American Experience," in Sarna, *The American Jewish Experience*, 212.

221. Ibid.

222. JHSD, Louis Finger letter, December 1898.

223. Ibid., letter, January 30, 1899.

224. Ibid., letter, May 29, 1899.

225. Ibid., letter, May 30, 1899. His letter of June 3 makes clear that the person was A. B. Cohen, the Reform rabbi.

226. Ibid., letter, June 3, 1899.

227. Melvin Urofsky, "Zionism: An American Experience," 214. The Federation of American Zionists had only 12,000 members out of a U.S. Jewish population of over 2.5 million on the eve of World War I. See also Sorin, *A Time for Building*, chapter eight and Irving Howe, *World of Our Fathers*, 204–8.

228. Schagrin, ("The Jews in Delaware," 2:621) used this estimate, which was then repeated by many researchers. Based on census, birth, death, and marriage records, Toni Young has identified at least 290 men, 253 women, and 570 children under the age of 20. In counting adults, I have used the age of 20 because in 1900, one had to be 20 years old to be a member of Adas Kodesch, the largest Jewish organization of the day.

229. In 1900, 76,508 people lived in Wilmington. *Abstract of the Twelfth Census,* 1900 (Washington, D.C.: Government Printing Office, 1902), 102 #80.

230. Ibid., 105 #81 and 108. Of the foreign-born population, 3,820 were from Ireland, 1,762 from Germany, and 1,307 from England, Scotland, and Wales. The fact that the total number from Poland, Russia, and other Eastern European countries is 2,269 could suggest that my estimate is low. The foreign-born population of Wilmington had increased from 9,099 to 10,478, and a large percentage of that increase was in the number of Jews.

231. Author's estimate from census, birth, death, and marriage records, based on approximately 230 of the 290 men and about 200 of the 253 women.

232. Data on age is from 237 of 290 men and about 200 of 253 women.

233. Data on date of arrival is based on information for about 259 of 290 men.

234. The WCD of 1901 lists 26 clothing stores; 19 were run by Jews.

235. Information on barbers is from WCD 1890s.

236. *Morning News,* 19 January 1900. The ball, which was opened by Governor Tunnell, was an enormous success and raised $400, significantly more than the previous year. According to Emile Topkis's notes on a December 31, 1899 article, Nathan Lieberman chaired a committee to invite Tunnell. Reverend A. B. Cohen, J. Harry Gordon, David Snellenburg, and Dr. A. D. Jacobsen, a doctor of literature or philosophy, were on the committee.

237. *Sunday Star,* 31 March 1901.

CHAPTER 5: BALANCING TWO WORLDS

1. *Morning News,* 7 September 1901.

2. *Morning News,* 9 September 1901. Leon Czolgosz had lived in Wilmington for about six months around 1895. A fellow worker at Harlan and Hollingsworth remembered Czolgosz as an "expert coppersmith." Although Czolgosz earned $22 a week, he considered it insufficient and resigned. *Morning News,* 14 September 1901.

3. *Every Evening,* 12 September 1901.

4. *Morning News,* 12 September 1901.

5. *Every Evening,* 14 September 1901.

6. *Morning News,* 17 September 1901.

7. *Morning News,* 20 September 1901. During most of the service, sunlight streamed through the windows of the Opera House; however, at 3:30, about the time McKinley was buried, the sunlight ceased, and a pall of darkness spread throughout the theater.

8. *Every Evening,* 20 September 1901.

9. *Sunday Star,* 29 September 1901.

10. Ibid.

11. *Every Evening,* 11 September 1901.

12. *Every Evening,* 15 January 1902. Levy was a well-known Reform rabbi. Many of the leaders of the Hebrew Charity Association were Reform-leaning Jews who had attempted the 1895 synagogue.

13. *Sunday Star,* 9 February 1902.

14. JHSD, Adas Kodesch Collection, Morris Chaiken, "History of Chesed Shel Emeth," in cornerstone of Adas Kodesch, 1907. Translated from the Yiddish by Rabbi Leonard Gewirtz. According to Rabbi Gewirtz the names are Moshe Konivskeh, Baruch Moshe Haikin, Moshe Dov Izraelsohn, and Dovid Hodesh.

15. Ibid., JHSD, petition to recorder of deeds, 24 December 1901.

16. Chaiken, "History of Chesed Shel Emeth." The Golden Jubilee Booklet on Chesed Shel Emeth, 1950, lists Morris Finger as vice-president and Morris Ezrailson as treasurer. Both of these men were involved in the founding of the synagogue but most likely had the function listed by Chaiken. WCD lists Jacob Mailman as secretary in 1902–3 and president in 1904, and Max Green as president in 1905. Chaiken does not mention either of these men as officers.

17. Golden Jubilee Booklet on Chesed Shel Emeth, 1950.

18. Sophie Chaiken Swimmer, interview by the author, February 1991.

19. Sophie Chaiken, interview; also Delaware Public Archives, birth records, and Census 1900 and 1910.

20. Sophie Chaiken, interview by author.

21. Ibid.

22. Census 1900.

23. Census 1900.

24. WCD 1900. The Stromwassers had four children after the infant born in 1898 died.

25. Census 1910. By 1910 Esther, three children (Jacob, David, and Helen) and his mother Sarah lived with Morris.

26. Delaware Public Archives, record of a marriage, 27 October 1889; Census 1900.

27. Census 1900; WCD 1898–1900.

28. Census 1900; Census 1920; WCD late 1890s–1902.

29. Census 1900.

30. Census 1910; WCD, 1898–1900; minutes of Adas Kodesch.

31. Census 1900 and 1910.

32. In the author's interviews (with Philip Simon, 12 March 1991; Sophie Swimmer Chaiken, February 1991; Bill Frank, April–June 1989; and Sol Polotsky, 8 June 1989), Chesed was described as following Sephardic ways. Rabbi Leonard Gewirtz, interviewed by the author 5 August 1997, clarified the meaning of Nusach Sepharad. "History of Adas Kodesch Shel Emeth" in *Generation Unto Generation*," called the synagogue Sephardic.

33. Rabbi Leonard Gewirtz, interview by the author, 5 August 1997. There are liturgical differences in certain prayers and psalms as well.

34. Handlin, *The Uprooted*, 105, 126–28.

35. Sophie Swimmer Chaiken, interview by the author, February 1991; Ben Cohen, Sadie Feinberg Cohen, and Esther Cohen, interview by the author, 3 July 1989.

36. Ben Cohen, Sadie Feinberg Cohen, and Esther Cohen , interview by the author, 3 July 1989; Mollye Sklut, interview by the author, July 1990.

37. Philip Simon, interview by the author, 12 March 1991.

38. Minute books of Adas Kodesch were kept in Yiddish except in 1900–1901 when William Topkis was secretary and wrote in English and for a few months at the end of 1901, when Louis Topkis was secretary and also wrote in English.

39. General opinion of all interviewed except Sophie Swimmer, who called Adas Kodesch Conservative.

40. Philip Simon, interview by author.

41. Rabbi David Geffen, conversation with author.

42. Chaiken, "History of Chesed Shel Emeth."

43. Jubilee Book, 1950.

44. JHSD, Adas Kodesch Collection, minutes of 22 December 1901.

45. JHSD, Adas Kodesch Collection, minutes of 21 October 1900.

46. JHSD, minutes of Adas Kodesch. Judah Barber was rejected on 30 June 1901. At the time, he was about forty-three years old. Morris Chaiken was rejected at 28 July 1901 meeting and Morris Kanewfsky at the 11 August 1901 meeting.

47. Ibid. minutes, 10 February 1901.

48. JHSD, Adas Kodesch Collection, minutes of 14 July 1901.

49. JHSD, Adas Kodesch Collection, minutes of 22 December 1901.

50. WCD, 1902–1914.

51. The membership book for 1900 lists 75 members. The *Programme for the Dedication* of the new synagogue in 1908 lists 155 members. A membership list in 1906 lists 165. From 1885 until at least 1929, Adas Kodesch was the largest synagogue and attracted some members who wanted to support the most dominant synagogue even if they didn't worship there.

52. Morris Chaiken, "History of Chesed Shel Emeth."

53. JHSD, Adas Kodesch Collection, minute and membership books.

54. *American Jewish Yearbook, 1900–1901,* 215.

55. Ibid. Louis Topkis was president, Elias Wetstein treasurer, and Dr. Sigmund Werner secretary.

56. Sophie Chaiken Swimmer, daughter of Morris Chaiken, remembers attending Hebrew school at Adas Kodesch about 1910 because Chesed Shel Emeth didn't have a school.

57. *American Jewish Yearbook, 1900–1901,* 215.

58. *Sunday Star*, 28 February 1904. See also Harry Bluestone, *A Historical Review of a Century of Jewish Education in Delaware 1876–1976*, 6.

59. Gluckman, "History of Adas Kodesch," 37.

60. Panitz, "In Defense of the Immigrant," 1965, 62.

61. *Reports of the Immigration Commission, Abstracts of Reprints of the Immigration Commission* (New York: ARNO and the New York Times, 1970), 1:215. In 1910, 1,911,933 immigrants came from Italy and 1,074,442 were Hebrew. Beginning in 1899, the Bureau of Immigration classified immigrants by race as well as by country of last permanent residence. "Hebrew" was a category. According to the report, all groups except the Hebrew or Jewish people accepted this method of classification.

62. Panitz, "In Defense of the Immigrant," 1965, 60.

63. Panitz, "In Defense of the Immigrant," 1965, 61. Sargent to Williams, William Williams Papers, Box I, 10 October 1902, New York Public Library.

64. *Every Evening,* 28 February 1903.

65. Sorin, *A Time for Building*, 203.

66. *Every Evening*, 28 May 1903; Census 1900.

67. *Every Evening*, 28 May 1903.

68. *Every Evening*, 29 May 1903.

69. *Every Evening*, 30 May and 2 June 1903. According to the *Sunday Star*, 31 May 1903, "The committee in charge of arrangements, Israel Wainer, Morris Miller, Samuel Green, Nathan Shtofman and Louis Finger, was honored and gratified by the support it received from the entire Wilmington community."

70. *Every Evening*, 2 June 1903. Rabbi David Geffen, "Take a Good Look at Delaware Jewish History II," a series of newspaper articles, interviews, and speeches on Delaware Jewry.

71. Ibid.

72. Jonathan D. Sarna, "The Myth of No Return: Jewish Return Migration to Eastern Europe, 1881–1914," *American Jewish History,* 71, no. 2 (December

1981): 257–63. Although Jews had a lower rate of return migration than other groups after 1908, it is important to recognize that no government figures exist for return migration before 1908.

73. Ibid., 262.

74. Sorin, *Tradition Transformed*, 44.

75. Ibid., 44.

76. Cohen, *Not Free to Desist*, 3.

77. *Every Evening*, 13 November 1905. The money was cabled to New York where Jacob Shiff was acting as national treasurer.

78. *Every Evening*, 22 November 1905.

79. ETC, notes on *Sunday Star*, 19 November 1905.

80. ETC, notes on *Every Evening*, 22 November 1905. The article mentions A. Hillison, but no such person is known.

81. Ibid.

82. Ed Glick, interview by author, 12 January 1997; Sadie Cohen Toumarkine, interview by author, January 1997.

83. *Every Evening*, 1 December 1905; *Sunday Star*, 26 November 1905.

84. ETC, notes on *Every Evening*, 1 December 1905.

85. ETC, notes on *Sunday Star*, 3 December 1905.

86. *Sunday Morning Star*, 4 February 1912. In an editorial lamenting the departure of Rabbi Abels, this was the explanation of why a secular paper would devote so much space to a rabbi's departure.

87. *Sunday Star*, 18 March 1906.

88. Ibid.

89. Handlin, "Introduction to the Report of the Immigration Commission," 1:ii–iii.

90. Ibid.

91. Report of the Immigration Commission, 11.

92. Ibid., 13.

93. Ibid.

94. *Morning News*, 18 June 1901.

95. ETC, notes on *Sunday Star*, 21 July 1901. Officers of Wilmington's B'nai Zion were Samuel Kasdin, president, William Satinsky, vice-President, Max Wainer, recording secretary, and Louis Finger, financial secretary.

96. Howe, *World of Our Fathers*, 204.

97. Ibid., 207.

98. JHSD, Adas Kodesch Collection, Cornerstone of Adas Kodesch Center, 1927, History of Moses Montefiore Mutual Beneficial Society, 1.

99. JHSD, Moses Montefiore Collection. Eleven men had signed in 1883. Nathan Lieberman had not signed in 1883, probably because of the death of his young son at the same time, but he did sign in 1903. Max Ephraim and Manual Richenberger were the only original incorporators who still lived in Wilmington. The others had died or moved.

100. History of Moses Montefiore Mutual Benefit Society, 1927, 2.

101. JHSD, unprocessed collections, agreement between Lombardy Cemetery company and the Moses Montefiore Mutual Benefit Society, 21 January 1907. The cemetery was dedicated in February 1908; see *Sunday Star*, 23 February 1908. The 1927 history of the Moses Montefiore Society says the cemetery was purchased in 1908. The bodies were moved in 1908.

102. The men included Morris Levy, Nathan Barsky, Sigmund Werner, A. B. Cohen, J. Harry Gordon, Louis Topkis, Israel Wainer, Joseph Lictenbaum, Lewis

Brown, Abraham Fogel, Joseph Reisman, M. Chertok, Jacob Faber, Solomon Grossman, Samuel Kasdin, and D. M. Lurge.

103. Sorin, *A Time for Building,* 63.

104. For a full description of life on the Lower East Side see Howe, *World of Our Fathers,* 148–54. Handlin in *The Uprooted,* chapter six, discusses the devastating effect of the overcrowded, filthy cities on the immigrants.

105. Sorin, *Time for Building,* 63, and *Tradition Transformed,* 58.

106. Ibid.

107. JHSD, J. Harry Gordon letter of 26 January 1903.

108. JHSD, Twentieth Century Jews; Morris Levy letter, 23 February 1903.

109. JHSD, Letter from IRO to Morris Levy, 4 March 1903.

110. Morris Levy letter, 6 March 1903. The hotel at 205 Market was run by Morris Leshem.

111. JHSD, Hebrew Charity Association Collection, 8 February 1904.

112. JHSD , Hebrew Charity Association, letters of 20 November 1905 and 9 April 1906.

113. JHSD, Hebrew Charity Association, letter of 27 December 1906.

114. JHSD, Morris Levy letter, 17 February 1904.

115. JHSD, Twentieth Century Jews; Morris Levy letter , 29 February 1904.

116. JHSD, Hebrew Charity Association Collection, letter of 24 March 1904.

117. JHSD, Hebrew Charity Association Collection, letters 20 July–8 August 1904.

118. Kessner, *The Golden Door,* 34–5.

119. Ibid., 165.

120. *Every Evening,* 19 February 1907.

121. JHSD, Sallie Topkis Ginns, "History of the Ladies Bichor Cholem Moshev Zekenim Society and The Hachnosas Orchim," 1; Harry Bluestone, *The Kutz Home, Inc.: A Historical Review 1902–1970* (Wilmington: The Kutz Home, Inc., 1974), 1.

122. Sallie Topkis Ginns, "History of the Ladies Bichor Cholem," 2; ETC Box II, Mrs. David T. Topkis, conversation with Emile Topkis, 4 January 1955. Ida Kanofsky is listed as Fannie or Frances in WCD.

123. Census 1900 and 1910.

124. In 1902, Hannah Ray Topkis had four children, Rose Barsky had three children, and Ida Kanofsky had three children. Author's statistics based on census records.

125. Sallie Topkis Ginns, "History of Ladies Bichor Cholem," 1–2. The account of Rosalie Hillersohn Schorr in JHSD, David Geffen Collection, credits Rabbi Blatt with the name.

126. JHSD, Adas Kodesch Collection, cornerstone, " History of Bichor Cholem Society of Wilmington."

127. Information in this paragraph is from ETC, Mrs. David Topkis, conversation with E. Topkis, 1955.

128. The fact that Mrs. David Topkis was the only one comfortable with English shows that the early Bichor Cholem did not include the American-born Jews or the more established German and Central European Jews.

129. JHSD, Bluestone Collection, Bichor Cholem, Constitution and By Laws.

130. Rosalie Hillersohn Schorr op. cit., JHSD; Geffen, and ETC, Mrs. David Topkis, conversation with E. Topkis.

131. *Every Evening,* 21 September 1908; *Programme of Dedication of the Synagogue, Adas Kodesch,* 20 September 1908; Sallie Topkis Ginns, "History of the Ladies Bichor Cholem."

132. Harry Bluestone, *A Historical Review of the Jewish Community Center 1901–1965* (Wilmington: Jewish Community Center, 1971), 2. See also JHSD, Adas Kodesch Collection, "History of Young Men's Hebrew Association," 1907. It is important to note that the Hebrew Charity Association, the Bichor Cholem Society and the YMHA were all organized within a short time of one another around the turn of the century. These three organizations grew into the Jewish Family Service, the Kutz Home, and the Jewish Community Center, which continued to be Delaware's major Jewish institutions until the end of the twentieth century.

133. JHSD, incorporation paper of YMHA, December 1901.

134. *Sunday Star*, 9 February 1902.

135. Information in this paragraph comes from WCD 1900–1903 and census records, 1900 and 1910.

136. Information on J. Harry Gordon is from the WCD's lists of officers of organizations. *American Jewish Yearbook, 1900–01*, 215.

137. WCD, 1904; Bluestone, "Historical Review of Jewish Community Center," 3.

138. WCD, 1905.

139. WCD 1904, 1905.

140. Bluestone, "Historical Review of Jewish Community Center," 3.

141. Ibid., ETC, notes on *Sunday Star*, 4 March 1906.

142. Bluestone, "Historical Review of Jewish Community Center," and YMHA list in cornerstone. At least twelve members were sons of the community leaders; other sons have the same initial as their fathers so it is not possible to determine which one was the member.

143. JHSD, cornerstone of Adas Kodesch Center 1927, Samuel Silver's handwritten history of the Workmen's Circle, 1. Research suggests that several of the "founders" arrived much later than 1907.

144. Ida Fineman Goldman, interview by author, July 1989.

145. Sorin, *Tradition Transformed*, 112.

146. JHSD, Bob Silver, interview by Jackie Rafel and Helen Goldberg, 1981.

147. WCD 1907.

148. JHSD, Bob Silver, interview by Jackie Rafel and Helen Goldberg, 1981.

149. Ibid.

150. Ida Fineman Goldman, interview by the author, July 1989.

151. *The Jewish Encyclopedia* (New York and London: Funk & Wagnalls, 1903), s.v. "Fraternities."

152. WCD 1902–4. Jacob Mailman, who is not listed in Chaiken's history, is listed in WCD as secretary of Work of Truth and president of Chesed Shel Emeth.

153. *Morning News*, 21 February 1910.

154. *Morning News*, 27 April 1904.

155. *Morning News*, 26 April 1904.

156. ETC Box 1, notes of Emile Topkis.

157. Esther Topkis Potts's letter to author, 9 August 1991.

158. *Sunday Star*, 29 December 1918.

159. JHSD, Samuel Saretsky, "History of the Jew in Delaware," 1922.

160. ETC, notes on *Sunday Star*, 18 February 1906.

161. Ibid.

162. JHSD, Twentieth Century Jews, Knights of Pythias.

163. *Sunday Star*, 24 October 1926.

164. Ibid.

165. Author's estimate based on census, birth, death, and marriage records. This number does not include approximately 70 men and women who were born in the U.S. but came to Delaware or came of age in the 1900s.

166. H. Clay Reed, *History of the First State: Volume III, Personal and Family Records*, 281. Charles Keil and Barbara Silverstein Keil, interview by the author, 2 July 1996.

167. Charles Keil and Barbara Silverstein Keil, interview by the author, 2 July 2, 1996, and WCD 1904–6. After Fannie died, Max married Rose Kluger.

168. ETC, notes on *Sunday Star*, 28 January 1906. By 1910, their brother-in-law Nathan Schlanger was also in the liquor business.

169. WCD 1895–1897.

170. Wilmington, Delaware, Board of Trade Journal, 1900, 49.

171. Census 1900.

172. Information on Altman is from Libby Zurkow, interview by the author, 19 April 1990.

173. JHSD, Bill Feinberg interview, 14 July 1988.

174. Ibid.

175. Census records of Herman Feinberg, 1900 and 1910.

176. WCD 1900.

177. Interview with Bill Feinberg (in JHSD) says the store was at 305, WCD says 309.

178. JHSD, Twentieth Century Jews; *Journal Every Evening*, 14 November 1956.

179. WCD 1903–5.

180. *Morning News*, 5 March 1910; WCD 1905.

181. *Sunday Star*, 1 April 1906, 31.

182. JHSD, Twentieth Century Jews, Miller Collection, *Sunday Star*, 31 May 1953.

183. Ibid.

184. *Morning News*, 5 March 1910.

185. Information on the Greenbaums is from Census 1910; Delaware Public Archives, probate of Samuel Greenbaum; birth record of Herman Greenbaum; WCD 1899–1918.

186. *Morning News*, 5 March 1910.

187. Data is from census, Delaware Public Archives, and WCD.

188. Sadie Cohen Toumarkine, interview by the author, 24 January 1997. Harry Cohen had received a traditional training in Russia and believed that no one who worked on Sabbath should be president of a synagogue so he never would serve as president of Adas Kodesch.

189. Sadie Cohen Toumarkine, interview by the author, 24 January 1997.

190. Ida Fineman Goldman, interview by the author.

191. Nathan Glazer, "The American Jew and the Attainment of Middle-Class Rank: Some Trends and Explanations," in *The Jews: Social Patterns of an American Group*, ed. Marshall Sklare (Glencoe, Ill.: Free Press, 1958) as repeated in Kessner, *The Golden Door*, 88.

192. Kessner, *The Golden Door*, 171.

193. JHSD, Nineteenth and Twentieth Century Jews—Breuer; *Every Evening* , June, 1935. In addition to his work, he was auditor of the Home Building and Loan Association and executive secretary of the Hebrew Charity Association.

194. Elbert Chance, "The Motion Picture Comes to Wilmington," part 1, *Delaware History* 24, no. 4 (Fall–Winter 1991–92): 259.

195. Sid Laub, interview by the author.

196. Ed Glick, interview by the author, 12 January 1997.

197. *Evening Journal*, 31 March 1930.

198. ETC, notes on *Sunday Star*, 12 August 1906.

199. David Geffen, *Seventy Five Years at the JCC* (Wilmington: Jewish Community Center, 1977).

200. *Sunday News Journal*, 3 December 1978, at Archives of JHSD, Twentieth Century Jews.

201. Mrs. Jacob Statnekoo, interview at the University of Delaware, special collections.

202. WCD 1900–1910; Ralph Tomases, interview by the author, 9 December 1996.

203. *Wilmington Board of Trade Journal*, 2, no. 3 (June 1900): 21.

204. *Every Evening*, 27 February 1907.

205. Data is from WCD 1900–1914 and census records.

206. *Board of Trade Journal*, June 1901.

207. Board of Trade Journal, 3, no. 11 (February 1902): 5.

208. Ibid. In 1906, Robert Binger of New York and Alden Sleepter of Boston replaced the earlier partners.

209. Obituary of Richard Patzowsky.

210. *Morning News*, 5 March 1910. The plant was between Eleventh and Twelfth and Poplar and Wilson.

211. WCD 1905.

212. WCD 1908. Morris Rees's son Andres was vice-president in 1910.

213. *Every Evening*, 5 September 1901.

214. *Every Evening*, 26 January 1932. A magistrate did not have to be a lawyer.

215. *Morning News*, 19 February 1902. The festivities included at least eleven toasts as well as remarks by Nathan Lieberman, David Snellenburg, David Levy, David Topkis, Israel Wainer, and Sam Slessinger.

216. Ibid.

217. *Sunday Star,* 2 July 1905.

218. Leslie H. Gluckman, "Memoirs of Wilmington at the Turn of the Century," *Jewish Voice*, 9 September 1975.

219. Ibid.

220. Ibid.

221. *Morning News,* 16 November 1933.

222. JHSD, Nineteenth and Twentieth Century Jews, Gluckman news clippings. Wilson Lloyd Bevan, *History of Delaware Past and Present*, volume 3, 166. Gluckman was the first magistrate to hold office for more than two terms.

223. According to Robin's obituary in the *Sunday Star* , 25 December 1927, Robin was state pathologist from 1899–1903 and city bacteriologist from 1903–1906.

224. JHSD, Robin Collection, Eva Robins, "Brief Biography of Albert Robin."

225. Ibid.

226. Ibid.

227. Ibid.

228. Ibid. In 1903, both of the synagogues in Wilmington were Orthodox.

229. Ibid.

230. Frances Goldstein, conversation with the author, 20 April 1997. In many Jewish families, the younger siblings were able to stay in school because families had become more stable and had more income.

231. Helen L. Winslow, ed., *The Delaware Bar in the Twentieth Century* (Wilmington: Delaware State Bar Association, 1994), 281.

232. JHSD, Aaron Finger Collection, *Wilmington Morning News,* obituary, 4 June 1969.

233. Ibid., and Winslow, *The Delaware Bar.*

234. JHSD, Biographical and Historical Information on Twentieth Century Jews, Gluckman, Louis Gluckman letter of 20 November, 1959.

235. Ibid. Also Gluckman obituary, *Morning News,* 6 July 1961.

236. Kessner, *The Golden Door,* 97.

237. Ibid., 97 and 173–74.

238. Ibid., 95–96.

239. *Sunday Star,* 16 September 1906 and 23 September 1906.

240. *Sunday Star,* September 16, 1906.

241. Ibid.

242. *Sunday Star,* 23 September 1906.

243. JHSD, Temple Beth Emeth Collection, circular. *Every Evening,* 16 May 1908.

244. JHSD, "History of the Organization of the Congregation Temple of Truth," 1908; *Every Evening,* 16 May 1908.

245. Curiously, some had recently joined Adas Kodesch; Albert Rothschild in October 1905 and David Snellenburg in November 1905.

246. JHSD, "History of the Organization of Congregation Temple of Truth."

247. ETC Box 1, Kate Pizor, postcard to Emile Topkis, 3 January 1955.

248. Information is from birth, death, marriage, and census records. There is no information on Jacob Malis.

249. ETC, notes on *Sunday Star* , 27 January 1907.

250. WCD 1905–7.

251. *Sunday Star* , 1 November 1906.

252. Temple of Truth, incorporation record, 1906. The incorporators included James J. Cohen, Max Breuer, Emanuel Frankle, Samuel Handler, Morris Rees, Samuel Harris, Ignatz Roth, and Reuben W. Wolters in addition to the board.

253. *Every Evening,* 20 September 1906.

254. Ibid. The fact that the temple celebrated two days shows a leaning towards Conservative.

255. *Sunday Star,* 1 November 1906.

256. *Sunday Star* , 27 January 1906.

257. *Every Evening,* 12 December 1906.

258. Kevin Proffitt, American Jewish Archives, letter to author, 14 March 1997.

259. *Sunday Star,* 13 October 1907.

260. Gluckman, "History of Adas Kodesch," 37.

261. *Every Evening,* 21 September 1908.

262. *Sunday Star* , 14 April 1907. The synagogue had been designed by Kennedy Brothers based on a design by David Topkis, according to *Sunday Star,* 3 February 1907 and *Every Evening,* 16 May 1908.

263. *Every Evening,* 21 September 1908.

264. *Sunday Star* ,14 April 1907.

265. JHSD, Adas Kodesch Collection, *Programme of the Dedication of Adas Kodesch,* 1908, 76–80.

266. Ibid. 77. Rabbi David Geffen points out the language was most likely Yiddish, since very few people understood Hebrew in 1908 but many spoke Yiddish.

267. Ibid. M. David Geffen, "An Introduction to the History of the Rabbinate in Delaware," in *Delaware and the Jews,* 72–73.

268. *Every Evening*, 19 August 1907. See also *Morning News*, 19 August 1907 and *Programme of Dedication*.

269. Ibid. The *Every Evening* mentions "the Jewish language." The *Programme* specifies English for Rosenthal.

270. Histories of the YMHA, Hebrew Charity Association, B'nai B'rith, Ladies Bichor Cholem, Chesed Shel Emeth, Ahawas Israel, and the Moses Montefiore Society were placed in the cornerstone and survived. Today they are among the earliest documents at the JHSD.

271. *Every Evening*, 19 August 1907.

272. *Programme of the Dedication*, 86–87.

273. Ibid., 87.

274. JHSD, Adas Kodesch Collection, "Golden Jubilee of Adas Kodesch, 1890–1940."

275. *Programme of the Dedication of Adas Kodesch.*

276. *Every Evening*, 16 May 1908; JHSD, Harry Topkis, "History of Temple of Truth," May 1908, in cornerstone of Temple of Truth.

277. Topkis, "History of Temple of Truth."

278. *Evening Journal* , 29 January 1908.

279. *Sunday Star* 5 April 1908.

280. *Every Evening*, 16 May 1908; *Sunday Star*, 17 May 1908.

281. *Sunday Star,* 24 May, 1908. Topkis's "History of Temple of Truth" was in the cornerstone.

282. Ibid.

283. *Every Evening,* 31 August 1908. The key was carried by Miss Mildred Shaul according to the *Every Evening,* but it was carried by Miss Helene Snellenburg according to the *Sunday Star*, 30 August 1908.

284. Ibid.

285. Ibid.

286. Ibid. See Handlin, *The Uprooted,* chapter five, particularly 126.

287. Ibid.

288. By the time of the dedication, the board had changed. Five new members, including Abe Rothschild, James J. Cohen, Max Ephraim, Samuel Harris, and M. Bernard Hoffman, had joined the board. Max Ephraim and Sam Harris had been part of the 1895 effort; both of them, as well as James J. Cohen, had attended the 1906 meeting to form a new synagogue. Abe Rothschild represented the Lieberman family.

289. Ibid.

290. *Every Evening,* 29 August 1908.

291. *American Israelite*, 10 September 1908.

292. *Sunday Star*, 20 September 1908.

293. *Sunday Star*, 20 September 1908. Topkis's remark implies that the existing Hebrew and Sunday schools were struggling to survive, if they even still existed. President Joseph Lictenbaum, Rabbi B. L. Leventhal of Philadelphia, Dr. Louis S Dunn, and Rabbi Joseph M. Gold also gave speeches.

294. *Programme of the Dedication of Adas Kodesch*, 1908.

295. Gluckman, "History of Adas Kodesch."

296. *Programme of the Dedication of Adas Kodesch*, 1908.

297. *Morning News*, 31 May 1909. See also JHSD, Bill Frank Collection, Bill Frank paper on the Hope Farm. The Hebrew Charity Association had collected funds for the Anti-Tuberculosis Society as early as February 1907 according the the *Every Evening*, 19 February 1907.

298. *Morning News*, 31 May 1909.
299. Ibid.
300. *Morning News*, 1 June 1909.
301. *Morning News*, 11 October 1909; *Evening Journal*, 11 October 1909.
302. Ibid. The dedicatory ceremony was lengthy because of many speeches. Rabbi M. J. Abels, Governor Simon S. Pennewill, Dr. Albert Robin, and Dr. Michael Ostro were among the speakers. Eva Barsky presented the key to the shack donated by the Barsky family to Emily Bissell.
303. Ibid.
304. Ibid.

CHAPTER 6: A THRIVING COMMUNITY

1. Abstract of the Fourteenth Census of the United States (Washington, D.C.: Government Printing Office, 1920), 52. According to the *Sunday Star*, 25 April 1920, the city had grown to a wartime peak of 130,000, but 10,000 to 15,000 had left Wilmington after the war, largely due to the inability to find houses here. For Jewish population, see footnote 489.
2. *Morning News*, 5 March 1910.
3. For background on the shirtwaist strike and other early labor strikes see Howe, *World of Our Fathers*, 295–304; Sorin, *Tradition Transformed*, 123–35.
4. *Morning News*, 8 February 1910.
5. Ibid.
6. *Morning News*, 28 February 1910.
7. *Morning News*, 4 March 1910.
8. Ibid.
9. *Morning News*, 5 March 1910.
10. *Morning News*, March 12, 1910.
11. *Morning News*, March 21, 1910.
12. Ibid.
13. *Morning News*, 5 March 1910.
14. *Morning News*, 11 March 1910.
15. *Morning News*, 4 February 1910.
16. Ibid.
17. Carol E. Hoffecker, *Corporate Capital: Wilmington in the Twentieth Century* (Philadlephia: Temple University Press, 1983) 11; *Sunday Star*, 6 October 1912.
18. Hoffecker, *Corporate Capital*, 11.
19. Ibid., 41.
20. Census records of 1910 and 1920 .
21. Sorin, *A Time for Building*, 69, 78.
22. Author's statistic based on census, birth, death, and marriage records. Of the 400 male Jewish immigrants who arrived in the 1910s and whose nationalities are known, 87 percent were from Eastern Europe and only 9 percent were from Germany, Austria, or England. Of 330 female Jewish immigrants, 84 percent were from Eastern Europe and only 10 percent were from Germany, Austria, or England.
23. Information on Morris Tomases is from Ralph Tomases, interview by author, 9 December 1996.

24. Philip Simon, interview by author, 12 March 1991; Ralph Tomases, interview by author; and Sarah Statnekoo, interview at University of Delaware.

25. Ben Cohen, Sadie Feinberg Cohen, and Esther Cohen, interview by author, 3 July 1989.

26. Gary Greenstein, interview by author, 18 April 1997; Frances Goldstein, interview by author, 20 April 1997.

27. Ibid.

28. Alfred Green, interview by author, 2 May 1997.

29. Information is from census, birth, death, and marriage records.

30. JHSD, Twentieth Century Jews, Benjamin Franklin Cohen, *News Journal*, 30 June 1986.

31. JHSD, Hebrew Charity Association collection, letter of 28 December 1910.

32. JHSD, Hebrew Charity Association, letter of 31 August 1912. On February 2, 1911, Levy said he had contacted the most important industrial companies including American Tobacco, Pullman Palace Car, Harlan and Hollingsworth, New Castle Leather, American Car Foundry, Pusey and Jones, Malleable Iron, Remington Machine, F. Blumenthal, duPont Power, American Bridge, United Leather, and Bancroft and Company.

33. JHSD, Hebrew Charity Association, letter of 31 August 1912.

34. Ibid., letter of 16 September 1912.

35. Ibid., letter of July 27, 1910. Twelve dollars a week would mean a little more than 21 cents an hour for 55 hours.

36. Carol E. Hoffecker, *Corporate Capital*, 63.

37. Ibid., 65.

38. Ibid., 63.

39. *Sunday Star*, 21 November 1915.

40. Ibid.

41. JHSD, Hebrew Charity Association, letter of 31 October 1916.

42. *Sunday Star*, 1 April 1917.

43. *Sunday Star*, 18 September 1918.

44. Ben Cohen, interview by the author, 3 July 1989, and conversation of 15 April 1997.

45. Ibid.

46. Philip Simon, interview by author, 12 March 1991.

47. By 1914 Platensky had left Pullman and was a roofer.

48. Philip Simon, interview by author, 1991.

49. Ibid.

50. *Sunday Star*, 26 March 1916.

51. *Morning News,* 27 November 1916, obituary of Patzowsky. In his will, Patzowsky left money to Jewish causes, but his obituary did not mention any Jewish affiliations.

52. Eleutherian Mills Hagley Foundation, New Castle Leather Collection, Scrapbook on New Castle Leather, *Morning News*, 23 July 1923. J. Wirt Willis had started with Patzowsky at F. Blumenthal and Company in 1898 and had moved to New Castle Leather when Patzowsky formed it.

53. Samuel Rachlin, "A History of the Jews in Wilmington," *The Reform Advocate*, Wilmington supplement, (Chicago: Bloch & Newman, 1916), 4.

54. *Sunday Star*, 26 March 1916.

55. *Sunday Star*, 24 June 1917.

56. Census 1920.

57. *Morning News*, 10 January 1917.
58. Ibid.
59. *Morning News,* 24 June 1917.
60. WCD 1916.
61. Hilda Cohen Codor, interview by author, December 1996; Census 1920. Daughters Gertrude and Rebecca were born in Wilmington.
62. Barbara Yalisove, conversation with author; and WCD 1916.
63. WCD 1919.
64. WCD 1916.
65. Marvin Balick, interview by author, 23 April 1997. See also Marvin Balick, *Genealogy of the Balick Family of Delaware For the Period Covering 1890– 1995* (Wilmington: N.p., 1995).
66. Miriam Balick Lieblein, conversation with author, 23 April 1997.
67. Marvin Balick, interview by author, 23 April 1997.
68. WCD 1916. At the time, there were more than 430 grocery stores in Wilmington, but 70 was still a disproportionate number of Jewish stores.
69. WCD 1916.
70. Ibid.
71. WCD 1906–1916; Arthur Menton, *The Book of Destiny* (Cold Spring Harbor, N.Y.: King David Press, 1996), 141–42. In 1916 Morris was at 16 and 20 East Front, Hyman Cohen was at 103 and 115 West Front, and Joseph Cohen was at 113 West Front.
72. Ibid.
73. Rachlin, "A History of the Jews in Wilmington," 7.
74. *Sunday Star,* 17 August 1913.
75. *Sunday Star*, 10 October 1915.
76. Rachlin, "A History of the Jews in Wilmington," 8
77. *Sunday Star,* 6 December 1914.
78. *Sunday Star*, 12 May 1916.
79. *Sunday Star*, 18 November 1917.
80. *Sunday Star*, 29 September 1918.
81. *Sunday Star*, 21 November 1915.
82. *Sunday Star*, 31 May 1953.
83. *Sunday Star*, 19 March 1916.
84. Bevan, *History of Delaware Past and Present* (New York: Lewis Historical Publishing Co., 1929), 4:418 says Nathan took control in 1922; Reed, *Delaware: A History of the First State*, iii, says 1917.
85. JHSD, Topkis Family Collection, *Morning News* clipping, circa 1962.
86. New Castle County, Recorder of Deeds, "Direct Deed Index" 1897–1912 and 1912–1920.
87. JHSD, Topkis Family Collection; *Every Evening*, 28 November 1939.
88. Ibid.
89. According to the *Evening Journal ,* 13 January 1919, by 1919 the store was known as Topkis Sons Department Store and operated from 420 Market Street, 417 King Street, and 10 East Fifth Street.
90. Elbert Chance, "The Moving Picture Comes to Wilmington Part II," *Delaware History*, 25, no. 1 (Spring-Summer 1992): 33; *Sunday Star*, 24 September 1911.
91. Ibid., 33–34.
92. JHSD, Yetta Chaiken, unpublished paper on Sallie Topkis Ginns.
93. Chance, "The Moving Picture Comes to Wilmington," 34.

94. *Sunday Star,* 9 May 1915.

95. Ibid.

96. Chance, "The Moving Picture Comes to Wilmington," 41–42; *Sunday Star* , 13 February 1916.

97. *Sunday Star,* 14 February 1917.

98. JHSD, William Topkis Collection. The receipts are presumed to be from the decade 1910–1920.

99. JHSD, William Topkis Collection, letter from Ralph to William Topkis explaining that a woman with a baby in arms had been allowed into the house.

100. JHSD, William Topkis Collection Box I, undated newspaper clipping.

101. *Sunday Star,* 16 May 1920.

102. JHSD, William Topkis Collection, Samuel Goldwyn letter to William Topkis, 1921.

103. Esther Topkis Potts and Topkis's great-nephew William Topkis, conversations with author.

104. Chance, "The Moving Picture Comes to Wilmington," 37.

105. Ibid., 39.

106. Ibid., 48.

107. Ibid., 53–55.

108. Delaware Public Archives, Physician's Register 1881–1934.

109. Frances Goldstein and Gary Greenstein, interview by the author; WCD, 1913.

110. WCD 1915.

111. Bevan, *History of Delaware Past & Present,* 4: 435.

112. *Sunday Star,* 14 July 1915.

113. *Sunday Star* , 17 June 1917.

114. Kessner, *The Golden Door,* 125.

115. Applications of David Rossman, S. M. Zion, and J. S. Keyser for membership in Medical Society of New Castle County at Academy of Medicine, Wilmington.

116. David Rossman's application for membership in Medical Society of NCC, 1914. Delaware Public Archives, A Physician's Register 1881–1934 says Rossman graduated on 20 January 1913.

117. S. M. Zion's application for membership in Medical Society of NCC, 1920. A Physician's Register 1881–1934 says Zion graduated 9 June 1914.

118. WCD 1916. A Physician's Register lists Keyser's graduation date as 21 January 1914.

119. Joseph Barsky's application for membership in the Medical Society of NCC, 1914. Physician's Register lists the date as 18 October 1915.

120. *Sunday Morning Star,* 20 June 1915.

121. Census 1920; Connie Kreshtool, conversation with author; WCD 1914.

122. Census 1920; Connie Kreshtool, conversation with author.

123. Census 1920; JHSD, Twentieth Century Jews, Gluckman article. In May 1917, Louis Gluckman joined the army, and afterwards practiced dentistry in Philadelphia until 1936, when he returned to Wilmington.

124. Census 1920; WCD 1921.

125. *Sunday Star,* 30 May 1915. Although the clinic's first listing in the 1916 city directory was under Hebrew Societies, the entry stated it was nonsectarian. Dr. Robin was acting on behalf of the Maimonedes Lodge of B'nai B'rith. Schagrin, "The Jews of Delaware," 622.

126. *Sunday Star,* 27 June 1915.

127. Ibid.

128. *Sunday Star*, 17 October 1915.

129. *Sunday Star*, 19 December 1915.

130. *Sunday Star*, 26 September 1915.

131. *Sunday Star*, 3 October 1915.

132. Schagrin, "The Jews of Delaware," 622.

133. JHSD, Robin Collection; *Medical Society of Delaware Journal*, 3, no. 1 (December 1911).

134. JHSD, Robin obituary, 25 December 1927.

135. JHSD, Robin Collection, E. R. Mayerberg dictation. His reference was to the fact that Jews were not welcome to practice there. Also duPont letter to Eva Robin, 14 May 1956.

136. Ibid.; JHSD, Robin Collection, Bill Frank notes on Robin talk given at Fall 1975 meeting of the JHSD. *Every Evening*, 28 April 1960.

137. JHSD, Robin obituary, 25 December 1927.

138. JHSD, Finger Collection, Aaron Finger obituary. Morris Levy, David Snellenburg and Charles Topkis were in charge of a banquet in his honor on 3 April 1917; *Sunday Star*, 1 April 1917.

139. JHSD, Finger Collection, article of 25 May 1918 that praised his action.

140. Bevan, *A History of Delaware Past and Present*, 3:36; *Morning News*, 4 June 1969.

141. Bevan, *A History of Delaware Past and Present*, 3:732.

142. ETC Box II, notes on Morris Levy.

143. Winslow, *The Delaware Bar*, 733.

144. Ibid., 641–42. Sybil Ursula Ward was also admitted in the class of 1923.

145. Ibid.

146. Rachlin, "A History of the Jews of Wilmington," 19. William Feinberg had become the first Jewish boy on Wilmington High's football team in 1916.

147. Ibid.

148. Handlin, *The Uprooted*, 226.

149. Ibid.

150. See list.

151. Hoffecker, *Delaware and the Jews*, 43.

152. Ibid. See also JHSD, Population Survey of the Jewish Welfare Board, 1929, 16–17.

153. Sol Polotsky, interview by author, 8 June 1989.

154. *Abstracts of Reports of the Immigration Commission*, 1:48.

155. Ibid., 45.

156. Ibid., 48.

157. Ibid., 47–48; Panitz, "In Defense of the Immigrant," 71; Cohen, *Not Free to Desist*, 48–49.

158. Oscar Handlin, introduction to *Abstracts of Reports of the Immigration Commission*, 1:viii.

159. Ibid., viii–ix.

160. Ibid.

161. Ibid., xxix.

162. Ibid., xxx.

163. *Abstracts of Reports of the Immigration Commission*, 41, 186.

164. Ibid., 1:49.

165. Panitz, "In Defense of the Immigrant," 73.

166. *Congressional Record*, 62nd Cong., 3rd sess., 1913, Vol. 49, pt. 4 and 5: 3269–70.

167. Ibid., 3270.

168. Ibid.

169. Ibid., 3318; *Morning News*, 19 February 1913.

170. *Congressional Record,* 62nd Cong., 3rd sess., 1913, Vol. 49, pt. 4–5: 3429.

171. *Morning News*, 28 February 1913.

172. Ibid.

173. *Congressional Record,* 63rd Cong., 3rd sess., 1914–1915, Vol. 52, pt. 1–3: 2481–82.

174. Ibid., 3077.

175. *Morning News*, 18 August 1915.

176. Panitz, "In Defense of the Immigrant," 84.

177. *Congressional Record,* 64th Cong., 2d sess., 1916–1917, Vol. 54, pt. 1–3: 2212–13.

178. Ibid.

179. Ibid., 2456–57.

180. *Morning News*, 2 February 1917.

181. Ibid.

182. *Congressional Record,* 64th Cong., 2d sess., 1916–1917, Vol. 54, pt. 1–3: 2629.

183. *Morning News*, 6 February 1917.

184. Ibid.

185. *Morning News*, editorial, 6 February 1917.

186. Ibid.

187. Nathan C. Belth, *A Promise to Keep: A Narrative of the American Encounter with Anti-Semitism* (New York: Times Books, 1979), 61.

188. Leonard Dinnerstein, *The Leo Frank Case* (New York: Columbia University Press, 1968), 5, 6.

189. Ibid., 32.

190. Ibid., 83.

191. Belth, *A Promise to Keep,* 64.

192. *Morning News,* 18 August 1915.

193. *Morning News,* 19 August 1915.

194. Ibid.

195. *Morning News,* 18 August 1915.

196. Belth, *A Promise to Keep,* 65.

197. The articles on Frank cast light on an interesting side issue, the *Wilmington Morning News'* competition with Philadelphia and New York newspapers. On August 19, the *Morning News* editorial pointed out that yesterday's Wilmington paper had carried a full front-page story on Mr. Frank's abduction and hanging while the out-of-town morning papers, which were earlier editions, did not. The editorial claimed, "This newspaper frequently gets important news items not in Philadelphia or New York morning papers that reach this city." Even the later editions of the out of town papers wouldn't have more information than the *Morning News* because the *Morning News* received the services of the Associated Press.

198. Sol Polotsky, interview by author.

199. *Golden Jubilee Chesed Shel Emeth Congregation 1900–1950*, Wilmington, 1950.

200. Ibid., *Morning News*, 23 June 1914.

201. Census 1920; Ed Glick, interview with author, 12 January 1997.

202. WCD 1914–1924.

203. WCD 1921–22.

204. *Morning News*, 22 June 1914.

205. *Morning News*, 22 June 1914. M. David Geffen explains the reference to their own tongue probably means Yiddish since most Jews at the time spoke Yiddish, not Hebrew.

206. Ibid.

207. *Morning News*, 22 February 1915.

208. Ibid.

209. Rabbi Levinthal, chief Orthodox rabbi of the district, Rabbi Sbritsky, Morris Chaiken, and J. Cohen also participated in the ceremony.

210. JHSD, typewritten membership list, dated 1927.

211. Bill Frank, interviews by author, April–July 1989, and Mollye Sklut, interview with author July 1990.

212. *Sunday Star*, 23 September 1917.

213. Bill Frank, interview by author.

214. Ibid.

215. *Sunday Star*, 28 February 1915, 26 September 1915.

216. *Sunday Star*, 7 and 14 November 1915.

217. *Sunday Star*, 16 January 1921.

218. JHSD, letter to Swiren relative; *Sunday Star* , 30 December 1917.

219. Ibid.

220. JHSD, Swiren letter.

221. Geffen, "An Introduction to the History of the Rabbinate in Delaware," in *Delaware and the Jews*, 74; *Generation Unto Generation*, Adas Kodesch, 1985. WCD 1923–28.

222. WCD 1910–1917.

223. *Sunday Star*, 29 September 1918.

224. Ibid.

225. Bill Frank, interview by author.

226. Ibid.

227. Ibid.

228. Ibid.

229. Ibid.

230. Korn's Reform leaning has been discussed. Rubenstein's background was provided by Kevin Proffitt, American Jewish Archives, letter to the author, 14 March 1997. According to the *Sunday Star,* editorial, 4 February 1912, "Prior to the arrival of Rabbi Abels, we had no regularly ordained rabbi in Wilmington."

231. *Sunday Star*, 4 February 1912. See also Davis, *The Emergence of Conservative Judaism*, 17–19.

232. Rabbi Mischkind, "A Brief History Commemorating the Twentieth Anniversary Congregation Beth Emeth," 12 November 1928, 17. According to Rabbi Drooz, the history was written by Rabbi Mischkind, who said that by 1928 Conservative synagogues had introduced the confirmation service. Apparently, the temple used the date of the construction of its building rather than the founding date for its anniversary.

233. *Sunday Star,* 4 February 1912. In 1912, when Abels resigned from Temple of Truth, a page one story in the *Sunday Star* and an editorial praised the rabbi and lamented the fact that he would be leaving Wilmington.

234. Ibid.

235. *Morning News*, 8 May 1911.

236. *Sunday Star,* 28 November 1915.

237. Cyrus Adler, ed., *American Jewish Yearbook, 1903–04* (Philadelphia: Jewish Publication Society of America, 1904), 96–97.

238. Dr. Emanuel Schreiber, *Abraham Geiger: The Greatest Reform Rabbi of the Nineteenth Century* (Spokane, Wash.: Spokane Printing Company, 1892).

239. Saretsky, "History of the Jew in Delaware."

240. Terry Barbaro, Union of Hebrew Congregations, New York, reported to author that according to a loose collection of early papers, Temple of Truth became affiliated on January 14, 1913 .

241. *Sunday Star*, 23 April 1916.

242. Rabbi Herbert Drooz, "A Brief Sketch of Beth Emeth's History," in *Congregation Beth Emeth 80th Anniversary, 5745,* (Wilmington: n.d.), 25.

243. Rachlin, "A History of the Jews of Wilmington," 11.

244. *Morning News,* 26 September 1916.

245. *Sunday Star,* 17 June 1917.

246. Twenty-five percent of members of 1928, whose country of birth is known, were born in the United States.

247. Nine of the seventy-two members about whom information is available belonged to Adas Kodesch and Chesed.

248. Esther Potts's letter to the author, 9 August 1991.

249. JHSD, Finger Collection, letter of 11 May 1921.

250. JHSD, Finger Collection, letters to Charles Topkis. Topkis had loaned $1,450.

251. Mischkind, "A Brief History Commemorating the Twentieth Anniversary," 23.

252. *Sunday Star,* 21 May 1922. Rabbi Drooz, in "A Brief Sketch of Beth Emeth's History," 25, says that Goberman had been told he was the only one who could hold the temple together.

253. JHSD, letter from Goberman, 1 June 1922.

254. *Sunday Star,* 6 August 1922, 17 September 1922.

255. Rabbi David Geffen, *Temple Beth Shalom Fifty-Year Historical Record, 1922–1972,* unnumbered pages. In their opinion, the need for such a synagogue had been felt for two or three years prior to 1922. See also JHSD, minutes of 11 June 1922 in minute book.

256. Ibid.

257. Bea and Sid Laub, interview by the author.

258. Ibid.

259. Geffen, *Temple Beth Shalom;* JHSD, minute book of Congregation Beth Shalom, 1922 .

260. Ibid.

261. Census records; Winslow, *The Delaware Bar in the Twentieth Century,* 733.

262. Unfortunately no lists of Temple of Truth membership between 1908 and 1928 are extant; therefore, it is not possible to determine membership. However, the Laubs and Levitts were members of Temple of Truth, according to the author's interviews with Sid Laub and Harold Levitt.

263. Geffen, *Temple Beth Shalom;* JHSD, minutes of 11 September 1922 and 10 October 1922.

264. *Sunday Star,* 16 July 1922.

265. Mischkind, *A Brief History Commemorating the Twentieth Anniversary of Beth Emeth,* 23.

266. Ibid., 25.

267. Ibid., 15.

268. *Morning News,* 5 March 1910.

269. Molly Cohen Sklut, interview by the author.

270. JHSD, Twentieth Century Jews, Nathan Miller, "Meet Nathan Miller," in *Delaware Today,* August, September 1969.

271. ETC Box 1, letter of Kate Wolters Pizor to Emile Topkis.

272. Bevan, *History of Delaware Past and Present,* 418–19.

273. *Journal Every Evening,* 14 November 1956 at JHSD, Twentieth Century Jews, Nathan Miller.

274. Philip Simon, interview by the author.

275. *Sunday Star,* 7 March 1915; WCD 1916.

276. Sorin, *Tradition Transformed,* 162.

277. Dr. Carol Hoffecker, conversation with the author, July 1997.

278. *Morning News,* 7 March 1915.

279. *Sunday Star,* 2 January 1916.

280. *Morning News,* 12 March 1917.

281. Ibid.

282. Ibid.

283. *Morning News,* 19 January 1917.

284. *Morning News,* 12 March 1917.

285. Ibid.

286. If the number of members who paid dues is correct, the Hebrew Charity Association had widespread support because there were probably not even 1200 Jewish households in the city. Some households may have had more than one member. Perhaps the wartime influx of Jews did increase the population to 1200 households for a time. The survey of 1929 by Jewish Welfare Board estimated 986 households at that time.

287. *Morning News,* 23 January 1917.

288. Ibid.

289. JHSD, Hebrew Charity Association Collection, IRO letter of 16 February 1914.

290. JHSD, Hebrew Charity Association Collection, letter of 17 February 1914.

291. Ibid., Gordon letter of 28 February 1914.

292. Ibid., letter of 3 March 1914.

293. Ibid., letter of 16 March 1914.

294. Ibid., letter of 9 June 1916.

295. Ibid., letter of 16 May 1916.

296. Ibid., letter of 23 May 1916.

297. Ibid., letter of 9 June 1916.

298. Ibid, letter of 17 May 1918.

299. Ibid., letter of 12 September 1919.

300. Ibid., letter of 16 February 1920.

301. JHSD, Bichor Cholem Society Collection, newspaper clipping 26 August 1941 and papers of Rosalie Hillersohn.

302. *Sunday Star,* 6 February 1916.

303. Ginns, "History of Ladies Bichor Cholem," 3.

304. Ibid.; Bluestone, *A Historical Review of the Kutz Home,* 2.

305. *Sunday Star,* 24 November 1918.

306. *Sunday Star,* 1 June 1919.

307. Ibid.

308. *Sunday Star,* 13 June 1920; *Morning News,* 14 June 1920. According to the *Sunday Star,* the home was at 209–211 West Street suggesting that additional property had been acquired.

309. *Sunday Star* , 13 June 1920.

310. *Morning News*, 14 June 1920.

311. *Morning News*, 12 June 1920.

312. Mollye Sklut, interview by the author, 1990.

313. Ginns, "History of Ladies Bichor Cholem," 3.

314. Bluestone, *History of Kutz Home*, 3; Ginns, "History of Ladies Bichor Cholem," 4.

315. *Sunday Star,* 13 May 1917; Ginns, "History of Ladies Bichor Cholem."

316. ETC, Mrs. David Topkis, conversation with Emile Topkis.

317. *Sunday Star*, 4 July 1920.

318. *Morning News*, 29 September 1913.

319. Ibid. Rabbi Abels was invited back as the main speaker because of his important role in the YMHA when he was in Wilmington. The rabbis who followed Abels at Temple of Truth continued to emphasize the importance of the YMHA to the community.

320. *Morning News*, 29 September 1913.

321. Ginns, "History of the Moses Montefiore Society," 4.

322. Harry Bluestone, *A Historical Review of the Jewish Community Center of Wilmington, Delaware 1901–1965,* 74; *American Jewish Yearbook,* 21, (1919–1920): 354.

323. *Sunday Star*, 12 March 1916.

324. *Sunday Star*,12 March 1916 and 19 March 1916. According to an application form, December 1917, Samuel Rachlin was the first leader; Harry Schagrin, age eighteen, was the assistant scout master. David Snellenburg, Nathan Miller, and Jacob Rosenblatt served as a committee of representative citizens. The scouts were between thirteen and sixteen years old.

325. WCD 1916. The YMHA was the first Jewish building for the use of all Jewish organizations. The federation Abels had organized in 1911 had hoped to open a Jewish building, but it did not succeed.

326. Geffen, "The Beginning 1902–1917," in *Seventy Five Years at the JCC.*

327. *Sunday Star*, 24 June 1917.

328. Geffen, "The Beginning 1902–1917."

329. *Sunday Star,* 18 October 1918.

330. Saretsky, *History of the Jew in Delaware.*

331. *The Dawn*, 19 March 1922, 8. Toni Young, "The Struggle to Exist," in *Seventy Five Years at the JCC;* Saretsky, *A History of the Jew in Delaware.*

332. *The Dawn,* 19 March 1922, 8.

333. Young, "The Struggle to Exist."

334. Ibid.

335. Ibid.

336. *The Dawn,* 12 December 1922.

337. Ibid. For a discussion of the growing gap between immigrant parents and children see Handlin, *The Uprooted,* chapter nine.

338. *The Dawn*, 19 March 1922.

339. *Sunday Star*, 19 February 1922; Young, "The Struggle to Exist."

340. *The Dawn*, 19 February 1922.

341. Saretsky, *A History of the Jew in Delaware;* Young, "The Struggle to Exist."

342. *Morning News*, 19 March 1922.

343. *Sunday Star,* 17 May 1922.

344. *The Dawn*, 20 May 1922, 14.

345. Ibid.

346. Saretsky, *A History of the Jew in Delaware.*

347. Ibid.

348. *Sunday Star*, 25 June 1922.

349. *Every Evening,* 30 June 1922.

350. *Sunday Star*, 12 March 1916.

351. Ibid. Louis Fox, Louis Platensky, Samuel Cannon, E. Leopold, A. Sosnoff, Max Rosenbaum, H. Evans, A. Silver, Max Court, and Nathan Shtofman were on the committee to purchase the building.

352. Irving Howe, *World of Our Fathers*, 203–4.

353. JHSD, Cannon Family Collection, obituary, Sam Cannon; *Evening Journal*, 13 September 1971.

354. JHSD, Bob Silver, interview by Jackie Rofel and Helen Goldberg.

355. *American Jewish Yearbook, 1919–20* (Philadelphia: Jewish Publication Society, 1919) 21, 354.

356. *Sunday Star*, 16 April 1916.

357. *The Jewish Encyclopedia,* 1903, s.v. "Fraternities."

358. *Sunday Star*, 25 November 1917.

359. *Sunday Star*, 9 June 1918.

360. JHSD, Sallie Ginns, handwritten History of National Council of Jewish Women, 1968, 2.

361. Yetta Chaiken, unpublished paper on Sallie Topkis Ginns.

362. *Morning News,* 10 June 1918. Sallie Ginns, History of National Council of Jewish Women, 3.

363. *Morning News,* 8 May 1911. Rabbi Geffen's notes on *American Hebrew,* 26 May 1911. Kehillah, the self-government of Jews in the Old World, denoted a disciplined community structure.

364. Howe, *World of Our Fathers*, 133–35; Sorin, *A Time for Building,* 91–92 and 214–18.

365. According to an article by Samuel Cannon in *The Dawn,* 31 March 1922, the committee was organized during the 1917 campaign. According to the 1929 Survey of the Jewish Welfare Board, it was formed during the 1918 campaign.

366. *Sunday Star*, 11 May 1919.

367. Ibid.

368. See Handlin, *The Uprooted,* chapter seven.

369. Melvin Urofsky, *American Zionism from Herzl to the Holocaust* (New York: Anchor, 1976), 1, 2.

370. Ibid.

371. Sorin, *A Time for Building,* 227–28.

372. Urofsky, "Zionism: An American Experience," 214–15; Sorin, *A Time for Building*, 227. The *Sunday Star* ,14 November 1915 reported on Brandeis's speech on Zionism in Washington.

373. Walter LaQueur and Barry Rubin, eds., *The Israel-Arab Reader* (New York: Penguin, 1969), letter from Arthur James Balfour to Lord Rothschild, 2 November 1917, 18.

374. *Morning News,* 1 December 1917.

375. *Morning News,* 1 December 1917 and 3 December 1917. David Snellenburg, Nathan Miller, Louis Topkis, and Rabbi Samuel Rabinowitz were among the organizers of the celebrations.

376. *Sunday Star*, 17 November 1918.

377. *Israel Reader*, 34.

378. *Sunday Star*, 2 May 1920.

379. *Sunday Star*, 9 May 1920.

380. Ibid.

381. *Sunday Star*, 17 June 1917; Sorin, *A Time for Building*, 211.

382. Sorin, *A Time for Building*, 212.

383. Geffen, "A Visit to the Land of the Patriarchs—The Diary of William Top-kis, 1923," in *Cathedra*, no. 13 (October 1979): 71–94. Quoted in Hillel Tryster, *Israel Before Israel: Silent Cinema in the Holy Land* (Jerusalem: Steven Spielberg Film Archive of Hebrew University, 1995) 147–49.

384. Ibid. The diary William Topkis kept while in Palestine is at the JHSD, William Topkis Collection.

385. *Abstract of the Census of 1920*, 324. In 1911–13, 2,743 arrived and in 1914, 705.

386. Between 1900 and 1910, as the number of immigrants increased, the number of Wilmingtonians unable to speak English tripled, according to the *Sunday Star*, 14 November 1915.

387. *Sunday Star*, 14 November 1915.

388. Ibid.

389. Howe, *World of Our Fathers*, 227,229.

390. *Morning News*, 29 June 1915, editorial.

391. *Morning News*, 29 June 1915.

392. *Morning News*, 6 July 1915.

393. *Morning News* , 29 June 1915.

394. *Morning News*, 29 June 1915.

395. *Morning News*, 5 July 1915.

396. Ibid.

397. *Sunday Star,* 14 November 1915.

398. *Morning News*, 22 December 1915,

399. *Morning News*, 31 December 1915.

400. *Sunday Star* , 30 January 1916.

401. *Sunday Star*, February 27, 1916.

402. *Morning News*, 13 September 1916.

403. *Sunday Star,* 15 December 1918.

404. *Sunday Star*, 4 April 1919.

405. *Sunday Star*, 23 February 1919.

406. Ginns, "History of Ladies Bichor Cholem," 3.

407. Saretsky, "History of the Jew in Delaware and of Men and Women Who Love Their Neighbors as Themselves," no pp.

408. JHSD, Wars Collection, list of Ralph Tomases, "Delaware Jews in American Wars," a slide show. See also Samuel Saretsky, *History of the Jew in Delaware*. Saretsky's list includes older men who served on welfare and draft boards.

409. Information is based on census records. Fifteen of the seventy men whose nationalities are known were foreign-born; most were from Russia.

410. *Sunday Star,* 29 December 1918.

411. *Sunday Star,* 1 September 1918.

412. *Sunday Star,* 29 December 1918.

413. JHSD, slide show "Delaware Jews in American Wars."

414. *Morning News*, 13 June 1917.

415. *Sunday Star*, 2 September 1917.

416. Ibid. George Slonsky had been born in Wilmington around 1896.

417. *Sunday Star*, 16 September 1917.

418. Ibid.

419. JHSD, Biographical and Historical Information on Nineteenth and Twentieth Century Jews, Barsky, obituary, 2 August 1948.

420. JHSD, slide show, "Delaware Jews in American Wars."

421. JHSD, War Collection.

422. Alfred Green, interview by author, 2 May 1997.

423. *Sunday Star,* 15 September 1918.

424. *Sunday Star,* 2 September 1917.

425. Saretsky, *A History of the Jew in Delaware.*

426. Ibid.

427. Ibid.

428. "Jewish War Relief Work," in Samson Oppenhiem, ed., *American Jewish Yearbook, 5678, 1917–18* (Philadelphia: Jewish Publication Society of America, 1917), 194.

429. Ibid., 194–96.

430. Ibid., 199–202.

431. *Sunday Star,* 19 September 1915.

432. *Sunday Star,* 19 September 1915, 19 December 1915, and 9 January 1916. At the dinner in celebration of the birth of a son to Mr. and Mrs. Ring, $11.36 was donated. At the Goldstein wedding, $33 was contributed. At the anniversary of Rebecca and Max Green, 20 February 1916, funds were donated.

433. *Sunday Star,* 9 January 1916.

434. Ibid; Henry H. Rosenfelt, *This Thing of Giving* (New York: Plymouth Press, 1924) 29,31.

435. Ibid. According to the *Sunday Star,* 13 February 1916, among those who worked in the Middletown drive were Joseph Berkman, Abraham Fogel, Solomon Burstan, Samuel Berg, Solomon Rosenberg, Lester M. Shestack, Morris Berg, Louis Froomkin, Benjamin Rosenberg, Ralph Berkman, and Miss Laura Fogel.

436. *Sunday Star,* 30 January 1916.

437. *Morning News,* 10 May 1918. In his moving story about the gift, Rosenfelt, (*This Thing of Giving,* 37–40) does not mention a condition on the contribution.

438. *Morning News,* 4 June 1917.

439. Morning News, 15 June 1917. Background on Josiah Marvel is from *Delaware Magazine* 2 (June 1919).

440. *Morning News,* 16 June 1917.

441. *Morning News,* 11 June 1917.

442. Ibid.

443. *Morning News,* 18 June 1917; *Sunday Star,* 17 June 1917. Wilmington received such recognition in spite of the fact that communities throughout the country were breaking all records and exceeding their quotas.

444. *Sunday Star,* 17 June 1917.

445. Rosenfelt, *This Thing of Giving,* 36.

446. *Sunday Star,* 28 October 1917.

447. *Sunday Star,* 16 December 1917.

448. Schagrin, "The Jews of Delaware," 622–23; Oscar Handlin, *A Continuing Task: The American Jewish Joint Distribution Committee 1915–1964* (New York: Random House, 1964), 28; Rosenfelt, *This Thing of Giving,* 73–77.

449. *Morning News,* 13 May 1918.

450. *Sunday Star,* 12 May 1918. Rossell's comment demonstrates the continued tendency to see all Jews as one unit.

451. Rosenfelt, *This Thing of Giving,* 75.

452. Carol Hoffecker, "Four Generations of Jewish Life in Delaware ," 44–45.

453. *Morning News,* 10 May 1918.

454. Rosenfelt, *This Thing of Giving,* 73.

455. For a description of the evening see JHSD, Geffen Collection, Rabbi David Geffen, "1918", a radio address; Carol Hoffecker, "Four Generations of Jewish Life in Delaware," 44–45; Rosenfelt, *This Thing of Giving,* 73–77; *Sunday Star,* 12 May 1918; *Morning News, Every Evening,* and *Evening Journal,* 13 May 1918.

456. *Sunday Star,* 12 May 1918.

457. *Morning News,* 13 May 1918. For further information on Mr. duPont's background see John K. Winkler, *The duPont Dynasty,* and JHSD, research by Emile Topkis, Bill Frank, and Louis Finger. Moses Homberg was the early Jewish ancestor.

458. At times this comment has been interpreted to mean Pierre duPont contributed the entire $75,000. *Every Evening,* 13 May 1918, suggests he meant he would make up the deficiency should there be one. The author believes Pierre duPont's statement was meant to inspire the Jews to action.

459. *Morning News,* 13 May 1918.

460. Ibid.

461. *Sunday Star,* 12 May 1918.

462. *Morning News,* 10 May 1918.

463. *Morning News,* 13 May 1918.

464. Ibid.

465. *Morning News,* 16 May 1918; JHSD, Snellenburg Collection, scrapbook contains the telegram.

466. *Morning News,* 16 May 1918.

467. *Morning News,* 18 May 1918.

468. *Sunday Star,* 19 May 1918. Elihu Schagrin and others cite a different total.

469. *Morning News,* 20 May 1918.

470. Rosenfelt, *This Thing of Giving,* 77. Rosenfelt was part of the national campaign staff.

471. *Sunday Star,* 19 January 1919.

472. Ibid.

473. Ibid. See also JHSD, Geffen, "1918," a radio address.

474. *Sunday Star,* 21 March 1920.

475. *Morning News,* 24 March 1930.

476. Ibid. Also *Sunday Star,* 14 March 1920. Others on the advisory committee included Mayor William G. Taylor, former governor Charles R. Miller, Secretary of State Everett C. Johnson, Reverend Charles I. Candee, William Coyne, George A. Elliott, John S. Rossell, and William P. White.

477. Ibid.

478. Ibid.

479. *Sunday Star,* 21 March 1920.

480. *Sunday Star,* 21 March 1920.

481. *Morning News,* 22 March 1920.

482. *Morning News,* 23 March 1920.

483. *Morning News,* 24 March 1920.

484. *Morning News,* 26 March 1920.

485. *Morning News,* 27 March 1920.

486. *Sunday Star,* 28 March 1920.

487. *Morning News,* 30 March 1920.

488. Ibid.

489. According to the *American Jewish Yearbook 1922–23*, the Jewish population in 1918 was 3,806; the book notes that the number may be low because it is
based on census numbers that are sometimes low because people don't answer religious questions. The 1929 survey by the Jewish Welfare Board said the Jewish
population in 1928 was 3,935. The Jewish population had remained static during
the 1920s in spite of an 11 percent growth in the general population. The survey
reports that in 1923 the Jewish population was 4,010, and a 1925 survey of National Council of Jewish Women said the population was 3,959. Based on data
from census records, birth, death, and marriage records, Toni Young believes the
estimate of about 4,000 in 1923 is correct. The city population was 110,000 according to the *Abstract of the Fourteenth Census of the United States* (Washington,
D.C.: Government Printing Office, 1923), 108.

490. The foreign-born population of Wilmington was 16,337 according to the
Abstract of Fourteenth Census, 109. The largest percentage of immigrants in Wil-
mington were from Poland, followed by Italy and Ireland. (*Abstract of Fourteenth
Census*, 316–17).

491. *Abstract of the Fourteenth Census*, 109. In all, 19,132 were of foreign parentage, 7,103 were of mixed parentage.

492. Author's research based on census, birth, death, and marriage records for
about 730 men and 640 women whose nationalities are known. See also Survey of
1929.

493. The 1929 survey says 90 percent of the children were born in the U.S., and
three-fifths of the Jewish population was native-born. The author estimates fewer
native born in 1920.

494. Author's research based on census, birth, death, and marriage records for
about 730 men and 640 women whose nationalities are known. The 1929 survey
says only 1 percent of the population was from Western Europe, while 37 percent
was from Eastern Europe.

495. The author's data based on census, birth, death, and marriage records suggests that at least 10 percent of the adult Jews in Wilmington had been here since
before the turn of the century. According to the 1929 survey, 50 percent of the
total population, including children, had been in the U.S. since 1903.

496. Author's research from census, birth, death, and marriage records .

497. Ibid. The survey of 1929 says 49 percent of the population was twenty-five
and under and 32 percent were between twenty-five and forty.

498. *Every Evening*, 2 November 1959.

499. Charles Keil and Barbara Silverstein Keil, interview with the author, 2 July
1996.

500. Charles Levy, interview with the author; *The Whisp*, 1922. Hyman Yanowitz became known as H. Albert Young.

501. Ibid.

CHAPTER 7: END OF AN ERA

1. Henry L. Feingold, *A Time for Searching: Entering the Mainstream*, vol. 4
of *The Jewish People in America* (Baltimore: Johns Hopkins University Press for
the American Jewish Historical Society, 1992), 6.

2. Ibid., 6–7.

3. *American Jewish Yearbook, 1921–22, 23*, 314.

4. Ibid., 7.

5. *Morning News*, 22 January 1921, editorial.

6. *American Jewish Yearbook, 1921–22,* 23, 314–15 and 367.

7. Feingold, *A Time for Searching*, 8.

8. Ibid., 9.

9. Feingold, *Zion in America*, 270.

10. Leo P. Ribuffo, "Henry Ford and *The International Jew,*" in Sarna, *The American Jewish Experience*, 180.

11. Ribuffo, "Henry Ford," 187; Feingold, *A Time for Searching,*13; Rufus Learsi, *The Jews in America: A History* (New York: KTAV, 1972), 291.

12. Feingold, *A Time for Searching,* 13.

13. Ibid.

14. Higham, *Send These to Me*, 53.

15. Ibid.

16. *Morning News*, 12 January 1921.

17. Morning News, 5 January 1921, editorial.

18. Ibid.

19. The Dover State News' opinion was reported in the *Morning News*, 22 January 1921.

20. Higham, *Send These to Me*, 54.

21. The Senate vote was 78 yes, 1 nay, 17 not voting. The House vote on May 13 was 276 yes, 33 nay, 1 present, and 120 not voting.

22. *Congressional Record,* 67th Cong., 1st sess., 1921, Vol. 61, pt. 1: 967–69.

23. *Congressional Record,* 67th Cong., 1st sess., 1921, Vol. 61, pt. 2–3: 1443.

24. The Senate vote was 69 yeas, 9 nays and 18 not voting. House vote was 308 yeas, 62 nays, and 63 not voting.

25. *Congressional Record,* 68th Cong., 1st sess., 1924, Vol. 65, pt. 9–11: 8589, 8652.

26. Feingold, *A Time for Searching*, 28.

27. Drooz, "A Brief Sketch of Beth Emeth's History," 24.

28. Young, "The Struggle to Exist." Ignoring the advice of the Jewish Welfare Board to wait for a unified effort, Adas Kodesch decided to build a center next door to its synagogue. The Adas Kodesch Center opened in 1928 and closed for lack of funds in 1932.

29. *Sunday Star*, 22 November 1925.

30. Ibid.

31. JHSD, 1929 Survey of Jewish Welfare Board.

32. Ibid.

Afterword

1. Sorin, *Tradition Transformed*, 238, 253.

Bibliography

Primary Sources

Archives of the Jewish Historical Society of Delaware. Includes minute books, programs, brochures, handwritten histories, personal correspondence, and newspaper clippings, as well as photographs, slides, and taped interviews. The archives are the best single source of information on Delaware Jewish history.

Cemetery Records of Adas Kodesch Shel Emeth, Beth Emeth, Beth Shalom, Chesed Shel Emeth, Machzikey Hadas, Old Montefiore, and Workmen's Circle.

Delaware Public Archives. Dover, Delaware. Birth, marriage, and death records.

Evening Journal. 1870s–1920s.

Every Evening. 1870s–1920s.

Gopskill's Philadelphia City Directory. Philadelphia: James Gospill, 1875.

HIAS. Philadelphia Branch. Index of People Resettled, 1884–1945.

Laws of the State of Delaware.

New Castle Leather Company, Scrapbook 1. Eleutherian Mills Hagley Foundation.

Recorder of Deeds. Direct Deed Indexes 1873–1897, 1897–1912, 1912–1920.

Saretsky, Samuel. "History of the Jew in Delaware and of Men and Women Who Love Their Neighbors as Themselves." 1922. at the JHSD.

Sunday Morning Star. 1880s–1920s.

United States Bureau of the Census. Tenth Census of the United States 1880. Manuscript Returns for Delaware.

———. Twelfth Census of the United States 1900. Manuscript Returns for Delaware.

———. Thirteenth Census of the United States 1910. Manuscript Returns for Delaware.

———. Fourteenth Census of the United States 1920. Manuscript Returns for Delaware.

Wilmington City Directories. 1870s–1921.

Wilmington Morning News. 1880s–1920s.

Interviews

The author has spoken with numerous members of the Jewish community. She has conducted more formal interviews with the following people.

Sam Arsht, 7 December 1993

Marvin Balick, 23 April 1997

Frances (Mutzie) Bellak, 31 July 1991
Martin (Peni) Berger, 7 November 1996
Ann Berkman, 9 April 1992
James and Edie Chaiken, 19 May 1991
Leon Chambers
Herb Cobin
Ben Cohen, Sadie Feinberg Cohen, and Esther Cohen, 3 July 1989
Bill Frank, April through July 1989
Ed Glick, 12 January 1997
Rea Golden, July 1989
Ida Fineman Goldman, July 1989
Frances Goldstein, 20 April 1997
Alfred Green, 2 May 1997
Billie Rudnick Greenberg, 1 February 1995
Gary Greenstein, 18 April 1997
Sybil Keil Harris and Lewis Harris, 8 December 1996
Barbara Silverstein Keil and Charles Keil, 2 July 1996
Bea Leibowitz Laub and Sid Laub, 7 July 1994
Dr. Charles Levy, 21 March 1991
Bernie Muderick, 10 December 1996
Sol Polotsky, 8 June 1989
Mollie Cohen Sklut
Mollye Sklut, 25 July 1990 and 2 August 1990
Itze Shapiro
Philip Simon, 12 March 1991
Sophie Chaiken Swimmer, 7 February 1992
Ralph Tomases, 9 December 1996
Sadie Cohen Toumarkine, 24 January 1997
Libby Zurkow, 19 April 1990

In addition, numerous oral histories at the Jewish Historical Society of Delaware
have been most helpful.

Bill Feinberg, 14 July 1988
Bill Frank's interview of I. B. Finkelstein
Ann Statnekoo Porter
Henry Schultz, 17 July 1978
Jackie Rofel and Helen Goldberg's interview of Robert T. Silver, 1981
Sadie Toumarkine, 8 July 1881
Harry Schagrin, 19 December 1880
Yetta Chaiken's interview with Jechebet Roos, 7 November 1983
Yetta Chaiken's interview with Harry David Zutz

Emile Topkis's notes on conversations held in 1955 with descendants of the earliest members of the community, deposited in the collection of the JHSD, have been
an invaluable resource.

SECONDARY SOURCES

Books

Abstracts of Reports of the Immigration Commission. Introduction by Oscar Handlin. New York: ARNO and The New York Times, 1970. [Original report: Washington, D.C.: Government Printing Office, 1911].

Abstract of the Fourteenth Census of the United States. 1920. Washington, D.C.: Goverment Printing Office, 1923.

American Jewish Yearbooks 1903–4 , 1904–5, 1907–8, 1910–11, 1913–14, 1914-15, 1916–17, 1919–20, 1939–40, 1956. Philadelphia: Jewish Publication Society of America.

Balick, Marvin. *Genealogy of the Balick Family of Delaware for the Period Covering 1890–1995.* Wilmington: N.p., 1995.

Belth, Nathan C. *A Promise to Keep: A Narrative of the American Encounter with Anti-Semitism.* New York: Times Books, 1979.

Berger, David, editor. *The Legacy of Jewish Migration: 1881 and Its Impact.* New York: Brooklyn College Press, 1983.

Bevan, Wilson Lloyd. *History of Delaware Past and Present.* Volume 3. New York: Lewis Historical Publishing Company, 1929.

Bluestone, Harry. *A Historical Review of a Century of Jewish Education in Delaware, 1876–1976.* Wilmington: Jewish Historical Society of Delaware, 1976.

———. *A Historical Review of the Jewish Community Center of Wilmington Delaware, Inc., 1901–1065.* Wilmington: Jewish Community Center, 1971.

———. *Jewish Family Service of Delaware: A Historical Reivew, 1899–1965.* Wilmington: N.p., 1966.

———. *The Kutz Home, Inc.: A Historical Review, 1902–1970.* Wilmington: The Kutz Home, 1974.

Clement, A. J. *Wilmington, Delaware: Its Productive Industries and Commercial and Maritime Advantages.* Wilmington: Delaware Printing Company, 1888.

Cohen, Naomi W. *Encounter with Emancipation: The German Jews in the United States, 1830–1914.* Philadelphia: Jewish Publication Society of America, 1984.

———. *Not Free to Desist: A History of the American Jewish Committee, 1900–1966.* Philadelphia: Jewish Publication Society of America, 1972.

Compendium of the Tenth Census. June 1, 1880. Part I and II. Washington, D.C.: Government Priniting Office, 1883.

Compendium of the Eleventh Census. 1890 Part III. Washington, D.C.: Government Printing Office, 1897.

Compendium of the Twelfth Census. Washington, D.C.: Government Printing Office, 1902.

Thirteenth Census of the United States 1910. Abstract of the Census. Washington, D.C.: Government Printing Office, 1913.

Congregation Beth Emeth 80th Anniversary. Wilmington: Temple Beth Emeth, 1985–86.

Davis, Moshe, ed. *America and the Holy Land: With Eyes Toward Zion.* Westport, Conn.: Praeger, 1995.

Davis, Moshe. *The Emergence of Conservative Judaism: The Historical School in Nineteenth Century America.* Philadelphia: Jewish Publication Society of America, 1963.

Delaware's Industries: An Historical and Industrial Review. Philadelphia: Keighton Printing House, 1891.

Diner, Hasia. *A Time for Gathering: The Second Migration, 1820–1880.* Volume 2 of *The Jewish People in America,* edited by Henry L. Feingold. Baltimore:

Johns Hopkins University Press for the American Jewish Historical Society, 1992.

Dinnerstein, Leonard. *The Leo Frank Case*. New York: Columbia University Press, 1968.

Edwards, Richard, editor. *Industries of Delaware: A Historical and Descriptive Review*. Wilmington: Richard Edwards, 1880.

Encyclopaedia Judaica. Jerusalem: Keter Publishing House, 1971.

Fein, Issac M. *The Making of an American Jewish Community: The History of Baltimore Jewry from 1773 to 1920*. Philadelphia: Jewish Publication Society of America, 1971.

Feingold, Henry L., gen. ed. *The Jewish People in America*. 5 vols. Baltimore: Johns Hopkins Press for the American Jewish Historical Society. 1992.

———. *A Time for Searching: Entering the Mainstream, 1920–1945. Volume 4 of The Jewish People in America*.

———. *Zion in America: The Jewish Experience from Colonial Times to the Present*. New York: Hippocrene Books, 1981.

Friedman, Murray, editor. *Jewish Life in Philadelphia 1830–1940*. Philadelphia: Ishi Publications, 1983.

———, editor. *When Philadelphia Was the Capital of Jewish America*. Philadelphia: Balch Institute Press; London and Toronto: Associated University Presses, 1993.

Friesel, Evyatar. *Atlas of Modern Jewish History*. New York: Oxford University Press, 1990.

Gabler, Neal. *An Empire of Their Own: How the Jews Invented Hollywood*. New York: Doubleday, 1988.

Gartner, Lloyd P. *Jewish Education in the United States: A Documentary History*. New York: Teachers College Press, Columbia University, 1969.

Generation Unto Generation. Wilmington: Adas Kodesch Shel Emeth, 1984.

Glanz, Rudolph. *Studies in Judaica Americana*. New York: KTAV Publishing House, 1970.

Goldhagen, Daniel Jonah. *Hitler's Willing Executioners: Ordinary Germans and the Holocaust*. New York: Alfred A. Knopf, 1996.

Guyer, Charles G., and Hardesty, Edmond C., reporters. *Debate and Proceedings of the* Constitutional Convention of the State of Delaware. Dover, Delaware: The Supreme Court of Delaware, 1958.

Hafner, Arthur W., editor. *Directory of Deceased American Physicians, 1804–1929*. Chicago: American Medical Association, Division of Library and Information Management.

Handlin, Oscar. *Adventure in Freedom: Three Hundred Years of Jewish Life in America*. New York: McGraw-Hill, 1954.

———. *The Uprooted*. Boston: Little, Brown and Company, 1951 and 1973.

Harris, Leon A. *Merchant Princes: An Intimate History of Jewish Families Who Built the Great Department Stores*. New York: Harper and Row, 1979.

Hertzberg, Arthur. *The Jews in America: Four Centuries of an Uneasy Encounter*. New York: Simon and Schuster, 1989.

———, editor. *The Zionist Idea: A Historical Analysis and Reader*. New York: Atheneum, 1959.

Higham, John. *Send These to Me: Jews and Other Immigrants in Urban America.* New York: Atheneum, 1975

Historical and Biographical Encyclopedia of Delaware. Wilmington: N.p., 1882.

History of Wilmington. Compiled by *Every Evening.* Wilmington: F. T. Smiley and Company, 1894.

Hoffecker, Carol E. *Corporate Capital: Wilmington in the Twentieth Century.* Philadelphia: Temple University Press, 1983.

———. *Delaware: A Bicentennial History.* New York: Norton, 1977.

———. *Wilmington, Delaware: Portrait of an Industrial City, 1830–1910.* Charlottesville: University of Virginia Press for Eleutherian Mills-Hagley Foundation, 1974.

Holland, Randy, editor-in-chief, and Rubenstein, Harvey, editor. *The Delaware Constitution of 1897.* Wilmington: Delaware Bar Association, 1997.

Howe, Irving. *World of Our Fathers.* New York: Simon and Schuster, 1976.

Jewish Encyclopedia. New York: Funk & Wagnalls, 1901–1906.

Jick, Leon. *The Americanization of the Synagogue, 1820–1870.* Hanover, NH: University Press of New England, 1976.

Kessner, Thomas. *The Golden Door: Italian and Jewish Immigrant Mobility in New York City 1880–1915.* New York: Oxford University Press, 1977.

LaMar, Eldin. *Clothing Workers in Philadelphia: History of Their Struggles for Union and Security.* Philadelphia: Joint Board of Amalgamated Clothing Workers of America, 1940.

Laqueur, Walter, and Rubin, Barry, editors. *The Israel-Arab Reader: A Documentary History of the Middle East Conflict.* New York: Penguin, 1969.

Laws of the State of Delaware. Volume XVIII, 1887–1889.

Learsi, Rufus. *The Jew in America: A History.* New York: KTAV, 1972.

Lincoln, Anna T. *Wilmington Delaware: Three Centuries Under Four Flags 1609–1905.* Rutland, Vermont: Tuttle, 1937.

Linfield, H. S. *United States Census of Religious Groups and Census of Jewish Groups.* New York: Jewish Statistics Bureau, 1947.

Linfield, H. S. *Communal Organizations of Jews in the United States.* New York: American Jewish Committee, 1930.

Marcus, Jacob Rader. *Early American Jewry, 1649–1794.* Philadelphia: Jewish Publication Society of America, 1951.

———. *Essays in American Jewish History.* Cincinnatti: The American Jewish Archives, 1958.

———. *Memoirs of American Jews, 1775–1865.* Volume 3. Philadelphia: The Jewish Publication Society of America, 1955.

Merton, Arthur. *The Book of Destiny.* Cold Spring Harbor, N.Y.: King David Press, 1996.

Meyer, Michael A. *Response To Modernity: A History of the Reform Movement in Judaism.* New York: Oxford University Press, 1988

Morais, Henry Samuel. *The Jews of Philadelphia: Their History from the Earliest Settlements to the Present Time.* Philadelphia: Levytype Company, 1894.

Munroe, John A. *Colonial Delaware: A History.* Millwood, N.Y.: KTO Press, 1978.

Munroe, John A. *History of Delaware.* Newark: University of Delaware Press, 1979.

Postal, Bernard, and Koppman, Lionel. *American Jewish Landmarks: A Travel Guide and History. Volume I, The Northeast.* New York: Flett Press Corp., 1954.

Preisler, Julian. *Jewish Cemeteries of the Delmarva Peninsula.* Westminster, Maryland: Family Line Publications,1995.

Reed, H. Clay. *Delaware: A History of the First State.* Volume 2. New York: Lewis Historical Publishing Company, 1947.

Revised Statutes of the State of Delaware. Wilmington: James & Webb. 1874.

Roskies, Diane K. and David G. *The Shtetl Book.* New York: KTAV, 1975.

Sarna, Jonathan D. *The Americanization of Jewish Culture, 1888–1988: A Centennial History of the Jewish Publication Society.* Philadelphia: The Jewish Publication Society of America, 1989.

———, editor. *The American Jewish Experience.* New York: Holmes & Meier, 1986.

Seventy Five Years at the JCC. Wilmington: Jewish Community Center, 1977.

Silberman, Charles E. *A Certain People: American Jews and Their Lives Today.* New York: Summit, 1985.

Silliman, Charles. *The Episcopal Church in Delaware, 1785–1954.* Wilmington: Diocese of Delaware, 1982.

Sklare, Marshall. *The Jews: Social Patterns of an American Group.* Glencoe, Ill.: Free press, 1958.

———. *Observing America's Jews.* Hanover, NH: University Press of New England for Brandeis University Press, 1993.

Sorin, Gerald. *A Time for Building: The Third Migration, 1880–1920.* Volume 3 of *The Jewish People in America,* edited by Henry L. Feingold. Baltimore: Johns Hopkins University Press for the American Jewish Historical Society, 1992.

———. *Tradition Transformed.* Baltimore: Johns Hopkins University Press, 1997

Spencer, Edward. *An Outline of the Public Life and Services of Thomas F. Bayard.* New York: D. Appleton & Company, 1880.

Tansill, Charles Callan. *The Foreign Policy of Thomas E. Bayard, 1882–1897.* New York: Fordham University Press, 1940.

Temple Beth Shalom 1922–1972. Wilmington: Temple Beth Shalom 1972.

Urofsky, Melvin I. *American Zionism from Herzl to the Holocaust.* New York: Anchor, 1976.

Weinberg, Sydney Stahl. *The World of Our Mothers.* New York: Schocken Books, 1988.

Who's Who in American Jewish History. New York: Jewish Biographical Bureau, 1926.

Wilkinson, Norman B. *Lammot Dupont and the American Explosives Industry, 1850-1884.* Charlottesville: University of Virginia Press for Hagley Foundation, 1984.

Winkler, John K. *The DuPont Dynasty.* New York: Reynal and Hitchcock, 1935.

Winslow, Helen L. *The Delaware Bar in the Twentieth Century.* Wilmington: The Delaware State Bar Association, 1994.

Wolf, Edwin II, and Whiteman, Maxwell. *The History of the Jews of Philadelphia from Colonial Times to the Age of Jackson.* Philadelphia: Jewish Publication Society of America, 1957.

Wolf, George A. *Industrial Wilmington*. Wilmington: Board of Trade of Wilmington, 1898.

Wright, Richardson. *Hawkers and Walkers in Early America*. Philadelphia: J.P. Lippincott, 1927.

Young, Toni, editor. *Delaware and the Jews*. Wilmington: Jewish Historical Society of Delaware, 1979.

Articles, Essays, and Other Works

Abeles, Emil J. "The German Element in Wilmington 1850—1914." Master's thesis, University of Delaware

Board of Trade Journal. Wilmington Delaware. II, no3(June 1900).

Chance, Elbert. "The Motion Picture Comes to Wilmington." Part I: *Delaware History* 24, no. 4 (1991–92); Part II: *Delaware History* 25, no. 1 (1992).

Diner, Hasia. "Like the Antelope and the Badger." In *Tradition Renewed*, ed. Jack Wertheimer. New York: Jewish Theological Seminary of America, 1997.

Geffen, M. David. "Delaware Jewry: The Formative Years 1872–1889." *Delaware History*, 16, no. 4 (1975): 269–97.

Glanz, Rudolph. "German Jewish Mass Emigration 1820–1880." *American Jewish Archives*, 22 , no.1 (April 1970): 49–66.

Glazer, Nathan. "The American Jew and the Attainment of Middle-Class Rank: Some Trends and Explanations." In *The Jews*, edited by Marshall Sklare. Glencoe, Ill.: Free Press, 1958.

Goldstein, Eric L. "Different Blood Flows in Our Veins: Race and Jewish Self-Definition in Late Nineteenth Century America." *American Jewish History* 85, no. 1 (March 1997):

Gluckman, Leslie. "Memoirs of Wilmington at the Turn of the Century." *Jewish Voice*, 9 September 1975.

Handlin, Oscar and Mary F. "The Acquisition of Political and Social Rights by the Jews in the United States." *American Jewish Yearbook* 56 (1955): 43–96.

———. "A Century of Jewish Immigration to the United States." *American Jewish Yearbook, 1948–1949*. Philadelphia: Jewish Publication Society of America, 1949.

Isaacs, Joakim. "Ulysses S. Grant and the Jews." In *The American Jewish Experience*, edited by Jonathan D. Sarna. New York: Holmes & Meier, 1986.

Kessner, Thomas. "Jobs, Ghettoes and the Urban Economy, 1880–1935." *American Jewish History*, 71, no. 2 (December 1981): 218–38.

Korn, Bertram Wallace. "A Preliminary Checklist of American Jewish Institutions and Organizations Named in Honor of Sir Moses Montefiore." In *America and the Holy Land*, edited by Moshe Davis. Westport, Conn.: Praeger, 1995.

———. "Seventy Five Years of Continuity and Change 1655–1901." Philadelphia: Federation of Jewish Agencies, 1976.

Kuznets, Simon. "Immigration of Russian Jews to the United States: Background & Structure." *Perspectives in American History* 9 (1975): 35–124.

Meyer, Michael A. "German-Jewish Identity in Nineteenth Century America." In *The American Jewish Experience*, edited by Jonathan D. Sarna. New York: Holmes & Meier, 1986.

Panitz, Esther. "In Defense of the Jewish Immigrant, 1891–1924." *American Jewish Historical Quarterly* 55, no. 1 (September 1965): 57–97.

———. "The Polarity of American Jewish Attitudes Towards Immigration." *American Jewish Historical Quarterly,* 53, no. 2 (December 1963): 99–130.

Rachlin, Samuel. "A History of the Jews of Wilmington." In *Reform Advocate.* Chicago: Bloch & Newman, 19 .

Sarna, Jonathan. "The Making of American Jewish Culture." In *When Philadelphia Was the Capital of Jewish America,* ed. Murray Friedman. Philadelphia: Balch, 1993.

———. "The Myth of No Return: Jewish Return Migration to Eastern Europe, 1881–1914." *American Jewish History* 71, no. 2 (December 1981): 256–68.

Schagrin, Elihu. "The Jews of Delaware." In *Delaware: A History of the First State,* edited by H. Clay Reed. Vol. 2, pp. 617–25. New York: Lewis Historical Publishing Company, 1947.

Schreuder, Yda. "Wilmington's Immigrant Settlement: 1880–1920." *Delaware History* 23, no. 2 (Fall-Winter 1988):

Weinryb, Bernard D. "East European Immigration to the United States." *Jewish Quarterly Review* 45 (April 1955): 497–528. "The German Jewish Immigrants to America." In *Jews from Germany in the United States,* New York: Farrar, Straus and Cudahy, Inc. 1955.

Yellowitz, Irwin. "Jewish Immigrants and the American Labor Movement, 1900–1920." *American Jewish History* 71, no. 2 (December 1981): 188–217.

Young, Toni. "Establishing Judaism in Delaware." In *Delaware and the Jews.* Wilmington: Jewish Historical Society of Delaware, 1979.

Index

Individuals are usually grouped by nuclear family. However, when there are short references to many members of an extended family, the individuals are listed under one family name. When a husband and wife are only mentioned together, they are listed as one entry. If a husband has individual references, these are listed first, followed by (and wife) or (and wife and family) for references to both of them. When a wife or child is discussed separately in the text, page references for the wife or child are separated from the husband's by a semicolon with the wife's entry preceding the child's. If a child is only mentioned as part of the nuclear family, he/she is not listed by name but as part of the family entry. When there are numerous references to an adult, previously mentioned as a child in a nuclear family, the adult is listed separately.